Rock and Roll, Desegregation Movements, and Racism in the Post-Civil Rights Era

Rock and Roll, Desegregation Movements, and Racism in the Post-Civil Rights Era

An "Integrated Effort"

Beth Fowler

LEXINGTON BOOKS
Lanham • Boulder • New York • London

Published by Lexington Books
An imprint of The Rowman & Littlefield Publishing Group, Inc.
4501 Forbes Boulevard, Suite 200, Lanham, Maryland 20706
www.rowman.com

86-90 Paul Street, London EC2A 4NE

Copyright © 2022 by The Rowman & Littlefield Publishing Group, Inc.

All rights reserved. No part of this book may be reproduced in any form or by any electronic or mechanical means, including information storage and retrieval systems, without written permission from the publisher, except by a reviewer who may quote passages in a review.

British Library Cataloguing in Publication Information Available

Library of Congress Cataloging-in-Publication Data

Names: Fowler, Beth (Beth Nicole) author.
Title: Rock and roll, desegregation movements, and racism in the post-civil rights era : an "integrated effort" / Beth Fowler.
Description: Lanham : Lexington Books, 2022. | Includes bibliographical references and index. | Summary: "This book uses archival research and analyses of musical performances and original oral histories to explore the uncertain legacies of the civil rights movement and early rock and roll music in a supposedly post-civil rights era"— Provided by publisher.
Identifiers: LCCN 2022003944 (print) | LCCN 2022003945 (ebook) |
  ISBN 9781793613851 (hardback) | ISBN 9781793613875 (paperback) |
  ISBN 9781793613868 (epub)
Subjects: LCSH: Rock music—United States—To 1961—History and criticism. | Rock music—United States—1961-1970—History and criticism. | Rhythm and blues music—History and criticism. | Music and race—United States—History—20th century. | Segregation—United States—History—20th century.
Classification: LCC ML3534.3 .F68 2022 (print) | LCC ML3534.3 (ebook) |
  DDC 781.660973/0904—dc23
LC record available at https://lccn.loc.gov/2022003944
LC ebook record available at https://lccn.loc.gov/2022003945

Contents

Acknowledgments	vii
"A Subtle Defiance in the Songs"	1
1 "Shufflin' 'Til the Break of Dawn," 1946–1953	25
2 "If It's a Hit, It's a Hit," 1954–1956	73
3 "A Teen Ager in Love," 1957–1960	137
4 "They'd All Be Dancing Together," 1961–1964	207
5 "A Drummer with a Totally Different Beat," The Post-Civil Rights Era	287
Bibliography	333
Index	353
About the Author	363

Acknowledgments

As much as I love my work, I have long grappled with the isolating nature of historians' work. Long hours spent sitting alone in archives, or in front of a blinking computer screen with few distractions other than one's own thoughts, can take a toll on anyone who otherwise thrives on social interaction and collaboration. And yet, as I look back on the decade and a half of work that went into this manuscript, I realize that I was never really doing anything on my own. Throughout my professional career, I have been exceedingly fortunate to receive the support of individuals and institutions providing motivation, stability, and, perhaps most importantly, intellectual curiosity. These relationships have helped me grow as an academic researcher, writer, teacher, and human being, and for that I am sincerely grateful. In the end, this book's publication would not have been possible without the contributions of those listed here.

    First of all, I would like to thank the archivists, librarians, and administrative staff at the Rock and Roll Hall of Fame Library and Archives, the American Folklife Center and Manuscript Division at the Library of Congress, the Bentley Historical Library at the University of Michigan, the Wisconsin Historical Society Library and Archives, the Columbia University Rare Book and Manuscript Library, the Schomburg Center for Research in Black Culture, and the Paley Center for Media. I consistently received pleasant and helpful assistance at each institution, and was even introduced to other researchers working on similar topics and invited to join staff members for lunch in certain cases. During research trips when time is in short supply, these instances of professional kindness and support are especially appreciated. These trips would not have been possible in the first place without generous financial support from the Office of the Vice President for Research, the Humanities Center, the Office for Teaching and Learning, and the Irvin

D. Reid Honors College at Wayne State University. Travel also would have been far more expensive and a lot less fun had I not been able to stay with Dillon Fowler and Gabriella Scipione, who graciously opened their home to me on several occasions, or hang out with Lesley Warren after long days sifting through historical documents.

I began work on this project several years ago as part of my MA degree at the University of Windsor. My adviser, Christina Simmons, was instrumental in getting me to see how culture and politics could affect one another, and to understand how concepts of whiteness and Blackness could shift within different historical periods. When I began my doctoral studies at Wayne State University, I was able to expand my work on this project in large part due to financial assistance from the Department of History, especially the Thomas C. Rumble Graduate Fellowship, and the Humanities Center. Support from both departments funded travel to archives, presentations at national conferences, and perhaps most importantly, semesters devoted to full-time research. But no amount of funding could replace the profound support provided by my adviser, Kidada Williams, who introduced me to the mechanics of academic work by prominent scholars doing cutting-edge research, encouraged me to promote my research on a number of different platforms, and never failed to provide the precise and honest criticism that is necessary for intellectual development. I am not exaggerating when I say that this project would never have amounted to much without the enormous amount of work she put into my growth as a scholar. I also very much appreciate how Liette Gidlow and Danielle McGuire assisted me with my research and writing throughout my years as a doctoral student, and how Andrew Newman stepped in as a committee member with very little time to prepare, yet still managed to provide thoughtful feedback on my dissertation. This gratitude extends to other professors in the Department of History as well, especially Tracy Neumann for friendship, emotional support, tough-talk guidance, and pop culture discussions; Andrew Port and Sylvia Taschka for holding the most entertaining scholarly reading group meetings imaginable; and Elizabeth Faue for rock-steady guidance in times of great need. I would also like to thank Eric Ash, Jennifer Hart, Hans Hummer, Marc Kruman, Janine Lanza, Aaron Retish, and Fran Shor, all of whom supported my academic and departmental endeavors, and Gayle McCreedy for helping me with too many administrative snafus to mention.

The process of turning this research into an actual, readable book would not have been possible without the financial, intellectual, and collegial support I have been so lucky to receive within the Irvin D. Reid Honors College at Wayne State University. Deans Jerry Herron and John Corvino have both put significant investment into my intellectual and professional growth by advocating for job stability and research support, allowing me to teach seminars on subjects related to ongoing research, and offering all-around support and guidance that has never failed to make me realize how fortunate I am to work under such amazing leadership. Kevin Deegan-Krause and Kevin Rashid have both provided unwavering assistance navigating the ins and outs of working in this department without ever sacrificing the kinds of kindness and humor that make you appreciate going into the office each day. Stuart May endured many hours of my sitting in his office while he ensured that any financial support for research trips and conference presentations was properly allocated. Ali Salamey, Kevin Piotrowski, and Tim Moran offered thoughtful responses to chapter readings during office Brown Bag presentations. And special thanks go out to Walter Edwards, director of the Humanities Center at Wayne State, for consistently championing my work, offering insightful feedback, and supporting efforts to share early drafts of this book with faculty members from departments across the university.

Writing can be a lonely exercise, but I have been fortunate to find friends who have been willing and able to meet for writing days, lunches, and coffee meetups in order to alleviate any sense of working in isolation. Over the years, I have been extremely fortunate to bounce ideas off of many extra-smart people whom I genuinely enjoy spending time with, including Stine Eckert, Kamahra Ewing, Nicole Gerring, Rashida Harrison, Andrew Hnatow, David Hopkins, Liz Hudson, Nate Kuehnl, Alex Lovit, Austin McCoy, Miriam Mora, Tracy Neumann, Elena Past, Alexandra Sarkozy, Stephanie Spielmann, and Jennie Woodard, all of whom provided motivation, essential perspectives on my work, and general conviviality over drinks and diner specials. Special thanks go out to my former officemates, Joelle Del Rose, Elizabeth Ryan, Cami Ward, and Amanda Walter, who helped create a comforting space filled with never-ending (and loud!) laughter, tears, queso, and a cute corner sofa for necessary rest breaks.

The day that Courtney Morales, assistant editor at Lexington Books, reached out to me was the day that I began thinking about this project as a potential manuscript that other people might actually read. Her patient and helpful guidance throughout the publication process consistently assured me that I was in good hands. When the pandemic broke out in early 2020, she helped me figure out a new timeline that would account for travel and research limitations, while simultaneously assuring me of her support for this project. Becca Beurer and Matthew Valades also responded to my numerous questions with promptness and clarity, granting me the confidence I needed to complete this manuscript in a timely manner. And I could not have gotten anywhere close to finishing this project without the awe-inspiring efforts of Bridget McDevitt. Bridget was in charge of posting and coordinating calls for oral history interviews, preliminary discussions with potential candidates, scheduling interview times, and transcribing recordings, and she did it all at an astonishingly quick pace. She also went out of her way to locate new respondents and to ask questions that shed new light on completed interviews. This book would never have been completed in the allotted time frame without her going above and beyond her stated duties, and I am sincerely grateful for her devotion to the project.

I would also like to extend my sincere gratitude to the 45 individuals who agreed to be interviewed as part of this project. Although almost every respondent was eager to talk about the music they loved when they were young, it is not always easy to discuss personal traumas associated with racist injustice or shifting racial politics with a stranger, especially during a contentious election year. Many of the questions that I asked were written long before the Black Lives Matter protests erupted across the globe in the summer of 2020, but they took on new resonance during this period, and many people admitted that they were thinking and learning about the effects of structural racism in new ways. Respondents who had themselves been active in social justice campaigns stressed that they were hopeful for transformative change this time, given the expansive and diverse nature of these protests, and the deeper level of analysis promoted in popular media and news accounts. Their willingness to spend hours of their time speaking with me about how their lives have been impacted by both civil rights struggles and popular music allowed me to think about my research questions in deeper ways and to consider how broader structures continue to affect individuals throughout their lives. But the hope that so many espoused in the midst of a devastating pandemic and some of the most disturbing resurgences of racial hatred in over half a century gave me faith that we would be able to continue fighting against these injustices, even as I watched the events of 2020 unfold with trepidation from my living room sofa.

I would also like to thank my best and most long-term friends, Catherine Colautti, Joelle Del Rose, Jessica Gallaway, Tessa Mancini, Lesley Warren, and Brooke Wells, for offering consistently sympathetic ears, cups of coffee, lunch dates, and shopping excursions when I needed breaks from work. Finally, I am forever grateful to my parents, Lynn and Neil, not only for imparting a love of music that I never grew out of, but for supporting my career choice even when it seemed like graduate school would never end, and for always reiterating the importance of treating all people with respect and dignity. It is because of their influence that I became invested in learning about the history of racism and racial politics in the United States, and in the fight for racial justice. Thank you also to my sister, Lauren, and my brother, Dillon, for being the best friends I could ever be related to, and for making me laugh even in the most unlikely circumstances. For all their continued love and support, I dedicate this book to my family.

"A Subtle Defiance in the Songs"

Each year The Rock and Roll Hall of Fame in Cleveland, Ohio, hosts a schedule of events celebrating Martin Luther King Jr. Day. Along with free admission to the museum, guests enjoy a range of performances and interactive activities celebrating African-American musical traditions and affirming Black voices. One event in particular, a presentation entitled "Rock and Roll and the Civil Rights Movement," shows visitors "how a range of artists, from Mahalia Jackson and Sam Cooke to Berry Gordy at Motown and rock and roll pioneer Fats Domino created a popular music that empowered African Americans to take their rightful place in American society." Here, the connection between Black freedom struggles and gospel, rhythm and blues (R&B), and rock and roll music created and performed by African-American artists is made explicit. The words "empowered" and "rightful place" echo many Black Power platforms, which emphasize racial pride and an unwillingness to assimilate to white norms. Indeed, many Black kids who grew up during the 1950s and 1960s admired these musicians, both for their positions as role models within mainstream popular culture and for creating professional opportunities for other Black Americans to work in the music industry. And yet so much of the accepted civil rights movement narrative focuses on racial integration, especially the eradication of Southern Jim Crow laws, as a major goal. Desegregation campaigns were waged just as early rock and roll music "desegregated" the radio airwaves, gaining young fans from all racial backgrounds and weakening cultural divisions. In both cases, the lines between protest and pop culture are depicted as reassuringly linear, even if they represent vastly different visions of racial politics.[1]

These connections have become increasingly visible in both public history presentations and contemporary culture. Popular museum exhibits make this link evident to visitors, with presentations that pair mass organization against

Jim Crow in the South and housing and economic inequality protests in the North with the joyous mixtures of African- and European-American musical contributions that made up early rock and roll. Visitors to Sun Studio in Memphis, which is advertised as "The Birth Place of Rock 'N Roll," are regaled with tales of how founder Sam Phillips, and his friend and sometime business partner, deejay Dewey Phillips, routinely broke through the color line in pursuit of both dollars and desegregation. The integration of sounds, songwriters, and audiences is also pivotal to Motown lore, where the museum's webpage explains how the record label "broke down racial prejudice," while similar claims are made in the tour's introductory film. And an exhibit entitled "Integrated Effort" at the Stax Museum in Memphis proclaims that "prior to Dr. Martin Luther King Jr.'s assassination, Stax was, in many respects, a manifestation of his dream. Color was not an issue: from Booker T. and the MGs in the studio to the employees in the corridors, Stax was racially mixed."[2]

Museums are not the only places where the general public can learn about rock and roll's dependence on, and contributions to, desegregation movements. On television, the 2013 PBS documentary *Sister Rosetta Tharpe: The Godmother of Rock and Roll* informs viewers that the gospel singer used both her performances and her iconic status as means of challenging white cultural norms, while *Ray* and *Walk the Line*, major studio film adaptations of the lives of Ray Charles and Johnny Cash, respectively, draw clear lines between fights to end segregation and the musical genre that encouraged this goal. The first major motion picture to tackle this subject, John Waters's 1988 cult classic *Hairspray*, which was remade in 2007, presents rock and roll music as a cheerful tool for prodding obstinate white teenagers into accepting their Black school mates as equals. Even specialized K–12 educational curricula designed for the Rock and Roll: An American Story program through Steven Van Zandt's Rock and Roll Forever Foundation, which aims to present recent American history through the lens of popular music, solidify this link. In an online teaching module entitled "Elvis and Race in 1950s America," for example, Elvis Presley's rise and subsequent popularity are presented against a backdrop of fights for school desegregation and counter-reactions to the *Brown v. Board of Education of Topeka* decision. An overview of the lesson explains how Presley's first single, a cover version of R&B star Arthur Crudup's "That's All Right Mama," "showed that black and white music could live side by side on a 45 RPM slice of vinyl in 1954, even if the men who wrote the songs were discouraged from doing so in public life." Despite this caveat, the author makes clear the political import of rock and roll during this decade: "In some ways, Elvis' first single did what the Supreme Court could only dream of doing at that moment, integrating black and white culture in one neat package that would have enormous influence on millions of

Americans." Contemporary popular culture is therefore rife with the notion that rock and roll music helped white people to appreciate Black culture, leading to support for the desegregation movements that civil rights activists were staging at the same time.[3]

This so-called integration of popular music did, in some ways, reflect shifting racial politics. Civil rights organizers focused on the desegregation of transportation, schools, and other public spaces during this period, rightly predicting that these campaigns would gain more support from white elites and government officials than with more radical calls for economic or bodily justice. Desegregation movements were supported by most Black teenagers, as well as many white teenagers during this period, a shift that was strengthened by the success of rock and roll records among multiple racialized demographics. But this narrow emphasis produced differing conceptions of racial equality among white and Black youth, a distinction which becomes clear when examining their responses to "integrated" rock and roll music. White listeners have often argued that music is capable of bringing people together, and that the racial identities of performers should not matter if their records are enjoyable. This focus on individual achievement was also crucial to desegregation strategies, prompting many white supporters to embrace a "color-blind" approach to race relations rather than recognizing the need for group-based solutions to structural problems. Some white rock and roll fans who grew up during this period make similar arguments about how listening to music by Black artists like Fats Domino and Chuck Berry led them to see African Americans as people who *deserved* to have their rights recognized based on their merits and contributions, revealing a connection between the ways they perceived desegregation campaigns and examples of integration in their everyday lives. Black listeners made these connections too, but they largely understood that desegregation was meant to be used as a tactic in the struggle for full citizenship rather than as an end goal, an acknowledgment that is paralleled by the ways they listened to rock and roll music. Although most Black kids were aware of the "integrated" nature of this music and enjoyed recordings by white artists like Presley and Jerry Lee Lewis, they were more likely to take pride in increased representation of Black artists and African-American culture within mainstream culture, as well as further opportunities for artists, writers, and business people in the white-dominated music industry. These contrasting responses to rock and roll music can shed light on how Black and white teenagers viewed the goals, methods, and lasting effects of legal desegregation in very different ways.

A celebratory connection between the energetic music of youth in rebellion and increased acceptance of desegregation campaigns supports most widely accepted narratives about the civil rights movement in the United States. According to movement lore, Martin Luther King Jr. emerged out of nowhere to take his rightful spot as leader of the Montgomery Bus Boycott in 1955. After the campaign's inevitable triumph, which, in reality, demanded over a year's worth of persistent organizing and agitating on behalf of Black women across the city, many of whom lost their jobs or suffered health problems because of their involvement, the stage was set for activists to demand equality on a broader scale. Black activists and white allies formed nonviolent direct action campaigns to protest segregation and racial discrimination in the Jim Crow South, which, when met with violent massive resistance, prompted the federal government to intervene. This happy result of activist perseverance was handed down from on high on July 2, 1964, with the passage of the Civil Rights Act, rendering racial segregation in public places illegal, and the Voting Rights Act a year later, allowing the use of federal power to prevent interference with a citizen's right to vote. The latter, passed after peaceful marchers were violently attacked in Selma, Alabama, and President Lyndon Johnson delivered a Special Message to Congress concluding with the freedom chant "We Shall Overcome," has particularly been identified as the moment when full political equality was finally granted to all American citizens.[4]

Yet, as comforting as this story of righteous, triumphant moral outrage might be, a narrow focus on integration and equal treatment gained through respectable, nonviolent protest as the only means of eradicating racism inadvertently convinced many whites that racial oppression disappeared upon the eradication of Jim Crow laws. But integration was never the ultimate goal of the civil rights movement. After World War II, activists grappled with many different strategies, including fights for economic justice, bodily integrity, housing rights, and internationalist movements, as part of a broader Black freedom struggle. Desegregation of public spaces and voting rights were identified as major goals for many organizations, including the National Association for the Advancement of Colored People (NAACP), Congress of Racial Equality (CORE), and, eventually, the Southern Christian Leadership Conference (SCLC) and Student Nonviolent Coordinating Committee (SNCC), because of increased access to resources, support from white political elites, existing laws and democratic structures, media interest, and legal capabilities, but they did not represent the breadth of Black struggle against white supremacy. Because of this focus, however, racially liberal white teenagers often conflated integration and voting rights with racial equality, allowing many to believe that racism ceased to be a major problem after this phase of the civil rights movement ended.

The methods that these groups used to protest racial injustice and inequities would also become the stuff of civil rights lore, even though decisions to use these tactics often resulted from uneasy compromises among activists who had to consider the safety of their participants, as well as the views of white audiences whose support could help their goals become reality. Respectability politics, which had been used by Black activists since the early twentieth century to try to "uplift" African-American communities while simultaneously showing whites that they deserved equal treatment based on adherence to middle-class values, shaped campaigns where participants dressed in their "Sunday Best," or expressed the need for desegregated schools because straight-A students deserved the same future career opportunities as their white peers. Appeals to the country's democratic political structure, which was supposed to guarantee equal rights to all citizens, were also prominently used by activists to relay how their demands were hardly radical but merely calls for the federal government to enforce laws that were already on the books. Finally, activists' use of nonviolent direct protest, heralded as a humane and moral ideology emanating from Mahatma Gandhi's political philosophies, and embraced by King and other Black church leaders, made white supremacist opponents look like easy villains when they attacked movement participants who refused to respond in kind. Each tactic was meant to protect activists from even greater violence, and from the harmful stereotypes that whites often lobbed at Black protestors in order to undermine their demands. These methods were also chosen because they were more likely to lead to successful outcomes by appealing to white sympathies, despite contentious disagreement among activists who questioned the effectiveness (and desirability) of white support. Campaigns that made use of these methods were, indeed, successful in gaining widespread support for moderate civil rights goals like desegregation of public spaces and voting rights, and in convincing many white Americans that equal rights and opportunities should be granted to all citizens, regardless of race. But they also implicitly rendered other goals and protest methods less acceptable, or even threatening, to many whites who otherwise viewed themselves as opponents of racial discrimination. As this part of the civil rights movement came to an end in the mid- to late 1960s, many whites believed that the most brutal forms of racial injustice had been eradicated, and that the country could move forward as a true democracy, unencumbered by its unseemly past. And yet this perspective would have devastating consequences for post-civil rights racial justice movements, as many continuing inequalities were ignored, and acknowledgment of the persistence of racism could be considered controversial, since it had supposedly disappeared along with Jim Crow signage and separate school edicts.

This post-civil rights narrative obscures how economic injustice and structural racism, neither of which were directly targeted by the eradication of state-sanctioned segregation, have continued to proliferate in the intervening decades. In his seminal 2014 article for *The Atlantic*, "The Case for Reparations," Ta-Nehisi Coates painstakingly shows how historical and current housing, lending, and tax policies, as well as overt resistance, have prevented even higher-income Black families from gaining proportionate levels of equity in their homes, sending their children to high-quality schools, and accessing the public and private resources that contribute to the success of their white contemporaries. White supremacy is still exercised every day, in decisions about housing, education, employment, medicine, banking, and finance, and upheld violently through systems of mass incarceration and over-policing, but because the civil rights movement supposedly eliminated most forms of racism, these problems are often attributed to individual or group inadequacies. The persistence of this belief system, even amid supposedly widespread support for racial equality, has been identified as a new form of racial liberalism, defined by C. W. Mills as "essentially egalitarian and inclusive, placing racism and racial oppression in the categories of the anomalous and deviant." This seemingly positive perspective led many whites to devise "various new strategies for circumventing antidiscrimination law," particularly a reimagining of traditional liberal ideals of "individual rights and freedoms" as the natural state of peoples of all racial backgrounds, in stark contrast to prewar beliefs that social welfare policies would be necessary to create and enforce racial egalitarianism.[5] This ideology has bolstered the illusion that civil rights successes banished racial prejudice to the so-called fringes of society. Yet coded language, first developed by Republican campaign managers in the late 1960s, has allowed whites to dismiss grievances of racial prejudice as "playing the race card," and, by the 2000s, to extol the virtues of a "post-racial society," all while pretending that, since racial inequality was supposedly eradicated, any concerns about continuing discrimination and injustice must be disingenuous. These attempts to divide what was already made whole, or to blame concerns about racism on an "unwillingness to move on from the past," comprise what Tim Wise refers to as the "rhetoric of racial transcendence," which renders any mention of systemic racism as not only disingenuous, but an attempt to dredge up a hurt that has supposedly been resigned to history.[6]

This ambivalent and often unacknowledged legacy of the civil rights movement has captured the attention of scholars across disciplines, many of whom argue that racial segregation and discrimination were not so much discontinued as they were reconfigured. The striking title of sociologist Eduardo Bonilla-Silva's book, *Racism without Racists*, almost viscerally depicts a society where, the author argues, "things work in a subtle and apparently non-racial way," and where white Americans "latch onto almost any racism-less explanation" to avoid confronting the persistence of structural racism and the benefits of white privilege. He describes this "color-blind racism" as distinct from "Jim Crow racism" due to naturalization of racial differences, often ascribed to supposed cultural distinctions without recognition of structural power imbalances, minimization of harmful impacts, and the ability to address these distinctions "in an abstract, decontextualized manner." As this wayward ideological framework has come to shape socioeconomic realities, large numbers of Black men have essentially had their civil rights stripped away by an expanding carceral state, and shifting state and corporate responses to demands for equality have limited African-American progress, all while the country has marveled at its capacity for tolerance by electing Barack Obama as the first Black president in U.S. history.[7] This perspective, created and supported by the dominant civil rights narrative, has led to incredibly harmful consequences, including the police shootings of unarmed Black citizens that prompted the Black Lives Matter (BLM) movement, and the 2013 *Shelby v. Holder* decision, where the Supreme Court ruled Section 4(b) of the Voting Rights Act, which allocated federal oversight to elections held in jurisdictions that had historically discriminated against African Americans, to be unconstitutional. Almost immediately, some states began instituting rules and identification requirements that prevented or dissuaded people of color from voting, leading to a Supreme Court battle over a voter suppression law in North Carolina, as well as investigations into new voting guidelines in 20 states. Defenses routinely rely on the post-civil rights myth that, since racism has been eradicated, it is unnecessary, and even harmful, to consider race when crafting voting stipulations, even if they have proven to stifle voices in non-white communities.[8]

The civil rights activism that took place during the 1950s and 1960s did, of course, lead to improvements for African Americans in numerous ways. Coates insists that "the lives of black Americans are better than they were half a century ago," citing greater political representation, the end of sanctioned public segregation, lifted bans on interracial marriage, and decreasing Black poverty rates as signs of progress. The hard work that civil rights activists engaged in throughout most of the postwar period forced the federal government and the country's white majority to take seriously the lack of equal rights among all citizens. Their efforts produced codified legal changes, increased Black representation in positions of power, implemented institutional diversity requirements, and provided general support for the concept of racial equality. These changes reveal real progress, yet they should not obscure continuing racial injustice, or de-emphasize the white supremacist backlash that existed just beneath polite societal norms before seemingly exploding in anticipation of the 2016 presidential election. The legacy of the Black freedom movement is therefore somewhat ambivalent. The racially integrated "beloved community" first promulgated by members of SNCC as a means of courting powerful white allies may have won the rhetorical war, but in many ways its goals seem more elusive than ever. While the supposition of a "post-racial society" begins to fall apart, an in-depth examination of the actual changes that occurred during the civil rights movement, and an assessment of how these changes created the particularly troubling racial politics we encounter today, is urgently needed.⁹

Historians like Jacquelyn Dowd Hall, Peniel Joseph, and Glenda Gilmore have criticized the dominant civil rights timeline, arguing that it denies the movement's more radical origins and goals, while many others have challenged the narrow focus on desegregation campaigns by looking at alternate strategies used by Black activists during the same time period. Other historians, including Matthew Lassiter and Lisa McGirr, have examined how neoconservative counter-movements that skillfully manipulated the tenets of individual rights to argue against state intervention in racial politics helped to shape this new form of racial liberalism. But a study of how Black and white Americans responded to the movement's focus on desegregation and supposed racial "equality," and how this legacy laid the groundwork for the racially liberal politics and beliefs that would emerge in its wake, has so far been overlooked. *Rock and Roll, Desegregation Movements, and Racism in the Post-Civil Rights Era: An "Integrated Effort"* aims to fill this gap by examining how some aspects of post-civil rights racial liberalism may be identified in the distinct reactions that white and Black teenagers had toward desegregation campaigns, and how the "integrated" rock and roll music that almost every teenager listened to during this period could encourage this perspective. These identifications help to show how many self-described "racially liberal" white Americans have continued to support supposedly "race-neutral" policies based on individual achievement, respectability, and democratic rhetoric rather than combating structural injustice, while also revealing the limitations of civil rights movement goals, even if the language of these campaigns has been used to abolish most legal barriers to full citizenship.¹⁰

Rather than simply accepting the supposed connection between early rock and roll music and the mainstream civil rights timeline, this study uses both contemporary and recent responses to both movement and music as tools to investigate shifts in culture and politics during this period, and to reveal distinctions between how white and Black Americans viewed desegregation movements, even if they used similar language to describe their beliefs. When rock and roll music first emerged in the mid-1950s, it did so within the context of desegregation movements, as musicians, songwriters, and producers of different racial backgrounds combined musical characteristics to create a genre that appealed to listeners across racial and class lines. In his book *The Seventh Stream*, sociologist Philip Ennis notes that the genre first originated when songs began to "cross over" on the Pop, R&B, and Country and Western music trade charts, representing a "desegregation" of popular music. These crossovers occurred because teenagers began listening to music that was created by, and marketed to, different racial groups other than their own in larger numbers. By the mid-1950s, adolescents represented such an important consumer demographic that nonplussed record executives were inclined to follow their customers' leads if they wanted to reach these markets. Rock and roll was not a fad created by the music industry to bilk gullible teenagers out of their allowances, at least not initially; instead, record labels responded to existing consumer demands. Jerry Wexler, a former music journalist who co-owned the Black-oriented Atlantic Records label from 1953 until the late 1990s, insisted that listeners were willing to cross racial lines *before* music executives recognized it could be profitable. "First came the fans, and not long after, the musicians," he said. "The collision between openly integrated music and a tightly segregated society created a new kind of energy. You can hear a subtle defiance in the songs." This defiance represented a challenge to the white supremacist status quo, as young people explicitly reaffirmed their support for the "integrated" sights and sounds of rock and roll before such "crossovers" were commodified and diluted by mainstream record labels.[11]

The popularity of this new genre made celebrities out of artists from different racial backgrounds and solidified African-American cultural traditions as integral to mainstream mass culture. Within the context of civil rights campaigns that were nearly ubiquitous news items by the mid- to late-1950s, rock and roll was depicted as racially transgressive right from the start, particularly as young whites began using the language of what Taeku Lee calls "cherished democratic principles," including "justice, equality, and universal rights," to explain their support for both the desegregation of public spaces and music that crossed racial boundaries.[12] Many white rock and roll fans attested that race should not matter when listening to music, and that music could be used to bring people together. The focus on individual achievement that was so crucial to integration strategies also urged many white supporters to embrace a "color-blind" approach to race relations rather than recognizing the need for group-based solutions to structural problems.

Shared musical affinities, however, did not demand from white teenagers the kinds of insight and sacrifice that an actual dismantling of structural racism would require. This was partly due to the commodification of rock and roll by major music labels in the late 1950s. As radio station operators and record executives realized the profits they stood to lose by ignoring the teenage market, a few acquiesced to customer demand by actively marketing songs by Black performers to white teenagers. Memphis deejay Dewey Phillips, for instance, challenged Southern segregation norms by engaging with white fans of his predominantly Black-oriented radio program, while, as one of the genre's earliest and most ardent proponents, Alan Freed consistently identified the African-American roots of rock and roll music as the reason that parents of his numerous white fans were so opposed to their listening habits.[13] Atlantic Records, which was created with the mission to sell jazz and R&B records to Black customers, appeared at the same time as what Wexler describes as "that fortunate point in American music when the lines between black and white were starting to fade. Things were getting blurry in a hurry, and Atlantic both benefited from and contributed to that breakdown."[14] But this method of "selling" diversity presented a view of society where racial discrimination would not exist if people did not actively engage in it themselves, an attempt to disavow the consequences of systemic racism by simply refusing to acknowledge its existence.

By responding to consumer trends and expanding the boundaries of the mainstream, these industry insiders normalized the concept of racially integrated music just as civil rights campaigns normalized desegregation in public spaces. Most of these campaigns needed support and resources from broad audiences, including white political elites, who would be more likely to support desegregation efforts since Jim Crow laws already violated the Fourteenth Amendment.[15] In order to gain this support, however, organizers had to present desegregation as a morally righteous and democratic goal that would not disrupt people's lives as white supremacists had predicted. Images of Black and white children attending school together, or shopping in the same spaces, were presented as unremarkable, unlike the more radical actions that would follow, like the 1974 decision to bus white children in Boston to majority-Black schools, which resulted in violent protest when white parents refused to alter their actions in order to create more integrated school systems.[16] This focus on integration and equality of opportunity, especially in the areas of education and consumerism, reinforced basic capitalist-democratic values that most white Americans already supported. Concepts of diversity and integration therefore gained approval among many young whites. But the belief that individuals could "purchase" or "feel" their way out of racial inequality, and that most elements of racial injustice disappeared once the Civil Rights Act abolished segregation in public places, shaped new, distorted visions of racism that would prove more difficult to uproot.

As the commercialization and expansion of rock and roll continued to define adolescent culture into the 1960s, white teenagers remained captivated by the music's overt embrace of interracial characteristics and performers. And yet its rebellious nature was dulled by its omnipresence and mainstream acceptance. Whereas white kids in the early to mid-1950s often had to surreptitiously seek out this music, it became the best-selling genre in many stores and radio stations only a few short years later, prompting even a few parents to start listening for themselves.[17] Furthermore, the overt message of rock and roll was to have fun with friends, not to challenge political structures. This music may have *encouraged* young white listeners to question established racial norms, but it *required* nothing of them other than to have a good time dancing to the beat. The origins of post-civil rights racial liberalism were already apparent, as large numbers of white kids disavowed what writer Mychal Denzel Smith calls the "impolite racism" of "say[ing] mean things about black people," and generally embraced equality through desegregation, all without recognizing just how deeply the roots of racial injustice run in almost all American institutions.[18] They could proudly proclaim that they were against racism without realizing that their individual beliefs did not eradicate the systems of oppression that continued to marginalize Black Americans. Rock and roll music therefore provided a cultural foundation for widespread acceptance of post-civil rights racial liberalism.

Black teenagers also engaged in cross-racial listening habits during this period, which, as Brian Ward explains, partly reflected hopes held by many Black kids that integration in the cultural realm would lead to increased racial justice overall.[19] Many teenagers purchased records by white musicians like Elvis Presley and Jerry Lee Lewis during this period because their music was clearly inspired by African-American traditions. However, Black kids largely understood that desegregation was meant to be used as a tactic in the struggle for full citizenship rather than an end goal. They advocated for individual dignity and group advancement, as well an end to state-sanctioned segregation laws, and their responses to rock and roll music reflect these nuances. Many Black listeners were inspired by increased African-American representation within mainstream popular culture, and by greater opportunities for artists, writers, and business people in the music industry, even as they simultaneously acknowledged that rock and roll's interracial origins could reflect broader support for integration in general. Although the gap between both income and stability among the Black and white middle classes remained substantial, kids who grew up with greater material wealth than their parents were more likely to expect equal treatment in the cultural realm and to view this form of integration as actual progress. Widespread disappointment with desegregation campaigns after the mid-1960s, however, encouraged some younger African Americans to eschew their beliefs that interracial cooperation could ever amount to real change, and to recognize that dominant systems could not simply absorb integrated processes, but would instead have to be entirely re-shaped. The limited abilities of desegregation, in both the cultural and political realms, to affect racial justice led some who grew up during this period to view rock and roll as a missed opportunity for real progress, while others deemed the genre yet another example of the cultural appropriation of non-white cultures, profiting white musicians and music executives at the expense of the Black artists whose innovations helped create this genre.

Historians of both the civil rights movement and mid-twentieth-century youth culture have identified shifting ideas about race as key to understanding the emergence and popularity of rock and roll music among teenagers in the 1950s and 1960s. Right from the start, Charlie Gillett, whose 1970 history of rock and roll, *The Sound of the City*, was the first serious examination of the genre, noted that "while interracial tension became more evident during the period when this book was being written, there also seemed to be increasing numbers of young white people who rejected traditional attitudes of superiority towards black people." He quickly reminded readers, however, that this observation did not necessarily indicate increasing racial tolerance among white teenagers overall.[20] After necessary distance from this period, other scholars, including Reebee Garofalo, George Lipsitz, and Glenn Altschuler, studied the connection between rock and roll and shifting racial values more directly, showing how the interracial nature of this music coincided with the timeline of the U.S. civil rights movement, ultimately promoting racial integration specifically, and African-American characteristics generally, as desirable values. Although these connections exist, they are complicated by distinct racialized perspectives on the fundamental meanings of integration. Other scholars, including Michael Bertrand, Grace Elizabeth Hale, and Matthew Delmont, have shown how, even though rock and roll music could encourage white teenagers to question racial norms, this questioning did not necessarily encourage them to become participants in civil rights campaigns or alter their perspectives on racial discrimination in meaningful ways. Brian Ward has examined how Black listeners briefly believed that white enthusiasm for Black musicians could presage support for broader civil rights initiatives, while Jack Hamilton has stressed that any opportunity for rock and roll to act as a racial common ground was abolished by the late 1960s, as major record labels and fans alike "whitewashed" the genre, cleansing historical memory of the music's African-American origins. I am indebted to each of these authors, and hope to build on their arguments by directly contrasting perspectives on desegregation movements with views on rock and roll music to show how white teenagers could sincerely believe that they were supporting racial integration and equality, even as their conceptions of an equal society were not what most Black Americans were actually working to achieve.[21]

This literature, then, requires a reexamination of the strategic decisions that civil rights activists made and the rhetoric they used when staging desegregation campaigns. Responses to these decisions, and to rock and roll music, from Black and white music fans can help historians identify their distinct perspectives on the civil rights movement in general, and on integration specifically. Many civil rights accounts have been hesitant to identify widespread movement support among young people since very few Black teenagers, and even fewer white adolescents, would go on to board buses to challenge segregated interstate travel or to sign up for voting rights canvassing in Mississippi. But a lack of overt political engagement does not mean that teenagers were ambivalent about these campaigns. When a nationwide survey of 2,000 to 3,000 teenagers of different racial backgrounds was taken in October 1954, five months after the *Brown v. Board of Education of Topeka* ruling that declared racial segregation in schools unconstitutional, the researcher found that 58 percent agreed with the statement "Pupils of all races and nationalities should attend school together everywhere in this country." An additional 19 percent maintained that they were undecided, or that they did not care one way or the other about movement outcomes. Ideas about racism and segregation were clearly changing among large groups of teenagers, even those who did not become actively involved in the movement. Examining teenage responses to music, however, can, as Ward argues, "offer a useful insight into the changing sense of self, community and destiny" that was occurring among adolescents during this period, even though they "rarely left the sorts of evidence, or undertook the sorts of activities, to which historians are usually receptive."[22] To understand this widespread shift, it is necessary to listen to what Black and white listeners have had to say about this music in the context of widely publicized desegregation movements and to consider how these responses have shaped their post-movement thoughts on racial politics.

Relationships between reactions to music and politics cannot be *proven* in any quantitative sense, but oral histories and contemporary accounts can be interpreted against the backdrop of civil rights campaigns in ways that suggest connections between rock and roll culture and shifting views on racism and desegregation. My research for this project includes 45 original oral histories with narrators who identify as either Black or white, were born between 1934 and 1956, raised in the United States, and listened to rock and roll music during this period. Calls for respondents were posted on multiple online sites, including the American Association of Retired Persons and SNCC Legacy message boards, nationwide radio and music nostalgia blogs, and community message boards in major urban areas, including New York, Detroit, Chicago, Los Angeles, San Francisco, Memphis, Nashville, Birmingham, Mobile, Jackson, and Atlanta. Since respondents chose to respond to these calls rather than being selected at random, many similarities are overrepresented in this group when compared to the general population. The vast majority of respondents hold advanced degrees, worked in professional positions, and often described themselves as middle class during our conversations. These demographic limitations are not confined to this specific project; much of the historical literature on rock and roll fandom during this period focuses heavily, if not exclusively, on middle-class audiences and consumers. In some ways, this parallels the fact that record companies and radio stations heavily catered their marketing strategies toward middle-class teenagers who had disposable income to spend on luxuries like records, concert tickets, music magazines, and products manufactured by the companies that sponsored shows and tours. Even though Black kids lagged behind their white peers in terms of spending abilities, many families did well enough during this period to allow their teens to engage in some of this fun consumerism while simultaneously expecting to benefit from the better educational and job opportunities that integration movements were fighting for. But this focus largely overlooks responses from working-class or lower-income teenagers who also enjoyed this music, and often helped to shape the dance trends that accompanied specific songs and styles. Their voices would clearly complicate the argument made here, not only because their spending habits were more constrained, but because of competing political and social ideologies and, often, increased interaction with people from other racial backgrounds. Although this is an area of research that requires further examination, I was unfortunately unable to do so within the confines of this project. Instead, the demographics of this group of respondents represent popular music marketing's main consumer targets.

Similarly, while respondents were not asked direct questions about their political affiliations, most self-identified as Left of Center, skewing anywhere between moderately liberal and progressive or socialist. None of the 33 people interviewed after the 2016 presidential election expressed approval of President Donald Trump and his administration, or otherwise voiced support for the Republican Party. Six respondents were actively engaged in civil rights or other progressive movements when they were younger, a percentage rate that is definitely far greater than that of the population as a whole. These individuals may not represent a random sampling of diverse American political ideologies, but their responses are helpful in determining how people who view themselves as antiracist and generally supportive of civil rights movements understand connections between music and racial politics. Since this study mainly looks at how both of these influences have helped create a new form of racial liberalism, it makes more sense to consider their stances, as opposed to those from people whose ideologies lie outside of this framework.

Interviews took place during two specific time periods, from November to December 2011, and September 2019 to July 2020. The first group was given a choice of responding to written questions or conducting the interview over the telephone, with most deciding on the former option. In some cases, respondents were sent follow-up questions to compensate for the lack of spontaneity and unexpected information that occurs more organically in conversation, but most chose not to submit answers to these questions. All participants in the 2019–2020 group chose to converse over the telephone until COVID-19 lockdowns, which began in March 2020, prompted many to elect for video calls instead. Each respondent is identified in this study by their first name and last initial in order to preserve a degree of anonymity, although all other identifiers remain unaltered. Each participant answered questions about their backgrounds and childhoods, what they knew about the civil rights movement growing up and how they felt about it, the music they listened to, and their current racial politics. The 2019–2020 respondents were asked additional questions about the Trump administration and the BLM movement, both of which did not yet exist when the first round of interviews took place. Finally, respondents who were interviewed between late May and July 2020 were eager to talk about the protests that erupted in the wake of George Floyd's and Breonna Taylor's murders at the hands of police officers, even though interview questions were not altered to address these specific cases. Racist violence and police brutality, as well as the protest methods used to demand justice, were very much on people's minds during this period, and may have affected the answers they provided in response to other interview questions.

Recollections of music and culture during this period, especially those of white men, are often dismissed as romanticization of the past. In some ways, this concern is one which affects all oral histories: narrators may idealize certain recollections, either consciously or unconsciously shaping their memories to present their past selves in the best possible light, and minimize any discomfort or regret they might feel. The unreliability of memory, especially after 60 odd years, is also an important consideration for all oral historians. In some cases, clear idealization is used to examine racial distinctions between responses to both civil rights goals and rock and roll music, and to explain persistent opposition to antiracist movements and policies even among racially liberal white Americans. I have examined narrators' past behaviors and actions based on their recollections while also considering how their interpretations of these past experiences have shaped their current beliefs on race and politics. By comparing these responses with archival and historical sources, including over 20 archived oral histories conducted by other interviewers, I have been able to identify connections between narrators' recollections of popular music in the 1950s and 1960s and their responses to civil rights campaigns focused on desegregation of public spaces.[23] Based on these responses, white narrators are more likely to romanticize both the music and the movement, nonviolent direct action, and the roles of individuals, all of which supports Grace Elizabeth Hale's argument that many disenchanted suburban white kids used Black culture as a means of shaping their own rebellions during the postwar period. While many acknowledge the importance of breaking with the parent culture, they also tend to focus on seeing others as actual people with supposedly inherent democratic rights, and on doing what is just according to their own moral codes. Their depictions of integration as based on the righteous decisions of diverse individuals obscured other civil rights strategies, providing the foundation for this new form of racial liberalism. Black kids, however, were inspired by greater African-American representation in both music and politics. As Brian Ward points out, many Black kids viewed mainstream acceptance of Black musicians and musical characteristics as a positive component of racial integration, while simultaneously hoping for an end to white dominance in both politics and popular culture, rather than simply integrating public spaces. A small but not unsubstantial number of white participants, mostly those who became active in civil rights and social justice movements themselves, fall somewhere in between, refusing a flat idealization of integration in either music or desegregation movements, and asking critical questions regarding the movement's successes, while still maintaining that bringing individuals together across racial lines is a mostly positive development stemming from this period.[24]

Other major sources for this project include archival materials and oral histories from The Rock and Roll Hall of Fame Library and Archives, the American Folklife Center at the Library of Congress, and the Columbia University Oral History Research Office, as well as civil rights organization records and interviews from the Manuscript Division at the Library of Congress, the Wisconsin Historical Society Library, Archives, and Museum Collections, and the University of Michigan Bentley Historical Library. I have also relied on a content analysis of *Billboard*'s Top-Selling Records charts between 1953 and 1964 as a means of determining purchase behaviors among different consumer demographics. The methodological process for this research involved logging the top 20 songs listed on the Popular chart and top 10 songs on the R&B and Country and Western charts listed in each issue of *Billboard* between January 3, 1953, just before crossover records began appearing frequently, and December 26, 1964, at the end of this study's timespan. The charts changed significantly during this period, most notably when editors introduced the 'Hot 100' chart in August 1958 and expanded the other charts to include 15 or 20 entries but to maintain integrity, I continued to include data from the top 20 spots, and the top 10 slots on the other charts. Although David Brackett, among others, has rightly criticized the publication's accuracy, given its subjective and, frankly, nontechnical data collection methods at the time, *Billboard* remains the most effective source for analyzing how young people shaped new musical trends with their consumer habits, as well as how those habits were reinforced by industry profit motives. Even though the publication never had an extensive readership among the general public and was briefly challenged by other trade publications, including *Cash Box*, the *Billboard* charts have set the standard for measuring music sales and radio play activity since the 1930s by heavily influencing record store purchasing decisions and radio and jukebox playlists, ultimately determining which music would become accessible to listeners. The publication's charts, while not a perfect research tool, still provide a fairly accurate account of the records that people purchased and the songs that they were hearing on the radio.[25]

Chapter 1 of this book details how the social and economic environment of the United States between 1946 and 1953 helped activists to identify desegregation as a major effort that could gain widespread support. Postwar civil rights strategizing coincided with the growth of Black and white middle classes, both of which were highly engaged with consumer culture, granting degrees of purchasing power that could influence corporate decisions. Businesses catering to Black customers, including independent record labels, proliferated in order to capitalize on this demographic, while larger record companies corporatized their operations and distribution patterns while simultaneously searching out new markets. These combined changes helped to shape a common, more commodified, yet somewhat more diverse, culture among distinct groups of Americans just as the effects of Depression and wartime era organizing directed many prominent civil rights groups to focus on desegregating public spaces. Rock and roll broke through these boundaries when it emerged as a distinct genre between 1954 and 1956. Chapter 2 looks at how a "crossover" effect that occurred as Black and white kids listened to and purchased pop, R&B, and country and western albums combined musical characteristics to create the new, "racially integrated" genre of rock and roll. This chapter also examines the reasons that white teenagers gave for seeking out records by Black musicians, and how they accessed this music, as well why Black listeners increasingly began purchasing records by white pop and country artists. At the same time, public transportation desegregation campaigns were gaining nationwide media coverage that inadvertently encouraged whites to view integration as the movement's ultimate goal. Local and national NAACP and CORE branch efforts used respectability politics and moral appeals to construct desegregation campaigns that appealed to both the Black middle classes and white political elites, ultimately gaining degrees of support from national mainstream media outlets. Movement leaders like Martin Luther King Jr. and Rosa Parks were chosen by rank-and-file branch members to make desegregation seem palatable to white political elites. This focus on the need for "respectability" in order to appeal to nominally white middle-class norms also affected the emergence of rock and roll, as Black R&B music was toned down or "covered" by white artists in order to adhere to these standards, even if the genre, and the audiences themselves, had technically "integrated."

Chapter 3 examines how the image of the teenager in American culture emerged amid school desegregation campaigns and increasing corporatization and "whitening" of rock and roll between 1957 and 1960. As Black and white adolescents both began to identify with the cultural attributes of the "teenager," school hallways became civil rights battlegrounds, students struggled to adjust within these ostensibly "integrated" spaces, and major record labels continued to dilute the Black influences in rock and roll to produce polished white pop rockers. And yet this genre continued to draw teenage listeners across racial lines. *Billboard* first introduced the Hot 100 chart because the

Pop and R&B charts looked so similar, an act that was widely viewed as "desegregating" racialized music markets.[26] Despite apparent integration on the charts and in some schools, however, Black and white kids responded to this shared teenage culture with different ideas of how a desegregated society should operate. Even though both groups used democratic rhetoric and consumer language to describe their goals and experiences, Black kids were still expected to assimilate into spaces where they often experienced harassment and neglect, not unlike the methods that mainstream record labels used to promote Black musicians and their music to largely white audiences by minimizing racial distinctions.

By the early 1960s, civil rights organizations adopted direct action methods, a shift largely due to the input of younger activists. Even though most teenagers and young adults did not actively participate in these campaigns themselves, widespread media coverage ensured that they were aware of student movements, and many came to admire these young protestors. Chapter 4 looks at how student activists formed SNCC, which became one of the most prominent civil rights organizations by fighting for desegregation and voting rights using nonviolent direct protest methods, even though many members disagreed with this tactic from the beginning. While Black kids largely understood that the organization's goals and methods were chosen because they were more likely to succeed within a political structure that was already supposed to uphold equal political rights, many white teenagers would come to believe that most racial discrimination was abolished by the federal policies that made segregation and interference with voting rights illegal, and to view nonviolent protest as the only acceptable means of demanding social change. These distinctions parallel teenage behaviors while listening to rock and roll music in public spaces. Direct action in these venues, segregated by either law or custom, could emulate movement strategies, although any political effects were blunted by their temporal, unorganized, and overtly social nature, even if participants felt as though they had effected change. Ultimately, as a number of young whites came to believe that the nonviolent actions of student protestors dismantled racial inequality, many Black kids became disenchanted by the fact that other protest methods and forms of oppression were being ignored. Finally, chapter 5 examines how both rock and roll and the impact of civil rights movement successes created considerable white support for what Wise calls the "rhetoric of racial transcendence," while neglecting to address the more difficult changes that were necessary to create a truly equitable society. Respondents' views on civil rights successes and where the movement fell short are contrasted with their thoughts about how music affected racial politics when they were growing up. Some white respondents reveal how their perspectives have been shaped by components of post-civil rights racial liberalism, while most Black respondents, along with some of their more progressive white peers, challenge this conception, especially in light of recent political and social movements. Ultimately, connections between the unfinished triumphs of the 1950s and 1960s and the racial challenges of the late twentieth and early twenty-first centuries, as detailed by reflections on the lasting significance of the civil rights movement, early rock and roll music, and contemporary racial politics among oral history narrators are made using the racially-liberal framework outlined by Mills, Bonilla-Silva, Wise, and other scholars.[27]

In May 1965, two months after the March on Selma, three months before President Lyndon B. Johnson signed the Voting Rights Act into law, and five months after *Billboard* magazine "re-segregated" its charts by publishing a "Soul" list that was separate from the Hot 100, *Time* magazine ran a 10-page article proclaiming rock and roll music "The Sound of the Sixties." The title might have indicated a resounding triumph on the part of a genre that had long been maligned as racially transgressive and youth oriented, but the article's tone is more suggestive of a once-rebellious child who has been tamed simply because they have continued to exist. "For the past ten years, social commentators, with more hope than insight, have been predicting that rock would roll over and die the day after tomorrow," the author began. "Yet it is still very much here, front, center, and belting out from extra speakers on the unguarded flank. Many cannot take 'rock 'n' roll,' but no one can leave it."[28] What was once deemed threatening, causing groups from the White Citizens Council to the American Psychological Association to issue warnings about how teenagers might be affected by this interracial music, had become mainstream.

This article seems to imply that integrationist goals, within the cultural realm at least, had become tacitly accepted in adult society. Those who did not care for this music largely found that it was fruitless to struggle, mirroring many white Southerners' resignation as the desegregation of public places became inevitable.[29] Rock and roll music from the 1950s and 1960s is still framed as a rebellious break from the past and as a means of bringing different groups of people together to engage in a shared culture. But what was once inherently transgressive has often been reduced to individualized nostalgia. Popular narratives connecting music to the civil rights movement reveal how young people's attitudes about race and segregation were in flux during this period, as many white kids broke with the norms of the parent culture to embrace ideals of fairness and diversity. Individual cultural preferences and artist success stories could transcend racial identity in certain instances, but a lack of structural awareness meant that racial injustice would continue to be reproduced, often by those who claimed to abhor racism, well after legal segregation was abolished.

NOTES

1. *MLK Exhibit Guide* (The Rock and Roll Hall of Fame Museum, Cleveland, OH); Chuck Yarborough, "Rock Hall Offers Free Admission, Programs on Martin Luther King Jr. Day," *The Plain Dealer*, January 7, 2016.
2. Sun Studio, Memphis, TN, author visited on October 17, 2015; "Motown Museum: Home of Hitsville U.S.A." last accessed at https://www.motownmuseum.org/story/motown/, on May 21, 2019; Stax Museum of American Soul Music, Memphis, TN, author visited on October 17, 2015.
3. *American Masters: Sister Rosetta Tharpe: The Godmother of Rock and Roll*, directed by Mick Csaky (PBS, 2013); *Ray*, directed by Taylor Hackford (Universal Pictures, 2004); *Walk the Line*, directed by James Mangold (20th Century Fox, 2005); *Hairspray*, directed by John Waters (New Line Cinema, 1988); *Hairspray*, directed by Adam Shankman (New Line Cinema, 2007); "Elvis and Race in 1950s America," *TeachRock.org*, last accessed at http://www.teachrock.org/lesson/elvis-and-race-in-1950s-america/, on June 22, 2016.
4. "And We Shall Overcome," President Lyndon B. Johnson's Special Message to Congress, March 15, 1965. National Archives and Records Administration, The Lyndon B. Johnson Library and Museum, last accessed at http://www.lbjlib.utexas.edu/johnson/archives.hom/speeches.hom/650315.htm, on May 16, 2019. For more in-depth analyses of the dominant civil rights narrative and its harmful consequences, please see Charles M. Payne, "View From the Trenches," in *Debating the Civil Rights Movement, 1945–1968*, ed. Steven F. Lawson and Charles M. Payne (Lanham, MD: Rowman & Littlefield Publishers, 2006) and Jacquelyn Dowd Hall, "The Long Civil Rights Movement and the Political Uses of the Past," *The Journal of American History* 91, no. 4, (March 2005).
5. Ta-Nehisi Coates, "The Case for Reparations," *The Atlantic*, May 21, 2014; Charles. W. Mills, "Racial Liberalism," *PMLA* 123, no. 5 (October 2008), 1380; 1390. See also Thomas J. Sugrue, "Breaking Through: The Troubled Origins of Affirmative Action in the Workplace," in *Color Lines: Affirmative Action, Immigration, and Civil Rights Options for America*, ed. John David Skrentny (Chicago: University of Chicago Press, 2001) and Ruth Feldstein, *Motherhood in Black and White: Race and Sex in American Liberalism, 1930–1965* (Ithaca, NY: Cornell University Press, 2000), 39.
6. Tim Wise, *Colorblind: The Rise of Post-Racial Politics and the Retreat from Racial Equity* (San Francisco: City Lights Books, 2010). Coded language, including terms like "forced busing," used to capture white ire toward desegregated schooling plans, and "law and order," to condemn violence committed by African Americans in urban centers, was first used to great success by Richard Nixon's 1968 campaign to capitalize on white discontent with civil rights progress without resorting to the overt racism of vilified massive resistance. This tactic has continued to be utilized, particularly by Ronald Reagan in 1976, when he spoke of a "welfare queen" who made a fortune off of government programs, and who was presumed to be Black, even though he did not mention her race. Please see Ian Haney Lopez, *Dog Whistle Politics:*

How Coded Racial Appeals Have Reinvented Racism and Wrecked the Middle Class (New York: Oxford University Press, 2014) and Ari Berman, *Give Us the Ballot: The Modern Struggle for Voting Rights in America* (London: Picador, 2016). For an example of how Black and white Americans "don't all experience history the same way," please see Hua Hsu, "Pale Fire," *The New Yorker*, July 18, 2016.

7. Eduardo Bonilla-Silva, *Racism Without Racists: Color-Blind Racism and the Persistence of Racial Inequality in America* (Lanham, MD: Rowman & Littlefield, 2009), xvii, fn 1 and fn 5; Eduardo Bonilla-Silva, "Color-Blind Racism in Pandemic Times," *Sociology of Race and Ethnicity* 1, no. 12 (2020), 1. For an examination of how the legal system has been utilized to disproportionately segregate and marginalize Black men, please see Michelle Alexander, *The New Jim Crow: Mass Incarceration in the Age of Colorblindness* (New York: The New Press, 2010). For a study of how Lyndon Johnson's Great Society programs could reinforce the marginalization of non-white citizens, please see Elizabeth Hinton, *From the War on Poverty to the War on Crime: The Making of Mass Incarceration in America* (Cambridge, MA: Harvard University Press, 2016). And for a look at how the myth of post-racialism was used during Barack Obama's campaigns and presidency, please see Thomas J. Sugrue, *Not Even Past: Barack Obama and the Burden of Race* (Princeton, NJ: Princeton University Press, 2010).

8. Jaweed Kaleem, "How Did the Weakened Voting Rights Act Impact Election Results?" *The Los Angeles Times*, November 8, 2016, last accessed at http://www.latimes.com/nation/politics/trailguide/la-na-election-day-2016-how-did-the-weakened-voting-rights-act-1478670026-htmlstory.html, on June 2, 2019; Mark Joseph Stern, "North Carolina's 'Monster' Voter-Suppression Law is Dead," *Slate*, May 15, 2017, last accessed at http://www.slate.com/articles/news_and_politics/jurisprudence/2017/05/north_carolina_s_voter_suppression_law_was_apparently_too_racist_for_the.html, on June 2, 2019; "New Voting Restrictions in America," *Brennan Center for Justice at New York University of Law*, last updated March 1, 2017, last accessed at http://www.brennancenter.org/new-voting-restrictions-america, on June 2, 2019.

9. Coates, "The Case for Reparations."

10. Hall, "The Long Civil Rights Movement"; Peniel Joseph, *Waiting 'Til the Midnight Hour: A Narrative History of Black Power in America* (London: Macmillan, 2007); Glenda Elizabeth Gilmore, *Defying Dixie: The Radical Roots of Civil Rights* (New York: W.W. Norton & Co., 2008); Matthew D. Lassiter, *The Silent Majority: Suburban Politics in the Sunbelt South* (Princeton, NJ: Princeton University Press, 2013); Lisa McGirr, *Suburban Warriors: The Origins of the New American Right* (Princeton, NJ: Princeton University Press, 2002).

11. Philip Ennis, *The Seventh Stream: The Emergence of Rocknroll in American Popular Culture* (Middletown, CT: Wesleyan University Press, 1992); Jerry Wexler and David Ritz, *Rhythm and the Blues: A Life in American Music* (New York: St. Martin's Press, 1994), 192–193.

12. Taeku Lee, *Mobilizing Public Opinion: Black Insurgency and Racial Attitudes in the Civil Rights Era* (Chicago: University of Chicago Press, 2002), 155–182.

13. Louis Cantor, *Wheelin' on Beale: How WDIA-Memphis Became the Nation's First All-Black Station and Created the Sound that Changed America* (New York:

Pharos Books, 1992), Louis Cantor, *Dewey and Elvis: The Life and Times of a Rock 'n' Roll Deejay* (Champaign, IL: University of Illinois Press, 2010); Alan Freed, "The Big Beat Has Arrived: Izzy Rowe's Notebook," *The Pittsburgh Courier*, 1955.

14. Wexler, *Rhythm and the Blues*, 90; Ennis, *The Seventh Stream*, 192.

15. Steve Valocchi, "The Emergence of the Integrationist Ideology in the Civil Rights Movement," *Social Problems* 43, no. 1 (1996), 116–130.

16. For more on the Boston busing crisis, please see Matthew F. Delmont and Jeanne Theoharis, "Rethinking the Boston 'Busing Crisis,'" *Journal of Urban History* 43, no. 2 (March 2017) and Matthew F. Delmont, *Why Busing Failed* (Berkeley and Los Angeles: University of California Press, 2016).

17. Alan Freed, "The Big Beat," 43. Alan Freed Papers, Box 1, Folder 55, The Rock and Roll Hall of Fame Library and Archives, Cleveland, OH.

18. Mychal Denzel Smith, "Donald Sterling's Impolite Racism," *The Nation*, April 28, 2014. Last accessed at http://www.thenation.com/blog/179559/donald-sterlings-impolite-racism#, on April 29, 2014.

19. Brian Ward, *Just My Soul Responding: Rhythm and Blues, Black Consciousness, and Race Relations* (Berkeley and Los Angeles: University of California Press, 1998).

20. Charlie Gillett, *The Sound of the City: The Rise of Rock and Roll* (Cambridge, MA: Da Capo Press, 1996), xix–xx.

21. Reebee Garofalo, "Popular Music and the Civil Rights Movement," in *Rockin' the Boat: Mass Music and Mass Movements* ed. Reebee Garofalo (Cambridge, MA: The South End Press, 1999); George Lipsitz, *Time Passages: Collective Memory and American Popular Culture* (Minneapolis: University of Minnesota Press, 2001); Glenn C. Altschuler, *All Shook Up: How Rock 'n' Roll Changed America* (New York: Oxford University Press, 2004); Michael Bertrand, *Race, Rock and Elvis* (Champaign, IL: University of Illinois Press, 2000); Grace Elizabeth Hale, *A Nation of Outsiders: How the White Middle Class Fell in Love with Rebellion in Postwar America* (New York: Oxford University Press, 2011); Matthew F. Delmont, *The Nicest Kids in Town: American Bandstand, Rock 'n' Roll, and the Struggle for Civil Rights in 1950s Philadelphia* (Berkeley and Los Angeles: University of California Press, 2012); Ward, *Just My Soul Responding*; Jack Hamilton, *Just Around Midnight* (Cambridge, MA: Harvard University Press, 2016).

22. H.H. Remmers and D.H. Radler, *The American Teenager* (Newport, RI: Charter Books, 1957), 202; Ward, *Just My Soul Responding*, 3–4.

23. For this research, I followed the Oral History Association's General Principles for Oral History, which may be accessed at http://www.oralhistory.org/about/principles-and-practices/. Although a relatively small number of participants responded to this study, my research is not based on proving causation, but on showing how people from a variety of backgrounds and regions remember their experiences so similarly that we may draw larger conclusions. This sample should therefore be viewed as representative rather than definitive.

24. Hale, *A Nation of Outsiders*; Ward, *Just My Soul Responding*.

25. David Brackett, "The Politics and Practice of 'Crossover' in American Popular Music, 1963 to 1965," *The Musical Quarterly* 78, no. 4 (1994), 775.

26. *Billboard*, August 4, 1958.
27. Wise, *Colorblind*.
28. "Rock 'n' Roll: The Sound of the Sixties," *Time*, May 21, 1965.
29. For an in-depth look at white Southern responses to desegregation movements and legislation, please see Jason Sokol, *There Goes My Everything: White Southerners in the Age of Civil Rights, 1945–1975* (New York: Vintage Books, 2007).

Chapter 1

"Shufflin' 'Til the Break of Dawn," 1946–1953

Louis Jordan ended the 1940s on an exceptionally high note. The "jump blues" pioneer had recorded several hits for Decca Records' "Sepia" series, which was specifically aimed at Black consumer markets, throughout the late 1930s and early 1940s. But his crowd-pleasing 1949 release, "Saturday Night Fish Fry," surpassed even those expectations. The song topped the *Billboard* R&B chart for 12 weeks, solidifying Jordan's celebrity among Black audiences. But it also hit number 21 on *Billboard*'s national Pop charts listing, indicating that it sold well among white listeners as well.[1] As many postwar civil rights organizations focused on making racial segregation of public spaces and institutions illegal, Jordan's success revealed that some forms of popular culture already possessed cross-racial appeal. This record could be interpreted differently based on listeners' racialized perspectives, though. In a nation wracked with anxiety over mounting Cold War tensions, and uncertain of its new position as global hegemon, Jordan's up-tempo dance tune got white audiences to their feet, his lyrics conjuring images of celebration where revelers could relieve their stresses with food, music, and socializing, a "rockin'" party with "shufflin' 'til the break of dawn" where "folks was havin' the time of their life." And yet the song also detailed the very particular experiences of many Black Americans who lived in Northern urban centers during this period. The song's setting is reminiscent of the "rent parties" thrown by many city dwellers since the Great Depression to supplement their meager incomes; indeed, Jordan directly refers to admittance prices and party-goers' low-paying jobs by noting that "You don't have to pay the usual admission/If you're a cook, a waiter or a good musician." Listeners of any background may have accepted Jordan's joyous musical invitation, but white fans likely overlooked the song's depiction of how urban Black workers celebrated community and self-reliance amid persistent racism and financial precarity.[2]

Jordan himself was well aware of his popularity among white audiences, as over 20 of his recordings made the Pop charts between 1942 and 1951. "I made just as much money off white people as I did colored," he was fond of saying. "I could play a white joint this week and a colored next."[3] What interested him most was not the promise of any kind of cultural integration, but the profits that Black performers were usually denied and the ability to provide for himself financially through his chosen vocation. He was therefore dismayed when he realized that his label was not marketing his records as aggressively as he would have liked. Milt Gabler, an Artists and Repertoire (A&R) representative at Decca who personally oversaw production of many of Jordan's biggest hits, explains how the musician "went into a lot of black record shops that didn't have his records and—well, when we checked it out with our sales departments, they said 'they're on hold, they don't pay their bills.' We had no control over a lot of the stores he went to. They didn't buy their records from us." Although this process was standard within the music industry at the time, Jordan was so incensed by this seeming lack of promotion that, in 1951, he left the label that had been his professional home for almost 15 years.[4]

As Jordan struggled within the confines of a racially segmented music industry that limited access to white consumers, activists working with the Congress of Racial Equality (CORE) and the Fellowship of Reconciliation (FOR) were organizing a campaign to challenge racial segregation on interstate transportation lines that would lay the groundwork for civil rights operations in the 1950s and 1960s. This "Journey of Reconciliation" would send eight white men and eight Black men on bus routes through Virginia, North Carolina, and Tennessee in order to show how the 1947 Supreme Court ruling, *Morgan v. Virginia*, which supposedly rendered segregation on interstate transportation lines illegal, was not enforced in Southern states. This decision was barely covered in the press, limiting potential for further organizing even when the court showed that it could be supportive of Black Americans' citizenship rights in some cases. Finally, another goal of this journey was to publicize the harassment and violence that riders faced despite the legal ruling.

The riders, including co-organizers Bayard Rustin and George Houser, faced violence and were threatened with arrest several times during their journey, but at each point they remained courteous to their attackers and refused to fight back, or even defend themselves. This tactic was partially informed by Rustin's and Houser's ideological commitments to do no harm, but it also benefited the cause by making the activists seem less like the "troublemakers" that Southern white supremacists consistently referred to and more like respectable citizens calmly asserting their rights. Although, as historian Derek Catsam notes, this early "freedom ride" campaign failed to elicit mass outrage and organization, it did set the template for more broadly successful movements in the 1950s and 1960s. These better-known campaigns would be shaped by the same struggles for desegregation, radical use of "nonviolence," collective action focused on individual decision-making, democratic rhetoric, and reliance on mass media coverage as the Journey of Reconciliation. Unlike the legal strategies favored by more established civil rights organizations like the NAACP and the Urban League, this combination of tactics was confrontational, yet remained appealing to potential supporters. These types of actions were capable of reaching people across the country and showing that Black activists were simply trying to practice rights that were already enshrined in law. They were simultaneously capable of encouraging Black Americans to engage in protests and gaining sympathy from whites who had the political power to effect some of these changes.[5]

During the late 1940s and early 1950s, the color line was becoming blurry in both popular music and in the public spaces where activists were overtly challenging segregation laws. The ways that these cultural and political challenges were shaped, however, would have lasting ramifications for how desegregation and civil rights struggles would be interpreted by Black and white Americans. Blacks were more likely to view the breakdown of Jim Crow as a formidable task, whether by activists enduring violence and arrest at the hands of law enforcement, or by artists struggling to break into more financially remunerative white consumer markets. Desegregation of these spaces could, however, lead to greater economic opportunities and respect for equal citizenship. Collective action was necessary, since, as the Journey of Reconciliation revealed, a handful of activists could not make the nation care about an unenforced law, and, as Jordan found out, one musician, no matter how successful, could not force radio stations and record shops to feature his music.

White Americans, who were largely shielded from these injustices, often viewed these challenges in simpler terms that adhered to, rather than challenged, the country's supposed democratic framework. Rustin, for instance, recalled sympathetic white passengers saying things like "I thought this was the United States" when he and other activists were getting hassled on the buses.[6] This type of well-meaning statement reveals how unaware many whites remained about the kinds of discrimination Black Americans were up against. And yet the statement also reveals a fairly simplistic expectation that everyone in the country should be treated fairly, even though the denial of basic rights to African Americans is an intrinsic part of the country's history, with the implication that merely being left alone to sit where one wishes on a bus would supposedly fulfill this democratic promise. These sympathetic reactions are reflected in how white listeners could enjoy the high spirits of Louis Jordan's music, even as it expressed a particular form of Black self-reliance. Jordan and his label were interested in "integrating" their audiences and getting his record into stores in majority-white areas not because of any hope for racial reconciliation, but because they wanted the profits and platforms denied to most Black musicians.

These differences are necessary to consider as a national mass culture emerged during the postwar period, consumer desires began to overlap across supposedly segmented demographic groups, and formerly decentralized record and radio industries attempted to solidify control among a handful of major companies. These shifts were direct responses to the incredible expansion of both white and Black middle classes, whose newly disposable incomes allowed them the ambiguous power of becoming what Lizabeth Cohen calls "citizen consumers."[7] As civil rights organizations advertised desegregation through nonviolent means as a way of gaining support from white political elites, participation in this new mass culture could provide a helpful picture of what an integrated society might look like. But even as some white Americans began to voice sympathy for this goal, they did not necessarily interpret either politics or music in the same ways as their Black contemporaries. As musical styles and actual records began to "cross over" among racialized groups, and major civil rights organizations stressed nonviolent struggles for desegregation as a central goal, Blacks and sympathetic whites began to talk about integration using similar language, even if they identified with different aspects and envisioned very different futures.

EARLY DESEGREGATION MOVEMENTS, 1830S–1940S

Civil rights activists engaged in a variety of strategies during and after World War II that were not necessarily predicated on integration, especially in Northern cities, where many Black residents used the rights that were available to them to fight different forms of racial injustice. They protested job discrimination that led to higher poverty rates by becoming active in labor unions, advocating for fair local employment laws, and conducting "Don't Buy Where You Can't Work" campaigns. They organized rent strikes when landlords charged exorbitant rates, knowing that Blacks were barred from living in white neighborhoods, and rallied against the real estate and lending practices that created these "redlined" areas in the first place. They argued that politicians needed to take police brutality and other forms of racial violence seriously, and agitated for greater and more accurate representation in politics, news, and entertainment. They staged consumer boycotts after incidents of ill-treatment or racial violence, forcing companies to either capitulate to their demands or risk the serious loss of profits, supported Black-owned businesses, and, in some cases, even formed "consumer collectives" to keep wealth in their own communities. "My youth preceded the civil rights movement, but we always had our way of responding in a subtle kind of way. And boycotting was nothing new," Edgar S., who grew up in Mississippi in the 1940s and 1950s, recalls. "When someone did something that we didn't like in the community, we would boycott that person." He explains how, even though an individual might not have enough power to fight back against, for example, the drugstore where a clerk gave him change for a dollar when he had paid with a five-dollar bill, group pressure could extract results or at least "keep our own pride [when] you don't treat me right."[8]

Some Black professionals practiced what Tomiko Nagin-Brown calls "pragmatism," supporting only those integrationist efforts that would directly benefit African-American communities, while working within Jim Crow structures to strengthen their economic positions.[9] Others looked to the Communist Party USA, which advocated complete racial equality, as a possible political alternative, to the extent that the party even managed to make inroads in Southern states throughout the 1930s and 1940s, especially after its legal wing represented the so-called Scottsboro Boys during their trials for sexual assault during the early 1930s. Many were inspired to action by Black Nationalist philosophies, including what Matthew Countryman describes as "intraracial cooperation, local neighborhood politics, and self-sufficiency," especially supporting Black businesses, homeowners, schools, and politicians. Finally, some activists argued that, in light of postwar decolonization movements in Africa and Asia, Black Americans ought to link their struggles to an internationalist movement recognizing white domination of people of color around the world. These distinct methods may reveal what Peniel Joseph has called "a contested social landscape" among activists, but they do share one thing in common: a focus on ensuring full citizenship and personhood rights for Black Americans within their own communities, rather than attempting to integrate.[10] And yet, as young activist James Farmer was considering the perpetuation of Jim Crow segregation in his 1941 proposal to create CORE, an organization dedicated to racial justice, he questioned:

> Why has it all persisted? Despite NAACP and the Urban League; despite Fred Douglass; despite [W.E.B.] DuBois and James Weldon Johnson; despite Charles Hueston, Thurgood Marshall, Bill Hastie, and a whole battery of superb lawyers; despite the bombardment of the nation's ears by writers who can stride into the human heart and orators who put Demosthenes to shame. Despite it all, segregation persists.[11]

His proposal seems to indicate that a mere focus on improving facilities for Black people would never be enough, and that true freedom could only be achieved once the political and social systems defined by segregation were torn down. CORE's goals, he wrote, would be not to make housing in ghettoes more tolerable, but to destroy residential segregation; not to make Jim Crow facilities the equal of others, but to abolish Jim Crow; not to make racial discrimination more bearable, but to wipe it out. . . . We must effectively repudiate every form of racism. We must forge the instrumentalities through which that national repudiation can be effected. We must not stop until racial brotherhood is established in the United States as a fact, as well as an ideal.[12]

Movements to desegregate public spaces, especially public transit, schools, and business districts, were not new; Black Americans in both Northern and Southern cities had been fighting to desegregate these areas since before the Civil War. But their goals and perspectives differed based on time period, region, and activist tactics. Demands for integration were sometimes viewed as elitist and accommodationist by working-class activists and supporters of Black nationalism, both of whom preferred to strengthen Black community institutions rather than make appeals for what they saw as white approval. But in other instances, especially in Southern cities, where challenging Jim Crow boundaries would more often be met with violence, desegregation movements were deemed more militant than other ideological struggles. In these instances, advocates argued for the affirmation of Black personhood in public spaces, the right to receive a quality education in properly funded schools, and the ability to get to work on time anywhere in the city. These goals aligned with Black Nationalist strategies of focusing on economic development within African-American communities and encouraging pride in Blackness. Depending on time and place, though, desegregation could be deemed the most effective means of achieving those particular ends. As Steve Valocchi argues, integration, "narrowly defined as challenging legal segregation in the South," became a predominant goal of the civil rights movement in the 1950s and early 1960s "because a political battle over competing ideologies had already taken place."[13] This battle also utilized new strategies after World War II, capitalizing on global horror over Nazi atrocities and sympathy for Mahatma Gandhi's Indian Independence movement, on the U.S. government's need to appear fair and equitable at the dawn of the Cold War, and an expanding national mass media, by using nonviolent protest methods to gain support from political elites.

Organizers focused on desegregation efforts thinking that, since these laws clearly violated the Fourteenth Amendment, they could be struck down in court with enough funding and support. This tactic could also garner white sympathy since segregation seemed so overtly wrong, and visceral examples of Blacks being forcibly kept out of public spaces could be easily captured on camera. In comparison, high rents and attacks on bodily integrity were easily hidden from white view and could be explained away by other causes.

Desegregation also did not challenge the capitalist-democratic fabric of the nation the way that socialist and internationalist campaigns did—rather, it strengthened these core national values. This perspective became particularly persuasive by the late 1940s, as the Cold War commenced, and anything hinting of communism was viewed with fear and distrust. Meanwhile, as Countryman notes, "the optimism of mid-century American liberalism about the uses of state power to protect individual rights and encourage upward mobility" led many prominent organizations, including the NAACP, the Urban League, and CORE to focus their efforts on eradicating racial segregation, thereby obscuring other goals and tactics from national view.[14]

Public facilities began employing segregation guidelines in Northern cities by the 1830s, and in the South during and after the Civil War, as larger numbers of free Blacks began moving to urban areas. Black residents almost universally viewed these guidelines as affronts to their dignity as citizens, but disagreements over how to challenge them could be divisive. One perspective focused on strengthening and enriching separate Black communities by fighting for local control over Black schools, hospitals, businesses, and banks, ultimately resulting in more positions for Black professionals. Critics of "separatism," however, argued that Black communities were consistently denied the resources, amenities, inherited wealth, and stronger tax bases they would require to fully thrive. Since white-controlled power structures would never allot the proper amount of resources to these institutions, integrated public facilities were often portrayed as the only way of ensuring fair treatment. Instead of focusing on insular communities, Black workers would be able to find jobs across the city, students could attend schools closer to their homes, and residents would not have to be feel inferior whenever they made use of public facilities. Successful challenges to segregated public spaces often did result in loss of control over local Black institutions and a decrease in the number of professional positions available to Black workers. Integration and separatist movements were not always diametrically opposed, though—as historian Blair L. M. Kelley notes, "community-based institutions fueled the movement to contest lynching, disfranchisement, and the daily humiliations of segregation on trains and streetcars," all of which involved engagement in broader political concerns. Similarly, despite tensions regrading protest goals, supporters of integration movements tended to embrace what David Gerber calls a "pragmatic midpoint" that would allow Black citizens the greatest amount of possible power under rapidly deteriorating political and social conditions.[15]

As with the Journey of Reconciliation, many campaigns focused on desegregating public streetcars since residents needed reliable transportation in order to navigate expanding urban areas. Throughout the 1840s and 1850s, Black residents of New York City, Philadelphia, San Francisco, and other

Northern urban centers protested racial restrictions on new public streetcars by boycotting lines and sometimes even refusing to vacate carriages. Unlike passengers on the Journey of Reconciliation, however, most did so on an individual basis, were not averse to fighting back against conductors who attempted to eject them, and even brought legal suit against streetcar companies. Legal associations and protest organizations, which were often linked to Black churches, were formed with the express intent of demanding desegregation on public streetcars, as public figures like Frederick Douglass, Sojourner Truth, and Robert Smalls shared their own—again, individual—stories of refusing to abide by segregation constraints to abolitionist audiences.[16]

In Southern states, protests emerged in direct response to the racial segregation enforced by Black Codes that were enacted in the late 1860s and 1870s as a means of keeping recently enslaved people in inferior positions. Republican politicians tried to prevent Southern states from enforcing these codes by passing the Civil Rights Act of 1875, which stated that "all persons within the jurisdiction of the United States shall be entitled to the full and equal enjoyment of the accommodations, advantages, facilities, and privileges of inns, public conveyances on land or water, theaters, and other places of public amusement," and which was "applicable alike to citizens of every race and color, regardless of any previous condition of servitude."[17] Although the act made no mention of schools or churches, institutions which played a central role in many citizens' lives, it often went unenforced even before being declared unconstitutional by the Supreme Court in 1883. Individual Black residents continued to challenge segregation on public streetcars in Southern cities, however. Douglass, Truth, and Ida B. Wells were among the more well-known figures who would refuse to give up their seats when conductors demanded that they move to either a lower class of carriage or onto the outside platform, while Black-oriented newspapers ensured that their protests were covered in great detail. Less famous people also made news by filing lawsuits against transit lines that refused them passage and conductors who violently ejected them, even when they had purchased appropriate tickets because their presence would integrate these spaces.[18] Many litigants received damages, but transit companies' right to discriminate on the basis of race was never directly challenged, prompting integrationist activists to plan a large-scale action around an instance of direct protest. Homer Plessy's famous refusal to vacate his first-class train car when the conductor found out that he had a mixed-race background, for instance, was orchestrated by the New Orleans Citizens Committee, an organization devoted to ending segregation in the city's public spaces, as a means of bringing the state law before the courts. By 1896, four years after Plessy's arrest, this "test case" failed in a devastating manner, as the Supreme Court ruled in favor of so-called separate but equal facilities, providing federal protection for state and local Jim Crow laws for the next 70 years. Yet, as Kelley shows, this ruling did not stop Black residents of Southern cities from protesting segregation on public transit. In New Orleans, where hopes were high that the *Plessy v. Ferguson* case would abolish segregation on the trains altogether, many Black Americans boycotted the city's streetcars after passage of a 1902 law allowing screens to be placed in carriages to separate white from Black passengers. People also boycotted streetcar lines in Montgomery, Mobile, Atlanta, Richmond, Savannah, and, as Kelley states, "in nearly every state that passed such laws."[19]

In each case, protestors argued that segregation on streetcars prevented them from enjoying the benefits of equal citizenship and infringed on their dignity as free people. This rhetoric, based on seminal American values of democracy, freedom, and equality in terms of citizenship, would come to exemplify desegregation campaign goals, particularly to white outsiders. But Black residents of both Northern and Southern cities also fought for integrated streetcars because of pragmatic concerns that they felt were not adequately addressed by separatism. Workers who lived in segregated neighborhoods would often have to travel great distances to get to their jobs, and therefore required reliable transportation. Parents needed assurance that they could quickly bring sick children to hospitals, and soldiers serving in the Civil War had to report to military bases across the city. Southern climates also made traveling in cramped segregated cars almost unbearable in the heat, while members of the growing middle class in Northern cities were concerned about being forced to ride with people they considered to be socially and economically inferior. Despite the democratic rhetoric so often used in court cases and newspapers, people protested segregation on streetcars for a variety of reasons that often had just as much to do with pragmatism or propriety as abstract notions of racial equality.[20]

In Northern cities, where acceptance of certain integrated spaces was not as intrinsically threatening to the racial order, desegregation policies slowly gained degrees of acceptance among white liberals and moderates throughout the late nineteenth and early twentieth centuries. During the Civil War, for instance, elements of racial tolerance became popular among whites who were eager to differentiate themselves from their Southern enemies, while Black support during World War I, which included increased military service, convinced some white moderates that Blacks had earned their citizenship rights through patriotic action. Because assurance of these rights was so rooted in assumptions of Northern moral supremacy and beliefs that Black Americans had earned their citizenship through wartime service, however, many white supporters failed to understand that integration was only one component in the struggle for racial justice. If white moderates did not see the harm in allowing Black residents who had earned their access to certain public spaces, they also neglected to understand how the housing shortages, economic oppression, and police violence that led to race riots in over 25 cities between 1919 and the early 1920s would continue to limit African-American citizenship rights, even if segregation could be completely abolished.[21]

Desegregation would come to be defined as a major focal point for civil rights activism by the 1930s, due in large part to the efforts of the NAACP. According to Steve Valocchi, the NAACP approached civil rights struggles

> from the vantage point of the failure to extend the principles of eighteenth century liberalism. This liberalism supposedly granted all citizens economic freedom in the acquisition and use of property and political freedom in the use of the vote. Blacks had been denied those freedoms as vividly evidenced in racial discrimination, Jim Crow segregation, and restrictions on and denial of the right to vote. As a remedy to the violations of these principles, the NAACP sought the extension of this liberalism to the nation's black citizens.[22]

This organization, which was founded in 1909 by Black and white activists, including W. E. B. Du Bois, worked to combat lynching and voter disenfranchisement in the South, and to ensure equal employment and educational opportunities for Black citizens. Despite its biracial board members and progressive mission, the organization was criticized for its overwhelmingly white leadership and need to appeal to moderate whites for support. Indeed, the NAACP's framework meant that it was able to garner resources and media attention and expand across the country fairly quickly, unlike Black-led organizations like the National Equal Rights League and Marcus Garvey's United Negro Improvement Association (UNIA). But even as the organization vehemently disagreed with accommodationist politics, its members also had to exercise caution so as not to offend white potential supporters. Integration policies, which many whites feared would lead to "social equality," a polite term for interracial relationships and marriages, were sometimes deemed too controversial by the association's white leadership, even as many members vocally supported these measures. Segregation challenges, including legal attempts to force school desegregation, and protesting President Woodrow Wilson's decision to begin enforcing racial divisions in White House employment, remained critical to the association's mission. The NAACP's first two decades, however, were also marked by efforts to improve the lives of Black Southerners within the confines of state-sanctioned Jim Crow laws, including demands for a federal anti-lynching law, legal challenges to voter disenfranchisement measures, and litigation to improve separate Black schools.[23]

The association's focus narrowed in the 1930s, as sympathetic white liberals who supported the NAACP began advocating for legal challenges to Southern segregation laws. Valocchi explains that these campaigns seemed more feasible under President Franklin Roosevelt's administration, which implemented New Deal programs largely based on liberal-democratic principles connecting citizenship rights with work and education, and included over 40 African-American advisers who would come to be known as Roosevelt's "Black Cabinet." Many of these advisers strongly supported desegregation policies themselves, partially because they saw themselves as beneficiaries of this strategy, but also to protect themselves from accusations of militancy by positioning their stance as moderate, and other tactics and ideologies as radical and potentially threatening. The NAACP's leadership directed operations toward donor requests, resulting in the creation of a legal department specifically focused on challenging Southern Jim Crow laws in 1935. Desegregation of public places, which had so often been considered more militant than separatism, was therefore reshaped as a fairly moderate strategy within progressive politics, as well as the NAACP's major organizing focus.[24]

This strategy, which could be branded as both moderate and militant, was again re-fashioned after World War II broke out, as activists continued to fight for equal citizenship while simultaneously promoting their loyalty to the Allied cause. More Black Americans signed up for military service than in any previous war, prompting disputes as soldiers from outside the South encountered Jim Crow restrictions on Southern bases. Right from the start, military officers were inundated with complaints of racial insults and violence from fellow soldiers, as well as direct challenges to segregated spaces and services. Thomas Joyce details instances where Black soldiers, incensed that they were preparing to fight for democratic principles on behalf of their country, walked out of racist presentations, staged sit-ins in spaces designated only for whites, and forcibly "desegregated" lunch tables in base cafeterias.[25] In these cases, soldiers' demands were based on the fact that they were denied basic rights while making sacrifices that were directly tied to their status as American citizens.

Activists waged protests based on this ideology on the home front too. Even though A. Philip Randolph's 1941 call for ten thousand Black Americans to flood the streets of Washington, D.C., until the city ground to a halt never came to pass, President Roosevelt was still moved to sign Executive Order 8802, which barred racial discrimination in hiring practices and wages among companies with federal contracts. Even though activists used language and tactics that were militant enough to provoke this action, David Lucander explains how the movement was defined by a combination of "explicit patriotism, confrontational rhetoric, and threat of disrupting public life." Randolph, he says, felt that "respectable" forms of protest like petitioning representatives could only go so far and was therefore encouraged to use bolder tactics to fight for economic opportunities among Black workers. But supporters also "expressed allegiance to the United States," he says, which "appealed to the vast majority of African Americans, who preferred a flawed United States with the capacity for improvement rather than living in a Nazi racial order under German rule."[26] This movement, then, used militant tactics as a means of affirming Black Americans' rights to participate in the economy and to fight on behalf of their country. This ideology also shaped *The Pittsburgh Courier*'s "Double 'V'" campaign, which encouraged readers of the renowned Black-oriented newspaper to support the war effort as a means of promoting democracy abroad and fighting racism at home. Black Americans could prove their loyalty by working in munitions factories, participating in scrap metal drives, planting victory gardens, and buying war bonds, and would then, theoretically, be rewarded with federal civil rights initiatives once the war was over. This campaign explicitly sought support from white politicians who could be convinced to support equal rights policies by promoting positive stories of wartime involvement, and positioned equal citizenship as something that Black Americans deserved because of their service. But this campaign was also not as strongly grounded in integrationist ideology as many previous movements; the *Courier*, for instance, was a Black-owned-and-operated newspaper with a history of vocal support for civil rights struggles, while the initiatives it highlighted were led by Black leaders from mostly segregated communities. The appeals to white politicians that would become hallmarks of the civil rights movement were therefore balanced by a strong focus on independent, Black-led efforts.[27]

These wartime initiatives prompted some federal officials to support the equal treatment that was already supposed to be assured by the Fourteenth and Fifteenth Amendments. This activism would lay the groundwork for the civil rights strategies of the 1950s and early 1960s. Most prominent civil rights organizations focused on getting the federal government and white allies to support laws that would desegregate public spaces and transportation in the South since these challenges had proved somewhat successful in the past, and because this goal was seen as a crucial first step toward achieving full and equal citizenship for all Black Americans. But this ideology was also very much shaped by more militant demands for the right to exist in these public spaces, and to exercise economic and political rights that were already supposed to be assured.

A NEW POSTWAR MOVEMENT, 1945–1953

Although popular narratives tend to situate the start of the modern civil rights movement in the mid-1950s, many movement historians instead point to its origins in the immediate aftermath of World War II.[28] This period is "too often overshadowed by the events of the late 1950s and 1960s," Jeanne Theoharis argues. "But there was nothing inevitable about the mass movement of the mid-1950s and early 1960s, which would not have been possible without this arduous spadework."²⁹ Much of this "spadework" was undertaken in the South by veterans and "Double V" supporters who were incensed by the indignities of living under violent white supremacy enshrined in Jim Crow laws after fighting a war for global democracy. Soldiers who fought in Europe had found that they were treated as *Americans* rather than as *Black Americans* while overseas, and were generally allowed to eat or congregate with white friends in nonsegregated spaces. Many of these soldiers had never left their hometowns or counties before, so these very different experiences in international spaces led them to see that racial segregation and brutality were part of a historically constructed system that could be challenged and changed. Amzie Moore, a soldier who would later become an NAACP leader in Mississippi, recalled seeing ancient Roman ruins when stationed in Italy and realized that they had been part of a great empire, just like the United States—and that that empire had fallen. If this beautiful and complex civilization could falter, then so too could Jim Crow.³⁰ Indeed, Beat writer and Black Arts Movement proponent Amiri Baraka argued that the realization "that social inequities suffered by the black [person] could for the first time be looked at somewhat objectively by [blacks] as an *evil*, and not merely as their eternal *lot*" ultimately led to more organized demands for equal treatment.³¹ The tensions of battle and the importance of relying on fellow soldiers for survival also revealed the absurdity of American racial divisions. "It was all so illogical," said David Dinkins, a Marine who would later become the mayor of New York City.

> Here we're going to fight this war to end all wars, yet we got second-class citizenship. As far as I knew, there weren't going to be white bullets and black bullets. There weren't going to be white graves and black graves. We were all going to be together—or so I thought. But when those Marines who may have thought Jim Crow was okay got pinned down under fire in places like Guam, boy—they just loved to see black Marines landing and bringing ammo. They were so relieved and delighted they hugged them.³²

This process was intensified when soldiers returned to the South from battlefields where their heroism had been more or less applauded, yet discovered that they were still treated like second-class citizens. These men were heroes and warriors; they were not coming back to pick cotton under the threat of racist violence.

Black Americans who did not leave rural Southern areas during the war were also inclined to challenge Jim Crow laws. Even in these areas, the juxtaposition between how Black residents were treated in comparison to German prisoners of war on local military bases was considered shocking. At one camp in Salina,

Kansas, for instance, Black soldiers who sat at a lunch counter were told that the establishment did not serve "colored" people—even though German POWs were eating at the same counter. Private Lloyd Brown, who encountered this spectacle, mused: "If we were untermenschen in Nazi Germany, they would break our bones. As 'colored' men in Salina, they only break our hearts."[33] On the Mississippi plantation where legendary blues musician B. B. King worked as a sharecropper in his youth, he recalls how "German prisoners-of-war used to come and pick cotton" alongside the usual workers. "They would come to work at eight or nine o'clock in the morning and they would go back 3:30 or four o'clock in the evening," he said. "We had to be there all day. They could eat at the cafes, but we weren't allowed to go there. Now, that I know. That's sort of sad when I think about that today, how we were treated."[34]

It is during this period that we begin to see a new direction in civil rights struggles take form. Even as civil rights organizations continued to fight against a variety of injustices, desegregation of public spaces dominated most campaign goals. The NAACP's decision to focus on integration played a large role here, but since it mainly focused on legal challenges, smaller civil rights groups took up the mantle by fighting for desegregation, often starting on public transportation, by building relatively large campaigns around instances of direct resistance. Irene Morgan's refusal to give up her bus seat in front of white passengers, which provided the catalyst for the *Morgan v. Virginia* case that would ostensibly end segregation on interstate travel lines, and the harassment that Wilson Head received when he refused to sit at the back of a bus from Atlanta to Washington, D.C., both provided initial inspiration for the Journey of Reconciliation.[35] And despite many Southern restrictions preventing Black servicemen from appearing in public in uniform, Isaac Woodard tried to board a bus in South Carolina in his military raiment and was subsequently beaten and blinded for his efforts. When the NAACP helped him finance his court case against the busing company, this brutal treatment of a Black soldier in the supposedly free and democratic United States made headlines around the world, ultimately prompting President Harry Truman to order a federal investigation into his case. Although South Carolina fought the investigation at every turn, Truman's administration was undeterred, creating the Committee on Civil Rights, which was tasked with investigating instances of racial discrimination, and the president himself passed Executive Order 9981, which desegregated the Armed Forces. This move fundamentally changed the nature of the Democratic Party, prompting the mass exodus of white Southern "Dixiecrats," while giving hope to Black Americans that, perhaps, they might be protected by some elements of the federal government.[36]

Organizational campaigns built around instances of nonviolent direct action would come to define the postwar civil rights movement. Pictures and stories of people being brutally ejected from buses and assaulted by police or white bystanders made the injustice of Jim Crow easily understandable for readers and viewers, and sensational news at a time when mass media was growing exponentially. Many protestors, including those mentioned here, were either veterans or defense plant workers, which identified them as patriotic Americans who had made sacrifices for their country and had therefore *earned* the right to be treated with dignity (a notion which neatly overlooked the fact that, in many cases, they were simply attempting to exercise rights that were already on the law books). These protests effectively increased awareness and sympathy from liberal whites outside the South, as well as limited support from the federal government.[37]

Direct action protests are difficult to ignore due to their confrontational nature, but since nonviolence was used as a strategy, white defenders of segregation were often castigated for harming people who refused to fight back. Struggles for racial justice have a long history of pacifist protests utilized by Quakers, but, as John D'Emilio explains, younger activists like James Farmer and Bayard Rustin, under the leadership of FOR leader A. J. Muste, felt the need to put their moral beliefs into action, and to transform society rather than simply refusing to partake in harmful institutions. "Where pacifism in the FOR had once been a message to preach," D'Emilio says, these members "understood nonviolence as a path toward action. Where the Christian pacifists of the FOR sought to end war, [younger activists] wished to eliminate injustice."[38] During this period, protestors around the world were particularly inspired by Mahatma Gandhi's use of *satyagraha*, a conscientious use of nonviolent resistance, during the Indian Independence Movement of the 1930s and 1940s. This form of protest, which requires directly confronting discriminatory institutions, and even preventing their operation, while rendering oneself vulnerable to physical violence, arrest, and financial ramifications without causing harm in return, differs from passive resistance, which merely involves refusing to engage with oppressive structures. It is this more confrontational form of civil disobedience which inspired Farmer to contend that "words are not enough; there must be action. We must withhold our support and participation from the institution of segregation in every area of American life—not an individual witness to purity of conscience, as [Henry David] Thoreau used it, but a coordinated movement of mass noncooperation as with Gandhi."[39] These members ultimately formed CORE in 1942 to specifically target racial injustice, as well as asserting, D'Emilio says, that "the cruelty, exploitation, and indecency inherent in racial caste systems were as much implicated in violence as were declarations of war and the maneuvers of armies."[40]

Rustin, who grew up in a household heavily influenced by Quakerism, and attended a Quaker college, viewed any participation in the war effort or the carceral system as a form of violence which needed to be eliminated in order for a more racially just society to be formed, declaring nonviolence as not only a "policy," but "a way of life."[41] And yet this decision was also tactical. Although he was similarly devoted to nonviolence on a moral basis, Farmer also argued that "we cannot achieve a raceless society through racist methods. We must demand of all who believe—whites, too—that they must, as a matter of conscience, as well as strategy, withdraw from participation in racist practices."[42] The concept of "strategy" was incredibly important as activists began to adapt nonviolent direct action as a tactic. Refusing to engage in violence, even as it was meted out by police and others acting as instruments of oppression, made protestors look like they were fighting for a just cause. These actions also seemed effective. James Forman, a director of the SNCC, recalled how he and his friends would get into fights with white kids when they crossed the segregated boundary in his Chicago neighborhood. One day, he told his friends "if we cross the street and they are constantly beating us, why don't we just duck down . . . and go underneath them and get to the store." His friends listened to him, and "they all sort of disappeared . . . we didn't have any more trouble with White people beating us for crossing the street."[43] On the surface, this form of protest could seem simpler and have a higher probability of success than other tactics, which were more likely to invite opposition—and if they did not work, then at least protestors would appear to have the moral high ground when their activities were covered by the media.

Despite its moral and tactical advantages, this shift toward nonviolent direct protest stirred controversy among many Black Americans, even those involved in other freedom efforts. The NAACP, for instance, continued to focus on using the legal system to challenge segregation as a violation of the Fourteenth Amendment. Many prominent members felt that direct action was too dangerous, including Justice Thurgood Marshall, who privately complained that the tactic would "get people killed." These fear were shared by older members of FOR.[44] Farmer's own father warned him against using direct nonviolence, telling him that the tactic only worked in India because the British were a minority in that country, while white Americans made up a majority of the population, and were not afraid to use violence against protestors since "in our culture, only women and sissies back away from a fight, and the big fist wins."[45] Furthermore, many communities feared that they would be punished for these direct action campaigns after activists had left the area, leaving them, Catsam says, "to face the wrath and recriminations of an enraged white community that lumped the alien protestors with even the most acquiescent of local blacks." In one case, middle-class residents even tried to prevent a mass meeting supporting the riders, even though it eventually drew a sizeable crowd.[46] And yet CORE activists pressed on with the tactic, as Farmer noted that "nonviolence and legal action must be twin weapons—either one being used when it seems to be most applicable, with each bolstering the other."[47]

As CORE expanded its direct action efforts to stage a sit-in at a Chicago restaurant that routinely denied service to Black customers or treated them with hostility, Farmer became increasingly aware of a racial imbalance at preparatory meetings. "There was no shortage of whites with an awareness of Gandhi and an interest in nonviolence," he claimed, "but where were the blacks? This could not be a white movement." White members tended to join these campaigns, he says, because of their moral beliefs in equality and "colorblindness, but "there were not many blacks . . . who were pacifists and socialists and interested in direct action of a nonviolent nature against racism." He further explained that "Negroes who came in would be ends-oriented rather than means-oriented. They would join the movement because the program worked, produced results; not because of an ideological commitment to nonviolence."[48] Even though CORE's commitment to "destroy[ing] residential segregation" and "abolish[ing] Jim Crow" was hardly a gentle proposition, it became increasingly clear that using nonviolent direct resistance as a tactic to challenge segregation would appeal in very different ways to sympathetic whites and Blacks who joined the movement, and that their ultimate goals would differ.[49]

CONSUMERISM AND THE RISE OF THE BLACK MIDDLE CLASSES

The "ends-oriented" goals that Farmer mentions very often seemed more obtainable to the increasing number of Black Americans entering the middle classes after World War II. Increasing employment and educational opportunities, as well as the Truman administration's support for some civil rights initiatives, led many to believe that the system was starting to work in their favor. Perhaps a truly democratic, integrated society where Black citizens were treated with dignity and could receive the same opportunities as their white counterparts was actually possible. Although doubts about the benefits Black Americans would receive from integration persisted, younger people especially became more likely to view desegregation efforts in both the North and the South as eliminating a crucial obstacle that barred them from enjoying full citizenship rights.

The American economy prospered to such an extent after World War II that this period has been dubbed "The Affluent Society." Although white Americans were the major beneficiaries, Black Americans also profited from this boom in wealth and consumer spending. Indeed, an expanding federal government, postwar employment and educational programs, labor union strength, and widespread industrialization in the South led to Black income rates growing faster than white rates in the mid to late 1940s. "The separation was still there," Edgar S. recalls of the Black community in Vicksburg, Mississippi, where his family relocated from a rural part of the state during this period. "But I found Blacks in different positions economically. . . . That's where I saw Black physicians, for instance. Black dentists. Still Black teachers. But in my small town, I had not seen a Black professional other than those that were in the school or in the churches."[50] By the mid-1950s, Secretary of Commerce Sinclair Weeks claimed that one-third of the African-American urban population were homeowners, earning up to four times more income than before the war, with employment rates holding steady at 90 percent.[51] The millions of Black Southerners who headed to Northern and western cities for wartime employment may not have left racial prejudice, segregation, or violence behind, but greater educational and professional opportunities, accompanied by the ability to vote in most areas, led to a sharp increase in numbers for the Black middle class. Some labor organizations, particularly the Congress of Industrial Organizations, ensured various levels of employment equality, allowing non-white workers to advance in their positions. These changes led sociologist E. Franklin Frazier to write that, after the war ended, "the economic status of the Negro, the Negro middle class, or the 'black bourgeoisie' has grown in size and acquired a dominant position among Negroes."[52]

This financial growth, while impressive, remained far shakier than that of white contemporaries. Black families who were able to take advantage of the still-limited economic and social opportunities which arose after World War II may have been able to enjoy some of the financial and social benefits of the middle class, but the firm economic foundation that solidified the positions of their white contemporaries, whose stability was subsidized by government programs, remained frustratingly out of reach for many.[53] Madison Foster, who became active in the League of Revolutionary Black Workers and the Black Arts Movement in the 1960s, was the son of a physician and a nurse, yet, despite his parents' professions, notes that his father did not leave behind an inheritance when he died "because he gave a lot of gratis medical care," while his mother's income remained fairly low. "On paper it looked as if I was well to do as a Southern black, but the contrary was true," he asserts. "I didn't learn to write until I was nine. I went to the public schools like all the black kids."[54] Black unemployment rates, while still incredibly low in the postwar period, were three times higher than white rates. Black families were much closer to losing their financial stability through job loss, racist employment practices that prevented people from finding new jobs, unequal incomes, and lack of home equity, and many had to work more than one position in order to pay the bills. Nat Williams, for instance, became famous as the first Black deejay at Memphis's renowned WDIA station, yet was only able to maintain his family's middle-class lifestyle by keeping his full-time job as a history teacher at Booker T. Washington High School.[55] If a growing number of Black households making a suitable living, working in professional or unionized jobs, and preparing their children for university could not exactly be deemed "middle class" in the same way that financially stable whites would be, they may instead be considered part of what historian Michele Mitchell terms the "aspiring class."[56]

This distinction was made abundantly clear in Black residential neighborhoods across the country, which were segregated by federal policies and real estate regulations that prevented many Black families from purchasing homes, as well as by Jim Crow state laws in the South. These policies instead benefited the scores of young white families who wanted to flee the confines of the city for the metaphorically and literally greener pastures of brand-new houses in suburban developments. In an attempt to ensure that the housing market, an integral aspect of a healthy economy, did not spiral out of control, the federal government intervened in the private sector to a remarkable degree, prodding many families who could not otherwise afford housing prices to purchase suburban homes. Through the Serviceman's Readjustment Act (more popularly known as the G.I. Bill), returning veterans were not only granted historically low interest rates on suburban mortgages, but the Federal Housing Administration (FHA) guaranteed their loans, meaning that applicants were almost always approved by banks and insurance companies. In many cases, a neat little suburban home with a backyard, close to shopping centers and schools, was less expensive than an urban apartment that was falling into disrepair. The choice to move to a new suburb, then, was also often the cheapest option.

These desirable economic spaces, however, were almost entirely white.[57] Despite the fact that over 1 million Black Americans served in the military during World War II and were therefore eligible for the same G.I. Bill benefits as their white counterparts, few were able to take advantage of them in the same way. Southern states codified racial segregation, of course, but in other areas of the country, the FHA would only guarantee loans for homes purchased in neighborhoods that were "stable"—a code word for "white." City maps were issued to banks and real estate and insurance offices with red outlines around neighborhoods that would not be supported by the FHA. "Redlining" areas became an efficient means of keeping Black homebuyers out of certain neighborhoods, which the FHA and lending organizations maintained was important for appeasing white residents' anti-Black racism, ensuring that residents would remain in their homes (and keep up with stable mortgage payments) for years to come, and, perhaps most importantly, ensuring support from Southern congressmen. Furthermore, Black families who asked to look at homes in new suburbs or otherwise all-white areas were effectively "steered" out of the neighborhood by real estate agents who sought to maintain the racial status quo set by the FHA. These decisions were not based on individual prejudices; they were part of a systemic attempt by the National Association of Real Estate Boards to maintain housing segregation, as shown in the 1924 Code of Ethics, where realtors are advised to "never be instrumental in introducing into a neighborhood . . . members of any race or nationality . . . whose presence will clearly be detrimental to property values in the neighborhood."[58]

Most suburban housing developments also had racially restrictive covenants written into each individual deed. Although restrictive covenants are commonly used to prevent fences from being built on the property, or owners from using the premises to maintain farm animals, these covenants strictly forbade homeowners from ever selling to someone "other than a member of the Caucasian race." Racially restrictive covenants, which were not deemed completely illegal until 1968 despite numerous efforts by the NAACP and other civil rights organizations to abolish them, effectively prevented Black Americans from purchasing homes in most suburbs. This racialized exclusion was painfully clear to Black residents of Northern cities, where communities did not require the Jim Crow signs that peppered the South. The folksinger Odetta, who grew up in Los Angeles, recalled that "I didn't see any colored signs and white signs, but I knew where I could and couldn't go," while academic and musician Tony T., who grew up in a majority-white neighborhood in Connecticut, remembers how "if you went to the store, you would be afraid you might not be treated properly, even if you always were treated properly."[59] Dootsie Williams, a former swing band leader and independent, Black-oriented record label owner based in Los Angeles, recalls Jim Crow-type segregation even in this supposedly progressive West Coast city. "Blacks were not allowed South of Slauson for many years," he says. "I remember a Black family had the nerve, the audacity, to move in at 92nd Street, and the whites gave them a terrible time."[60] Similarly, legendary record producer and music impresario Quincy Jones says he "didn't understand racism too well" growing up in a mostly white community in Washington State, where he was popular enough to be voted student class president, but he did begin to question why Black residents lived "way outta town . . . you'd get off the bus, we had to walk up a hill for three miles."[61] Respondents who grew up in the South also recall how they became aware of these divisions, even if they were more overt and all-encompassing. Ed B., for instance, remembers being threatened with violence and racist epithets whenever he ventured into a white neighborhood that abutted his own in his hometown of Memphis. When he was very young, he says, "We would fight, run, fight, run, fight, run. That type of stuff. When I look back, it was all fun. I never looked at it as racism that much." And yet, as he grew up, "it resonated on me, hey, that's what that was."[62] And while Edgar S. explains that he always knew that his family was poor, he did not necessarily see their economic situation as resulting from racial discrimination at the time. "I knew we were separate because we lived on one side of the track, and white people lived on the other," he says. "I knew something was wrong with that. I didn't have any personal encounter [with racism] in Hollandale [MS], but I was a victim of what was going on because my family was prohibited from advancing, and [had] to live in certain kinds of conditions. Quite different from the white." And yet, he asserts, "I didn't feel inferior. I knew they were separate, but [I felt like] we were being held down. Not because we were not capable. But I knew it was wrong."[63] Black kids in redlined cities and Jim Crow states alike therefore grew up aware of the injustices that shaped their lives and the very spaces they were allowed to inhabit.

These restrictions meant that most Black people could not build equity by purchasing homes the way their white counterparts did, limiting abilities to grow personal and inheritable wealth. Residential segregation also cut Black families off from well-funded schools and job opportunities, which state governments purposely situated in white areas, and which remained inaccessible if regular transportation was unavailable. Finally, major retail outlets were also based in white suburbs or in downtown business districts, restricting many Black consumers to smaller shops with more limited access to goods, and, if they were owned by whites who lived outside of the area, often charged exorbitant prices. These limits meant that Black consumers were seldom courted by businesses and advertisers, and, as Robert Weems and Robert Weems Jr. note, were "subjected to 'second-class treatment'" when they shopped for goods and services. "African Americans' overall socioeconomic status warranted the widespread disrespect shown them," they explain. "Moreover, any group desire for upward mobility appeared to be thwarted by the existence of American apartheid, popularly known as 'Jim Crow.' Consequently, American businesses believed they could ignore and disrespect African American consumers with impunity."[64]

And yet as the affluent society spread (unevenly) across racial boundaries, the Weemses note that "a once predominantly rural people with limited disposable income were increasingly seen as a potentially lucrative market." Intrepid advertisers aimed to convince potential clients of the vast profits they could collect by targeting Black markets. A widely read two-part article, published in the radio-advertising trade publication *Sponsor* in the fall of 1949, for instance, urged stations and potential corporate patrons to consider the "Forgotten 15,000,000" Black Americans as an untapped demographic. Their newfound financial stability created potential consumers, but they were still being ignored because of old-fashioned assumptions about Black impoverishment. "In numbers and in buying power the American Negro market is growing by the proverbial leaps and bounds," the article's author exhorted, clearly under the assumption that misguided notions about income levels would overcome corporate hesitation to target Black markets.[65] Although many businesses continued to disregard Black consumers, fearing that they would become known as a "Negro" company, and that whites would take their money elsewhere, several large corporations did begin to target campaigns to lure Black customers to purchase their products, advertising in Black-oriented media outlets, conducting studies to determine their needs, and even hiring Black employees in selective locations. Some businesses also began to encourage respectful treatment of all customers, regardless of race, since Black customers were quick to boycott discriminatory companies.[66]

More often than not, advertisements aimed at Black consumers bore a striking resemblance to those found in general interest publications, but with one major difference: they featured Black models. Children smiled after brushing with Crest toothpaste; well-adorned, middle-class wives covered grays with hair dye; and men in business suits enjoyed choice liquor at the office. The copy did not differ from "mainstream" white advertisements, and an orderly, middle-class lifestyle was upheld as the ideal.[67] This form of advertising reflected some of the hopes that civil rights activists had for desegregated spaces: it increased African-American representation, and depicted people engaged in relatable daily activities rather than relying on harmful stereotypes that could perpetuate discrimination. It showed that large companies were taking their needs seriously and treating them as what Lizabeth Cohen calls "citizen consumers." It reflected the increased income that Black Americans were ready to spend, and the status that better-paying jobs and higher educations had brought members of this growing middle class. Indeed, Grace Elizabeth Hale has shown that "consumer culture could undermine white supremacy" to the extent that Southern states passed increasingly harsh Jim Crow laws as more and more Black consumers were able to participate. Although Black-oriented marketing campaigns were still relegated to African-American media outlets and shops in Black neighborhoods, the fact that large, mainstream corporations were making efforts to sell the same products, often using the same tactics, to both Black and white customers seemed to anticipate a future where the ability to live, work, and play would not be hindered by race; where, as Hale so eloquently puts it, Blacks could proclaim "'We are not inferior' above the din of segregation's daily humiliations."[68]

This limited form of racial tolerance was only granted to those with means, echoing one of Black activists' major concerns with desegregation campaigns. This type of integration equates citizenship with money and consumerism and can therefore act as a commodity rather than a fundamental right. Access to the mass consumption enjoyed by middle-class whites during this period was tenuous for many Black Americans, even those whose incomes had increased after the war, particularly since their poverty rates were still far higher relative to white rates. This marketing also emphasized assimilation with white and middle-class norms even as Black representation technically increased, while Black business owners feared that larger corporations could easily lure away their customer bases with lower prices and more varied product selections, forcing them to close their doors. This dynamic provided a source of tension among many members of the Black middle classes, for whom, Andrew Flory explains, "success was often equated with distance from authentic blackness."[69] While some feared that Black communities could be drained of their culture and wealth while profiting white-owned and operated corporations, the idea that integration could be purchased within the existing capitalist-democratic system if one simply worked hard enough to afford it and behaved according to acceptable middle-class standards would begin to take hold in more liberal white circles.

CORPORATE VS. INDEPENDENT: RACIAL DISTINCTIONS WITHIN A GROWING MUSIC INDUSTRY

Although the market for Black-oriented music continued to grow throughout the 1940s and into the early 1950s, the mainstream music industry proved stubbornly resistant to any form of integration among racialized genres or audiences. Decades earlier, in the 1920s and 1930s, major labels Columbia, Decca, and RCA Victor had been so eager to capitalize on the musical tastes of Black and white Southern migrants to urban centers that they purchased the catalogs of smaller labels that catered to these audiences, and even opened their own specialized divisions, including Decca's Sepia series, which had signed Louis Jordan in the 1930s. Country acts like the Carter Family and Jimmie Rodgers, and Black artists like Louis Armstrong and Duke Ellington, performed well for their respective labels, although Black musicians and songwriters were almost always paid less than their white counterparts, viewed merely, Steve Chapple and Reebee Garofalo maintain, "as something a little extra by the record companies." It would therefore become easy to neglect these divisions after the war, as rapidly corporatizing labels began demanding assured profits from broadly white audiences.[70]

Record and radio sales were booming in a way that no one could have imagined in the years after the war. By the end of the 1940s, radio sales amounted to about $224 million, as 95 percent of American homes owned at least one radio.[71] "The war! We couldn't produce enough records," Decca Records producer Milt Gabler recalls. "You couldn't get enough material to satisfy the demand. Everybody had money—they're working in plants and everybody was doing business, so records were selling."[72] But just as war-weary and newly affluent Americans developed an incredible hunger for records, the purchasing and distribution powers of major record labels contracted. Most major-release records at the time were made of shellac, a substance from India that was strictly rationed for war usage. Even when the war ended, this shortage drastically reduced the number of acts each label would be able to sign and promote, so the majors decided to focus on white pop acts that were proven best sellers rather than gamble on new artists who would need time to build audiences or on R&B musicians, whose Black target market was decidedly smaller and less profitable.[73] "Larger companies wouldn't sign a lot of acts because you couldn't press enough records," Gabler continues. "You could sell a million by Bing [Crosby] and the Andrews Sisters, and you only had so much material." Overall, the major record companies at the time, Decca, Capitol, Columbia, Mercury, and RCA Victor, seemed unable to fulfill consumer demand for different kinds of music, even as the companies themselves began to expand.[74]

The six major labels also gained tighter control over their artists, merged with other companies, and invested in new technologies to gain larger market shares, sell overseas, and compete with rivals. Prior to World War II, record companies attempted to sell to a broad demographic while reinforcing the segregation of both markets and actual physical spaces, a plan that ostensibly garnered higher profits. But by the late 1940s, record labels expanded control over production and distribution to further profit from the nation's increased purchasing power, while, at the same time, the industry as a whole decentralized in order to target newly identified segmented markets. These shifts would theoretically allow many artists to reach larger audiences, and the musical genres of marginalized groups to be marketed and available as part of this new national mass culture. The major labels, however, began manufacturing and distributing records as well as producing them, leading to tighter control over market share, and increased competition among six rapidly expanding companies. This process was easier and cheaper than it had been before the war, partly due to technological advances, but also because nationally based media and marketing allowed companies to reach larger consumer bases than ever before. Luring artists away from other labels was a long-standing tradition, so most companies began locking their talent in with contracts that were difficult to break. In the midst of a battle over record formats, Columbia and RCA opened television departments that allowed cross-promotion on CBS and NBC, while Decca merged with Universal Pictures in 1952 and British music publishing company EMI purchased Capitol in 1955.[75] Specific departments were created to distribute records on a wider basis, and, particularly, to find and groom new talent. This task was conducted by A&R agents, who wielded incredible power at their respective labels during the postwar period. These executives discovered and signed artists, but also acted as proto-producers, forming a bridge between songwriters, musicians, and recording personnel by deciding which songs would be recorded, hiring technicians, and sometimes even determining musical arrangements. The popular music industry was strongly crafted by what Chapple and Garofalo refer to as "the centralization of A&R control," for, by the late 1940s, they almost exclusively determined what the major labels would sell to record shops and radio stations around the world.[76]

While A&R representatives were eager to root out any artists who could increase their companies' profits, they were more likely to focus on only a few singers and songwriters whom they believed had mass appeal, and to ensure that they recorded often and were heavily publicized. This minimized the risk of trying to sell the public on unknown quantities, and assured a base level of profit. Another way of avoiding risk was to assure that musical styles did not shift much from record to record. Most pop recordings were 32-measure songs with an 8-bar chorus that was repeated, led to a bridge and release, then repeated once more. They were melodic, meant to encourage sing-alongs, and usually offered few musicological surprises, though they were specifically engineered to get stuck inside people's heads and leave them humming along for the rest of the day. The genre was also almost entirely white. Even if a few pop artists like Nat King Cole or Johnny Mathis happened to be Black, A&R reps were mindful of the risks of marketing unknown artists to majority-white markets, which further segmented their consumer bases, and reproduced racial hierarchies by catering to presumed white preferences. Artists signed to these labels had little control over their output, and A&R reps were mostly interested in signing new performers who looked and sounded like ones who had already proven popular with consumers. This process was engineered to deliver fool-proof profits to major labels, but it was predicated on the somewhat misguided assumption that customers merely wished to purchase the same records over and over again without fear of being challenged or surprised by the music they listened to. By following these segmented marketing plans, the postwar popular music industry became an increasingly narrow conduit for musicians to connect with their audiences.[77]

A&R reps also acted as gatekeepers for the mainstream music industry by allowing only non-threatening, mostly white musicians singing innocuous lyrics like "All I want is having you/And music, music, music" and "How much is that doggie in the window/I do hope that doggie's for sale" to pass through.[78] These songs were created by professional songwriters who worked exclusively for major labels and were overwhelmingly based in New York. These professional positions required writers to hold regular schedules in their offices, and to churn out as many chart-topping hits as possible. This formula both restricted and encouraged innovation, as artists were reluctant to stray too far from the status quo, yet, at the same time, were quick to capitalize on a trend if they believed it would sell and distinguish them from their competitors. Most were also represented by the American Society of Composers, Authors, and Publishers (ASCAP), an organization formed in 1914 to ensure that artists were properly compensated when their music was published or used in hotels, restaurants, jukeboxes, films, and, by the 1950s, on television. Members were able to earn a living making music, but the organization could hardly be described as egalitarian. ASCAP only protected dues-paying members, and in order to achieve this rank, one had to be fairly established as a songwriter for a major record label. By 1939, the society was comprised of 1,100 writers and 140 publishers, all of whom were linked to major music or film companies, and was only accepting members who had already published five songs. These stipulations barred blues and gospel musicians, whose offerings were collectively dubbed "race records," and country and western artists, who were (somewhat pejoratively) known as "hillbilly" singers. If one of these artists did happen to be signed to ASCAP, they often received low flat fees rather than the more lucrative royalty contracts common among established pop singers. This closed system ensured that about 15 large music publishing companies, which dealt almost exclusively with white pop artists and marketed almost entirely to white, middle-class audiences, controlled about 90 percent of the market.[79]

ASCAP's hold on the music industry was challenged in the postwar years by two distinct developments: the establishment of Broadcast Music, Inc. (BMI), an alternative music performing rights organization, and the proliferation of several smaller, independent record labels and music publishing firms that responded to consumer demands for the blues, gospel, and country music, especially among Black and rural listeners. BMI, which was founded by Sydney M. Kaye and other broadcasters in 1940, was created as a lower-cost organization that recognized the opportunity to represent "race" and "hillbilly" performers, as well as younger, nonprofessional artists, who often lived outside the confines of New York or Los Angeles, by negotiating complicated agreements with radio and television stations and "enterprises that rely on music as an important part of their business," like hotels, restaurants, and music clubs. Since BMI's fees were cheaper than ASCAP's, many lower-profile stations and venues were eager to sign agreements, even if it meant giving airtime to little-known artists. In some cases, these agreements even meant that places of leisure, including bars, dance clubs, skating rinks, and bowling alleys, which were often racially segregated, even in the North, started featuring music by both Black and white artists in jukeboxes and on music systems.[80] Music that was previously unavailable in many parts of the country was now being heard in public spaces, radio stations, and record shops by larger and more diverse audiences. This process, Andrew Flory explains, helped to create "the infrastructure that supported black popular music as a distinct, self-contained market" in the years after the war.[81]

This process had the potential to challenge segregated production and distribution systems within the music industry as major advertisers in other fields were beginning to court Black consumers. A 1949 study conducted by a Charleston advertising agency found that roughly 80–95 percent of Black Americans across the country owned radios and purchased more records per capita than any other racial group.[82] With a postwar economy flush in both dollars and dreams, and tape recording technology making it easier and cheaper than ever to produce records, enterprising businesspeople accepted the core concept of segmented marketing by opening independent labels which specialized in what were considered "niche" genres. More than one thousand independent record labels debuted between 1948 and 1954, approximately half of which focused almost exclusively on sales to Black customers.[83] Most of these companies were started by white men who had developed an affinity for African-American culture and wanted to immerse themselves in this world while helping their favorite musicians reach more Black customers. Art Rupe, who founded Specialty Records in Los Angeles in 1946, opened his storied label because "some of this music moved me so much it brought tears to my eyes."[84] Phil and Leonard Chess, sons of Polish immigrants, were similarly affected by the music they heard in predominantly Black neighborhoods in their native Chicago and opened Chess Records to record the traditional Southern blues that was often confined to live music scenes in urban Black communities.[85] And Atlantic Records, which would ultimately join the ranks of the major labels, was started in 1947 by Ahmet Ertegun and Herb and Miriam Abramson. Ertegun, the son of a Turkish diplomat, was so inspired by African-American culture that he decided to stay in his adopted hometown of Washington, D.C. after his father died, and devote his life to the music he loved. "At age ten I saw Duke Ellington at the London Palladium," Ertegun recalled. "This was my first encounter with black people, and I was overwhelmed by the elegance of their tuxedos, their gleaming instruments, and their sense of style. But mostly it was the music. . . . I fell under the spell of black music. A new world opened up for me." He was soon joined by *Billboard* editor Jerry Wexler, who had started journeying up to Harlem as a kid to see live music and collect records by Black artists. Soon, Ertegun and Wexler were running one of the most thriving independent labels in the country, responsible for recording hundreds of mostly younger artists whose work would otherwise have been restricted to local audiences.[86]

By the late 1940s, most music created by Black artists was classified as R&B. This catchall term was mostly used as a euphemism for anything recorded by and for Black Americans, but it did encompass particular characteristics that both aligned and broke with African-American musicological traditions. R&B was a lively genre, written in the gospel (8-bar) or pop (16-bar) tradition rather than the classic blues 12-bar. A new reliance on instruments such as the saxophone, piano, drums, and electric guitar made for a fresh, dynamic sound. Lyrics were more sexually and emotionally direct than in mainstream popular music, extolling the exuberance of parties and clubs with biting cynicism and wit. Jump blues star Stick McGhee, for instance, had an early R&B hit in 1947 with "Drinkin' Wine Spo-Dee-O-Dee." The verses regaled listeners with the trouble that comes from too much drink: "Drinking that mess to their delight/When they gets drunk, start fighting all night/Knocking down windows and tearin' out doors/Drinkin' half a gallons and callin' for more." This was no cautionary tale, however, but a humorous, tongue-in-cheek description of a raucous party. "Wine spo-dee-o-dee, drinkin' wine, bop ba," McGhee croons in the chorus. "Pass that bottle to me."[87] But the lyrics were almost beside the point. If pop songs encouraged listeners to sing along, R&B was, as former music publishing executive Arnold Shaw attested, "vocal music to dance to—and the rhythm of the words is more important than meaning, if a choice had to be made."[88] While the music of white America was supposed to speak to the heart, the music emanating out of Black communities went for the soul instead.

This music exemplified both the optimism and the hardships that Black people often experienced, continuing in the tradition of what historian Robin D. G. Kelley defines as "cultural opposition." He explains that Black people created music that would provide a "social space free from the watchful eye of white authority or, in a few cases, the moralizing of the black middle class." Edgar S., who grew up near a "juke joint," explains how "the blues rocked me to sleep every Saturday night because I could hear the music right across the road." The so-called Blues People were "the people with whom I grew up," and therefore integral to his community. "Once I heard it, you know, I liked it," he says. "To me, blues is a feeling. You know if you feel it, and I feel it, and I could listen to it and relate to it because of the things that they were talking about. The kinds of things that I saw around me."[89] A sense of community that expressed the particularities of Black life in America, as well as realistic, down-to-earth themes, imperfect diction, raw emotions, and often sexual implications, were imparted into R&B performances to help listeners cope with experiences of racism and economic disparity while celebrating the joy they were still able experience. The tradition of "call and response," which Craig Werner calls "the core of gospel politics," was also ingratiated into postwar R&B, giving voice not only to the central performer, who issues a call in the vein of the preacher, but to the "congregants" who provide vocal responses.[90] This technique mirrors communal aspects of many Black churches, signaling that the singer is not alone and can look to others in the community for support. Listeners may also become participants in the song's meaning-making, as the call issues an invitation to identify with the artist, and to see one's own problems within the broader scope of a community of suffering.[91] This new genre, however, also had to distinguish itself from its predecessors in order to communicate new wartime and postwar experiences in urban areas. Although R&B could act as covert resistance to white middle-class mores, Kelley asserts that these people did not exist in a vacuum either, and that cultural overlap between races continued well into the twentieth century. "Black culture represents at least a partial rejection of the dominant ideology," he notes, and yet it was simultaneously "forged within the context of struggle against class and racial domination."[92] Many found more stable, permanent jobs and were ready to celebrate their more prosperous lives in the city. Jump blues drummer and bandleader Roy Milton displayed this new attitude when he remarked that "the trick was to get all that crazy fun we had backstage out to the public."[93] Most R&B songs, then, combined the joys of living in close-knit communities with an acknowledgment of how people continued to struggle under severe racial discrimination. Although R&B was often described as "party" music, it also allowed Black writers and performers a means of expressing very real pain and endurance within rapidly changing political and social climates.

This music resonated mostly with Black audiences at first, partly because of its ability to articulate particular experiences, but also because most record labels were uninterested in trying to sell across racial divisions. Markets were mostly segmented in the 1940s, and companies relied on new research that encouraged them to target specific markets for their products. If R&B was supposedly music for urban Black Americans, and country and western appealed to whites in the rural South and Southwest, then many labels were content to put most of their energies into selling pop since the demographic numbers translated into higher profits. These other genres were relegated to specialty divisions with fewer resources, and, in the case of Black artists, hampered by adherence to segregation laws, which limited touring capabilities and record store availability, leading, partially, to Louis Jordan's predicament with his label.[94] But music producers overall did not plan for the blurring of racial and class divisions among genres, even though they were not without warning. As early as 1945, executives were surprised to learn that R&B singer Cecil Gant's single, "I Wonder," was a hit in both white and Black markets, foreshadowing some of the boundary crossing that was set to occur within the next few years.[95] Jerry Wexler, who still wrote for *Billboard* at the time, noted that "it sold hundreds of thousands of copies each week, reminding white executives that a record by and for blacks only could still make a mint."[96] And yet, for the time being, most failed, or refused, to take notice. Two years later, when Black White Records A&R representative

Ralph Bass was marketing jazz band leader Jack McVea's "Open the Door, Richard" to Los Angeles-area radio stations, he stresses, "I couldn't give it away, the DJs just wouldn't play black music." When he finally found a popular deejay willing to play the record, it immediately caught the attention of white audiences, and other stations were forced to ask Bass for copies. The song became the first since "I Wonder" to be listed on *Billboard*'s Pop charts, yet it was indicative of the new, racially transgressive musical tastes and consumer trends that major labels would soon be forced to directly confront.[97]

As independent labels were cropping up to provide Black consumers with the music they were so eager to purchase, Black-oriented radio stations also began to flourish. This occurred during a period when, as Albin Zak explains, "American radio entered a period of decentralization," resulting in "an abundance of cultural expression" and "a pluralistic cornucopia" on the airwaves. But even though a few stations, like WLAC in Nashville, allowed white deejays to play Black artists at night to great success, fears of offending white listeners prevented stations from fully switching over until 1948, when WDIA-Memphis became the first in the country to convert to a fully Black-oriented format. The station, which hit the airwaves with an innocuous mix of pop and country the previous year, responded to sluggish sales by shifting to R&B music, as well as news and human interest programs, that would resonate with the city's large Black population. The station's owners also decided to hire Nat Williams, who emceed at local music clubs on nights and weekends, as (by most accounts) the first on-air Black deejay in the country. Both WDIA and Williams became hits, not only with the local Black audiences the station's owners targeted, but also with African-American listeners in the surrounding rural areas, and, somewhat surprisingly, the city's white teenage population, ultimately resulting in one of the highest listenerships in the country throughout the 1950s.[98]

By the following year, the number of Black deejays in the country increased from 16 to over 100, while some white deejays began affecting what they believed to be Black speech patterns and slang in order to draw young, hip audiences. Independent radio stations wholly devoted to Black-oriented programming also started cropping up across the country in an attempt to emulate WDIA's success, almost all of them run by white owners and operators, with some exceptions, including WERD-Atlanta headed by J. B. Blayton Sr., the only Black certified public accountant in Georgia. Within 10 years, over 600 stations across 39 states featured some form of Black programming, while a "National Negro Network" was established by Chicago accountant, Leonard Evans, at WCHB in Inkster, Michigan, the first Black-owned and operated radio station to be built from the ground up.[99] Some critics complained that these stations promoted segregation, noting that all-Black programming perpetuated the racist notion that African

Americans were different, and needed to be kept separate from whites, but *Sponsor* magazine claimed that these stations appealed to listeners because they helped bolster Black pride, as both citizens and consumers. The new Black customer "has the money to respond to the sales messages leveled at him," the copy crowed. "And because he has always felt discriminated against, the very fact that a station removes some of that feeling of discrimination by 'talking' directly to him is almost enough to guarantee that he will spend his money on the products and services advertised on that station."[100] The significant popularity of these stations revealed the increased purchasing power of Black consumers while simultaneously providing a space for African-American culture and voices. And even though their audiences remained mostly Black during this period, airwaves could not be segregated, and these stations began hearing from small numbers of white listeners right from the start, providing a neat parallel for the forthcoming "integration" of music and listeners. But since most were white owned and operated, the proliferation of Black culture on the radio would remain mired within existing economic structures, beholden to segregation laws that limited where they could play and sell, and reliant almost entirely on the profits that could be accrued for white owners.

R&B was not the only musical genre affected by the surge in listenership possibilities, the decentralization of the radio industry, and BMI's challenge to ASCAP during this period. Independent labels and radio stations also began producing and distributing country and western or "hillbilly" music during this period. Just as with race records, this genre had proven highly profitable to major record labels in the decades before World War II, particularly among Black and white Southern migrants to Northern urban centers. As James Gregory explains, this "strikingly regional" music was linked almost entirely to the South, while "modeling behaviors and understandings that have helped in the refashioning of Southern white culture and identities." Although the major labels did not disregard country music as quickly as they had with "race" records, the shellac shortage and corporate modeling focused on "mainstream" white middle-class tastes still affected distribution within the genre. Most of the country music released by these labels after the war came from film soundtracks and was written by ASCAP songwriters to be just as sentimental as any pop tune, yet with a romanticized "twang" and longing for a rural life that often no longer existed. These songs had little in common with the folk-based country music that emanated from performers in the South and Southwest, which used what Gregory defines as "theatricality" and "comedic-historical play" while simultaneously depicting what Diane Pecknold describes as "realism, sincerity, and frank depictions of everyday life." Major labels were not interested in distributing this more controversial form of the genre, at least not at first, resulting in further opportunities for independent producers.[101]

Country music's popularity increased during World War II, possibly due to a heightened sense of patriotism and "interest in all things American."[102] The establishment of Nashville, home to several country music stations, as the putative home of country music production, and radio recordings of Grand Ole Opry performances that were beamed into homes across the country allowed the genre to prosper, even amid the proliferation of poppy and derivative tunes released by the majors in New York. By its very nature, country was meant to express the unadulterated desires and frustrations of rural Americans, using pared-down instrumentation and elements from old folk and blues songs to create a passionate yet faintly unpolished style.[103] Whereas pop lyrics appealed to themes that were comforting and familiar to the white middle class, country music's focus on real people in disquieting situations appealed to listeners who were troubled by the uncertainties of postwar America. Love, for instance, was not given the glossy coat it received in pop music, but was often presented as unrequited or caught in a triangle, with partners not the dreamy caricatures of romance novels, but, instead, liable to drink, cheat, and fight.[104] Hank Williams, a rural Alabama-bred musician who became one of the most popular country artists of all time, had a monumental hit in 1951 with "Cold, Cold Heart," sadly intoning "The more I learn to care for you, the more we drift apart/Why can't I free your doubtful mind and melt your cold, cold heart."[105] His mournful, deeply personal rendering of lost love stands in stark contrast to the heartbreak detailed in the year's major pop hit, "Cry," where Johnnie Ray emotes: "If your heartaches seem to hang around too long/And your blues keep getting bluer with each song/Remember sunshine can be found behind the cloudy skies/So let your hair down and go on and cry."[106] Ray's sadness here seems faceless and almost sweetened. The song was a major success, but it could not resonate on the same emotional level as Williams's self-penned, deeply personal lyrics that, as Richard Leppert and George Lipsitz explain, broke "with the traditional romantic optimism of popular music as crafted in Tin Pan Alley."[107]

Independent labels that specialized in country and western recordings were founded between the late 1940s and early 1950s to capitalize on consumer demand, especially as marketers realized that Southerners who had migrated to Northern cities during the war had taken their musical proclivities with them.[108] Acuff-Rose, started by Tin Pan Alley songwriter Fred Rose and country star Roy Acuff, had strong connections to major labels, while Dot Records, formed in 1950 by Gallatin, Tennessee record store and radio station owner Randy Wood as a means of creating new stars he could then sell and advertise himself, was such an overnight success that Wood was able to move to California in 1956 and sell Dot to Paramount the following year. But it was radio announcer Sam Phillips's Sun Records that revolutionized the country and western genre by melding it with R&B characteristics. Phillips created Sun in 1950, operating out of a small shop near Memphis's Black district, and recording the city's blues and country singers for a fee. The label did not turn a profit for the first few years, but it did allow younger artists who were too unpolished for the majors to record, and possibly distribute, newer and more revelatory sounds.[109] What these labels did, according to BMI's first country music division head Frances Williams Preston, was ensure that country music became an essential component of the national music industry. Country artists "wrote their songs and kept them in shoeboxes," she says. "They wrote about their everyday lives. They didn't think about writing a song as a way to make money."[110] The money would come in droves, but in order for that to happen, artists had to appeal to listeners who were looking for something that sounded more genuine and less commodified than what they were used to hearing in a pop-dominated cultural climate.

CROSSING OVER ON THE CHARTS, 1951–1953

These combined changes helped to shape a common, more commodified, yet somewhat more diverse, mass culture on the air waves and in record stores. This shift became evident when two new music marketing charts appeared in the pages of *Billboard*, the music industry's preeminent trade publication. By the early 1940s, the publication featured a "Music Popularity Chart" dividing hit songs into subcategories, including "Songs with Most Radio Plugs," "National and Regional Best Selling Retail Records," "Leading Music Machine Records," and "National and Regional Sheet Music Best Sellers." These charts had 10–20 positions each and were compiled listing the top radio plays from "the four major New York outlets" and by surveying a handful of record stores in the New York City metropolitan area, as well as featured cities in the East, South, and on the West Coast. The limited source material, stemming from major radio and retail outlets inlarge urban centers with majority-white customers, ensured that pop songs performed by familiar white artists would dominate. In March 1945, *Billboard* also began listing an "Honor Roll of Hits," which combined radio play, inclusion in films, and sales of records and sheet music to provide a more holistic acknowledgment of the top 15 or 20 hits in the United States, but the predominant "Best Selling Pop Singles" chart would not debut until September 30, 1950. Although the title and charting processes shifted, the Pop charts represented the standard by which other genres would be measured, even if the sales figures that provided the rankings were skewed in favor of large record stores in close proximity to major urban areas. A&R reps kept track of their success by consulting

Billboard, which became ever more integral in determining consumer trends during the war, while also ensuring that major-label output would dominate the airwaves.[111]

By the late 1940s, however, *Billboard* recognized the increasing prominence of both R&B and country and western by listing best-seller charts that measured and listed hits just like the Pop charts. Although "American Folk Records" columns were printed as early as 1942, the Country and Western chart, which measured sales in stores, did not debut until May 15, 1948, with charts measuring jukebox and radio play appearing the following year.[112] The R&B charts were not far behind, appearing on June 25, 1949, to replace the "Harlem Hit Parade" and "Race Records" charts used earlier in the decade.[113] Philip Ennis explains that, since *Billboard* used the same format when printing all three charts, and readers could easily see what was popular in any genre, this change indicated that all genres were part of the same consumer system of music distribution, rather than mere demographic curiosities.[114]

And yet, the methods with which records were tracked in the years before computer technology took over placed R&B and country and western records at a distinct disadvantage. *Billboard* chart managers would first identify sellers that fit the genre's specifications—the Pop chart, for instance, would list stores in majority-white areas, while the R&B chart would track those in majority-Black neighborhoods. Because residential areas were largely segregated, these shops generally sold to racially homogenous customers. Store managers would then manually rank the best sellers in their shops each week and send the information to *Billboard* editors, which would be used to compile the lists. This not-exactlscientific method was easily susceptible to both error and corruption, and implicitly reinforced racial segregation in housing and public areas by identifying sales based on race rather than musicological genre. It was also based entirely on the assumption that people would only purchase music within their own racially prescribed genre.[115] Bill Gavin, a contributing editor at *Billboard*, questioned this process in a 1964 opinion piece, explaining that "as it is used in the music business, rhythm and blues refers to almost any music that is preferred by Negroes" and declared "such classification of music according to its audience rather than its style and content" to be "unfair" even if it "emphasize[d] the importance of the Negro in record sales as well as in radio programming."[116] The process of charting musicians by their race was a bit more complicated than that—Nat King Cole consistently hit the Pop chart, for instance, while Johnnie Ray's Okeh-recorded pop tunes received high marks on the R&B charts. But ultimately the Pop chart measured the tastes of the white middle class that most record companies and radio stations were so eager to reach by counting sales at larger record stores and airtime on popular music stations. The result, Motown Records founder Berry Gordy explains, is that "Black records weren't always charted like white records. Even though many black artists sold more records in the black stores, the people who tracked sales for the different Pop charts would usually call the white stores more than they did the black stores."[117] Records by Black artists, especially those released by independent labels, were mostly shipped to smaller record stores in Black neighborhoods and were often kept out of jukeboxes in majority-white areas. Sales figures were often skewed in favor of pop songs, usually performed by white artists, hurting the bottom lines of smaller independent labels, which lacked the distribution channels that the majors had at their disposal.[118]

Physical and spatial segregation created parallel segregated music charts, then, as *Billboard*'s methodology presumed a division between Black and white musical tastes. And yet the very methods that reinforced this division would also be used to tear it apart. Since store managers merely listed the top sellers in their stores, regardless of genre or the artist's racial background, the concept of segregated genres became muddied. If a pop record by a white artist happened to sell well in Black neighborhoods it would hit the R&B chart; conversely, R&B songs that became popular in majority-white areas would be listed as pop hits. These "crossover hits" were rare before the early 1950s, but, as the decade progressed, the *Billboard* charts revealed that a surprising number of music fans were willing to transcend genre-specific racial boundaries in order to "desegregate" the charts. This unexpected shift would occur just as civil rights organizations that had committed to desegregation as a major tactic were planning massive legal and direct action campaigns that would soon become widely known across the country and around the world. Racial integration, at both the political and cultural level, would come to be intertwined in many ways for teenagers who would grow up listening to this music and learning about movement struggles on television and in newspapers and magazines.

In March 1952, *Billboard* published an article entitled "Hit Tunes and Good Talent are Keeping the Boxes Busy" featuring different authors writing separate columns on "The Pops," "Country and Western," and "Rhythm and Blues." The "hit tunes" referred to in the title came not only from the Pop chart, which was *Billboard*'s preeminent listing of mainstream recordings by established musicians and released by major record labels, but also from the other two categories as well. The article's focus on "the tremendous influence of r.&b. styles on the pop market" and R&B and country and western success among white mainstream audience revealed surprising new directions within popular music listenership. White pop stars Johnnie Ray and Kay Starr were both mentioned as examples of artists whose "singing style [is] close to r.&b. vocalists," which leads to "sell[ing] just as well in both fields." One author even questioned whether the days of charting records based on separate categories were numbered, musing that "while it seems as tho [*sic*] the line of demarcation among the various types of music are not as clearly defined as they used to be, it is not a certainty yet whether the line has permanently been breached and, perhaps, erased." Ultimately, the author concluded that deejays and radio station operators "cannot eliminate country artists or rhythm and blues artists or their songs only because they do not fit into what has been called the pop category. Anyone and at anytime can make a strong juke box record."[119] These charts were not yet as diverse as these authors claimed. But this article provided a telling premonition of how crossover records would take the music industry by storm in the mid-1950s.[120]

It wasn't just the musical stylings of pop that appealed to Black kids, however—savvy advertisers were starting to market Black musicians who were popular with teenagers in the same way they did with white heartthrobs. Percy Mayfield, for instance, was billed as "America's Newest Blues Balladeer" when Specialty Records signed him in 1950. The label's marketing department nevertheless released a promotional poster with a photograph of the singer staring sweetly into the camera, surrounded by animated Black girls dressed in the latest fashions with towering beehives atop their heads. A swirl of cartoon hearts completes the picture. The marketing team that designed the poster was clearly trying to brand the blues singer as an acceptable romantic idol for middle-class Black—and possibly even white—girls.[121] This depiction of Black musicians was new, especially for the artists who performed in more traditional African-American idioms. Marketers, however, were drawing on the same symbols and tropes to sell to both Black and white teenagers because these were the common images that middle-class kids with disposable incomes could relate to across racial lines. In some cases, Black teenagers were even inspired to start listening to white pop artists. As early as 1946, for instance, white deejay Alan Freed was pictured in an Ohio newspaper handing out Perry Como records to teenage contest winners—both were high school students, one Black, one white.[122]

Pop still accounted for about half of all record sales throughout the early to mid-1950s, but Philip Ennis explains that, since *Billboard* charted all three pop, R&B, and country and western sales the same way, and published them in the same format, they appeared equal to one another and were thus primed for songs to "move" easily among them by this period. And yet direct crossovers were incredibly uncommon; most songs would only place on more than one chart if they were covered by artists performing in different genres. Hank Williams's emotive 1951 country hit, "Cold, Cold Heart," for instance, only hit the Pop chart when Tony Bennett's more melodic and heavily produced version came out, and the R&B chart when Dinah Washington's jazzy cover, complete with piano, saxophone, and smooth background vocals, was released. That same year, Washington had an R&B hit with her version of Frank Sinatra's pop phenomenon, "I'm a Fool to Want You," while Kay Starr placed on the Pop chart with a revved-up version of R&B group the Clovers' "Fool, Fool, Fool." But the coming popularity of direct crossovers was also apparent. The Clovers record, for instance, hit the Pop chart soon after Starr's record did, which meant that white kids sought out the original even after they were introduced to the poppier cover.[123]

One of the earliest, and most successful, Black musicians to have records cross directly over from the R&B to the Pop chart was Fats Domino. The "boogie-woogie" piano player was promoted as an R&B performer after being signed to Imperial Records in 1949, even though his friend and producer Dave Bartholomew admitted that "we all thought of him as a country and western singer." If his race prevented him from claiming this mantle, his ability to mix elements from the different genres he heard while growing up in a musical family in New Orleans led him to create very different sounds capable of traversing racialized boundaries. Domino's first big hit, "The Fat Man," sounded so unlike anything else on the R&B charts at the time that BMI, The Rock and Roll Hall of Fame, and even Wikipedia, have identified the 1949 hit as one of the first true rock and roll recordings. The song debuted at number 4 on *Billboard*'s R&B chart in February 1950, and ultimately reached the second spot, firmly solidifying Domino as a star among Black listeners. Its rollicking piano bars reflected the ebullient party culture of New Orleans's Creole communities, while retaining more traditional blues elements like short verses detailing everyday struggles and triumphs ("All the girls they love me/'Cause I know my way around" and yet "I'm goin', goin' to stay/'Cause women and fast life/Train carrying this soul away"), and lack of a pop-style chorus. The bridge consists not of lyrics, but of a series of "wah-wah" sounds inflected with Domino's inimitable twang, which hinted at the country and western influences to which Bartholomew alluded. Even though "The Fat Man" never placed on the Pop chart, Domino's easy ability to mix musical genres seemed to forecast his future crossover success; according to BMI's official history, "youngsters white and black alike heard delicious echoes of the country and r&b fusion that was breaking loose all across the nation" in his music.[124]

The next big crossover to take the music industry by surprise was Johnnie Ray's "Cry," a fairly traditional pop ditty sung by a white artist that also scored on the R&B chart. Ray grew up loving Billie Holiday and was not shy about admitting that she influenced his emotionally direct singing style. This mixture of characteristics appealed to both Black and white teenagers, who helped "Cry" and its follow-up, "The Little White Cloud That Cried," remain atop both the Pop and R&B charts from 1951 well into 1952.[125] But it was "Sixty-Minute Man," performed by Billy Ward and the Dominoes, an adolescent doo-wop group, which really illuminated the groundbreaking nature of crossover records. This single took the top spot on the R&B charts during the spring and summer of 1951, while simultaneously making the top 20 on the Pop chart, and ultimately earning the title "Song of the Year."[126] Given the record's Black gospel-tinged musicality and tongue-in-cheek lyrical ode to teenage sexual exploits ("I rock 'em, roll'em all night long/I'm a sixty-minute man"), its success among white teenagers was surprising, acting as a harbinger of what this demographic craved in their musical choices. "In contrast to a more respectable emotional repression, white teenagers increasingly valued the expression of passion and desire," Grace Elizabeth Hale explains. "In place of their parents' controlled and polished forms of entertainment, they sought the raw and frenetic."[127]

The following year, "Crying in the Chapel," a country-gospel song written by Artie Glen and initially recorded by his son Darrell, revealed the extent of cover song popularity across genres. The record was almost immediately re-recorded by country star Rex Allen and by pop ingénue June Valli, as well as by the Orioles, a young Black doo-wop group. As expected, the Glen, Allen, and Valli versions immediately hit the Pop chart, while the Orioles steadily climbed up the R&B chart. And yet, within three weeks of its initial appearance on the R&B chart, the Orioles' version appeared at number 20 on the Pop chart. For the next month, all four versions of the song appeared on the Pop chart—and by the third week, the Orioles version had surpassed all but Valli's record in popularity. White audiences were apparently searching out the Orioles cover after first hearing the pop and country versions of the song and were eager to purchase the record in multiple genres rather than simply accept the racialized version marketed to their demographic.[128] This striking development seemed unique at first: another 1953 hit, "Rags to Riches," for instance, which was written by Broadway legends Adler and Ross, and performed by white pop legend Tony Bennett, was covered the same year by the Dominoes. The group's bass-heavy version allowed the song to hit the R&B charts months after Bennett's original debut, which had failed to cross over from the Pop chart. In this case, listeners abided by the racial and regional divisions dictated by record labels: white listeners were more likely to purchase the pop record, and Blacks were more likely to go with the Dominoes. And yet "Crying in the Chapel" may be seen as a harbinger of the rapid changes that would soon drive consumer patterns. Although divisions among genres had never been absolute, racialized boundary lines were becoming increasingly blurry.[129]

Very few music industry professionals expected that much would come of these early crossovers; they were widely viewed as one-off novelties, or as proof that a great song could briefly transcend boundaries because listeners would want to own every recorded version, regardless of the performer. But the increased availability of R&B and country and western recordings, either on the air or through independent labels, provided more opportunities for dissolute young listeners to be introduced to new music that better resonated with their lived experiences. Records would continue to cross over throughout the mid-1950s, just as desegregation campaigns began changing the country's legal structures and appearing on national (and global) news. These crossovers would ultimately help define how listeners from different racial groups would come to perceive the goals of a civil rights movement aimed at desegregating public spaces using nonviolent direct action.

NOTES

1. Joel Whitburn, *Top R&B/Hip-Hop Singles: 1942–2004* (Menomonee, WI: Record Research, 2004), 310. For most of the 1950s and 1960s, Pop, R&B, and C&W charts were divided into three categories: Best Sellers in Stores, Most Played in Jukeboxes, and Most Played by [Disc] Jockeys. Most of the research for this book focuses on the Best Sellers in Stores charts, since they were featured most prominently in *Billboard*'s pages, acted as the primary resource for music industry executives, and defined fans as active consumers of music rather than (possibly) passive listeners.

2. Louis Jordan and Ellis Lawrence Walsh, "Saturday Night Fish Fry," Decca, 1949.

3. Louis Cantor, *Dewey and Elvis: The Life and Times of a Rock 'n' Roll Deejay* (Champaign, IL: University of Illinois Press, 2010), 136–137.

4. Ralph Gleason, interview with Milt Gabler, 1974, 12–13, Box 4, Folder 18, Milt Gabler Collection, The Rock and Roll Hall of Fame Library and Archives, Cleveland, OH.

5. Derek Catsam, *Freedom's Main Line: The Journey of Reconciliation and the Freedom Rides* (Lexington, KY: The University Press of Kentucky, 2008), 13–45.

6. Catsam, *Freedom's Main Line*, 29.

7. Lizabeth Cohen, *A Consumer's Republic: The Politics of Mass Consumption in Postwar America* (New York: Vintage, 2003). The research in this book will focus mainly on white and Black teenagers, and on European-American and African-American culture. Although I am aware of the inadequacies of these labels in defining people's racial and ethnic identities, this dichotomy dominated racial discussions in the mid-century United States, as assimilation of European and some Middle-Eastern and Latin cultures into an all-encompassing "white" identity signaled increased class status. "White" was meant to stand in stark contrast to "Black" in these early years of massive civil rights organizing. These racial categories were used as the basis for everything from market segmentation to housing and school stipulations, and so, despite their shortcomings in distinguishing important aspects of people's experiences and identities, I am choosing to focus on them here as a means of replicating the cultural categories that teenagers would have understood during this period. For more on this, please see Thomas A. Guglielmo, *White on Arrival: Italians, Race, Color, and Power in Chicago, 1890–1945* (New York: Oxford University Press, 2003) and Matthew Frye Jacobson, *Whiteness of a Different Color: European Immigrants and*

the Alchemy of Race (Cambridge, MA: Harvard University Press, 1999). I am also aware of other contributions to the genre of rock and roll, stemming from Latin, Asian, and Polynesian sources. But since rock and roll predominantly emerged from a combination of pop, country and western, and R&B musics, which were (and still are) racialized as "white" and "Black" respectively, and most prominent artists identified with one of these racial identities, I am choosing to focus mostly on these groups. For more on this process, please see Philip H. Ennis, *The Seventh Stream: The Emergence of Rocknroll in American Popular Music* (Middletown, CT: Wesleyan University Press, 1992). For more on the considerable contributions of Latin musicians to the genre of rock and roll, please see George Lipsitz, "Land of a Thousand Dances: Youth, Minorities, and the Rise of Rock and Roll," in *Recasting America: Culture and Politics in the Age of Cold War*, ed. Lary May (Chicago: University of Chicago Press, 1988) and George H. Lewis, "Ghosts, Ragged but Beautiful: Influences of Mexican Music on American Country-Western and Rock 'n' Roll," *Popular Music and Society* 15, no. 4 (1991), 85–103.

8. Matthew J. Countryman, *Up South: Civil Rights and Black Power in Philadelphia* (Philadelphia: University of Pennsylvania Press, 2007), 7; Peniel E. Joseph, *Waiting 'Til the Midnight Hour: A Narrative History of Black Power in America* (London: Macmillan, 2007), 12; Edgar S., in discussion with the author, June 25, 2020. For an account of civil rights campaigns in the Northern United States, please see Thomas J. Sugrue, *Sweet Land of Liberty: The Forgotten Struggle for Civil Rights in the North* (New York: Random House, 2008). For an examination of civil rights strategies used by New York residents during the 1930s and 1940s, including "Don't Shop Where You Can't Work" campaigns, rent strikes, and better media representation, please see Martha Biondi, *To Stand and Fight* (Cambridge, MA: Harvard University Press, 2009). For extensive studies of redlining practices, including protests against housing discrimination, please see David Freund, *Colored Property: State Policy and White Racial Politics in Suburban America* (Chicago: University of Chicago Press, 2010), Thomas J. Sugrue, *The Origins of the Urban Crisis: Race and Inequality in Postwar Detroit*, Vol. 6 (Princeton, NJ: Princeton University Press, 2014), and Richard Rothstein, *The Color of Law: A Forgotten History of How our Government Segregated America* (New York: Liveright Publishing, 2017). For an examination of different forms of economic protest, please see Robert E. Weems and Robert E. Weems Jr., *Desegregating the Dollar: African American Consumerism in the Twentieth Century* (New York: New York University Press, 1998). For a history of how Black women protested racialized sexual violence, please see Danielle L. McGuire, *At the Dark End of the Street: Black Women, Rape, and Resistance—A New History of the Civil Rights Movement from Rosa Parks to the Rise of Black Power* (New York: Vintage, 2010). For examinations of Black Power politics and social movements before the 1960s, please see Countryman, *Up South*, Joseph, *Waiting 'Til the Midnight Hour*, and Robert O Self, *American Babylon: Race and the Struggle for Postwar Oakland* (Princeton, NJ: Princeton University Press, 2005).

9. Tomiko Brown-Nagin, *Courage to Dissent: Atlanta and the Long History of the Civil Rights Movement* (New York: Oxford University Press, 2011), 2–4.

10. For an examination of Black support for the Communist Party in the South, please see Robin D.G. Kelley, *Hammer and Hoe: Alabama Communists During the Great Depression* (Chapel Hill, NC: University of North Carolina Press, 2015). And for excellent studies of how American activists positioned the U.S. movement within a global context, please see Nikhil Pal Singh, *Black is a Country* (Cambridge, MA: Harvard University Press, 2004) and Glenda Elizabeth Gilmore, *Defying Dixie: The Radical Roots of Civil Rights* (New York: W.W. Norton & Co., 2008).

11. James Farmer, *Lay Bare the Heart: An Autobiography of the Civil Rights Movement* (Fort Worth, TX: TCU Press, 1998), 75.

12. Farmer, *Lay Bare the Heart*, 75.

13. Steve Valocchi, "The Emergence of the Integrationist Ideology in the Civil Rights Movement," *Social Problems* 43, no. 1 (February 1996), 126.

14. Mary L. Dudziak, *Cold War Civil Rights: Race and the Image of American Democracy* (Princeton, NJ: Princeton University Press, 2011), 47–78; Countryman, *Up South*, 4.

15. Blair L. M. Kelley, *Right to Ride: Streetcar Boycotts and African American Citizenship in the Era of Plessy v. Ferguson* (Chapel Hill, NC: University of North Carolina Press, 2010), 9; David A. Gerber, "Education, Expediency, and Ideology: Race and Politics in the Desegregation of Ohio Public Schools in the Late 19th Century," *The Journal of Ethnic Studies* 1, no. 3 (1973), 15–16.

16. Kelley, *The Right to Ride*; Philip Foner, "The Battle to End Discrimination Against Negroes on Philadelphia Streetcars: (Part I) Background and Beginning of the Battle," *Pennsylvania History* 40, no. 3 (1973), 261–291; Euan Hague, "'The Right to Enter Every Other State'–the Supreme Court and African American Mobility in the United States," *Mobilities* 5, no. 3 (2010), 331–347.

17. The Civil Rights Act of 1875, History Art and Archives, United States House of Representatives. Last accessed at https://history.house.gov/Historical-Highlights/1851-1900/The-Civil-Rights-Act-of-1875/ on June 16, 2021.

18. Kelley, *The Right to Ride*, Hague, "The Right to Enter Every Other State," Nell Irvin Painter, *Sojourner Truth: A Life, A Symbol* (New York: W.W. Norton & Co., 1996), 210–211.

19. Kelley, *The Right to Ride*, 87; Jay Winston Driskell Jr., *Schooling Jim Crow: The Fight for Atlanta's Booker T. Washington High School and the Roots of Black Protest Politics* (Charlottesville, VA: University of Virginia Press, 2014), 10.

20. Foner, "The Battle to End Discrimination Against Negroes on Philadelphia Streetcars," 266–273; Kelley, *The Right to Ride*.

21. Gerber, "Education, Expediency, and Ideology," 6–7; Lawrence Grossman, "George T. Downing and Desegregation of Rhode Island Public Schools, 1855–1866," *Rhode Island History* 36, no. 4 (1977), 103; William Jordan, "'The Damnable Dilemma': African-American Accommodation and Protest During World War I," *The Journal of American History* 81, no. 4 (1995), 1562–1583; Driskell, *Schooling Jim Crow*, 20–21; Equal Justice Initiative, "Red Summer of 1919." Last accessed at https://eji.org/reports/online/lynching-in-america-targeting-black-veterans/red-summer, on September 7, 2019.

22. Valocchi, "The Emergence of the Integrationist Ideology in the Civil Rights Movement," 120.

23. Jordan, "The Damnable Dilemma"; National Association for the Advancement of Colored People, NAACP, "A Letter to President Woodrow Wilson on Federal Race Discrimination," August 15, 1913, NAACP Records, Library of Congress, last accessed at https://www.loc.gov/exhibits/civil-rights-act/segregation-era.html on September 12, 2019; Barbara Joyce Ross, "JE Spingarn and the Rise of the NAACP, 1911–1939," *Atheneum* 32 (1972); John J. Donohue III, James J. Heckman, and Petra E. Todd, "The Schooling of Southern Blacks: The Roles of Legal Activism and Private Philanthropy, 1910–1960," *The Quarterly Journal of Economics*, February 2002; Stacy Pratt McDermott, "'An Outrageous Proceeding': A Northern Lynching and the Enforcement of Anti-Lynching Legislation in Illinois, 1905–1910," *The Journal of Negro History* 84, no. 1 (1999), 61–78; Gloria J. Browne-Marshall, *The Voting Rights War: The NAACP and the Ongoing Struggle for Justice* (Lanham, MD: Rowman & Littlefield, 2016), 39–60.

24. Valocchi, "The Emergence of the Integrationist Ideology in the Civil Rights Movement," 116–125.

25. Thomas Joyce, "The 'Double V' was for Victory: Black Soldiers, the Black Protest, and World War II," dissertation, The Ohio State University, 1993, 235; 258–274.

26. David Lucander, *Winning the War for Democracy: The March on Washington Movement, 1941–1946* (Champaign, IL: University of Illinois Press, 2014), 2–4.

27. Pat Washburn, "The 'Pittsburgh Courier's' Double V Campaign in 1942," presented at the Annual Meeting of the Association for Education in Journalism, 1981.

28. Jacquelyn Dowd Hall first introduced the concept of a "long" civil rights movement in her seminal article, "The Long Civil Rights Movement and the Political Uses of the Past," *The Journal of American History* 91, no. 4 (March 2005), but many other historians, including Danielle McGuire in *At the Dark End of the Street* and Glenda Gilmore in *Defying Dixie*, have identified the origins of the civil rights movement either during World War II or in the immediate post-war period.

29. Jeanne Theoharis, *The Rebellious Life of Mrs. Rosa Parks* (Boston: Beacon Press, 2015), 18.

30. Michael Garvey, "Oral History with Mr. Amzie Moore, Black civil rights worker," The University of Southern Mississippi Center for Oral History and Cultural Heritage Digital Collections, 31. Last accessed at http://digilib.usm.edu/cdm/ref/collection/coh/id/5707, on July 17, 2013.

31. Imamu Amiri Baraka (LeRoi Jones), *Blues People: The Negro Experience in White America and the Music that Developed From It* (Edinburgh: Payback Press, 1995), 113.

32. "David Dinkins," *My Soul Looks Back in Wonder: Voices of the Civil Rights Experience*, ed. Juan Williams (New York: Sterling: 2004), 43.

33. Lloyd L. Brown, "Brown v. Salina, Kansas," *The New York Times*, February 26, 1973, 31.

34. Joe Nick Patoski, "Blues Man Interviewed in Jacksonville FLA," interview with B.B. King, December 27, 2003, 14. Voices of the CRM Project, 2005/015, American Folklife Center, the Library of Congress, Washington, DC.

35. Catsam, *Freedom's Main Line*, 14–20.

36. Andrew Myers, "The Blinding of Isaac Woodard," *The Proceedings*, 2004, 63.

37. Examinations of how civil rights activists used Cold War rhetoric emphasizing democracy, freedom, and equality to prompt action from the federal government have been thoroughly covered by historians including Mary Dudziak and Nikhil Pal Singh. Dudziak artfully explains that, during the Cold War, American officials had to maintain an image of freedom and democracy in order to convince other nations to repudiate communism and ally with the United States. Other countries, especially the Soviet Union, routinely criticized how the United States treated its Black citizens, and if the country did not try to solve its racial dilemma, nation after nation would turn to communism rather than support what was increasingly seen as a false democratic power. Coverage of the civil rights movement was so all encompassing that the racial hypocrisies embedded in American democracy were becoming blatant around the world, and many federal officials felt an urgent need to rehabilitate the country's stance on race relations. The first step was to acknowledge the dignity of the movement and the activists who propelled it, and to actually listen to some of their objectives. As Singh explains, "For a brief period, the demands and critiques of black intellectuals, activists, and masses of black people who took to the streets could not be ignored by a nation-state intent on legitimizing its claims to global power and domestic consensus." For more, please see Singh, *Black Is a Country*, 13, Dudziak, *Cold War Civil Rights*, and Gilmore, *Defying Dixie*.

38. For more on Quaker abolitionism and the uses of pacifism, please see James S. Stewart, James Brewer Stewart, and Eric Foner, *Holy Warriors: The Abolitionists and American Slavery* (London: Macmillan, 1996), 155–156; John D'Emilio, *Lost Prophet: The Life and Times of Bayard Rustin* (New York: Simon & Schuster, 2003), 41–50.

39. D'Emilio, *Lost Prophet*, 50; Farmer, *Lay Bare the Heart*, 74.

40. D'Emilio, *Lost Prophet*, 54.

41. D'Emilio, *Lost Prophet*, 24; 107.

42. Farmer, *Lay Bare the Heart*, 74–75.

43. James Forman, interview with Vincent Harding, November 8, 1999, 14, James Forman Papers, Box 92, Folder 2, the Library of Congress, Washington, DC.

44. Brown-Nagin, *Courage to Dissent*, 2–4; D'Emilio, *Lost Prophet*, 53.

45. Farmer, *Lay Bare the Heart*, 79–80.

46. Catsam, *Freedom's Main Line*, 26–27.

47. Farmer, *Lay Bare the Heart*, 98–99.

48. Farmer, *Lay Bare the Heart*, 76; 94.

49. Farmer, *Lay Bare the Heart*, 75.

50. Edgar S., in discussion with the author.

51. Louis Cantor, *Wheelin' on Beale: How WDIA-Memphis Became the Nation's First All-Black Station and Created the Sound that Changed America* (New York: Pharos Books, 1992), 144.

52. E. Franklin Frazier, *Black Bourgeoisie* (New York: Simon & Schuster, 1997), 22–23.

53. For more on how white Americans were able to gain financial security through government-sponsored programs and policies, please see Ira Katznelson, *When Affirmative Action was White: An Untold History of Racial Inequality in Twentieth-Century America* (New York: W.W. Norton & Company, 2005), Sugrue, *Origins of the Urban Crisis*, and Freund, *Colored Property*.

54. Bret Eynon, interview with Madison Foster, July 1978, 5–6; Contemporary History Project: The New Left in Ann Arbor, Bentley Historical Library, The University of Michigan, Ann Arbor, MI.

55. Cantor, *Wheelin' On Beale*, 27.

56. Michele Mitchell, *Righteous Propagation: African Americans and the Politics of Racial Destiny After Reconstruction* (Chapel Hill NC: University of North Carolina Press, 2004), 9–10.

57. Despite the fact that both public and private regulations ensured that residents of suburban developments were overwhelmingly white throughout the 1950s and 1960s, these spaces were not exactly as homogenous as historians (and popular memory) often make them out to be. Black Americans and other people of color entered suburbs too, mostly as workers, and occasionally as residents. In the introduction to his edited volume, *The New Suburban History*, ed. Kevin M. Krause and Thomas J. Sugrue (Chicago: The University of Chicago Press, 2006), Thomas Sugrue makes the crucial point that "suburbs were shaped as much by the presence of racial minorities as by their absence," while Andrew Wiese argues that "historians have done a better job excluding African Americans from the suburbs than even white suburbanites." It is not my intention to add to this process of exclusion, but to comment on the very real segregation that was codified by both law (until 1968) and private practice in Northern suburbs, and to show how the Black-white racial divide was exemplified by this form of housing segregation, despite the fact that people were never completely isolated from other racial groups. For more on non-white suburban experiences, please see Andrew Wiese, "'The House I Live In': Race, Class, and African American Suburban Dreams in the Postwar United States," in Krause and Sugrue, *The New Suburban History*, 99–120 and Bruce D. Haynes, *Red Lines, Black Spaces: The Politics of Race and Space In a Middle-Class Suburb* (New Haven, CT: Yale University Press, 2001).

58. Code of Ethics adopted by the National Association of Real Estate Boards, June 6, 1924, last accessed at http://archive.realtor.org/sites/default/files/1924Ethics.pdf on February 6, 2020. For more on the construction of American suburbs, including racial politics, federal and state intervention, real estate regulations, and shifting racial attitudes of white suburbanites, please see Jessica Trounstine, *Segregation by Design: Local Politics and Inequality in American Cities* (Cambridge UK: Cambridge University Press, 2018), Freund, *Colored Property*, Self, *American Babylon*, Rothstein, *The Color of Law*, Sugrue, *Sweet Land of Liberty*, and Sugrue, *Origins of the Urban Crisis*.

59. Camille Cosby, interview with Odetta, May 26, 2003, 7–8, National Visionary Leadership Project, American Folklife Center, the Library of Congress, Washington, DC; Tony T., in discussion with the author, November 9, 2011.

60. Johnny Otis, *Upside Your Head!: Rhythm and Blues on Central Avenue* (Middletown, CT: Wesleyan University Press, 1993), 19.

61. Camille Cosby, interview with Quincy Jones, September 23, 2003, 5, National Visionary Leadership Project, American Folklife Center, the Library of Congress, Washington, DC.

62. Ed B., in discussion with the author, June 23, 2020.

63. Edgar S., discussion with the author.

64. Weems and Weems, *Desegregating the Dollar*, 1.

65. "The Forgotten 15,000,000," *Sponsor*, October 10, 1949, 24–25.

66. Weems and Weems, *Desegregating the Dollar*, 2–3; 32–34.

67. Cohen, *A Consumer's Republic*, 112–192.

68. Cohen, *A Consumer's Republic*; Grace Elizabeth Hale, *A Nation of Outsiders: How the White Middle Class Fell in Love with Rebellion in Postwar America* (New York: Oxford University Press, 2011), 34; Grace Elizabeth Hale, *Making Whiteness: The Culture of Segregation in the South, 1890–1940* (New York: Vintage Books, 1998), 95.

69. Andrew Flory, *I Hear a Symphony: Motown and Crossover R&B* (Ann Arbor: University of Michigan Press, 2017), 5.

70. Steve Chapple and Reebee Garofalo, *Rock 'n' Roll is Here to Pay: The History and Politics of the Music Industry* (Lanham, MD: Rowman & Littlefield Publishers, 1978), 7–8.

71. Paul Kingsbury, *BMI 50th Anniversary: The Explosion of American Music 1940–1990* (Nashville: The Country Music Foundation 1990), 19; Ennis, *The Seventh Stream*, 132.

72. Gleason, interview with Gabler, 18.

73. Jerry Wexler and David Ritz, *Rhythm and the Blues: A Life in American Music* (New York: St. Martin's Press, 1994), 78.

74. Gleason, interview with Gabler, 17. Decca, originally formed in Britain, became a separate American label in 1937 and was one of the original labels that merged to become the Universal Music Group. Capitol and Mercury were both formed during the war and are now part of the Universal Music Group. Columbia, founded in 1887, and RCA Victor, founded in 1929, were both originally formed to sell gramophones and are now subsidiaries of Sony Music Entertainment.

75. Chapple and Garofalo, *Rock 'n' Roll is Here to Pay*, 15–17; Cory Messenger, "Record Collectors: Hollywood Record Labels in the 1950s and 1960s," *Media International Australia* 148, no. 1 (2013), 119.

76. Ennis, *The Seventh Stream*, 99; Chapple and Garofalo, *Rock 'n' Roll is Here to Pay*, 14–18.

77. Ennis, *The Seventh Stream*, 99; 120; Albin Zak, *I Don't Sound Like Nobody: Remaking Music in 1950s America* (Ann Arbor: University of Michigan Press, 2010).

78. "Music! Music! Music!" Stephen Weiss and Bernie Baum, 1949, version by Teresa Brewer, London Records, 1949; "(How Much Is) That Doggie in the Window?" Bob Merrill, 1952, version by Patti Paige, Mercury, 1953.

79. Kingsbury, *BMI 50th Anniversary*, 6–11.

80. Kingsbury, *BMI 50th Anniversary*, 8; 12–13.

81. Wexler, *Rhythm and the Blues*, 60; Flory, *I Hear a Symphony*, 17.
82. "The Forgotten 15,000,000," 25.
83. Ennis, *The Seventh Stream*, 176; Kingsbury, *BMI 50th Anniversary*, 39; 19; 21; Zak, *I Don't Sound Like Nobody*, Intro and Chapter 1.
84. Billy Vera, "Specialty Records 40th Anniversary 1946–1986: Celebrating Four Decades of Leadership in Rock, R&B, and Gospel Music," 17, Specialty Records Collection, Box-Folder OS1-OF6, The Rock and Roll Hall of Fame Library and Archives, Cleveland, OH.
85. Kingsbury, *BMI 50th Anniversary*, 24.
86. Kingsbury, *BMI 50th Anniversary*, 19; Wexler, *Rhythm and the Blues*, 52; 56–57; 76–77.
87. Stick McGhee, "Drinkin' Wine Spo-Dee-O-Dee," Atlantic Records, 1949.
88. Arnold Shaw, *The Rockin' 50s: The Decade That Transformed the Pop Music Scene* (New York: Hawthorn Books, 1973), 80.
89. Robin D. G. Kelley, *Race Rebels: Culture, Politics, and the Black Working Class* (New York: Simon & Schuster, 1996), 36; 44; Edgar S., in discussion with the author.
90. Craig Werner, *A Change Is Gonna Come: Music, Race and the Soul of America* (New York: Penguin Putnam, 1998), 14.
91. Ennis, *The Seventh Stream*, 71; 27.
92. Kelley, *Race Rebels*, 36; 44.
93. Otis, *Upside Your Head*, 46.
94. Flory, *I Hear a Symphony*, 18. Many major record labels created subsidiaries between the 1920s and 1940s to produce and distribute Black "race" records and country and western "hillbilly" tunes to African-American and rural white audiences. Prominent race and hillbilly record labels include RCA Victor's race records line, introduced in 1927; Okeh, acquired by Columbia in 1926; Vocalion by Warner Brothers in 1931; Mercury's Keynote line, which focused on jazz artists, in the 1940s; and Decca's Sepia and Hill Billy series, released in 1941. By 1951, RCA also instituted its Groove label to sign and sell R&B artists. For a more in-depth discussion of subsidiary race and hillbilly labels, please see Brian Ward, *Just My Soul Responding: Rhythm and Blues, Black Consciousness, and Race Relations* (Berkeley and Los Angeles: University of California Press, 2012), 27–29, Evelyn Brooks Higginbotham, "Rethinking Vernacular Culture: Black Religion and Race Records in the 1920s and 1930s," in *African American Religious Thought: An Anthology*, ed. Cornel West and Eddie S. Glaude Jr. (Louisville, KY: Westminster John Knox Press, 2003), 210; 214, William G. Roy, "'Race Records' and 'Hillbilly Music': Institutional Origins of Racial Categories in the American Commercial Recording Industry," *Poetics* 32, no. 3–4 (June–August 2004), 265–279, and "'St. Louis Blues': Race Records and Hillbilly Music," in *American Popular Music: From Minstrelsy to MP3*, 3rd ed., ed. Larry Star and Christopher Alan Waterman (New York: Oxford University Press, 2009).
95. Charlie Gillett, *The Sound of the City: The Rise of Rock and Roll* (Cambridge, MA: Da Capo Press, 1996), 165–166.
96. Wexler, *Rhythm and the Blues*, 64.

97. John Fleming, "Ralph Bass, Synopsis" in "A Life Recording," Ralph Bass Papers, Folder 2, The Rock and Roll Hall of Fame Library and Archives, Cleveland, OH; Arnold Shaw, *Honkers and Shouters* (New York: Macmillan, 1978), 226–227.

98. Zak, *I Don't Sound Like Nobody*, 10–11; 35–36; Cantor, *Wheelin' On Beale*, 146; 159; 155.

99. Weems and Weems, *Desegregating the Dollar*, 45; Zak, *I Don't Sound Like Nobody*, 35; Cantor, *Wheelin' On Beale*, 161; 169; 171; Ennis, *The Seventh Stream*, 174–175; "The Forgotten 15,000,000, Part Two: How to Build Negro Sales," *Sponsor*, October 24, 1949, 30; Cantor, *Dewey and Elvis*, 205.

100. "The Forgotten 15,000,000, Part Two," 54.

101. James N. Gregory, *The Southern Diaspora: How the Great Migrations of Black and White Southerners Transformed America* (Chapel Hill, NC: University of North Carolina Press, 2006), 175; Kingsbury, *BMI 50th Anniversary*, 10; 20; 23; 1; Diane Pecknold, *The Selling Sound: The Rise of the Country Music Industry* (Durham, NC: Duke University Press, 2007), 2.

102. Ennis, *The Seventh Stream*, 168.

103. Kingsbury, *BMI 50th Anniversary*, 10; Ennis, *The Seventh Stream*, 25; 169, Pecknold, *The Selling Sound*, 4–6.

104. Shaw, *The Rockin' '50s*, 14.

105. "Cold, Cold Heart," Hank Williams Sr., Sterling, 1951.

106. "Cry," Churchill Kohlman, Okeh Records, 1951.

107. Richard Leppert and George Lipsitz, "Age, the Body and Experience in the Music of Hank Williams," in *All That Glitters: Country Music in America*, ed. George H. Lewis (Bowling Green, OH: Bowling Green State University Popular Press, 1993), 28.

108. Gregory, *The Southern Diaspora*.

109. Michael Lydon, *Rock Folk: Portraits from the Rock 'n' Roll Pantheon* (New York: Citadel Press, 1971), 32; Kingsbury, *BMI 50th Anniversary*, 20; 26.

110. Kingsbury, *BMI 50th Anniversary*, 37. Diane Pecknold has challenged this conception of country and western as an "authentic" music produced outside of corporate structures. Despite the fact that country stars' down-to-earth nature was part of their appeal, she argues that both artists and audiences were aware of the machinations needed to record these musicians and distribute their music on a wider, national scale. For more, please see Pecknold, *The Selling Sound*.

111. Whitburn, *Top R&B/Hip-Hop Singles*, 310.

112. Kingsbury, *BMI 50th Anniversary*, 20.

113. Ennis, *The Seventh Stream*, 25; 172; Wexler, *Rhythm and the Blues*, 62.

114. Ennis, *The Seventh Stream*, 184–185.

115. "Charting the Charts," *On the Media*, WNYC, October 23, 2009, last accessed at http://www.wnyc.org/story/132541-charting-the-charts/#transcript, on April 12, 2018; Chapple and Garofalo, *Rock 'n' Roll is Here to Pay*, 237.

116. Bill Gavin, "No Musical Color Line," *Billboard*, April 25, 1964, 64.

117. Berry Gordy, *To Be Loved: The Music, the Magic, the Memories of Motown* (New York: Warner Books, 1994), 189.

118. Flory, *I Hear a Symphony*, 18; Chapple and Garofalo, *Rock 'n' Roll is Here to Pay*, 236–237.

119. Bob Rolontz, "Hit Tunes and Good Talent are Keeping the Boxes Busy: Rhythm and Blues," *Billboard*, March 15, 1952, 82; Joe Martin, "Hit Tunes and Good Talent are Keeping the Boxes Busy: The Pops," *Billboard*, March 15, 1952, 82.

120. Albin Zak explains that there are two distinct types of crossovers: "Song" crossovers could include "cover" versions performed by different artists, while "record" crossovers meant that the same recording by a particular artist appeared on two or more charts. For the sake of simplicity, I will respectively refer to these records as "covers" and "direct crossovers". For more, please see Zak, *I Don't Sound Like Nobody*, 114–115.

121. Vera, "The Specialty Story," 26.

122. "How to Stop Vandalism?"1946, Alan Freed Archives, last accessed at http://www.alanfreed.com/wp/archives/archives-1943-1949-radio-broa/, on August 3, 2013.

123. Ennis, *The Seventh Stream*, 184–185; 200; 215.

124. Kingsbury, *BMI 50th Anniversary*, 24; 28–29; "Fats Domino," The Rock and Roll Hall of Fame, last accessed at https://www.rockhall.com/inductees/fats-domino, on June 16, 2018; "Fats Domino," *Wikipedia* page, last accessed at https://en.wikipedia.org/wiki/Fats_Domino#Recordings_for_Imperial_Records_(1949%E2%80%931962), on June 16, 2018; *Billboard*, February 18, 1950; Fats Domino and Dave Bartholomew, "The Fat Man," J&M Studio, 1949.

125. Kohlman, "Cry"; Ennis, *The Seventh Stream*, 215; Shaw, *The Rockin' 50s*, 7.

126. Billy Ward and Rose Marks, "Sixty Minute Man," Federal Records, 1951; Whitburn, *Top R&B/Hip-Hop Singles*, 168.

127. Hale, *A Nation of Outsiders*, 16.

128. *Billboard* Pop, R&B, and C&W charts, July 18, 1953–October 3, 1953.

129. *Billboard* Pop, R&B, and C&W charts, July 18–November 14, 1953; September 19, 1953–February 27, 1954.

Chapter 2

"If It's a Hit, It's a Hit," 1954–1956

In 1952, Decca Records took out a full-page advertisement in *Billboard* announcing the release of not two, not three, but *four* different versions of a new and potentially chart-topping song. "Honest and Truly" was written by professional pop songwriter Fred Rose, but the song was released in all three major music marketing categories that *Billboard* measured: an R&B version by Little Donna Hightower, a country interpretation by Roland Johnson, and what the ad describes as "two in the popular idiom": one by white bandleader Guy Lombardo and the other by the Ink Spots, a Black vocal group that had gained considerable success among white listeners. The faces of all four acts are featured prominently on the page, while the copy boldly declares:

> WE BELIEVE that HONEST AND TRULY is so memorable a song that it can be a simultaneous success in all fields: pop, country and western, rhythm and blues. ACTING ON THAT BELIEF, we have recorded HONEST AND TRULY four ways: two in the popular idiom, one country and western style, and one rhythm and blues. WE THINK each is a standout. ALL FOUR VERSIONS go on release the same day—March 10, 1952. WE BELIEVE that when you hear these four records you will agree that they are all candidates for the best-seller lists.[1]

Decca tried to increase profits from the song by selling different recordings to audiences that were presumably divided and defined by race, class, and age. The R&B version, featuring Hightower's sweet vocals set against a dynamic background of horns and percussion, was expected to sell to Black customers. The country single, with Johnson's twangy vocals backed by string instrumentation, was marketed to predominantly rural corners of the South and to Southern migrants in urban centers. And while both were labeled "pop" songs, Lombardo's precise big-band rendering and the Ink Spots' delicate crooning accompanied by a piano melody were both considered old-fashioned by burgeoning youth markets.[2] The practice of having multiple performers "cover" the same songs, allowing labels to profit without the uncertainty of releasing an original record, was hardly remarkable for this period. And yet Decca's assumption that the same song, performed by different artists and with altered arrangements, would appeal to both white and Black listeners from urban, suburban, and rural markets, provides a telling premonition of how "crossovers," defined by Denis-Constant Martin as records that "find common elements in the tastes of distinct groups," would take the music industry by storm in the mid-1950s.[3]

Crossover records began showing up on *Billboard* charts in greater numbers just as major civil rights victories like the *Brown v. Board of Education of Topeka* ruling in 1954 and the Montgomery Bus Boycott, which lasted from 1955 to 1956, captured national and international attention. Accounts of these hallmarks are often presented as the inevitable triumph of righteous and unimpeachable activism, with hallowed figures like Martin Luther King Jr. and Rosa Parks emerging out of nowhere to peaceably demand integration on Montgomery, Alabama's public transit system, and messages of tolerance broadcast throughout the world to approving audiences. The Bus Boycott did indeed force a confrontation with the violence of the Jim Crow system, help to build a broader coalition of Black activists, and turn King, the new 26-year-old pastor at Dexter Avenue Baptist Church, into a charismatic, yet controversial, media figure. Media coverage of the boycott also promoted the nonviolent protest techniques that were gaining further traction among activists after World War II, which King spoke of as both moral imperative and tactical advantage, telling a group of supporters that "if we as Negroes succumb to the temptation of using violence in our struggle, unborn generations will be the recipients of . . . a long and desolate night of bitterness. And our only legacy to the future will be an endless reign of meaningless chaos."[4] These tactics, undertaken with the goal of desegregating public spaces, would ultimately come to define the civil rights movement during this period, even if activists' intentions were far more complex and multilayered than mere peaceful demands for a seat on a bus.

Decisions to focus on nonviolent activism were also shaped by what Evelyn Brooks Higginbotham calls the "politics of respectability."[5] This strategy, which advocates for Black adherents to practice a combination of middle-class manners, behaviors, and customs, and religious or moral values, has long "appealed to African American reformers," Victoria Wolcott explains, in order "to communicate messages to both African American urban newcomers and the white community."[6] Indeed, respectability politics were used in the 1950s civil rights campaigns to both mobilize Black support and to protect activists from racist invective with what E. Frances White calls "narratives that African Americans develop to counter racism" while simultaneously, Fredrick C. Harris says, "prov[ing] to white America that blacks were worthy of full citizenship rights."[7] These appeals to propriety and order helped to mobilize and organize Black Americans across the country to fight for desegregation, but they also projected messages to whites that movement activities would be mainly defined by nonviolence and by middle-class values that supported dominant societal systems rather than disrupting them, and which focused on desegregation as a final and absolute goal rather than a piece of a longer and more difficult battle to dismantle racial injustice in all forms.

This focus on integration and respectability extended to popular music during this period, as listeners from different racial and regional demographics enjoyed not only the same musical genres, but also the same artists, songs, and recordings, in greater numbers than ever before.[8] The language of "desegregation," which was purposely used to describe records which sold well among Black and white listeners across national markets, directly referenced the civil rights campaigns that were beginning to make front-page news at the same time. *Billboard* writers and editors almost uniformly praised these crossovers, indicating a level of acceptance for desegregation in music that could extend more broadly in politics and public spaces. The publication aimed, of course, to sell and promote as many records as possible. If consumers were purchasing records traditionally sold to other demographics, it stood to reason that *Billboard* and its advertisers and subscribers would profit from higher sales numbers. Increased commodification of Black music was troubling, especially since artists and producers rarely received fair pay or acknowledgment for their work, but the dominant culture within the music industry began to convert R&B records into "respectable" artistic and consumer products. This shift could possibly convey respectability onto civil rights politics overall, even as it denied Black artists, writers, and producers payment and acknowledgment.

If the racialized genre divisions promoted by the music industry had reinforced the existence of racially segregated spaces, then their breakdown could reveal a growing interest in the possibilities of desegregation. But this "integration" of popular culture through crossover records would not ultimately lead to the fundamental investigation of structural white supremacy that deeper change would require. These parallels are complicated by the narrative of how rock and roll originated and became popular and ultimately "respectable" among white listeners.[9] In the context of early to mid-1950s desegregation campaigns, crossover hits could be viewed as positive templates for the integrated public spaces that civil rights activists were visibly fighting for during the same period. But white focus on the "respectability" of both activists and artists, which almost always obscured other aspects of Black personhood, led to missed opportunities for deeper institutional change to occur.

Overall, Black artists were not treated equally within this supposed desegregation of musical genres. Many white listeners were first drawn to R&B music because of its "non-respectable" attributes; the lyrics were more sexually direct than those in romanticized pop songs, and the genre's reliance on electric guitars, drums, and horns encouraged physical movement rather than passive listening. Singers' voices were celebrated for their honest emotion and ragged vocals rather than pop singers' strict tonal adherence. This attraction could, as Brian Ward and Nelson George have argued, reinforce the kinds of racist stereotypes that respectability politics were supposed to undermine—that Black people were more overtly sexual and less ambitious or intelligent than whites, that they possessed natural aptitudes for dancing and singing, and that the joy in their performances meant they could be happy living under a white supremacist system.[10] At the same time, some white listeners recall how they related to the struggles and joys that Black artists sang about, and that they were able to see them as fully fledged people who should not have to suffer the indignities of second-class citizenship. These responses were further complicated by major record label attempts to make Black music "respectable" by getting white pop artists to cover R&B and early rock and roll songs. In these cases, original writers and artists would receive minor compensation for their works, while white cover artists and their representation would profit handsomely. Even Elvis Presley, whose exaggerated gyrations and overtly Black-influenced style and vocal delivery caused some level of consternation among parents and cultural critics, benefited from his "respectable" whiteness by becoming wealthier and more famous than Black contemporaries like Chuck Berry, Little Richard, and Sam Cooke, even when their record labels adjusted their appearances and performance behaviors to appeal to middle-class white audiences. Tellingly, Presley became the first artist to have a record reach the number 1 spot on all three *Billboard* charts simultaneously, meaning that a white man would be credited with "desegregating" the charts.[11]

These depictions, however, obscure the shifting dynamics among consumers, artists, executives at major and independent record labels, deejays, radio station managers, and music journalists that produced a far more complex creation that otherwise belies easy description. According to Steve Chapple and Reebee Garofalo, whose book, *Rock 'n' Roll is Here to Pay*, was the first scholarly work to examine how corporate structures shaped the distribution of the genre, "Even preceding major radio play, white kids were buying up 'race' records," creating "a mysterious phenomenon for the major powers within the record business."[12] Philip Ennis also challenges the accepted narrative by focusing on listener agency. "Did the music industry force-feed teenagers into the acceptance of rocknroll?" he asks. "To the contrary, it was almost the reverse." He reminds readers that most elements of the mainstream music industry were "at that point either blind, indifferent, or hostile to the rocknroll 'craze' or 'fad,' as it was called. No one in particular wanted it, and most fought it for years before they belatedly sought to get a piece of the action."[13] And Brian Ward argues that young consumers initially influenced music production through their desire for cross-genre records. "Black and white audiences could not only shape the social and political meanings of musical products by the manner of their consumption," he says, "but in choosing to consume some styles in great quantities while ignoring others, they could even encourage the industry to move Rhythm and Blues in new directions which reflected the changing moods and needs of its customers."[14]

Major labels and larger radio stations did not instigate their customers' appetites for Black music; rather, many were forced to accommodate this cultural shift. Increasing popularity of R&B music among Black audiences meant that it was more readily available in some record stores, jukeboxes, and on the airwaves. Even if distributors and marketers only meant to reach Black customers, white youth also began listening to and enjoying this music. A few deejays like Alan Freed and Dewey Phillips purposely played R&B music for their white audiences, but most people who worked in the music industry were perplexed by the number of records that began crossing over in 1954, and assumed this fad would pass. By 1956, however, white demand for Black and Black-inspired music and artists was undeniable, all but forcing many major labels to find some way of marketing crossover music to white teenagers. These labels' decisions to purchase hit songs by Black artists for a nominal fee, have white pop singers re-record them, and sell these "cover" records to white teenagers succeeded at first, but quickly lost appeal as fans began to seek out original recordings instead. Bibb E. explains how he and his friends "began to assert the power to listen to the music we wanted to" in the mid-1950s, of which "few of our parents seemed interested in. As we made it ours, the market kicked in."[15] White teenagers did not mindlessly consume products marketed by major record labels and radio broadcasting syndicates, but instead helped broaden what was considered acceptable within the pop mainstream by choosing records by Black artists, and, by 1956, largely eschewing cover versions.

These kids' decisions to listen to records by Black artists, even when they often had to seek them out on their own, could therefore indicate support for an integrated popular culture during a period when any form of racial mixing challenged political and social boundaries. But exploitation of Black musical professionals, and the expectation that African-American musical traditions would assimilate into, rather than challenge, "respectable" white-dominated frameworks, limited potential for Black representation and white acknowledgment of structural racial injustice. Appropriation, defined by Diarra Osei Robertson as "a process of a nongroup member employing the culture of another group in cultural production," robbed Black musicians of credit and profits, even as their sounds and techniques shaped the genre that would define a generation. "The architects of early rock 'n' roll such as Little Richard and Chuck Berry were less concerned with the fact that white musicians were playing their music, but rather with an environment in which white rock musicians such as Jerry Lee [Lewis] or Elvis Presley received more recognition or financial gain than black artists," she explains. "While some may complain about issues of misrepresentation or reifying stereotypes, the most salient factor when it comes to appropriation is financial."[16]

Even so, Black and white teenagers quickly began listening to the same records by the same artists during this period, but they did so for different reasons, and their interpretations of the same lyrics, beats, and melodies were often distinguished by racialized life experiences. Black listeners who grew up during this time recall excitement over increased representation on the radio and in record stores, which could, as Brian Ward has argued, augur increased support for other forms of equality and inclusion, as well as professional opportunities within the music industry.[17] The white fans who ultimately favored original recordings by Black artists over white cover versions generally did not share these responses. Some describe listening to this music as a "gateway experience" that prompted them to question their perspectives on racism and racial justice. But most remember being drawn to songs that were fun, energetic, rebellious, honest, and "authentic" without recognizing that these qualities were shaped by artists' experiences with racial oppression and inequality. The vast majority also began listening to this music once their friends did so, or when they started to hear Black voices on the radio, both of which reshaped R&B as respectable, or at least part of mainstream adolescent culture. These distinctions parallel many white responses to the respectability politics used by Black activists to shape awareness of desegregation campaigns. Responses to both music and movement among young Black and white listeners therefore reveal a far more complicated relationship between the rock and roll created from these musical mixtures and changing ideas about racial politics than has previously been identified.

RESPECTABILITY POLITICS FROM THE PROGRESSIVE ERA TO WORLD WAR II

After Reconstruction policies were gutted in the 1870s and 1880s, Jim Crow laws were passed throughout the South and in parts of Northern cities, and instances of white violence against Blacks, including lynching and sexual assault, increased. Black reformers realized that their abilities to effect real political and social change would be compromised, so instead many focused on what Michele Mitchell terms "self-perceptions, habits, and lives" in order "to create better habitats for a healthier, more wholesome people."[18] These reforms, which focused on education, hard work, morality, cleanliness, etiquette, and traditional gender roles would, proponents argued, allow Black Americans to improve life for their own families and their communities alike by helping formerly enslaved people learn how to live as free citizens, building wealth within Black neighborhoods, and ensuring the overall health and well-being of the race. Reformers also hoped that respectability politics would limit violent white reprisal by showing how Black Americans deserved full citizenship based on adherence to acceptable middle-class customs and behaviors, while at the same time encouraging racial pride by extolling the achievements of Black leaders in politics, education, business, and the church. This focus, Martha Jones explains, "offered a counternarrative about African-American history and culture that challenged both the popular images and the political degradations of the early Jim Crow era." The admonition to "lift as we climb," which became a popular slogan for middle-class Black reformers, aimed to work within the strict and dangerous confines of turn-of-the-century white supremacy to simultaneously strengthen Black pride, protect people from racialized violence, and appeal to white power structures for the full citizenship that Reconstruction policies had promised, yet failed to deliver.[19]

Many of these reformers came from the growing Black elite, the so-called Talented Tenth of African-American society, who were supposedly tasked with helping their apparently less talented contemporaries with achieving their potential and "improving" the race overall.[20] But, as Victoria Wolcott has argued, respectability politics were "particularly open to competing definitions, inflections, and meanings" that were dependent on "social, political, and cultural context." She explains how members of the working classes tended to emphasize "family survival and individual self-respect" while middle-class reformers focused on "public propriety."[21] Ideologies of Black women especially differed depending on whether they organized through social clubs, which tended to draw elite and middle or "aspiring" class members, or church congregations, which included higher numbers of working-class patrons.[22] Although their tactics and messages may have differed, women from both groups advocated for better education and for morality and refined manners in Black communities, especially lower-income areas. Reformers also viewed education as a means of social, as well as economic, advancement.[23] The idea was to increase the number of professional positions and to provide segregated Black communities with the services residents needed, but also, echoing some of the points made by Booker T.

Washington in his 1895 Atlanta Compromise Speech, to make the best of the job opportunities that already existed, and to do them well. These reformers, Evelyn Brooks Higginbotham explains, believed that "a well-educated vanguard constituted a buffer between white society and the black masses" since "uneducated or half-educated" people were seen as more likely to embrace "a militant and extremist position," rendering entire communities vulnerable to racist violence. But a better educated population, she says, could also strengthen Black communities from within by allowing people to "demand respect" and by improving their economic and physical health. The value of a good education also "appeared irrefutable to men and women denied legal access to learning under the slave's regime," therefore allowing adherents to draw a definitive line between past oppression and hopeful futures as full citizens.[24]

Reformers believed that better education could also, Higginbotham explains, help "even the poorest to maintain orderly, intelligent homes. It prepared them to teach their children to read, appreciate knowledge, and develop self-discipline and lofty ideals."[25] Notions of "correct" bourgeois morality and manners were clearly intertwined with learning for many middle- and aspiring-class reformers who were genuinely concerned about high rates of disease, infant mortality, teenage pregnancy, and alcohol abuse harming their communities. But they were also aware of how "degenerate" behaviors could reinforce racist stereotypes of Black people as immoral, lazy, over-sexualized, and criminal.[26] Concerned activists therefore embarked on campaigns to "improve" people's manners, hygiene, and morality by encouraging them to follow guidelines in keeping with both dominant white society and Black churches. Some of these supposedly behavioral changes were contingent on access to material goods that were difficult to attain amid widespread poverty. Michele Mitchell, for instance, shows how poor housing was such a concern among club women that they routinely organized home visitations in poorer neighborhoods to train parents in cleanliness and parenting skills, and sometimes even "slated race households for renovation."[27] Similarly, Jennifer Jensen Wallach shows how "respectable" food and dining choices were promulgated both as a means of strengthening health and hygiene in Black families and as a means of what she calls "creating a new narrative for freedom." Adherents hoped that new "food practices . . . would create a distance between themselves and the painful past of slavery." Reformers believed that these foods and practices were healthier, but they were also "intended to serve as a refutation to ongoing stereotypes about black culinary difference and inferiority."[28] As with housing, however, few outside of the so-called Talented Tenth could afford these more expensive foods and furnishings, and many remained uninterested in abandoning their own culinary traditions.

Since manners and moral practices were not directly tied to material wealth, and many had roots in Black religious traditions as much as they did the white middle classes, both elite and aspiring-class reformers believed that they could more easily effect changes in these areas. Higginbotham points to the campus activities at Spelman College, a Baptist institution created in 1881 for Black women, as an example. At Spelman, students could attend "social purity meetings, Christian endeavor societies, converts' meetings, and the Young Women's Christian Association with its missionary and temperance bands" while expected to be present for daily Bible study classes.[29] But proper behavioral and moral comportment was advocated for everyone, Mitchell says, through the publication of manuals and "prescriptive literature" which aimed to teach outside of the classroom. These manuals, she says, often discussed the dangers of alcohol, flirting, infectious diseases, crime, and teenage pregnancy, and advocated temperance, marriage and parenthood, and strict adherence to gender roles as means of combating these social ills. Again, reforms were meant to ensure the physical health and moral strength of Black families since death and disease rates were often disproportionately higher than those in white neighborhoods. Alcoholism and teen pregnancy rates among Black and white populations were roughly similar, but members of the aspiring class also aimed to debunk white stereotypes which "generally portrayed black women as indiscriminate and insatiable, black men as oversexed and bestial, and black children as so sexually precocious as to preclude innocence." Since these racist depictions were believed to incite violence and provide rationalizations for denying Black Americans their rights, these responses, Mitchell claims, "formed a politicized and cohesive genre" when other forms of protest were rendered difficult and dangerous.[30]

These reforms were heavily directed toward lower-income or working-class Black Americans, who did not always approve of respectability politics. Higginbotham notes how "some blacks rejected their Victorian ideals and viewed their 'assimilationist' goals as divisive in families and communities" while Mitchell adds that reformers' distaste for "unbelievers," "drunkards," "loafers," and those in "poor health and circumstance" led people to feel judged for their lifestyle choices or for aspects of their lives that were beyond their control.[31] But others responded favorably to respectability politics, both because individual actions were easier to control than structural issues, and because of a desire to "advance" as a race, particularly among religious churchgoers and those who strove for upward mobility. As the twentieth century progressed, respectability politics would inform both Black Nationalist and integrationist ideologies. Honor Ford-Smith, for instance, says that Marcus Garvey's UNIA was "proletarian, but also pursued respectability." UNIA members were expected to adhere to strict gender norms, with women in particular instructed "to produce a disciplined elite with sexual mores that conformed to those of nineteenth-century respectability," and to practice manners that would not have been out of place in middle-class white households, such as keeping proper meal times.[32] Meanwhile, Victoria Walcott finds that women in Detroit during the interwar years continued to embrace respectability politics as a way to challenge segregation policies as well as "enhance their reputation, ensure social mobility, and create a positive image for their communities."[33]

This focus on respectability also spread to culture, as many reformers in the early to mid-twentieth century castigated the blues for glorifying immorality and vice, and for centering experiences with poverty, racism, and helplessness rather than the industriousness and upward mobility they wanted all Black Americans to embody. The blues, descended from songs created by enslaved people, became popular in the South in the late nineteenth century, and ultimately spread to Northern cities as migrants began their journeys to urban centers, taking their musical customs with them. This genre utilized an unadorned instrumental technique, usually accompanied by an acoustic guitar, and focused on the fallible human voice as a means of voicing sorrows within a 12-bar structure. The use of a chorus, which was standard in popular music, was eschewed in favor of songs made up entirely of verses, with the third line of each verse providing a sense of closure to the lyrics. The structure of these songs implies that the person singing them will be able to go on living simply because he or she is able to recognize the pain in life, and to deal with it accordingly. Singing, listening to, and performing the blues was used, according to Lawrence Levine, not to actually end misery, but to "[create] the necessary space between the slaves and their owners and [become] the means of preventing legal slavery from becoming spiritual slavery."[34]

This message was also implicit in what Tera Hunter calls the "blues aesthetic," which she describes as "positive affirmations of cultural memories and racial heritage, and the envisioning of new possibilities and new racial realties." Here, she explicitly talks about the popular dances that would accompany blues performances in dance halls in 1910s Atlanta, where middle-class reformers and pious church people alike were concerned that "the halls, the activities, and the people were often associated with urban "vice"—crime, drinking, and illicit sex," and how they would harm their efforts at projecting images of propriety.[35] They were also concerned with the genre's supposedly offensive subject matter and emotive delivery. Angela Y. Davis notes how "those aspects of lived love relationships that were not compatible with the dominant, etherealized ideology of love—such as extramarital relationships, domestic violence, and the ephemerality of many sexual partnerships—were largely banished from the established popular musical culture," but Black reformers also considered these subjects to be derogatory and a means of reinforcing harmful stereotypes. B. B. King explained that mainstream depictions of blues singers emphasized the poverty, illiteracy, and vice that reformers aimed to distance themselves from: "With a cap on his head that's faced east and you got a jug a liquor on the west side, west of him. And his pants is tore in the south part. And he have a cigarette hanging on his lip somewhat on the northeast side of his mouth and he can't read or write. He don't speak very well."[36] Although record labels marketed blues records as "authentic" Black folk music from the South, many Black reformers across class lines rejected this genre as disreputable, presenting members of their race in an unflattering light.

But the blues was not the only popular music form enjoyed by Black listeners. Gospel music, which originated in Southern churches in the early nineteenth century and began moving outside the spiritual realm by the early twentieth century, was distributed by the same labels as "race records," and often even advertised in the same spaces. Much like the blues, gospel emphasized truth and used stories from the past as means of coping with present pains. But the religious nature of gospel music necessitated distinctions from secular blues songs that divided some listeners. Instead of focusing on the hardships of poverty, cheating romantic partners, and attempts to find solace in collective sadness as the blues did, gospel emphasized the love of God and the promise of salvation after enduring the cruel slings of fate on earth. Instead of relying on the voice of one singer like the blues did, Philip Ennis says that "gospel is almost entirely a vocal music," making use of soloists or groups of singers. Where the blues insisted on simplicity, gospel celebrated the ecstatic. Craig Werner argues that the use of "call and response" was integral to these recordings, since responses were largely left up to congregants. "The response can affirm, argue, redirect the dialogue, raise a new question," he says. "Any response that gains attention and elicits a response of its own becomes a new call. Usually the individual who issued the first call responds to the response, remains the focal point of the ongoing dialogue. But it doesn't have to be that way."[37] The importance of community and collective endurance was made even more plain in this genre. Listeners expanded beyond their traditional confines to become participants in making meaning, and their thoughts and emotions were deemed just as important as those of the primary performer. The democratic nature of gospel therefore appealed to many adherents, as did its promise of deliverance to the faithful.

Gospel was usually written in the more rollicking 8-bar progression rather than the traditional 12-bar blues pattern, and therefore tended to sound more joyous and upbeat, even when the lyrics told of sorrow and struggle. Many young musicians, including B. B. King, recall being first drawn to music at church. "When you go to the sanctified church and hear the people sing, in the area where we grew up everybody was very poor and the only instrument there was the guitar," King asserted. "That's the only instrument. And tambourines. The things you beat like that. . . . And they had, to me, the best rhythm."[38] A firm divide was supposed to exist between gospel music, performed as part of religious services to show adoration for God, and the blues, which was routinely referred to as "the devil's music" by aspiring-class Blacks and by the devoutly religious, who disapproved of the genre's earthier themes and seeming approval of sinful behavior. Robin Kelley explains that "the church's strict moral codes and rules for public behavior often came into conflict with aspects of black working-class culture. Baptists and Methodists disciplined members for patronizing gin joints, for wild dancing, and for gambling."[39] Johnny Otis also wrote about this conflict, noting that "many Black preachers carried on about what they called 'the devil's music,'" although these admonitions rarely did any good. "Black churchgoers, especially the young, listened to the anti-blues sermons and went out and enjoyed themselves anyhow."[40] Many listeners made the common assertion that the lyrics represented the main dividing line between otherwise similar forms of music. Otis asserted that "if you got close enough, you could separate the club sounds from the church. If you heard the word 'baby' a lot it was the club. If you heard 'Jesus,' it was the church."[41] Ray Charles talked about the two genres in a 1973 *Rolling Stone* interview. "I don't know what it is," he said. "Gospel and the blues are really, if you break it down, almost the same thing. It's just a question of whether you're talkin' about a woman or God. I come out of the Baptist Church, and naturally whatever happened to me in that church is gonna spill over. So I think the blues and gospel music is quite synonymous to each other."[42]

Even as some listeners enjoyed both the sacred and the profane in harmony with one another, Evelyn Brooks Higginbotham notes that gospel adherents tended to emphasize both the spiritual and "respectable" elements of the records they enjoyed. The respectability politics aligned with religious music may have appealed to middle- and aspiring-class reformers, but Higginbotham stresses that working-class listeners were also avid proponents of the genre and its corresponding moral dictates. Whereas the former wanted religious music to be used as a "civilizing force," she notes how the latter "challenged the middle-class ideology of racial uplift" by "drawing upon and promoting the very folk traditions that the middle class had sought to eradicate," including "highly emotional preaching, moaning, ecstatic audience response" and other characteristics that were clearly "rejecting a rational, dispassionate style." And yet "the religious culture" that these songs and sermons emanated from, she says, "embraced a strict moral code that denounced the fast and free lifestyle of blues culture. In the dialect, imagery, and rhythms of the Black poor, the religious race records repudiate sexual freedom, gambling, drinking, womanizing, and general defiance of the law."[43] Just as working-class church women emphasized the importance of respectability outside, and sometimes in contradiction with, middle- and aspiring-class uplift during the Progressive Era, these values continued to be upheld into the middle of the twentieth century.

Although Victoria Walcott argues that the economic desperation and renewed focus on unionism and anticapitalist politics shifted reformers' attentions away from respectability during the Great Depression, many tactics, values, and goals would combine with a wartime focus on civil rights and self-determination to shape protest politics in the 1950s, partially, as Danielle McGuire argues, to protect against Cold War accusations of communist subversion.[44] Decisions to utilize the ideals of respectability politics were partially meant to appeal to the many Black families who continued to use values of thrift, industriousness, propriety, and morality as means of protecting themselves culturally and economically. Singer Cissy Houston remembered her parents, who came to Newark, New Jersey, from Georgia, as being very strict with regard to education. "We went to school every day," she said. "You didn't not go to school, now. That was not a—um-mm. You went to school and you did your homework."[45] Many Black parents took pains to ensure that their children were nicely dressed to reflect their values to the outside world. "We didn't beg. We went to school dressed neat," Little Richard recalls of his childhood.[46] Although singer Gladys Knight asserts that, in her family, "we were all church-bound, so to speak. . . . It wasn't like you had a choice to go to church," she also stresses that her parents let her sing popular music as well as gospel. But they taught her and her siblings that "in certain things you've still got to have morality, you've still got to have class, you've still got to have quality."[47] And much like white suburbanites, who rushed to invest in new homes, actress and singer Diahann Carroll said that when her family "bought a brownstone on 148th Street . . . that's where I began to understand what property meant to my father. Property meant *everything* to my father."[48] In this way, many working- or aspiring-class Black parents espoused many of the same values and exerted many of the same demands on their children as middle-class white parents, even if their lived experiences were starkly different.

Most of the Black respondents involved in this study possess university degrees, and all of them held professional positions for most of their working lives. Many grew up in middle-class households in the first place, but even those who did not clearly obtained this class status through education or occupation. It is therefore unsurprising that so many in this group recall the impact of middle-class respectability norms on their lives when they were growing up in the 1950s and 1960s. "My ethic to work was in my face all day, every day," says Cheryl J. of how her middle-class professional parents ran their family's household. "I knew that I had to grow up, go to school, get a job, and go to work." Her parents also signed her up for extracurricular classes and activities, including art classes at the Detroit Institute of Arts, to ensure that she was always busy and always "learning something different." There was no question about whether or not she would go to college, she says, because "school was your job, and that's what you were going to do if you intended to survive in this country." She says she took this lesson to heart growing up, thinking "you've got to succeed, you've got to have your own everything, you know, never put yourself in the position to have to bug somebody or need something and you can't get it." Carol A. explains how her parents had a similar perspective on the connection between economic independence and respectability norms. They "may have thought kind of like W. E. B. Du Bois, like, pull yourself up by your bootstraps," she says. She recalls how "we grew up in a house that was kind of . . . not militaristic, but [my father] was really into this [belief that] you can't be lazy. You've got to wake up early in the morning. You've got to make sure that your bed is made." The reason for this, she says, is that, like many Progressive reformers who came before, her father "wanted to live a life of disproving any Black stereotypes." Joseph J. concurs, noting how he was born into a second generation of professionals with college degrees in New Orleans. "It was a motivation," he says of his family's "drive for you not to slack off. . . . You only had one direction, and it was forward." Each respondent is clear that their family's views were borne not out of any desire to appeal to white populations, but out of a sense of self-protection and a need for economic independence within a culture that set them up to fail. "A big part of Black ideology [is] that you don't want to conform to stereotypes white people have about Black people that are bringing down the race," Tony T. says of his mother's and grandmother's views on the subject. "You want to be . . . a credit to the race."[49]

RESPECTABILITY POLITICS AND THE MONTGOMERY BUS BOYCOTT, 1955–1956

Black activists who were trying to desegregate public spaces in the South therefore had every reason to use respectability politics to shape their movements in order to gain Black supporters who had invested in these values, as well as to appeal to white sympathies by proving that they deserved to have their freedoms recognized and to (hopefully) protect protestors from the worst kinds of backlash. These politics shaped the ways that Montgomery activists organized a bus boycott that would bring city transit to a breaking point, capturing national and international attention for 12 months between 1955 and 1956. This boycott, which had long been planned by members of the city's local NAACP office and the Women's Political Council, did not aim to integrate the bus lines at first, but instead demanded that drivers treat Black passengers with courtesy and respect, that seats be granted on a "first-come, first-served" basis, and that the transit company hire Black drivers for predominantly Black routes. These demands, which mostly operated within a segregationist framework, were meant to improve daily life for the Black women who were forced to endure humiliating remarks and sexual harassment as they rode buses to work in white neighborhoods. The initial goals of the boycott were therefore shaped from the start by a focus on respectability, particularly among working-class women who felt that white bus drivers and passengers were violating their rights to be treated with decorum.[50] Organizing tactics were also devised with an eye toward respectability politics. Although Black women were routinely arrested for challenging Montgomery's rule that Black passengers must give white passengers their seats if none were available in the front of the segregated section, few of these cases seemed suitable catalysts for a widespread boycott that would require the majority of Black riders to avoid the buses in order to get to work. Jeanne Theoharis explains how both Claudette Colvin and Mary Louise Smith were rejected as "not the proper plaintiff for a suit," as "the press would 'have a field day' with a less upstanding plaintiff."[51] Smith came from a working-class household and had an alcoholic father, while, Danielle McGuire explains, NAACP head E. D. Nixon worried that the 15-year-old Colvin would not be suitable either. His mind was made up, she says, after visiting Colvin's home in a very poor section of the city. When Colvin opened the door and Nixon saw that she was pregnant, he realized that an unwed teenage mother would not only fail to garner support among Black community members who were instrumental to the boycott's success, but that she could be used by white supremacists to further harmful stereotypes about Black Americans in general, preventing the movement from making a broader impact.[52]

When Rosa Parks was arrested on December 1, 1955, for refusing to give up her seat to a white man, however, both Nixon and Jo Ann Robinson, the head of the Women's Political Council, knew that she would provide the movement with necessary respectability. Parks, Taylor Branch attests, "was without peer as a potential symbol" for the boycott and the people who would support it, "humble enough to be claimed by the common folk, and yet dignified enough in manner, speech, and dress to command the respect of the leading classes."[53] A seamstress at Montgomery Fair, the city's major department store, Parks was married, well educated, soft spoken, a regular at church services, and a conservative dresser. Even if she and her husband had trouble making ends meet and could not be considered middle class in any economic sense, her comportment fit gendered expectations for respectability across racial lines, rendering her an appealing figure for both Black protestors and potential white allies. As Nixon said in a later interview, "She was perfect for what was needed. There was nothing they could point the finger at with her. Her character was untouchable."[54] Organizers were careful to hide much of her activist past from the public, however, since her experiences as an NAACP field reporter and attending interracial trainings at the controversial Highlander Folk School did not support the image of a tired woman who simply refused to give up her seat when she was asked to do so.[55] This tactic worked—a few months later, *New York Times* reporter Wayne Phillips declared that the boycott "might have happened no matter who Mrs. Parks was. But it was certainly strengthened by the fact that Mrs. Parks was an intelligent, hardworking woman with a strongly developed conviction that segregation was evil, a leader in her church, and one of the leaders in the local chapter of the National Association for the Advancement of Colored People."[56] Parks herself noted the importance of respectability politics as a tactic, telling a National Council of Negro Women gathering that "the people of the community knew me. . . . They knew that I was not a person to say very much. I was not an agitator or troublemaker." To arrest such a person, she implied, meant that everyone's dignity was at stake, no matter how well they adhered to middle-class values or moral dictates.[57]

Indeed, within 24 hours, nearly empty buses were traversing the streets of Montgomery after members of the Women's Political Council papered the streets with flyers proclaiming "another Negro woman has been arrested and thrown in jail because she refused to get up out of her seat on the bus for a white person to sit down." Activists knew that they would need a similarly appealing leader to keep the boycott going for as long as necessary, especially since participants faced economic distress, harassment, and physical exhaustion from having to walk to work or find alternate transportation.[58] Despite Parks's potency as a catalyst for protest, her sex would prevent her from being taken seriously as a leader. Instead, organizers looked to Martin Luther King Jr. as the boycott's motivating force. As the new pastor at Dexter Avenue Baptist Church, King had yet to establish himself in the city, which meant that he could easily leave if the protest failed, and that longtime leaders would be left relatively unscathed. But King was also appointed as a leader, and as the ultimate head of the Montgomery Improvement Association (MIA), created to fund and promote the boycott and other civil rights endeavors, because of his similarly respectable character. The son and grandson of prominent Atlanta ministers, King was married, had two children, and had recently earned his PhD from Boston University. His credentials as a well-educated, middle-class, and morally upright family man seemed indisputable across racial lines. His appeal became obvious within the pages of mainstream presses outside the South, as the *New York Times* described him as "a rather soft-spoken man with a learning and maturity far beyond his twenty-seven years. His clothes are in conservative good taste and he has a small trim mustache. He heads an upper middle-class group of Negro Baptists with dignity and restraint," while the *Washington Post and Times Herald* declared him "soft-spoken, always neatly dressed. He moves with deliberate speed, and is an excellent speaker."[59] This coverage had the desired effect on young people like Emily W., who is white and grew up in Florida. "I think MLK was an amazing man," she says. "I think his eloquence really caught a lot of people by surprise in the thoughtful man he was, and how well-spoken and kind, and I think that was huge for a lot of people who had other perceptions of Blacks."[60]

Independent Black presses also highlighted his claims to respectability. Claudette Colvin told *Baltimore Afro-American* reporter Ted Poston that "the Rev. Mr. King was picked as a spokesman because he was an intelligent man. There are many of us who don't like segregation. Many people who can't read and write don't like segregation on the buses but can't express themselves like Rev. Mr. King."[61] His background deviated from the often-celebrated "rags-to-riches" stories, and was instead presented as stable, loving, and prosperous. The *New York Amsterdam News* asserted that he was an "avid reader of history and philosophical books" and that "most of his youth was spent with few desires which his parents weren't able to secure for him," while the *Pittsburgh Courier* explained that King's childhood home "was warm and happy. They were well-to-do and they were all influenced and motivated by a strong religious emphasis."[62] The *Chicago Defender* even stated plainly that "many of the white citizens of the community are completely bewildered by the character of the boycott leadership and by the pronouncements of the Reverend Martin Luther King. The education, the poise and general behavior of Reverend King simply does not square with the long-held notions of many whites regarding the Negro, particularly the southern Negro about whom they thought they knew so much."[63]

King was rightly identified as someone who could both galvanize Montgomery's Black community to action and captivate the mainstream press, a leader who could retain his middle-class respectability even when he was brandished a communist and arrested, along with 90 other organizers, for staging what the state of Alabama claimed was a conspiracy to "injure the transit company's business."[64] This arrest prompted activists to begin fighting for desegregation on the bus lines, since it became increasingly clear that the white power structures in the city would not submit to separatist demands. "Far from intimidating them, the indictments stirred the Negroes to even greater unity," a *Life* magazine profile proclaimed. "At the mass meeting they roared approval as one of their leaders said, 'The right to protest is the glory of democracy.'" At the same time, King told a *New York Times* reporter, "Frankly, I am for immediate integration. . . . Segregation is evil, and as a minister I cannot condone evil."[65] This shift meant that integration as an abject civil rights goal and moral imperative would become inextricably linked with the boycott's respectability politics, even though it was not initially the driving issue behind the boycott. King's focus on Gandhian nonviolence as a protest tactic also became seen as a "respectable" means of protest in news accounts outside the South, even as boycotters were routinely identified as radical in the same pieces. The *New York Times* characterized King as "a Baptist preacher in a great southern tradition of resounding, repetitive rhetoric," for instance, but also whose "convictions are these: That all men are basically good; that ultimately good will triumph over the evil in their nature; that segregation in all its aspects is evil, and that ultimately it must be swept away."[66] The *Washington Post and Times Herald* asserted that "his passive resistance to segregation on buses in Montgomery, with the resulting frustration of opposing whites, has given him the aura of an American Gandhi."[67] Even after his family suffered a terrifying bomb attack in their home, "Dr. King appeared and told the crowd that especially those who threw the bomb needed love, that those who lived by the sword must die by the sword." The reporter added that "his words quickly brought peace. His words are also positive on the rights of all men. From the pulpit, his call for love and courage stresses the rightness of the Negro struggle. His language is Bible-belt language that both whites and blacks understand."[68] Both Black and mainstream presses, then, revealed their support for King's particular brand of nonviolent Judeo-Christian protests against segregation, implicitly distilling his values and tactics into the only successful and respectable means of advocating for civil rights.

White supremacist backlash was strengthened in many ways by the widespread support for this boycott, but white journalists mostly focused on the triumphs of desegregation after the 1956 *Browder v. Gayle* Supreme Court case. Days before the ruling that declared segregation on the city's transit lines illegal was put into place, *New York Times* reporter George Barrett visited the city to gauge resident reactions. "There is a tacit agreement by the bulk of both the Negro and white communities that violence must not erupt," he noted, explaining how residents of both races either ignored or made fun of three Ku Klux Klan (KKK) members in full regalia walking through the downtown area. Although he does not consider the reactions of Black citizens very closely, he tries to connect white responses to an emerging, and supposedly organic, racial tolerance. "The whites now express amazement at—and a reluctant admiration for—the yearlong campaign," he attests. Many of the white people he spoke with "confide—usually in private, however—that they are giving agonizing reappraisals to their Dixie-conditioned concepts of the black man." Barrett claimed that their outward contempt for Klan members revealed this change, and yet many also said that they did not use the buses anyway, so the ruling would not affect them; that segregation would continue despite the law; and that school desegregation was "where we're gonna draw our line."[69] Barrett continued his optimistic outlook a few days later when the ruling was actually implemented, declaring that "nothing happened to indicate that Montgomery's 75,000 whites and 50,000 Negroes looked upon the historic event as anything but a natural development." Upon riding the buses himself, he emphasized the polite yet impersonal exchanges among riders: "At first there was no exchange between whites and Negroes as they took up the strange pattern of mixed seating," he wrote. "But often the stiffness gradually disappeared. A Negro turned in one bus to ask a white passenger sitting behind him—the mark of the new order—what time it was and got a quick courteous reply. A white man who had been sitting next to a Negro, said later he did not understand what all the fuss and the difficulty had been about." Barrett witnessed only one example of hostility, as a white man tried to prevent a Black woman from taking her seat, but he also detailed what he considered a fairly powerful exchange as "two white men in one bus today found themselves sitting behind a Negro, and one of the whites said, loudly: 'I see this isn't going to be a white Christmas.' The Negro looked up, and smiled. He said, with good humor but firmness: 'Yes, sir, that's right.' Everybody in the bus smiled, and all the rancor seemed to evaporate."[70] Even the *Chicago Defender*, one of the most widely read Black- and civil rights-oriented papers of the period, observed "no resentment on this bus as Negro and white passengers boarded and took seats throughout the vehicle," adding that only one white "agitator" "tried hard to start a riot between Negroes and whites at a bus transfer point" before being "ignored, then routed by newsmen and a photographer."[71]

The notion that integration on the buses was a nonissue to most white passengers is evident in these accounts, as is the belief that white Southerners were almost organically starting to disavow racist beliefs, even after a yearlong campaign where many protestors were harassed, attacked, intimidated, and arrested. It was hard to deny the righteousness of protestors' demands when news outlets across the country broadcast images of calm, well-dressed Black people being assaulted by snarling white police officers and their supporters. Many believed that King's messaging, shaped by bourgeois respectability, democratic norms, and Judeo-Christian values, would inevitably convince Southern whites to embrace degrees of desegregation, even if any real attempt to improve economic and educational opportunities for Black residents was avoided. These perspectives would shape the ways that many young white Southerners would come to view the civil rights movement and to understand issues of racial justice overall. "I just did not *get* why what Blacks wanted was so bad, and created such a stir. I felt no threat," recalls Bibb E., who grew up in rural Virginia. "Children develop a very tightly wound sense of things not being *fair*. I saw no fairness in using the color of an individual's skin to determine how to treat them." Of the movement to desegregate in particular, he says, "It became obvious that these barriers had to come down. It was simple, the right thing to do."[72] Ann W., who grew up in rural Alabama, says she "didn't understand why we couldn't be part of the same 'place'" and that "there was finally a peace for me personally when barriers were removed.... Without really realizing it, I guess my views had been fairly constant that these things were wrong."[73] Those who grew up outside of the South are more likely to link their responses to a broader struggle, yet they still tend to use the same language of right and wrong when describing their responses to desegregation campaigns. Fran S. says he "felt like this was just a matter of fairness and very much identified with the whole civil rights agenda as a matter of justice," while Arnie Bauchner admitted that "for whatever reasons—I don't know what the roots were—I always felt I basically had liberal sentiments rather than feeling like people were fucked over. And probably feeling sorry, for a lot of it was internal, but it was like a basic sympathy." Victor F. concurs, explaining how "my moral code was, treat everybody equally," which did not make sense given what he saw going on in the South. "That ain't what Jesus said to do," he exclaims. "It's like, this isn't what we were raised, this isn't what our founding fathers had in mind."[74] Michigan native, and future radical activist, John Sinclair spoke about the movement's "air of moral purpose so strong and so pure that almost everyone could see that the blacks had right on their side." He explained that many white middle-class kids "found themselves in sympathy with the black man's struggle with unjust authority" after seeing "American citizens being beaten and arrested simply for asking for their constitutionally guaranteed rights." Mary R. explains how the realization that those supposedly guaranteed rights were not granted to Black people affected her entire family's views on the movement. "It's fundamentally un-American," she says of their response to these campaigns. "I was raised to see the South as a land of hypocrites who were irrationally anti-American because of the way they treated Negroes... it was just, you know, we hold these truths to be self-evident that all men are created equal. That was just foundational to our understanding of what life should be and what our ideals were. And there was a very clear understanding that we weren't living up to our ideals." She also uses moral language when describing her aversion to racial segregation, however, claiming that "this was America's cardinal, original sin, and it had to be changed."[75]

Many white respondents also talk about how these earlier protests introduced them to civil rights struggles that they otherwise would not have known much about. "I don't think that white people had a conscious racial civil rights kind of awareness," says Ron R. of his experiences growing up in the Midwest. He explains that his "awareness kind of coincided with the movement" in the mid-1950s when his classroom first integrated, and he was able to connect this development to the Montgomery Boycott. Marcia P. explains how she became increasingly uncomfortable with and confused by the racist jokes her extended family members would make during this period, even if she was not immediately aware of the movement's impact.[76] White respondents who grew up outside of the South are also likely to talk about their family's influences when learning about the movement. "Our politics have always been very liberal, they continue to be liberal," says Ellis B., who grew up in New York. "We were very supportive in the civil rights movement [including] Martin Luther King." Walter S. and Victor F. both describe their upbringings as "color blind," which they explain made it easier to support these campaigns since they fundamentally could not understand why Black people in the South were not treated equally. "It just seemed to me that all people were basically the same, and I always looked at Blacks as just having darker skin," Victor says. "So I wasn't brought up with prejudices. And when I became aware of them because of my early training, what my mother taught me, I didn't buy into."[77]

But these responses, which were overwhelmingly rooted in moral outrage and concerns that the country's democratic values were not upheld for everyone, overlooked much of what Black organizers of early desegregation campaigns like the Montgomery Bus Boycott were trying to accomplish. The city itself had long been viewed as an oasis of racial moderation in the South, leading many white authorities to express surprise at the size of the protests and to falsely assert that most of the organizing work was due to "outside agitators." "White Montgomery boasts of the schools and housing it has provided for colored citizens and seems chagrined that they are not profoundly grateful," Ted Poston reported for the *Baltimore Afro-American* during the boycott. And yet the Black residents he interviewed "answer by saying 'They are so used to not giving us anything, that when they do a little, they think it's the greatest thing in the world.'"[78] Goals switched to desegregation in the face of white resistance, but *Pittsburgh Courier* journalist Trezzvant W. Anderson spoke for many Black participants when he outlined frustrations with the boycott's outcomes in a 1957 series of reports for the famed Black-oriented paper. "Cold, hard facts are sometimes difficult to face, especially if they do not show one in a favorable light, or a satisfactory one," he proclaimed in his November 23 piece. "Yet cold, hard facts are indisputable. That was true here in the yearlong bus boycott. Some of the facts are harsh and unpleasant, yet true." Here, he argues that organizers' successful attempts to gain media attention "took the play away from the basic purposes of the boycott" and "became a show for the outsiders," yet "proved beyond a shadow of doubt it was not good for the Negroes of Montgomery, Ala." The following week, Anderson reported that lower-income Black residents have suffered from an "economic job squeeze," as fewer help wanted ads sought

Black employment, and white-owned financial institutions were refusing to extend credit to Black borrowers, presumably as retribution for the boycott. His December 21 report, however, really exemplified frustrations a full year after the buses were forced to desegregate. "None of the buses is manned by Negroes," he explained, referencing one of the campaign's initial demands. An MIA leader told him that "the bus company had made a sort of promise that Negroes would be hired when the time is right," but when he asked the superintendent of the transit company, he was told that there were no plans to do so in the near future. He also spoke to members of the Black business community who had been in stalled discussions with the MIA to advocate for a Black-owned credit union or bank. "What the heck good is it to me to be able to sit anywhere on the bus if I don't have fare to get on it?" one business owner asked in exasperation. Anderson noted that "the white drivers have adopted a policy of courtesy. This reporter did not see a single instance of any form of discourtesy or inconsiderateness." He supplemented this observation, however, with a discerning look at the strengths and weaknesses of using respectability politics to work toward desegregated public spaces. "This country and the world have had their minds and consciences set aflame by the picture of men and women walking the streets rather than riding segregated—but walking with such dignity that their very walking served as an indictment against the system which they protested," he asserted. And yet "the aim of the MIA has been achieved, but buses were not the only medium through which Negroes were segregated and intimidated, so the fight must go on."[79]

While sympathetic whites celebrated what they perceived to be the end of a yearlong struggle, many Black kids agreed with Anderson's assertions and questioned whether residents really benefited from desegregation rulings. Cheryl J., who grew up in Detroit, acknowledges that the boycott "set a precedence. That ended that. Black people suffered to get where they got. Can you imagine how hard it was for people that had been accustomed to riding in the back of the bus, now were walking to work? . . . And that went on for months and months." While she notes that "a lot of things were worth it," she also recalls how her parents barely discussed desegregation campaigns at home. "They were so caught up in, I don't want to use the term their dream, but . . . they had moved forward in life, and if any of that was getting on them, they were letting it roll off their back."[80] Many people who grew up outside the South recall feeling somewhat distanced from Jim Crow struggles, although Scott F. recalls preachers at his grandmother's church "taking incidents that happened . . . whether it was something that Martin Luther King had said . . . and expounding on it and also relating it to the way that we lived our lives in this New Jersey community. And how the events that took place a thousand miles away actually related to us as Black people as well."[81] Bunyan Bryant, who grew up in Little Rock, Arkansas, before moving to Flint, Michigan, as a teenager, recalled how "when King started picketing in the South, in the 1950s, I didn't understand. I knew that was a bad scene, but it was almost an embarrassment, you know, that somebody had to go out there and picket and demonstrate for their rights. I was pretty confused. My consciousness was not that sharp." Ultimately, he remembered thinking, "Why does King want to integrate anyway?"[82]

Many found it hard to see how the absence of state-sponsored segregation had benefited people's lives in Northern states, and therefore did not view Southern victories as any real form of racial justice. Plus, as Joseph J. explains, even for Southerners like his family, "the likelihood of that changing your life was very remote. And so the focus was on making sure you got what you needed using what you had." He remembers how his father "took the position that integration was probably going to be one of the worst things that would happen to Black people. And here's why: Because growing up, we went to Black doctors, we had lawyers, we shopped basically at stores where Black people owned and ran them."[83] A focus on integrating public spaces without working to ensure economic and leadership opportunities for Black people would, as earlier anti-integration activists predicted, only harm African-American communities and the businesses and networks they had worked so hard to build. Carol A., whose family is from Detroit, seconds this concern, recalling how the city's Black economic hubs were destroyed, mostly by the construction of highways, but also because, as she explains, consumers "think the white man's ice is colder. So when people had a choice, oh, I can go buy over here, and then you didn't get the same support, the same cohesion that a lot of minority communities have." She notes that her great uncle, who owned a string of successful party stores, "had a lot of Black patrons, but he cited desegregation as one of the reasons that there was the demise of the Black community." Civil rights activist Larry R. received similar reactions when talking to Black Southerners about their needs and goals. "America is a nation of nations, and we're all Americans together. And so everybody should have the right to vote," he says. But "the people I worked with, they did not experience life like that. They experience[d] life through being Black. So, you know, when they heard 'melting pot' or 'integration,' what it meant was people were telling them everybody has the right to be white." What he often heard instead was that "we do not want to melt. We are proud of being Black. And . . . as Black people, we are equal to anybody else. We don't have to change our culture."[84]

Some respondents also felt discomfort with desegregation campaigns' focus on respectability politics and nonviolent action. Najee M., who grew up in New York, says that if activists "were sincere, serious, and committed, I was proud of them and supported them." He stipulates, however, that "I was not a follower of Martin Luther King's approach. [I] understood that it was probably the way to go, but I didn't like treatment of Black people who were protesting to just live unencumbered."[85] Miche B., who also hails from Detroit, disliked how church leaders praised nonviolent protest as a moral approach. "I thought, it just looked bad," she recalls. "Because the nonviolent thing . . . for me, didn't really work. I think it got pestered into giving us equal rights. . . . But for them to kill people for wanting to be peaceful?" She does admit that "at the time, it brought us all together. And that was important. There was no way in the world that we were going to succeed with anything in any kind of way without doing it together."[86] These respondents recall questioning the efficacy and morality of respectability politics and nonviolent protest while, at the same time, applauding protestors' bravery and ability to unify against violent white resistance. These reactions were almost always overlooked by the mainstream press, though, and misunderstood by white sympathizers who were quick to praise the movement's focus on moral righteousness and integration of public spaces as an ultimate goal. This divide would come to shape not only how Black and white youth developed distinct perspectives on the civil rights movement in the 1950s, but how they listened to the "integrated" rock and roll music that was created during this period as well.

CROSSOVER RECORDS AND THE ORIGINS OF ROCK AND ROLL, 1954–1956

As news of desegregation movements spread throughout the country, *Billboard*'s charts revealed that increasing numbers of consumers were refusing to adhere to rigidly racialized marketing categories. Between 1954 and 1955, the publication revealed an 83 percent increase in the number of records that crossed over between the top 20 Pop hits and the top 10 R&B listings, and a stunning 175 percent increase in the number of artists whose songs placed on both charts. This shift did not result from any kind of preordained marketing strategies, and instead came as a surprise that many music industry officials struggled to explain. One of the most explosive records of 1954 was "Sh-Boom," an old jailhouse song recorded by the Chords, a group that Atlantic Records co-owner Jerry Wexler discovered singing together at a Bronx subway station. This record, which was supposed to be the B-side to a cover of Patti Paige's "Cross Over the Bridge," immediately hit the R&B chart upon its release in March and stayed there throughout the spring. Four months later, the song unexpectedly hit the Pop chart, despite the fact that the record label did not do any extra advertising aimed at white markets.[87] "Sh-Boom" alerted the music industry to the possibilities of crossover hits, but Black doo-wop groups like the Charms and Four Tunes also drew white listeners with "Hearts of Stone," "Marie," and "I Understand Just How You Feel." Some of these crossover hits were "racialized" cover records, which means that a version performed by a white artist hit the Pop chart after a Black artist's original made the R&B chart. By 1955, however, five records managed to cross over directly between the Pop and R&B charts without the aid of cover renditions, including the Platters' "The Great Pretender," Bill Haley's "Rock Around the Clock," and Chuck Berry's "Maybellene." Nine Black artists saw their records hit the Pop chart in 1955, whereas only four had achieved this feat the prior year. These records revealed that Black and white audiences really were listening to the same records, despite consistent attempts to separate genres by race.[88]

Doo wop groups like the Chords and the Four Tunes, who released some of the first big crossover hits, provided, in many ways, an ideal introduction to R&B for white teenagers weaned on "respectable" pop. A form of R&B that relies on group vocal performances, doo wop first emerged in the late 1940s, when Black teens gathered on urban street corners to pass the time by creating beautiful harmonies.[89] These songs tended toward the melodic, encouraged sing-alongs, and generally dealt with romantic love and heartache. Even the publicity images of these groups were in keeping with the conservative gender roles and social norms that dictated polite Atomic Age behaviors. Male members of groups like the Chords posed for album covers and promotional materials in elegant suits just like those donned by their white counterparts, while female singers, like Ruth Brown, or the Platters' Zola Taylor, would model lacy cocktail dresses that would not have been out of place at a prom or other formal event. These young Black performers, then, dressed and performed in ways that were familiar to white teenage audiences, while simultaneously promoting the respectability that continued to inform many middle- and working-class Black perspectives.[90] But these depictions could also encourage more positive self-images among Black teenage listeners. According to Robin Kelley, "Seeing oneself and others 'dressed up' was enormously important in terms of constructing a collective identity based on something other than wage work, presenting a public challenge to the dominant stereotypes of the black body, and reinforcing a sense of dignity that was perpetually being assaulted."[91] The fact that Black doo wop groups were depicted as respectable young people in promotional materials inspired Black teenagers, who wanted to be treated with dignity within the culture at large while still maintaining pride in their own cultural backgrounds.

At the same time, many white kids who listened to Black artists identified with the emotions they heard in their songs by focusing on the similarities in their responses to difficult or overwhelming adolescent experiences. The lyrics of the Platters' 1955 hit song, "The Great Pretender," for instance, could resonate with this age group, as lead singer Tony Williams conjured up feelings of confusion and alienation familiar to teenagers of any racial background with lines like "I seem to be what I'm not, you see."[92] The song's success on the Pop chart revealed that this Black group appealed to white listeners, who could identify with these emotions. But this focus on similarities across racial divisions could also obscure the painful experiences that gave doo wop its incredible power: Williams's "wail," for instance, which Decca producer Milt Gabler says set the Platters' vocalizations apart from those of white pop groups, came straight from expressions of anger in blues and R&B traditions. Similarly, the meaning behind Smiley Lewis's energetic 1955 single "I Hear You Knocking" could also be shaped by the race and experiences of each listener. The chorus, which repeats the lines "I hear you knockin' but you can't come in/I hear you knockin', go back where you been" may remind teenagers of trying to protect their privacy by keeping their parents out of their bedrooms or civil rights activists of defying police orders during protests. The second part of the chorus, "I begged ya not to go but you said goodbye/Now you come back tellin' all those lies," belies the fact that the song actually fit into a long history of blues songs depicting relationships gone bad and those who survive them, sometimes by enacting revenge on their paramours. While white kids could undoubtedly sympathize with emotions so overwhelming that they could cause a loss of control, few recognized that this musical style was rooted in the pain caused by racialized violence and oppression.[93] It is hardly surprising, then, that so many whites who grew up during this period have preferred to focus on the easy similarities among people of different races ever since, emphasizing feel-good stories of people of different races riding the same bus in peaceful silence, while avoiding the more uncomfortable discussions of the injustices African Americans continue to face.

While most crossovers between 1954 and 1955 occurred when R&B records by Black musicians hit the Pop chart, a handful of white artists also became popular enough with Black listeners to place on the R&B chart. Boyd Bennett, for instance, was a rockabilly pioneer whose bouncy single "Seventeen" crossed over from the Pop to the R&B chart for two weeks in the late summer of 1955. But it was former country singer Bill Haley who really signaled a shift in teenage listening habits. Haley and his band, the Comets, debuted on the Pop chart in September 1954 with his cover version of Joe Turner's "Shake, Rattle, and Roll." The record became a massive hit among white audiences, yet failed to challenge the original on the R&B chart. But Haley's follow-up, "Dim, Dim the Lights," an original record written for his band, broke through the top 10 on the R&B chart in February 1955 and remained in the top 15 for the next two weeks. His genre-defining hit, "Rock Around the Clock," solidified his appeal among both racial groups. The record, which had originally been unsuccessful upon its debut in 1954, returned to the Pop chart at number 14 on May 21,

1955, after being featured on the soundtrack for the film *Blackboard Jungle,* and remained there for five months, sitting at number 1 for seven weeks in mid-to-late summer. Although "Rock Around the Clock" would not achieve such phenomenal success among Black listeners, it did place at number 8 on the R&B chart on July 2, before disappearing for three weeks, then returning for an additional month in the top 10.[94]

Executives at Black-oriented labels and radio stations were not actively marketing to white consumers. Most emphasized that they were only interested in selling to Black audiences and had little interest in breaking into white markets, especially since racist backlash might lead to their downfall.[95] Jerry Wexler explained how "the notion of selling black music to whites . . . wasn't yet in the air. When I started working at Atlantic, I certainly had no such notions." Atlantic, he maintained, "was pointed at black adults. If white people went for it, fine; if not, we'd survive." His business partner, Ahmet Ertegun concurred, noting that "sales were localized in ghetto markets. There was no white sale and no white radio play. . . . We never cared about a white market. We didn't look for it." Ralph Bass, who worked as an A&R representative at independent, Black-oriented labels like Chess, Savoy, and King, even titled his tentative memoirs "I Didn't Give a Damn if Whites Bought It." "We never made [records] for kids, but for adults, black adults," he said. "I wasn't aiming at a teenage market, just a general market, kids from eighteen and up, we didn't have no twelve, thirteen year old kids listening to our records, and of course, the Blues were only for black adults, we didn't even have whites in mind. I didn't give a damn if whites bought it—if they did groovy!" It quickly became clear, however, that white teenage listeners were driving the market for crossover records regardless of, and sometimes even in opposition to, music industry marketing strategies. By 1954, Wexler and Ertegun told *Cash Box* magazine that deejays who played high school dances arrived "with a satchelful of Eddie Fisher's and Jo Stafford's," yet "found the kids asking for the Clovers and Fats Domino" instead. The result, they explained, was that deejays now had to "find out who and what the kids had in mind and to produce the records. For every two or three Como's and Patti Page's, the record hop jockeys now have to put on a cat [R&B] record so that the kids can swing out."[96]

Since R&B records by Black musicians were not initially marketed to white kids and were rarely played on mainstream radio stations or available for purchase in majority-white areas, most white teenagers were introduced to R&B music on Black-oriented radio stations. Even though these stations were explicitly directed at Black listeners, radio waves transcended color lines, and accounts of young white people in the South happening upon R&B music while turning the dial were incredibly common.[97] Bibb E. frankly admits that "stories of southern white young people of the period clandestinely listening to music their parents did not approve of—'race' music—are too numerous to count. It is just what we did." Journalist John Fleming recalls how difficult it was to listen to the "Negro" records he loved while growing up in Georgia since his mother disapproved of this music. "I can't count the number of hours I spent in my room 'grounded' from play, my friends and the phone because I got caught listening to music or practicing a new dance step," he says. The fairly widespread access to these stations' programming had a profound effect on young white listeners, many of whom describe feelings of elation and rebellion upon first hearing R&B music on the radio. Rick T. remembers the exact moment he started listening to his favorite radio station as a teenager in suburban Richmond, Virginia. "I was turning the dial one morning, and I heard this radio jingle," he recalls. "And for some reason, that jingle hit me like a ton of bricks. So I would listen at the top of the hour and the bottom of the hour every day for that jingle 'cause I liked it so much." The jingle he heard was for WANT-AM, the city's first Black-oriented radio station. While keeping his radio tuned to this station in order to catch the jingle, he began listening to the actual playlists, ultimately realizing that "I like this music!"[98] Bill W. recalls using a transistor radio to listen to the three Washington, D.C.-area Black-oriented stations and purchasing his favorite records by mail order, or by asking his father, who stocked a jukebox at the restaurant he owned, to bring home discarded tracks. "I was looking for this stuff, and these guys played it, and I was there listening to it," he says. "That was the major part of it, was access to these fabulous Black radio stations that were where I lived. And I came across them just be flipping the dial." Not all white Southern kids listened to R&B on Black-oriented stations, of course, but the music's new accessibility definitely had an impact on listening patterns. "In Atlanta, music was one area where white teenagers listened to a lot of Black music even on mainstream radio," Jeff T. explains, "because it was there."[99]

White listeners found new ways to listen to Black-oriented stations outside of the South as well. Bruce C., who says that he always tried to find R&B and gospel stations that broadcast out of Newark, New Jersey, would listen tacitly just like his Southern peers. He explains how an "earpiece was great because when your parents went to sleep you could get under your covers and stick that in your ear." Others used transistor radios to tune into stations from larger cities that were more likely to broadcast Black music. Ron R.'s hometown of Marion, Indiana, for instance, featured only one radio station that "wouldn't play what they called race records," so he listened in to broadcasts from Detroit, Cincinnati, and Indianapolis instead. But many respondents who lived outside the South also recall how radio station playlists were not quite so segregated, especially as crossover records became major sellers among white audiences. "Early in my childhood, I remember that it was not very common to hear [Black artists] on the radio," recalls David S. "And then, as the '50s moved on, it got more common." Bob S. concurs, remembering that "early on, a lot of Black music wasn't played on the radio. You had Black radio stations, and the only other music was Black jukeboxes." As crossover records began appearing on the charts more and more, however, "that's when you had a lot of Black artists that were played on white radio, if you can call it that. . . . And that, to me, really took down a lot of walls between the Black and white." Michael P. also recalls hearing interracial playlists on the radio. "Fortunately in New York we heard race records too, so it wasn't like music was segregated," he says. Using racialized terms to describe this music is fairly common among this group, as is a focus on the lack of boundaries that allowed them to hear new sounds without having them automatically racialized. "I listened to Black deejays and I listened to Black music," says Victor F. "And it just all became a hodgepodge to me. This is America. It all started in the music." Walter S. has a similar reminiscence, noting how "when I grew up listening to New York City radio, there were no color barriers in what was on those playlists. None. [Because] New Yorkers don't think that way, never thought that way. If it's a hit, it's a hit."[100]

These seemingly "color-blind" reactions are also apparent when white respondents insist that they often could not tell the singer's race over the radio. Michael P. says that "As an early child I could not discern the difference between what they called 'race records' and what they called the lily-white records." Victor F. explains that he and his friends were "color blind," which often led them to be surprised when they found out what their favorite artists looked like. "All my favorite artists, I didn't know what color they were, turned out to be Black," he says. "Elvis, he was white. Little Richard and Chuck Berry, they were Black. Do you think I knew what color they were? I had no idea that Chuck Berry was Black. I had no idea that Little Richard was Black until I saw them." He says that this uncertainty extended to deejays as well. "You didn't know they were Black," he recalls. "I mean, their elocution and everything was the same as the white deejays." Ultimately, he says, "I was just surprised that I was too stupid to even give it any thought in the first place. Like, why was I making an assumption that [an artist] was white." Others may have been aware of artists' racial identities but claim they did not care if they liked the music. David P., who listed white artists Dion and the Belmonts and Gene Pitney and Black R&B singer LaVern Baker as his favorites in high school, explained that even if he could usually figure out the race of the artist—"not always though"—it made no difference to him if he liked the song. Bob S. concurs with this reaction, claiming, "if it was a good song, it was a good song. It doesn't make any difference who does it."[101] New technologies combined with an increased focus on Black Americans as consumers inadvertently made R&B music more accessible to white listeners, who were increasingly choosing to "integrate" their popular media consumption by tuning into these stations. Their responses show that they treasure these memories of supporting integration within this realm, even at young ages, during the early stages of the civil rights movement, and that their supposedly color-blind embrace of Black artists reveals an almost natural aversion to judgments predicated on racial distinction. However much these recollections have been affected by intervening decades and changing memories, what becomes clear is how much white rock and roll fans' concepts of race and desegregation were shaped by activists' decisions to focus on integration as an absolute goal, and on the underlying humanity shared by both Black and white citizens.

And yet what drew so many white teens to R&B music in the first place was hardly "color blind"—the "energy" and "rhythm" that led them to surreptitiously listen to these stations were firmly rooted in Black musical traditions. As they grew up in new suburbs that were removed from any historical roots and from dynamic city life, the vibrant beats of Black-oriented music connected them to what they believed was a more lively existence.[102] Throughout the 1950s, white families flocked to these neighborhoods, which were almost immediately associated with feelings of boredom and alienation based on their racially and economically homogenous residency requirements. Most suburban children would grow up among people much like their own families, with no one else to compare themselves to, and no acknowledgment of people from different cultures. Even the aesthetics of suburbia contributed to a growing sense of alienation, as mass-manufactured housing and consumer products created conformist and, many argued, uninspired environments that counterintuitively prompted a desire among many young people to learn about life beyond the boundaries of their neighborhoods.[103] "I think there was also a motive of guilt for being middle class and white, and unserious," Students for a Democratic Society (SDS) president Todd Gitlin recalled in a 1978 interview. "There was some notion that the world we inhabited was unreal and sterile."[104] The "respectable" pop music that wafted through these neighborhoods seemed to mirror this sterility. Rock icon Janis Joplin proclaimed that "it seemed so shallow, all oop-boop. It had *nothing*," while folk-pop singer Janis Ian asserted that she "listened to everything but white pop music, which my friends and I looked on with disdain."[105] Marcia P. describes this music as "too squeaky clean. It was, like, my parents liked [it], so I thought, ugh. You know, I don't want to be like them, so I don't want to like the same music. It was too beige." And although he asserts that "mainstream pop music was about all we heard on TV," Bibb E. recalls that "what I heard did not speak to me, so I heard rather than listened."[106]

Many white kids were therefore drawn to R&B music by Black artists because of what they describe as genuineness. This belief was partially shaped by the fact that most Black-oriented music was released through independent record labels that were supposedly concerned with quality rather than larger, more powerful corporations that were merely concerned with profit. This dichotomy is too deceptively simple to be true, as Black-oriented record labels *had* to earn money in order to stay afloat. But even the musicological foundations of R&B struck white kids as more authentic than the overtly manufactured pop music they were used to hearing. "In Western music—music of the European tradition—[the major scales contain] the only 'legal' pitches; most instruments are designed to play these pitches and not others," explains neuroscientist Daniel Levitin. "Sounds in between are considered mistakes ('out of tune') unless they're used for expressive intonation (intentionally playing something out of tune, briefly, to add emotional tension) or in passing form one legal tone to another."[107] These "in-between" pitches were not often used in melodious pop music, but since R&B utilized some non-Western musical characteristics, these songs were more likely to surprise the listener with unexpected notes that were better able to express the wide spectrum of human emotion than more simplistic pop music scales. At the same time, most R&B and country songs were built on major chords, which are more dynamic and energetic than minor chords. This structure led many white kids to associate the music with positive emotions and a sense of realness that seemed to be lacking in mainstream popular culture.[108]

This depiction led many white listeners to question established racial beliefs based on the humanity they identified in artists' voices. "Blacks always sounded *real*, even if it just was a party song," Bibb E. asserts. "I think it was who was making the music I loved that caused me to think of blacks as people just like me. And it was just simply wrong to treat them differently." This concept of sounding "genuine" and therefore relating to Black performers as human beings reveals what C. W. Mills describes as belief in a supposedly "natural" individual rights and humanity which exists outside of political and temporal space. These struggles drew such a definitive line between support for white supremacy and for racial integration that listening to Black artists encouraged many middle-class white kids, most of whom felt largely detached from issues of racial injustice, to start thinking about the unfair treatment African Americans received. Jeff T. explains that crossover music "must have affected my views on race by broadening my knowledge of black people and their abilities and accomplishments," while Fran S., who grew up in Pittsburgh, "thought that, here is this really vital, vibrant music being created by people who still don't have first-class citizenship, how is that possible? It was as simple as that." Victor F., who grew up in New York, says that listening to this music led him to realize that an artist's skin color was "the only difference" that separated them and "that's the way I was with the musicians: Oh, they're so good, or oh, they're so beautiful, or that guy is so talented. So music is the great leveler." He goes on to explain that "if it wasn't for the music, I wouldn't have discovered [the civil rights movement]. It made me very politically aware. It made me politically interested," while Bill W. explains how his growing teenage obsession with R&B and early rock and roll starts like the Platters, the Dominoes, Ruth Brown, and LaVern Baker "start[ed] leading me to a place of, at least a slight bit of consciousness about African-American life and thoughts." Even though he explains that he "almost always found myself immediately sympathetic towards Black culture and Black politics," he says that "once I realized how great this music was, and how much it motivated and moved me, [stereotypes that] the rest of Blacks are lesser, they can't learn as much, they're this or that, no longer resonated with me. Because I'm going, well, wait, that can't be true. Look at the music that they're writing. Look at their performing. How can they be this great and they can't do anything in this area?" Ultimately, Stan W., who grew up in rural Alabama, claims, "white kids became big fans of a lot of black musicians and made them very successful. Once they were mainstream music, we just considered them people."[109]

For these listeners, hearing voices that they deemed authentic, and therefore relatable, made clear the absurdity of denying equal citizenship to talented musicians who, like the Montgomery protestors, had clearly earned the right to be treated with dignity. Black culture, and some of the people who delivered it to them, could be viewed as acceptable and normal rather than completely cut off from mainstream white society. They could then be understood as people *in the same way that whites were people* rather than as a completely different group outside of their expected reality. And yet the belief that artists were owed this equality based on the supposed genuineness of their musical performances and similarities to white listeners not only belied the concept that everyone, regardless of talent, deserved basic rights, it could reinforce the stereotype that Black Americans had a "natural" predisposition for music and dance—a connection that Progressive reformers had consistently tried to sever by promoting Black intellectual and religious aptitude instead.

By the middle of the decade, as the mainstream media was forced to grapple with the genre's popularity among young white listeners, Black R&B artists and the music they were creating were often described in terms that supported many of the harmful racialized stereotypes that so many Progressive Era reformers had railed against. When the first Congressional Committees on rock and roll were held in 1953, for instance, social commentator Vance Packard, a paid witness for the Songwriters of America, remarked that it "was inspired by what had been called race music modified to stir the animal instinct in modern teenagers."[110] Three years later, the *New York Times* quoted "noted psychiatrist" Dr. Francis J. Braceland's views that the music was "cannibalistic and tribalistic" and that it could be likened to a "communicable disease," while *Downbeat* magazine featured disc jockey Art Ford's opinions that Little Richard's "Long Tall Sally" was "rock and roll at its wildest and lustiest," and Elvis Presley's "I'm Left, You're Right" had a "sort of a savage, animal-like quality in his performance, in a way which is lacking in the usual theatrical refinements of show business, sort of a naturalistic school of singing."[111] In each case, the author or speaker's use of terms like "primitive," "jungle," "tribal," and "cannibal" easily conjured pervasive racist imagery of Black Americans as less civilized and intelligent than white Americans, all of which were meant to strengthen the hold of white supremacy on nationwide popular culture. Even Martin Luther King Jr. used this language to describe rock and roll music, telling a young musician that the genre was "transitory" and "so often plunges men's minds into degrading and moral depths," although in this case he was trying to steer the teenage inquisitor toward making respectable gospel music rather than signifying these less acceptable qualities as inherently Black.[112] These racialized allusions were not always framed in a decidedly negative way, but they nevertheless imparted messages that Black Americans were disreputable, and therefore inferior. In the summer of 1956, *Time* magazine printed an article about the growing popularity of R&B and rock and roll among young listeners. Although it was accompanied by a photograph of the smiling, white Bill Haley, the author describes the music as having an "obsessive beat," and informed concerned parents that "Rock 'n' roll got its name, as it got some of its lyrics, from Negro popular music, which used 'rock' and 'roll' as sexy euphemisms."[113]

Many white listeners, however, found this supposed lack of refinement and celebration of emotionality and sexuality appealing rather than offensive. John Lennon recalled that he was first drawn to 1950s R&B because "it is primitive enough and has no bullshit, really, the best stuff, and it gets through to you its beat. Go to the jungle and they have the rhythm. . . . You get the rhythm going, everybody gets into it," while Mick Jagger recalled how "my father used to call it 'jungle music' and I used to say, 'Yeah, good description.'"[114] John Fleming remembered his mother hating the music he liked, calling it "sinful," with a "'jungle beat' and the filthy words. 'It could brainwash you!' she'd scream. 'Don't you know they make the drums set the pattern of your heartbeat to put you in a trance?'" Victor F. explains how "the music up until [the late 1950s] was really rather simple and primitive" but that he was drawn to it because it "just kind of reached down into me."[115] Even when these terms were used in an approving manner, middle-class white kids ascribed the overt sexuality, lack of civilized decorum, and inability to fulfill the obligations of full citizenship that advocates of respectability politics, from the early twentieth century to the front lines of the Montgomery Bus Boycott, had vigorously challenged, onto African-American culture. "There's no question that we did see that culture as exotic, and we did see it kind of as primitive," Bruce C. asserts. "Not in the way that racists would see it as primitive, but primitive in all of its better qualities, and being honest and true and of the earth, and those sorts of things.... A romanticized attraction to this other culture. Because it represented everything that our culture wasn't."[116]

Black reformers had determined that the blues and jazz, two of R&B's antecedents, would incite immoral behaviors because of their focus on rhythmic movements and the body, but it was these very qualities which appealed to white kids who were uninspired by melodic pop music. "All good music calls for some level of participation by the listener," Bibb E. asserts. "If it did not move my body it needed to engage my mind. A perfect song did both." Patricia J. agrees that "it was just very visceral.... That percussion appeals to me. That beat appeals to me," while Ron R. notes that "the music was a good way for us to bond with each other, because we had to learn to dance." Henry I., who says that listening to music by his favorite artist, Ray Charles, "just reached down into my gut and ripped it out," says that he was drawn to R&B and early rock and roll because it "made me want to tap my feet. Get up and dance. Clap my hands."[117] "Wherefore this predilection?" Jerry Wexler and Ahmet Ertegun pondered with regard to white desire for the R&B records produced by Atlantic. "In our opinion, it stems from the kids' need for dance records."[118] At Decca, Milt Gabler also remarked on the connection between youth and movement. "The kids picked up on it right away and it became their kind of music," he said. "They like to have things that are associated with them—young singers and that kind of song, and they were dancing."[119]

Many white kids also found the genre's more explicit treatment of sexuality refreshing and alluring, especially since the subject was largely verboten in most areas of 1950s popular culture. Bibb E. recalls that "the first record I bought was Fats Domino's 'Blueberry Hill.' ... At 10 years old I had no idea what kind of thrills could be found on Blueberry Hill, but I was beginning to have my suspicions."[120] The lyrics to Domino's 1956 crossover hit, however, are hardly pornographic; in fact, the "thrill" that Bibb identifies is really the only line that even hints at sexual activity. Most of the song, instead, uses more respectable, romanticized pop imagery to impart how "The wind in the willow/Played love's sweet melody/But all of those vows you made/Were never to be."[121] Domino's measured, low-key delivery is also not indicative of the more rollicking boogie-woogie piano numbers he initially became famous for in the earlier part of the decade. And yet merely the hint of what might occur in a private moment between lovers on a purportedly secluded hill was enough to incite the interest of white teenagers who tired of a culture that tried to repress anything remotely sexual. More overt references could be heard in other R&B lyrics, of course. Hank Ballard and the Midnighters scored a hit with "Work with Me, Annie," which, if the title alone was too subtle, featured Ballard emitting a variety of shrieks and exhortations between verses like "Let's get it while the gettin' is good" and "Give me all my meat" while his backup singers hummed along to a driving beat (meant, some reformers asserted, to simulate the rhythms of sexual activity).[122] Fran S. explains his preference for this song, and its consequential follow-up, "Annie Had a Baby": "It was so overtly sexual and so, when your hormones are raging, you're like, I don't want to listen to 'How Much is that Doggie in the Window.'"[123] Bill W. also recalls this appeal, describing his favorite records as "more explicit" than mainstream pop music. "It wasn't just this ideal, oh I'm in love, there was an element that love is also involved, physical love, not just this ideal kind of thing," he says. "So that kind of thing was also appealing because your hormones are raging."[124]

For teenagers experiencing (or anticipating) the trials and tribulations of burgeoning physical intimacy, R&B music provided both a useful guide on how to navigate unfamiliar romantic situations, and the sense that listeners were not alone in their desires and frustrations. This music could act as a sexual stimulant, which was almost impossibly enticing to frustrated teenagers. White kids were able to see these artists as people like themselves, who desired physical affection, and who experienced emotional highs and lows. "This emphasis on feelings made authenticity into an internal rather than an external quality," Grace Elizabeth Hale explains. "Being alike on the inside, as people who shared emotions and the need for self-expression, replaced being alike on the outside, as people who shared a history of oppression and isolation. Emotionalism replaced materialism."[125] Yet, at the same time, white embrace of this music could also reinforce stereotypes of Black Americans as over-sexualized and overly emotional, which reformers had worked so hard to destroy using respectability politics. Beyond these stereotypes, white listeners were often unable to understand how this music was created within an oppressive societal framework that worked to rob them of joy. Rather than viewing R&B as a means of allowing Black musicians to express some of the aspects of their personhood that had to be obscured in white-dominated society, many instead associated performers with an inherent increased emotionality and sexuality. John Sinclair, for instance, wrote that he was drawn to Black music because it "expressed the unity of the black world view. There was less separation between body and mind, less separation of one person from other people, and less separation between people and their environment. It was a culture that recognized the uncertainty of life and was prepared to accept it."[126] These stereotypes not only reinforced some of the racist rhetoric that pervaded American culture since the Reconstruction era; they diminished the pains and injustices that Black people had to endure when living within white supremacist structures. As Bruce C. explains, "I think there was a certain amount of, kind of, an odd racism in our fascination with African-American culture . . . the 'exotic other.'"[127]

R&B BECOMES "RESPECTABLE"

Major record label responses to the initial popularity of R&B records by Black musicians among white audiences reveal how the broader racial anxieties and concerns over respectability politics that shaped civil rights movement politics also informed the creation and distribution of popular culture during this period. By the mid-1950s, the mainstream music industry could no longer ignore the profits they were losing by continuing to market old-fashioned pop music to disinterested teenagers, even if they were reluctant to actually begin signing larger numbers of Black artists. Some labels and radio stations began to compromise by reframing R&B as respectable if distribution could be controlled by white-owned companies, marketed to white audiences as rock and roll, and, in the case of racialized cover records, performed by white artists. The latter option succeeded at first before mostly collapsing by the end of the decade, but the very attempt to make R&B "respectable" by placing the genre under white control robbed Black artists and producers of both credit and compensation. These processes de-emphasized Black representation within popular music, while presenting R&B, and the rock and roll that would emerge from these crossovers, as an integrated, yet whitewashed, art form meant for everyone rather than a specifically African-American cultural creation.

This depiction has been strengthened by the fact that white deejay Alan Freed is consistently credited with "inventing" rock and roll in 1952 by playing R&B records for white audiences on "The Moondog Show," his late-night radio program on WJW in Cleveland.[128] Freed even claimed to have named the genre while spinning the "rock 'em/roll 'em" chorus of "Sixty Minute Man" on air.[129] John A. Jackson and Brett Lashua have both disputed this account, noting that Freed only began playing R&B music after Leo Mintz, who owned an independent record store in one of the city's predominantly Black neighborhoods, offered to sponsor the program in order to sell more records to his African-American clientele. They also noted that Freed's early audiences were mostly Black until he moved to New York in 1954 and began building a white fan base.[130] Even if these accounts challenge Freed's image as the creator of rock 'n' roll, they still show how Black music only became acceptable within the mainstream music industry when it appealed to white listeners.

This story is troubling in that it posits that a white man was the first to identify rock and roll as a separate genre, and to name it despite the fact that he did not write the lyrics that provided this inspiration, or possess any other type of ownership over the music. Freed consistently paid credence to the Black musicians who shaped these sounds, telling the *Pittsburgh Courier* that "the great and accomplished Negro song writers, musicians and singers . . . are responsible for this outstanding contribution to American music," and the *New York Times* that rock and roll "began on the levees and plantations, took in folk songs, and features blues and rhythm."[131] His show introduced thousands of young white listeners to Black sounds that they may otherwise have missed and provided a rising platform for the musicians who were frequent guests. And yet the structure of the show, and the positioning of Freed as the founder and guiding force of rock and roll, presented the music as a mere consumer good, divorced from the pain, joy, history, and traditions that Black Americans expressed through this art form. This presentation could only reinforce the initial responses that drew white listeners to R&B without really understanding the genre's role in African-American communities.

This narrative was also crafted in Memphis, where WHBQ deejay Dewey Phillips started infusing playlists of pop and country tunes with R&B and gospel on his *Red, Hot and Blue* show as early as 1951. Even though the program was meant to appeal to Black listeners at night, after the Black-oriented WDIA signed off, station employees quickly realized that white listeners were also tuning in. Louis Cantor, who worked at WHBQ as a teenager, notes that "at least some whites who were strongly attracted to the black music were still constrained enough by their traditional prejudices to feel uncomfortable listening to an all-black station." Phillips was able to hook these listeners, he says, because he was "a white announcer who would appeal to blacks, either by attempting to mimic what they considered a black dialect or by playing almost exclusively the new so-called race music." *Red, Hot and Blue* was never intended to appeal to white teenagers, but as they began to tune in in greater numbers, Cantor explains, Phillips's program helped legitimize Black music among white youth culture. The station therefore reinforced the notion that R&B could be a trendy and acceptable cultural alternative to mainstream pop, and that music could be "integrated" over the airwaves when controlled by white interests.[132]

These deejays defended their white teenage listeners' choice to embrace Black music to different degrees. Freed, who would go on to state explicitly that "the race question . . . is the real reason for all the hue and cry about rock and roll," explained that commotion over how the racially integrated teenage audience behaved at the first "Moondog Ball" in 1952 resulted from racist perceptions rather than any real threat of violence. "Those Cleveland affairs appealed most to colored people," he noted. "In fact, after I ran them, I received batches of poison-pen letters calling me a 'n****r-lover.'"[133] Phillips, who lived in a Southern city, and therefore faced greater repercussions than Freed would in Cleveland, did not explicitly discuss integration campaigns, yet, according to his biographer, he "was perfectly comfortable going into black clubs, churches, and juke joints," and often entertained Black people at his home.[134] These deejays had direct lines into the bedrooms and brainwaves of thousands of white teenagers, granting them very real potential to transmit positive portrayals of integration. The very fact that white listeners were introduced to Black voices allowed them, in some cases, to view Black artists as human beings with similar wants, needs, and perspectives. But the ways they listened to and appreciated this music were also highly reliant on white approval of Black respectability, revealing that this form of "desegregation" in the name of whitened respectability politics was anything but equitable.

If white youth, a large and increasingly integral consumer demographic, were gravitating toward more emotionally direct R&B records rather than the pop songs that major labels were mainly producing, then business would inevitably suffer, but few were willing to sign Black artists and directly distribute R&B records since racist backlash from whites who feared any form of integration could threaten profits. Cover songs seemed to present a solution to this conundrum. Covers are almost always racialized in popular memory, but prior to 1954 they were used by labels in all three marketing genres to profit more than once from the same hit record. Some white pop artists covered country and R&B songs, but untested ingénues covering the work of more experienced pop artists provided the most common type of cover song during this period, since established hits were more likely to ensure returns on investments among the same audiences. Country songs like "Cold, Cold Heart" and "Crying in the Chapel" and pop hits like "I'm a Fool to Want You" and "Honest and Truly" could, however, also be recorded by both Black and white artists in a variety of marketing categories to sell proven hits to different listener demographics. *Billboard* charts from the early to mid-1950s are therefore incredibly repetitive, as songs often made the top 20 Pop chart multiple times in the same week, and versions of the same songs performed by different acts appeared on different charts. These cover songs were racialized to the extent that performers were only expected to sell to audiences who came from their own racial backgrounds, but they were not conscious attempts to profit from white demand for Black music.

By 1954, however, increasing demand encouraged major-label executives to engage in exploitative practices that would deny many Black musicians ownership of their own songs and musical identities in order to consciously sell Black music to white audiences. Producers would purchase (or steal) R&B songs that had already become hits, alter the tempos and lyrics so that they would be considered more "suitable" for white audiences, and record these new arrangements as performed by white pop stars. "What we used to do, if a record would be started by some girl on a little label and we thought it had something, we would take it and make it," Milt Gabler later explained, clearly referring to Black-oriented companies when he mentions "little labels." "We made a more musical version and copied the pattern of the arrangement, but did a brand new arrangement, and [the cover artist] got the glory."[135] One of Decca's—and the major label music industry's—biggest cover hits was Bill Haley and the Comets' remake of Joe Turner's 1954 R&B hit, "Shake, Rattle and Roll." Gabler knew that white kids would love Haley's bouncy and energetic performance, but he also realized that the lyrics would have to be "clean[ed] up," not because white kids would be scandalized by sexual content, but because "I didn't want any censor with the radio station to bar the record from being played on the air. With NBC a lot of race records wouldn't get played because of the lyrics."[136] And so suggestive-to-the-point-of-obvious wording like "Get out of that bed" and "Well you wear low dresses,/The sun comes shinin' through" were changed to "Get out in that kitchen" and "You wear those dresses/Your hair done up so nice" in the cover version, which, according to Steve Chapple and Reebee Garofalo, effectively "domesticated [the song's] sexual content, moving the action from bedroom to kitchen."[137] Mildly adventurous middle-class white listeners were therefore able to get their helping of R&B through singles designed especially for the Pop chart, sung in what Charlie Gillett calls "the simple 'sing-along' mode, emphasizing the melody with little concern for the more complicated feelings contained in the original versions by the black groups."[138] Popular music was "integrating" to the extent that R&B characteristics from African-American musical traditions were becoming somewhat acceptable within mainstream culture. But actual Black people, and the more unbridled emotion and sexuality evident in many R&B songs, continued to be viewed as "disreputable," and therefore unworthy of representation by major music labels.

This tactic, which temporarily succeeded among pop music consumers in the mid-1950s, denied a lot of what Gabler calls "glory" to Black performers, songwriters, and producers, often cutting them out of the musical history they were helping to create while simultaneously denying them the financial rewards that would instead enrich major-label coffers. Black artists and writers were routinely paid next to nothing for songs that would go on to earn massive profits for major labels once they were covered by white pop stars. Enterprising record executives also had white artists re-record hits by Black musicians without any permission or payment. When challenged, high-priced company lawyers often drafted spurious arguments that the song in question was actually a traditional blues ballad and belonged to the public domain. Even when these claims were patently false, most Black artists or independent labels did not have the resources to fight back.[139] This practice promoted diversity through the mixture of musical genres, yet also encouraged white power structures to prosper from exploitation of non-white artists and businesses.

This tactic seemed to work at first—most R&B crossover records were bested by white cover versions on the Pop chart, and many records that had proven successful among Black listeners failed to make inroads with white audiences once covers were released. In 1954, for instance, two white cover versions sold so much better than their Black originals that they would be heralded as standards. The Chords' mega-hit "Sh-Boom" jolted many record executives, who realized that white teenagers were actively seeking out R&B music when it hit the Pop chart in March, even as it continued to dominate the R&B chart for several weeks. This pop-inflected single inspired executives at Mercury Records to recruit white pop group The Crew Cuts for coverage duties. The Crew Cuts' version hit the Pop charts on July 10 and immediately beat out the Chords' original record, even though both remained on the Pop chart for several weeks.[140] During the same time period, Joe Turner's "Shake, Rattle and Roll" hit the R&B charts in May 1954, but failed to cross over to the Pop chart on its own. The cover version by Bill Haley and the Comets, however, exploded onto the Pop chart four months later, and would ultimately become early rock and roll canon. Among many other examples between 1954 and 1955, Ruth Brown's R&B hit "What a Dream" was written by Okeh songwriter Chuck Willis and released on the Columbia subsidiary's label before Mercury executives picked it up for pop star Patti Paige, while the Crew Cuts also scored a hit with "Oop Shoop," which was originally recorded by Black girl group Shirley Gunter and the Queens.[141] But the man who would become most associated with racialized covers was undoubtedly Pat Boone. Randy Wood, founder of Dot Records in Gatlinburg, Tennessee, found a way to make the R&B music his white customers enjoyed more "respectable" by signing Boone, a white pop singer and country great Red Foley's son-in-law, to cover hits by Black artists. His first release, a cover of the Charms' "Two Hearts," hit number 16 on the Pop chart. But his follow-up record, a version of Fats Domino's "Ain't That a Shame," replete "with slightly 'corrected' lyrics and a pop styling," overtook Domino's place on the Pop chart fairly quickly, spending several weeks at number 2, while the original topped out at number 16.[142] Response from white teenagers was immediately and overwhelmingly favorable, turning Boone into one of the most popular "rock and roll" stars of the mid- to late 1950s, as well as the unofficial face of white cover stars.

And yet even as early as 1954, some cover records actually bolstered the popularity of Black originals among white audiences. The Charms' "Hearts of Stone" made the Pop chart for eight weeks after the Fontane Sisters released a cover version, while Domino's "Ain't That a Shame" only became a Pop hit after Boone's release, despite having been released months earlier. In some ways, this progression made perfect sense: Arnold Shaw, whose job at Edward B. Marks Music Corporation entailed purchasing popular R&B songs to be covered by white pop stars, explained that "In this transition period, young white listeners were reacting to black records," but, having grown up on the simpler melodies of pop and big-band music, "only a small percentage were ready for the raw and exuberant earthiness of rhythm and blues."[143] Again, these adjectives harmfully implied that Black Americans were less respectable or civilized than whites, but those were also the exact traits that young white listeners craved. By 1955, "Tweedle Dee" by LaVern Baker and Etta James's "Wallflower (Work With Me, Henry)" both hit the Pop chart after cover versions by Georgia Gibbs appeared, and Smiley Lewis's iconic "I Hear You Knocking" only crossed over when white pop star Gale Storm released a less dynamic cover for Dot Records. The Crew Cuts' rendition of "Earth Angel" eventually bypassed the Penguins' original record, but only after the Penguins had already enjoyed seven weeks atop the chart. And after eight weeks of success at the top of both the Pop and R&B charts, the Platters' "Only You" was ostensibly challenged by the Hilltoppers' cover, which never managed to break into the top 10.[144]

The turn-around time between a record placing on the R&B chart and its white cover version making the Pop chart also began to decrease between 1954 and 1955. Six weeks elapsed between Fats Domino's debut of "Ain't That a Shame" on the R&B chart and Pat Boone's version appearing on the Pop chart, but it only took a month for Boone's cover of the Charms' "Two Hearts" to do the same thing, while a mere week passed between Nappy Brown's "Don't Be Angry" showing up on the R&B chart and the Crew Cuts' rendition making the Pop chart. Even more shocking was the introduction of "Ko Ko Mo (I Love You So)" on both charts during the same week, February 5, 1955, with an additional pop version debuting the week afterward. Although the song was written by Gene and Eunice, the so-called "Sweethearts of Rhythm and Blues," and released by the independent Aladdin Records, RCA Victor and Mercury released cover versions by Perry Como and the Crew Cuts so quickly that they were able to place on the chart at the same time. This truncated time period shows that major-label A&R representatives were paying closer attention to the songs that did well on the R&B chart, and even taking note of rumors about which songs would do well among Black customers, in order to guide their own production and marketing decisions. Major-label executives shied away from selling Black music directly to young white listeners, but they clearly believed that white kids would invariably gravitate to the songs that succeeded on the R&B chart.[145]

In these cases, white kids seemed willing to purchase both original and cover versions, although many were also inspired to seek out R&B records by Black artists after being introduced to mainstream renditions by white singers. Others had already heard the original versions by tuning into Black-oriented radio stations. "Most of the Black artists just appealed to me. Their music appealed to me," Henry I. asserts. "It was sweet, their voices were great. You could dance to it. Just all those factors that—it was more fun." He explains how cover versions of original recordings "would get more play on the radio when I was a kid than the Black artist would, and it's so inferior. You know, it was just so inferior. There's no other way to say it. The originals were so much better." Although cover songs remained popular at his high school into the 1960s, Rick T. asserts that he was never interested in listening to them. "[Other kids would] ask me what I think and I'd say nah, I didn't listen to any of that," he says. "I'd say, 'Well I listen to WANT,' which is the Black station. And oh, that was just like, 'You're a weirdo.'" Fran S. recalls how he and his friends didn't "want to listen to the cover" of Hank Ballard and the Midnighters' "Work With Me Annie" on Pittsburgh's Black station. "The white cover song for that was 'Dance With Me Henry.' So to me, it was just much more vital, much more dangerous, in a sense, because of its overt sexuality." Bob S. states that he "didn't think that was fair" for white artists to release hits originally performed by Black musicians, and that his friends seemed to feel the same way. "The kids all went for the Black versions. They knew what the real thing was," he says. "The kids, including myself, we knew what the real thing was, and we wanted the real thing." Ron R. says that he always preferred the original recordings by Black artists "not because of color necessarily, but because they were the ones doing the innovating," and that whenever he heard a cover record, "I knew that the white's version wasn't as good as the original Black version." Bibb E. seconds that point, noting how "When I heard two versions of the same song—which was very common back then—I preferred the Black artist. . . . Even my pre-teen self could tell the difference between Pat Boone and Ivory Joe Hunter, LaVern Baker and Georgia Gibbs."[146] In each case, the traits that drew these listeners to original recordings were the same ones that major-label record producers tried to strip away: sexuality, genuineness, and feelings of being an outsider. These supposedly disreputable signifiers of Black inferiority continued to appeal to white kids who were tired of having to suppress many of these feelings within themselves.

The very reason for the cover phenomenon was to increase profits for mainstream record labels and radio stations by making R&B seem more respectable to white audiences. Producers made conscious decisions to embrace elements of African-American culture, including energetic dance beats, dynamic rhythms, and lyrical subject matter of interest to teenagers, while surgically removing Black people themselves, along with any supposedly "undesirable" racialized qualities. These qualities were the very same ones that Black reformers argued were perpetuating racist stereotypes, but white music industry officials were attempting to erase Black culture and people entirely to ensure white control and profit rather than reforming their behaviors in the name of uplift. "The offensive part is that black music that has been denied can be accepted because guys in white skin are doing it," Jerry Butler, lead singer of the Impressions, told *Rolling Stone* in a 1969 interview. Like many other musicians, Butler was not trying to discourage white interest in African-American musical forms—in fact, he adhered to the widely held belief that white admiration of Black music could reflect diminishing racial prejudices more broadly. "To be copied—imitation is the first sign of greatness," he added. "So if anybody imitates something that I do, I feel a little flattered. For me, for a guy to say, 'Wow, that's great music I want to learn how to play it,' that's a compliment." But, he continued, for listeners to "accept it from [white cover artists] and not accept it from me is a putdown."[147] When Phil Spector was asked if he encountered any Black resentment while he was working at Atlantic Records, which was both owned and operated by whites, he immediately replied, "Oh yeah, man." Black musicians, he said, would proclaim, "We bought your home, goddamn, and you don't forget it, boy. You livin' in the house we paid for, you drivin' a Cadillac we got, man. It's ours. You stole it from us."[148] Ray Charles asserted that covers and many early crossover records "were white hits, but based on black sounds and black rhythms going round years before," although he was also quick to note "It wasn't that I was angry at those white cats for taking from blacks. I've always said, just 'cause Alexander Bell invented the phone don't mean Ray Charles can't use it. I gave the ofay boys credit for having good ears."[149] Respect for the person who *makes* the art rather than just for the art itself would be key. But only the latter was present in racialized cover records, which limited opportunities for actual antiracist work. This process reflects the tentative support many young whites espoused for movement struggles to desegregate public spaces, so long as polite society rooted in capitalist-democratic ideals would more or less remain the same. The idea of integration could be applauded so long as activists behaved appropriately, and did not try to fundamentally alter the racial balance, like the Montgomery residents who demanded jobs for Black bus drivers or stable access to credit.

Even if Black kids were not identified as major consumer groups in the same way as white teenagers and Black adults, they were also responsible for increasing sales of R&B and pop records, even if they mostly avoided covers. Many respondents recall responding favorably to the same attributes that drew white listeners to the music, particularly the energetic dance beats and the emotion in singers' voices. "We weren't calling it rhythm and blues, we were calling it popular music," says Edgar S. "To me, it was more danceable than anything else." Even though he also enjoyed "popular love songs," recalling how "everybody wanted to make out with Ruth Brown," he stresses the particular importance of movement when a song played. "Music to me was more like a utility," he says. "It provided a relief. A pleasure. A relief valve. You know, from stresses." Cheryl J. says that she was also drawn to a song because of "the groove" and "the beat" before focusing on the lyrics and would then "listen to that song for a few days, loving it."[150] These "disreputable" qualities seemed rebellious and appealing to Black kids as well as white, especially those who grew up in middle- or aspiring-class homes shaped by respectability politics; a number of respondents, for instance, recall hearing mostly religious music growing up, even if their parents did not specifically object to R&B. The cross-racial appeal of respectability politics led to both Black and white kids enjoying the R&B music that flouted supposedly non-respectable characteristics. But they also reveal how music was still used as a means of dealing with the pressures of living in a racist society in an expressive, often communal way, just as earlier blues musicians had originally intended. Black kids never assumed that these concepts reflected the entirety of the African-American experience—how could they, when so many noted the differences between the worlds conjured by their favorite singers and the realities of their own lives? Black listeners also did not have to be convinced of these artists' humanity in order to relate to them like so many white respondents reported. They were, however, heartened by the increased representation of Black artists in particular, and of R&B music in general. Brian Ward has argued that this representation within mainstream music culture "reflected a mood of rising optimism about the possibility of Black integration into a genuinely equalitarian, pluralistic America," which echoes responses from white fans who grew up during this period.[151] Increasing white demand for R&B meant more opportunities and greater exposure for Black musicians, writers, and producers, even if they remained limited by the focus on white cover artists. It also meant that Black culture was promoted as fun and exciting rather than inferior. Just like with desegregation movements, music that allowed Blacks and whites to share the same sonic spaces was not an ultimate goal, but it could allow for greater appreciation of Black Americans as people, which could hopefully create the social and economic opportunities necessary to challenge certain racial inequities.

Even though white cover records never appeared in any great number on the R&B chart—and really only appeared at all after 1956 with the advent of white rockabilly artists like Elvis Presley and Carl Perkins—some respondents recall how they could inspire more awareness of original versions by Black artists. Najee M. recalls listening to Alan Freed's radio program so that he could hear his favorite Black doo-wop groups, including Frankie Lymon and the Teen Agers, the Flamingos, and Little Anthony and the Imperials. But he also remembers listening to Bill Haley's "Shake, Rattle and Roll," which he supported since the original record by Big Joe Turner also got more airtime, and "more Black music was being played" overall. Tony T. echoes these memories, noting that many of the radio stations he listened to played a variety of singles across genres. He "tended to like more of the Black tunes if they were played," which was not common, he says, until the arrival of Elvis Presley. "There was more Black music as part of that," he says. "Elvis was kind of like Black music. . . . But it was looked upon as a favorable thing because Elvis, Jerry Lee Lewis, they all went to the top of the R&B charts with their big hits." Many people listened to music by these white musicians, he says, because they reminded listeners of R&B performers, and also because their popularity inspired greater demand for music by Black artists. But listeners also realized that Black musicians were exploited with this supposed "exchange." "What bothered me was not that they were playing the music, because music is out there for everybody to play, for everybody to like. Music is the universal language," Edgar S. asserts. What did upset him, however, was that "we were being ripped off, you know what I mean? And they were making money from it. It was a commercial advantage to whites." He explains how "if there was an equal distribution of the benefits or the profits, it wouldn't matter to me at all. But who was profiting by it? Not the people from whom it originated." In both music and politics, Black kids could acknowledge the positive elements of desegregation, particularly the importance of representation, and the respect due to Black artists, within mainstream culture. And yet they declined to romanticize either music or movement politics, especially when "integration" meant that white musicians were unfairly profiting from the labors of Black artists.[152]

While most crossovers during this period consisted of R&B records by Black artists placing on the Pop chart, a few white pop and country artists did manage to cross over to the R&B chart. Those who were able to make this leap usually combined elements of two or more of these genres in both their music and performances. By the mid- to- late 1950s, this combination of genres would be identified as rock and roll, partly because it actually did combine characteristics to create something new, but also to re-classify any music with African-American roots as safe for young white consumption. Bill Haley was one of the first performers to be described as a rock and roll artist. Unlike the white pop singers handpicked by major-label A&R reps to cover R&B songs for young white audiences, Haley grew up in Pennsylvania singing country music—at one point he was even known as "Silver Yodeling Bill Haley." Yet he also loved Black gospel and R&B, especially records by "jump blues" king Louis Jordan. When he began touring as a professional musician, he included some of these songs in his set lists, performing with what Philip Ennis calls "black theatricality," and ensuring that the Comets were trained to play in the same style as Jordan's band, "thrashing their instruments and leaping about." Although this mixing of genre characteristics was uncommon when the band began touring in the early 1950s, record executives began to take notice, especially after Philadelphia "hillbilly" radio stations began playing his recordings, which were clearly influenced by R&B records. "Bill Haley is the one that—well, it wasn't black, and it wasn't country and western, and it was really a thing that he'd come up with on his own," recalls Milt Gabler, who oversaw Haley's recordings after he was signed to Decca in 1954.[153] Here, this new genre is explicitly identified as a mixture of major music marketing genres, created by an individual artist who is responsible for combining supposedly separate sounds.

Identifying Haley as the first "rock and roll" artist may have made it easier for Decca to sell records to white audiences, but it denies the genre's African-American heritage and the artists, writers, and producers who created this music. Two years after he exploded onto the national pop music scene, Haley's manager, James Ferguson, told *Downbeat* magazine that even though "the term rock 'n' roll originated with New York disc jockey Alan Freed," his client had "the distinction of having originated the actual music."[154] This assertion is patently false, of course, and reinforces the narrative that white men were responsible for creating rock and roll by "borrowing" Black sounds. Haley was, however, the first artist whose music was widely labeled "rock and roll." Many writers, including *Billboard* editors, did not quite know what to make of a white musician who combined pop, R&B, country, and gospel characteristics so neatly that the dividing lines between these genres seemed to dissolve, but it would be easier to market this music as acceptable to the mainstream when performed by a white artist like Haley. Listeners had no doubt that Haley was white, as he kept "the country twang" in his voice, but, as Arnold Shaw explained, "like blues singers, he shouted rather than vocalized." This method, which conveyed the pains and sorrows of laboring within racist structures as well as the joys present in close-knit Black communities sounded energizing to white teenagers who tired of what Shaw described as "the polish and varnish, the velvet and satin of big orchestras and syrupy crooning." Haley's more aggressive vocalization echoed that of R&B artists and implied that sharing raw, personal emotions was a legitimate form of expression, even among white musicians. According to Shaw, however, "his voice lacked the bluesman's burden of time." The structural white supremacy that led blues singers to create music as a sort of coping mechanism and communal adhesive, allowing them to express emotions they could not reveal elsewhere for fear of economic and physical reprisal, continued to go unheard by white listeners. They could appreciate the style, and even grasp some of the substance of this vocal method, without ever having to confront the racialized pain that shaped its creation. Again, white listeners focused on the emotional similarities common among people of all races rather than the oppression and injustice that rendered the format distinctly pertinent to Black Americans.[155] Integration within popular culture was therefore marked more by an insistence that Black Americans enjoy greater access to white-dominated spaces rather than demands for their destruction and replacement—much in the same way that Montgomery buses made room for Black passengers while so many city residents lost jobs or access to credit under continued white supremacist institutions.

Even if African-American culture was exploited in the service of white profit, the genre's reliance on Black influences did not go unacknowledged. Media outlets ensured that listeners knew exactly where the roots of Haley's music could be found: a June 1956 article in *Time* magazine, for instance, declared that "Rock 'n' roll is based on Negro blues, but in a self-conscious style which underlines the primitive qualities of the blues with malice aforethought." The author, while skeptical of Haley's popularity, saves most of his own "malice" for the African-American culture that informs his music. But the seeming contradiction between the author's harsh, racist rhetoric and the accompanying picture of a beaming white Haley signifies the ambivalent views on desegregation movements that were becoming common among many young white listeners. White support for both desegregation and musical crossovers was too often based on the notion that Black people could be granted equal rights so long as they focused on the "acceptable" aspects of their culture, and on advocating a common humanity among all races, without any expectation that white lives would be disrupted or made uncomfortable in any way. This meant accepting some Black artists and sounds into a white supremacist framework—exemplified by both the country's existing capitalist-democratic institutions and the consumer-driven major record labels and media outlets that supported them—rather than shattering the structure altogether.[156]

But shifts did occur within this structure. In the waning days of 1955, a song written and performed by a church deacon's son from Macon, Georgia, began steadily climbing the ranks of the *Billboard* R&B chart. Within a month, "Tutti Frutti," an explosive tune about the joys of queer sex, punctuated with singer Little Richard's inscrutable, irresistible call, "A wop-bop-a-loo-mop, a lop-bam-boom!" had reached number 2 on the chart. A few weeks later, a more sedate version by Pat Boone, who readily admitted that he had no idea what the song's lyrics were about, was released. The record debuted at number 15 on the Pop chart, but disappeared the following week. Meanwhile, Little Richard's original version crossed over to the Pop chart; although it never rose above number 18, it remained there for two weeks, replacing Boone's version. Song titles alone do not reveal the whole story here, however: the flip side of Boone's "Tutti Frutti" record, a cover of The Flamingos' "I'll Be Home," made the Pop chart every week between February 16 and May 12. Since both songs were included on the Boone single, it is difficult to ascertain which was more popular among white teens. Three months later, however, Richard's follow-up record, "Long Tall Sally," crossed over to the Pop chart after hitting number 1 on the R&B chart and remained there for a month. Unsurprisingly, Boone's label, Dot Records ensured that he released a cover, yet this time neither the cover version, nor its B-side, "Just So Long As I'm With You," made the Pop top 20 chart. In either case, it is difficult to state that one recording completely triumphed over another; as Albin Zak notes, for many white teenagers, "two recordings represented not an either/or choice but a spectrum of possibility" which could lead them to purchase and enjoy both versions. The fact that white listeners could choose an original record by a Black artist one week did not necessarily mean that they stopped listening to white covers. But the choices they could make as consumers within an integrating musical landscape did not necessarily adhere to racialized patterns, which helps explain how Boone could continue to dominate the charts for the remainder of the decade, while Little Richard's popularity on both charts presaged how increasingly integrated popular music would become by the late 1950s.[157]

Major labels continued to release racialized cover records well into the early 1960s, but original records became so popular that executives were forced to view releases by Black artists as viable consumer products within white markets. By the late 1950s, Milt Gabler admitted that "Georgia Gibbs doesn't copy anything anymore, the McGuire Sisters don't—because they'd get killed. The original record goes all the way."[158] Major labels could therefore remain profitable as social responses to cross-racial listening habits shifted, which clearly annoyed Alan Freed, who, despite attempts to be recognized as the founder of this genre, consistently promoted original recordings by Black musicians. He told *Pageant* magazine that "youngsters showed great maturity and understanding during the great copy-record scandal. When leading record companies tried to fool you kids into buying arrangements of Rock 'n' Roll tunes that had been copied note for note from originals done by authentic rhythm and blues artists, you fans listened to me and bought only the first released arrangement." Part of his frustration here clearly stems from the fact that major-label cover records had the potential power to diminish his self-appointed role as a sort of Pied Piper to white teenagers, leading them to discover dynamic Black music. And yet, while he credited himself with warning white kids about the follies of purchasing cover records, he was also quick to point out that these same listeners followed their own instincts when deciding which music they wanted to purchase. "The hit tunes are picked exclusively by the boys and girls themselves," he continued, "youngsters whose loyalty at the record counter saved the careers of dozens of struggling artists in the early days when big name stars tried to steal the arrangements of then unknown rhythm and blues singers." Although "this learning took time and for almost a year the artists suffered," Freed listed Fats Domino and Little Richard as examples of artists "who fell victim to the copy cats at first," but who ultimately enjoyed widespread support among white fans. He even targeted Pat Boone and Dot Records indirectly, slyly noting that "other companies copied [Domino's] first hit record *Ain't That a Shame*, and outsold him on the market. But it took just one synthetic and the kids were wise. Today he has one hit on top of another. No one has cared to ape his catchy *I'm Walkin'*."[159]

White teenage listeners were beginning to assert themselves as consumers with particular tastes, and, despite the lingering popularity of cover artists, original recordings by Black artists started to gain more traction on the Pop chart by 1955. But the way that Freed positioned both himself and white teenagers as saviors of Black musicians is troubling, even though he thought it augured a natural and peaceful connection among young people of different races. His explanation here reflects a belief that the careers of Black artists would only rise and fall at the whims of white listeners. The many Black musicians who had enormous popularity with majority-Black audiences for decades were invisible to whites in the music industry like Freed, who appeared to view white appeal as the only means of true financial and artistic success. His explanation of how crossover and cover records both challenged and upheld racial norms during this period provided a foundation for the new perspectives on race that were gaining traction among white youth. All people could be considered equal, so long as they engaged in the same socially acceptable praxes, just like the polite passengers observed on Montgomery buses by mainstream journalists, or Martin Luther King's and Rosa Parks's gender-appropriate manners and dress. But any attempts to address, or even acknowledge, the historical roots of racial inequities and injustices, and how they are reproduced on multiple political and social levels, were actively ignored. By the mid-1950s, increasing numbers of white teenagers would support desegregation movements because they felt it was the right thing to do, and because they did not understand what was wrong with allowing "respectable" Black artists and professionals into desegregated public places. And yet many of their Black peers would soon be dismayed to realize that this fairly nonchalant attitude would not extend to efforts meant to seriously confront deeper issues of economic inequality and racialized violence.

If *Billboard* dubbed 1955 "The Year R&B Took Over the Pop Field," then the following year prompted the publication to declare that "Desegregation of Chart Categories Earmarks '56.'" White demand for R&B records had become so undeniable that it was cited as the reason for a 43 percent increase in record sales between 1955 and 1956 when the prior industry norm was only a 4 percent annual growth. Of the 25 records that crossed over from the R&B top 10 to the Pop top 20 in 1956, only two were white covers of Black originals, and in one case, the original record also crossed over, appearing on the Pop chart before the cover version appeared.[160] Fourteen Black artists, including the Platters, Fats Domino, and the Teenagers, had records that made the Pop chart, while, in an abrupt shift from the previous year, six white artists appeared on the R&B chart. After Bill Haley was the sole white artist able to broadly appeal to Black listeners in 1955, the explosive popularity of Elvis Presley and other white artists like Carl Perkins and Gene Vincent, whose careers were ignited by first appearing on the Country and Western chart, resulted in five records that appeared on all three charts at the same time. Indeed, white respondents who are old enough to remember Presley's debut describe hearing or seeing him for the first time as a pivotal moment in their own personal musical histories. "I definitely remember Elvis Presley," Clara A. recalls "I remember that as being the absolute highlight of my life. Anytime I could see him, *Ed Sullivan Show*, or anything. But again, my parents were probably thinking, like a lot of people were, that you shouldn't move like that. How he danced, or whatever." Bill W. is more direct about the impact Presley's music had on his worldview, explaining how hearing "Hound Dog" for the first time "reverberates incredibly inside of me. And I never look back to the 'Doggie in the Window' again." Listening to Elvis, he says, only deepened his interest in Black music, while simultaneously leading him further away from the pop music that still comprised most mainstream radio station playlists.[161]

Although Presley in particular has been accused of exploiting African-American culture to sell to white audiences, his lifelong interest in gospel and blues music earned him a devoted following among many Black teenagers in the 1950s. Presley's first *Billboard* appearance, "Baby, Let's Play House," remained on the Country and Western chart, but "Heartbreak Hotel," which made the Country chart on March 3, 1956, crossed over to Pop after a week, and to R&B roughly a month later. The newly minted teen idol from Memphis appealed to young listeners across racial, class, and geographic boundaries, as his recordings of "Love Me Tender," "Don't Be Cruel," and "Hound Dog," a cover of Willie Mae Thornton's R&B hit, graced the top of the Pop, R&B, and Country and Western charts throughout the year. By October, "Don't Be

Cruel" became the first record to simultaneously achieve the number 1 spot on all three charts, and "Love Me Tender" appeared on each chart the first week it was available in stores.[162] Aside from Presley's inimitable crossover success, Carl Perkins achieved a chart-topping trifecta with the country- and blues-tinged record "Blue Suede Shoes," while Marty Robbins's country hit "Singing the Blues" was covered by English pop singer Guy Mitchell, whose version made both the Pop and R&B charts.[163]

The increasing number of records by white artists that originated on the Country chart, yet crossed over to the R&B chart, also surprised the music industry. Black kids were clearly more eager to purchase records stemming from this genre than from mainstream pop performers. Tony T., for instance, recalls that, of the "white songs," he "tended to like . . . the more country-oriented songs," because of the instrumental and emotional similarities the genre held in common with R&B. Cheryl J. says that she enjoyed country music because "they always had something to say. They whined about different things. I used to call their music whining." She was also impressed by the more serious topics that were addressed in many song lyrics. "I was like, damn, how could they sing about that?" she explains. "But they did, and it worked. And so that's why I liked country music. I felt like we could sing about relevant shit."[164] Ray Charles spoke of these parallels as well, explaining that country "was the closest music, really, to the blues—they'd make them steel guitars cry and whine, and it really attracted me."[165] In terms of both emotional tone and lyrical content, R&B and country and western music had much in common. Indeed, Black people who lived in the South had long been fans of white country artists, to the extent that, as Louis Cantor explains, "attempting to draw a clear distinction between 'black' and 'backwoods' can often lead to trouble. The entities were never entirely isolated from one another, and an effort to separate them can be as misleading as it is frustrating." Ed B. talks about how he grew up listening to the *Grand Ole Opry* radio shows, where he "learned to like Red Foley," and how he and his friends would try to sneak into white clubs to see Jerry Lee Lewis perform before he became a star. B. B. King, who grew up in the same Mississippi Delta area, also explained how he grew to enjoy country music when he was young. "I was familiar with Roy Acuff and Minnie Pearl and people like that—Merle Travis, Bill Monroe," he said in a 2001 interview. "They was cowboys. I liked them. Why shouldn't. . . . I have thought of them if they wasn't black, why would I like them? But I didn't think that way."[166]

This heritage may help to explain why Elvis Presley became popular among Black audiences almost immediately after his album's debut in 1955. Presley grew up in Memphis listening to country, gospel, and the blues. The city's segregated boundaries were somewhat more porous than in other places, especially for whites, and so he was able to listen to Black musicians in both clubs and churches, and even began shopping at clothing stores with majority-Black clienteles. He was therefore heavily influenced by African-American cultural norms in both sound and appearance, which endeared him to Sun Records founder, Sam Phillips, who had been looking for "white country boys who could sing the blues" that he could sell to white listeners.[167] As Presley began recording for Sun, he incorporated elements of country, R&B, and gospel to such an extent that few knew how to categorize his performances. "With . . . the explosion of Elvis those clear distinctions began to get fuzzy," Motown Records founder Berry Gordy recalled. "Elvis was a white artist who sang black music. What was it?"[168] Jerry Wexler asserted that Presley "combined hillbilly and rhythm and blues," ultimately producing "the harmonious marriage of two tough styles destined to coexist for decades to come."[169] His records became popular with both Black and white audiences because they sounded like they *belonged* on all three charts, even if they incorporated elements from other genres. Cantor details a 1956 concert sponsored by WDIA where the all-Black audience was so excited for Presley's performance that he did not even get a chance to perform before concertgoers "leaped to their feet and started coming directly toward [him] from both sides of the auditorium."[170] This concert revealed what the charts had been noting for a year and a half: as Arnold Shaw attested, "He was *dynamite* in personal appearances, affecting Southern girls, white and black—as Sinatra once had."[171]

And yet the fact that Presley's emotional vocal delivery, hyper-sexual performances, and theatrical hair and clothing made him so popular that he was dubbed "The King of Rock 'n' Roll" simultaneously upset many Black listeners, who saw that he was recruited to act as a safer vessel to deliver Black music to white listeners, even if he could hardly be described as "respectable." Upon meeting the singer for the first time in 1954, B. B. King was impressed with both his talent and his manners, yet was still concerned that, after he covered "That's All Right, Mama" by blues legend Big Boy Crudup "sounding just like him. Sounding black. . . . I noticed that things that hadn't been done for us started to be done for him."[172] In a 1982 interview, Little Richard noted that "when I came out . . . they wasn't playing no black artists on Top 40 stations. . . . It took people like Elvis . . . to open the door so I could walk down the road."[173] Ed B. asserts that "Elvis was a nice guy. And he was used. I don't have any negative feelings about him, it's just how he was used, how he was taken to the top playing the music, for instance, music from 'Big Boy' Arthur Crudup." And while Johnny Otis admitted that Presley's title as the "King of Rock and Roll" was "not without some justification because he brought a lot of originality with him," he still maintained that "the true kings of rock 'n' roll—Fats Domino, Little Richard, [and] Chuck Berry" were overshadowed by Presley's looming, hip-swiveling stature. "What happens is black people—the artists—continue to develop these things and create them and get ripped off and the glory and the money goes to white artists," he said.[174] Presley was therefore able to become more popular than his Black contemporaries because he allowed white teenagers to enjoy African-American music and dance styles without having to deal with the presence of an actual Black body. Even if his overtly sexual and supposedly vulgar performances were considered disreputable characteristics, his whiteness made him more respectable within mainstream culture than the Black musicians who informed his music and style. Grace Elizabeth Hale even notes how his off-stage politeness and unfailing Southern manners were meant to soften the image of his stage theatrics, distancing him even further from any behaviors that might be viewed as threatening or "primitive" if embodied by Black artists.[175] Presley's coronation as the King of Rock and Roll may have ushered in new acceptance for some African-American musical and performance characteristics and even urged major labels to sign more Black performers and radio stations to play their music. But the fact that a white artist was necessary to disseminate this music reveals the limits of integration for many white people, especially regarding actual Black bodies, who, unlike Presley, were unable to behave in "disreputable" ways while maintaining respectable personas."

The preponderance of records that crossed over among marketing genres perplexed the music industry in the mid-1950s, but increasing white demand for R&B records and Black support for white pop and country artists reflected the push for integration displayed by civil rights activists in Montgomery. Black people who acted "respectable" enough within a white-dominant society, or who became respectable through the profits accrued by their records selling among white audiences, could become integrated into a culture that would otherwise remain fairly unaltered. Black characteristics were more easily accepted through the conduit of white bodies like Elvis Presley or the bevy of cover artists recruited by major record labels. This form of integration, based on respectability, and limited to what the white mainstream was willing to accept, did not address the needs of Montgomery residents who could not afford to ride on the buses because their jobs were taken away, or the musicians who made next to nothing when their songs were given to profitable white artists to cover. Respectability politics worked to grant acclaim and credibility to people like Martin Luther King Jr., Rosa Parks, Fats Domino, and members of popular doo-wop groups. But where reformers had worked to "uplift the race," by the 1950s, respectability politics were instead used to ensure that small numbers of Black people in both music and the movement would become accepted by white society, even as the concerns of most Black Americans were obscured. Parks, for instance, was forced to flee the South in 1957 for Detroit because she was unable to find work because of her activism, while, as Ed B. points out, "Elvis said that he learned what he did from Black folk, but they still weren't getting them dollars."[176] Black teenagers could enjoy mainstream pop culture, as displayed by their support for Presley and other early rock and roll artists. But their pride in the fact that Black musical contributions were largely shaping popular music for young listeners across racial boundaries was tempered by the music industry's exploitation and negation of most Black musicians. Music began to desegregate just as civil rights campaigns began making national news, but the emergence of rock and roll as the cornerstone of youth culture, just as school desegregation battles wracked the country, would continue the process of unequal treatment on supposedly equal grounds.

NOTES

1. "Decca Advertisement," *Billboard*, March 15, 1952, 85.
2. Fred Rose, "Honest and Truly," Decca Records, 1952.
3. Denis-Constant Martin, "Music Beyond Apartheid?" in *Rockin' the Boat: Mass Music and Mass Movements*, ed. Reebee Garofalo (Cambridge, MA: South End Press, 1992), 205.
4. Zeke J. Miller, "Why Martin Luther King Jr.'s Lessons About Peaceful Protests Are Still Relevant," *Time*, January 12, 2018.
5. Evelyn Brooks Higginbotham, "African-American Women's History and the Metalanguage of Race," *Signs: Journal of Women in culture and Society* 17, no. 2 (1992).
6. Victoria W. Wolcott, *Remaking Respectability: African American Women in Interwar Detroit* (Chapel Hill: University of North Carolina Press Books, 2013), 6.
7. E. Frances White, *Dark Continent of Our Bodies: Black Feminism and Politics of Respectability* (Philadelphia: Temple University Press, 2010), 15; Fredrick C. Harris, "The Rise of Respectability Politics," *Dissent* 61, no. 1 (2014), 33.
8. Martin, "Music Beyond Apartheid?" 205.
9. Reebee Garofalo, "Popular Music and the Civil Rights Movement," in *Rockin' the Boat: Mass Music and Mass Movements*, ed. Reebee Garofalo (Cambridge MA: South End Press, 1999); Glenn C. Altschuler, *All Shook Up: How Rock 'n' Roll Changed America* (New York: Oxford University Press, 2004); Brian Ward, *Just My Soul Responding: Rhythm and Blues, Black Consciousness, and Race Relations* (Berkeley and Los Angeles: University of California Press, 1998); George Lipsitz, *Time Passages: Collective Memory and American Popular Culture* (Minneapolis: University of Minnesota Press, 2001).
10. Ward, *Just My Soul Responding*; Nelson George, *The Death of Rhythm and Blues* (New York: Penguin Books, 1988).
11. *Billboard*, October 27, 1956; June Bundy, "Desegregation of Chart Categories Earmarks '56," *Billboard*, January 26, 1957, 48.

12. Steve Chapple and Reebee Garofalo, *Rock 'n' Roll is Here to Pay: The History and Politics of the Music Industry* (Lanham, MD: Rowman & Littlefield Publishers, 1978), 231.

13. Philip Ennis, *The Seventh Stream: The Emergence of Rocknroll in American Popular Culture* (Middletown, CT: Wesleyan University Press, 1992), 31.

14. Ward, *Just My Soul Responding*, 2–3; 5.

15. Bibb E., in discussion with author, November 13, 2011.

16. Diarra Osei Robertson, "Cash Rules Everything Around Me: Appropriation, Commodification, and the Politics of Contemporary Protest Music and Hip Hop," in *Soul Thieves: The Appropriation and Misrepresentation of African American Popular Culture,* ed. Tamara Brown and Baruti Kopano (New York: Palgrave Macmillan, 2014), 33–34.

17. Ward, *Just My Soul Responding*, 5.

18. Michele Mitchell, *Righteous Propagation: African Americans and the Politics of Racial Destiny After Reconstruction* (Chapel Hill, NC: University of North Carolina Press, 2004), 12; 148.

19. Harris, "The Rise of Respectability Politics," 33; Evelyn Brooks Higginbotham, *Righteous Discontent: The Women's Movement in the Black Baptist Church, 1880–1920* (Cambridge, MA: Harvard University Press, 1993), 26; Martha S. Jones, *All Bound Up Together: The Woman Question in African American Public Culture, 1830–1900* (Chapel Hill, NC: University of North Carolina Press, 2009), 179.

20. Harris, "The Rise of Respectability Politics," 33.

21. Wolcott, *Remaking Respectability*, 4–7.

22. Mitchell, *Righteous Propagation*, 9.

23. Higginbotham, *Righteous Discontent*, 42–45; Jennifer Jensen Wallach, *Getting What We Need Ourselves: How Food Has Shaped African American Life* (Lanham, MD: Rowman & Littlefield, 2019), 87–88.

24. Higginbotham, *Righteous Discontent*, 19–26.

25. Higginbotham, *Righteous Discontent*, 29.

26. Mitchell, *Righteous Propagation*, 10.

27. Mitchell, *Righteous Propagation*, 142–149.

28. Wallach, *Getting What We Need Ourselves*, 9; 78–80.

29. Higginbotham, *Righteous Discontent*, 35.

30. Mitchell, *Righteous Propagation*, 108–111; 123.

31. Higginbotham, *Righteous Discontent*, 38; Mitchell, *Righteous Propagation*, 119.

32. Honor Ford-Smith, "Unruly Virtues of the Spectacular: Performing Engendered Nationalisms in the UNIA in Jamaica," *Interventions* 6, no. 1 (2004), 20–28; Wallach, *Getting What We Need Ourselves*, 110.

33. Wolcott, *Remaking Respectability*, 4–9.

34. Chapple and Garofalo, *Rock 'n' Roll Is Here to Pay*, 243–244; Angela Y. Davis, *Blues Legacies and Black Feminism: Gertrude 'Ma' Rainey, Bessie Smith, and Billie Holiday* (New York: Vintage Books, 1998), 33; 5; Lawrence Levine, *Black Culture and Black Consciousness: Afro-American Folk Thought From Slavery to Freedom* (New York: Oxford University Press, 1977), 80. Although these

characteristics tend to define what we now call "the blues" or at least late nineteenth- to early twentieth-century iterations, Karl Hagstrom Miller argues that Southern music genres during this period were created based on marketing to particular racial demographics rather than any true musicological attributes. He argues that both Black and white musicians "played blues, ballads, ragtime, and string band music, as well as the plethora of styles popular throughout the nation. . . . Many performed any music they could, regardless of their racial or regional identities." As the record industry began centralizing during this period, company scouts were sent to Southern states to identify artists playing "authentic" Southern music, where they would "compartmentalize southern music according to race. . . . Music developed a color line. The blues were African American. Rural white southerners played what came to be called country music. And much of the rest of the music performed and heard in the region was left out" (1–2). Although it is therefore somewhat reductive to discuss the blues as a unified genre, and the parts that reformers considered unsavory would have transgressed racial lines, the focus here is on how these characteristics were mapped onto Black artists and listeners in ways that were deemed unrespectable. For more, please see Karl Hagstrom Miller, *Segregating Sound: Inventing Folk and Pop Music in the Age of Jim Crow* (Durham, NC: Duke University Press, 2010).

35. Tera W. Hunter, "'Sexual Pantomimes,' The Blues Aesthetic, and Black Women in the New South," in *Music and the Racial Imagination*, ed. Ronald M. Radano, Philip V. Bohlman, and Houston A. Baker (Chicago: University of Chicago Press, 2000), 148–152.

36. Davis, *Blues Legacies and Black Feminism*, 3; Camille Cosby, interview with B.B. King, 42, National Visionary Leadership Project, The Library of Congress American Folklife Center, Washington, DC.

37. Ennis, *The Seventh Stream*, 27; 71; Craig Werner, *A Change Is Gonna Come: Music, Race and the Soul of America* (New York: Penguin Putnam, 1998), 11.

38. Cosby, interview with B.B. King, 5.

39. Robin D. G. Kelley, *Race Rebels: Culture, Politics, and the Black Working Class* (New York: Simon & Schuster, 1996), 46.

40. Johnny Otis, *Upside Your Head!:Rhythm and Blues on Central Avenue*, by Johnny Otis (Middletown, CT: Wesleyan University Press, 1993), 60.

41. Otis, *Upside Your Head!* 91.

42. Ben Fong-Torres, "Ray Charles," in *The Rolling Stone Interviews, 1967–1980*, ed. The Editors of *Rolling Stone* (New York: Rolling Stone Press, 1981), 262.

43. Evelyn Brooks Higginbotham, "Rethinking Vernacular Culture: Black Religion and Race Records in the 1920s and 1930s," in *American Studies: An Anthology*, ed. Cornel West and Eddie S. Glaude (Louisville, KY: Westminster John Knox Press, 2003), 225–228.

44. Wolcott, *Rethinking Respectability*, 4–9; Danielle L. McGuire, *At the Dark End of the Street: Black Women, Rape, and Resistance—A New History of the Civil Rights Movement from Rosa Parks to the Rise of Black Power* (New York: Knopf, 2010), 94.

45. Renee Pouissant, interview with Cissy Houston, December 14, 2006, 11, National Visionary Leadership Project, American Folklife Center, the Library of Congress, Washington, DC.

46. Charles White, *The Life and Times of Little Richard: The Quasar of Rock* (New York: Da Capo Press, 1994), 6.

47. Brent Edwards, interview with Gladys and Merald "Bubba" Knight, New York, New York, January 9, 2011, 1–2; 1–5, The Apollo Theater Oral History Project, Columbia University Rare Book and Manuscript Library, New York, NY.

48. Camille Cosby, interview with, Diahann Carroll, 18, National Visionary Leadership Project, American Folklife Center, the Library of Congress, Washington, DC.

49. Cheryl J., in discussion with the author, January 9, 2020; Carol A., in discussion with the author, February 24, 2020; Joseph J., in discussion with the author, January 30, 2020; Tony T., in discussion with the author, November 9, 2011.

50. Please see "Prologue," xv–xxii and Chapter 3, "Walking in Pride and Dignity," 84–134 in McGuire, *At the Dark End of the Street*.

51. Jeanne Theoharis, *The Rebellious Life of Mrs. Rosa Parks* (Boston, MA: Beacon Press, 2015), 122–123.

52. McGuire, *At the Dark End of the Street*, 91–93.

53. Taylor Branch, *Parting the Waters: America in the King Years, 1954–1963* (New York: Simon & Schuster, 1988), 130.

54. Ted Poston, "This is Montgomery: No Hat in Hand," *The Baltimore Afro-American*, August 25, 1956.

55. Theoharis, *The Rebellious Life of Mrs. Rosa Parks*, 118–130; McGuire, *At the Dark End of the Street*, 100–107.

56. Wayne Phillips, "Montgomery is Stage For a Tense Drama," *The New York Times*, March 4, 1956, 10.

57. "Race Urged to Keep Faith in Its Fight: Rosa Parks Makes Plea in Capital," *Chicago Defender*, June 9, 1956, 6.

58. Theoharis, *The Rebellious Life of Mrs. Rosa Parks*, 124–125.

59. "Battle Against Tradition: Martin Luther King, Jr." *The New York Times*, March 21, 1956, 28; "Montgomery's Patience Praised by Boycott Chief," The *Washington Post and Times Herald*, December 7, 1956, C15.

60. Emily W., in discussion with the author, June 30, 2020.

61. Poston, "This is Montgomery: No Hat in Hand."

62. James Booker, "Who is Martin Luther King?" *New York Amsterdam News*, March 31, 1956, 2; Evelyn Cunningham, "Martin Luther King, Jr.: 'A Young Minister Marked for Leadership,'" *Pittsburgh Courier*, April 7, 1956, A29.

63. "The Reverend Martin Luther King," *Chicago Defender*, March 25, 1956, 11.

64. "Prepare for Boycott Trials," *Chicago Defender*, March 30, 1956, 1.

65. "A Bold Boycott Goes On," *Life*, March 5, 1956, 40; "Battle Against Tradition," 28.

66. "Battle Against Tradition," 28.

67. "Montgomery's Patience Praised by Boycott Chief," C15.

68. George Barrett, "Montgomery: Testing Ground," *The New York Times*, December 16, 1956, SM5.

69. Barrett, "Montgomery: Testing Ground," SM5.

70. George Barrett, "Bus Integration in Alabama Calm," *The New York Times*, December 22, 1956, 1.

71. "Montgomery Boycotters Usher in New Era of Democracy For South," *Chicago Defender*, December 26, 1956, 10.

72. Bibb E., in discussion with the author.

73. Ann W., in discussion with the author, November 9, 2011.

74. Fran S., in discussion with the author, November 15, 2011; Bret Eynon, interview with Arnie Bauchner, December 1978, 4–5, Contemporary History Project: The New Left in Ann Arbor, Bentley Historical Library, The University of Michigan, Ann Arbor, MI; Victor F., in discussion with the author, September 30, 2019.

75. Bret Eynon, "John Sinclair: Hipster," November 21, 1977, 24, Michigan Historical Collections, Contemporary History Project Papers, Bentley Historical Library, The University of Michigan, Ann Arbor, MI; Mary R., in discussion with the author, May 11, 2020.

76. Ron R., in discussion with the author, June 9, 2020; Marcia P., in discussion with the author, December 6, 2019.

77. Ellis B., in discussion with the author, September 26, 2019; Walter S., in discussion with the author, October 4, 2019; Victor F., in discussion with the author.

78. Ted Poston, "This is Montgomery," *The Baltimore Afro-American*, July 21, 1956, 20F.

79. Trezzvant W. Anderson, "How Has Dramatic Bus Boycott Affected Montgomery Negroes?" *The Pittsburgh Courier*, November 23, 1957, B1; Trezzvant W. Anderson, "How Has Dramatic Bus Boycott Affected Montgomery Negroes?" *The Pittsburgh Courier*, December 4, 1957, B3; Trezzvant W. Anderson, "How Has Dramatic Bus Boycott Affected Montgomery Negroes?" *The Pittsburgh Courier*, December 21, 1957.

80. Cheryl J., in discussion with the author.

81. Scott F., in discussion with the author, April 20, 2020.

82. Ellen Fishman, interview with Bunyan Bryant, January 1979, 5, Contemporary History Project: The New Left in Ann Arbor, Bentley Historical Library, The University of Michigan, Ann Arbor, MI.

83. Joseph J., in discussion with the author.

84. Carol A., in discussion with the author; Larry R., in discussion with the author, October 4, 2019.

85. Najee Muhammad, in discussion with the author, November 20, 2011.

86. Miche Braeden, in discussion with the author, April 25, 2020.

87. *Billboard*, July 3–September 11, 1954; Ward, *Just My Soul Responding*, 1; 19; 20; 46; 49.

88. *Billboard*, December 18, 1954–February 11, 1956. Black artists and writers were routinely paid next to nothing for original songs that would go on to earn massive profits for major labels once they were recorded by white pop stars. And yet covers could also bolster the popularity of original recordings among white teenagers. For more, see Ennis, *The Seventh Stream* and Chapple and Garofalo, *Rock n' Roll Is Here to Pay*.

89. John Michael Runowicz, *Forever Doo Wop: Race, Nostalgia, and Vocal Harmony* (Amherst, MA: University of Massachusetts Press, 2006).

90. Runowicz, *Forever Doo Wop*, 1.
91. Kelley, *Race Rebels*, 50.
92. Buck Ram, "The Great Pretender," Mercury Records, 1955.
93. Bob Franklin, interview with Milton Gabler, Oral History Research Office, Columbia University, November 1959, 41–42, Milt Gabler Papers, Box 4, Folder 19, The Rock and Roll Hall of Fame Library and Archives, Cleveland, OH; Dave Bartholomew and Pearl King, "I Hear You Knocking," Imperial Records, 1955.
94. *Billboard*, February 5–October 15, 1955.
95. Louis Cantor, *Wheelin' on Beale: How WDIA-Memphis Became the Nation's First All-Black Station and Created the Sound that Changed America* (New York: Pharos Books, 1992), 194–196; Ward, *Just My Soul Responding*, 135.
96. Jerry Wexler and David Ritz, *Rhythm and the Blues: A Life in American Music* (New York: St. Martin's Press, 1994), 78; 207–208; Arnold Shaw, *The Rockin' 50s: The Decade That Transformed the Pop Music Scene* (New York: Hawthorn Books, 1973), 77; *Reader, Chicago's Free Weekly*, Friday May 17, 1991, 8, Ralph Bass Papers, Box 1, Folder 1, The Rock and Roll Hall of Fame Library and Archives, Cleveland, OH; Ralph Bass with John Fleming, "A Life Recording," 7, Ralph Bass Papers, Box 1, Folder 2, The Rock and Roll Hall of Fame Library and Archives, Cleveland, OH; Jerry Wexler and Ahmet Ertegun, "The Latest Trend: R&B Disks are Going Pop," *The Cash Box*, July 3, 1954, 56, Jerry Wexler Papers, Box 1, Folder 8, The Rock and Roll Hall of Fame Library and Archives, Cleveland, OH.
97. J. Fred MacDonald, *Don't Touch That Dial! Radio Programming in American Life from 1920 to 1960* (Stamford, CT: Wadsworth Publishing, 1979), 368 in Louis Cantor, *Dewey and Elvis: The Life and Times of a Rock 'n' Roll Deejay* (Champaign, IL: University of Illinois Press, 2010), 223–224.
98. Bibb E., in discussion with author; Fleming, "A Life Recording," 9; Rick T., in discussion with the author, November 20, 2011.
99. Bill W., in discussion with the author, June 1–2, 2020; Jeff T., in discussion with the author, November 5, 2011.
100. Bruce C., in discussion with the author, June 8, 2020; Ron R., in discussion with the author; David S., in discussion with the author, September 16, 2019; Bob S., in discussion with the author, September 25, 2019; Michael P., in discussion with the author, October 4, 2019; Victor F., in discussion with the author; Walter S., in discussion with the author.
101. David S., in discussion with the author; Michael P., in discussion with the author; Victor F., in discussion with the author; Bob S., in discussion with the author.
102. Lipsitz, *Time Passages*, 5; 99–100; 122.
103. For more on the creation of racialized suburbs in the United States after World War II, please see David Freund, *Colored Property: State Policy and White Racial Politics in America* (Chicago: University of Chicago Press, 2007) and Kenneth Jackson, *Crabgrass Frontier: The Suburbanization of the United States* (New York: Oxford University Press, 1985). And for analyses of young white responses to growing up in these suburbs, please see Wini Breines, *Young, White, and Miserable* (Boston: Beacon Hill Press, 1992) and Doug Owram, *Born At the Right Time: A History of the Baby Boom Generation* (Toronto: University of Toronto Press, 1997).

104. Bret Eynon, interview with Todd Gitlin, September 16, 1978, 9, Contemporary History Project: The New Left, Bentley Historical Library, The University of Michigan, Ann Arbor, MI.

105. Edward Willett, *Janis Joplin: Take Another Little Piece of My Heart* (Berkeley, CA; Heights, NJ: Enslow Publishers, 2008), 29; Janis Ian, *Society's Child* (New York: Tarcher, 2008), 21.

106. Marcia P., in discussion with the author; Bibb E., in discussion with the author.

107. Daniel Levitin, *This Is Your Brain on Music: The Science of a Human Obsession* (New York: Plume Printing, 2006), 27–28.

108. Levitin, *This Is Your Brain on Music*, 38.

109. Bibb E. in discussion with the author; Charles W. Mills, "Racial Liberalism," *PMLA* 123, no. 5 (October 2008), 1380; Bob C. in discussion with the author, December 13, 2011; Jeff T. in discussion with the author; Fran S. in discussion with the author; Victor F., in discussion with the author; Bill W., in discussion with the author; Stan W., in discussion with the author, December 20, 2011.

110. Paul Kingsbury, *BMI 50th Anniversary: The Explosion of American Music 1940–1990* (Nashville: The Country Music Foundation 1990), 31.

111. "Rock-and-Roll Called 'Communicable Disease,'" *The New York Times*, March 28, 1956, 33; Les Brown, "Elvis Presley: Can Fifty Million Americans Be Wrong?" *Downbeat*, September 19, 1956, 42, Alan Freed Papers, Box 1, Folder 55, The Rock and Roll Hall of Fame Library and Archives, Cleveland, OH.

112. Martin Luther King Jr. "Advice for Living," April 1958, The Martin Luther King, Jr. Research and Education Institute, Stanford University last accessed at https://swap.stanford.edu/20141218225520/http://mlk-kpp01.stanford.edu/primary-documents/Vol4/Apr-1958_AdviceForLiving.pdf, on July 2, 2021.

113. "Yeh-Heh-Heh-Hes, Baby," *Time*, June 18, 1956, 54.

114. Jann Wenner, "The Rolling Stone Interview: John Lennon," *Rolling Stone*, December 1970, last accessed at http://www.johnlennon.com/music/interviews/rolling-stone-interview-1970/, on September 15, 2021; John D. Wells, "Me and the Devil Blues: A Study of Robert Johnson and the Music of the Rolling Stones," in *American Popular Music: The Age of Rock*, ed. Timothy E. Schuerer (Bowling Green, OH: Bowling Green State University Popular Press, 1989), 165.

115. Fleming, "A Life Recording," 7; Victor F., in discussion with the author.

116. Bruce C., in discussion with the author.

117. Bibb E., in discussion with the author; Patricia J., in discussion with the author, March 9, 2020; Ron R., in discussion with the author; Henry I., in discussion with the author, October 30, 2019.

118. Wexler and Ertegun, "The Latest Trend: R&B Disks are Going Pop," 56.

119. Franklin, interview with Milt Gabler, 36.

120. Bibb E., in discussion with the author.

121. Vincent Rose, Larry Stock, and Al Lewis, "Blueberry Hill," Imperial, 1956.

122. Hank Ballard, "Work With Me, Annie," Federal Records, 1954.

123. Fran S., in discussion with the author.

124. Bill W. in discussion with the author.

125. Grace Elizabeth Hale, *A Nation of Outsiders: How the White Middle Class Fell in Love with Rebellion in Postwar America* (New York: Oxford University Press, 2011), 98.

126. Eynon, "John Sinclair: Hipster," 5.

127. Bruce C., in discussion with the author.

128. Alan Freed, "Alan Freed Says: 'I Told You So . . .'" *Downbeat*, September 19, 1956, 44, Alan Freed Collection, Box 1, Folder 55, The Rock and Roll Hall of Fame Library and Archives, Cleveland, OH; Alan Freed, "The Big Beat is Here to Stay," *TV Radio Mirror*, November 1958, 70, Alan Freed Collection, Box 1, Folder 56, The Rock and Roll Hall of Fame Library and Archives, Cleveland, OH.

129. Ennis, *The Seventh Stream*, 18.

130. John A. Jackson, *Big Beat Heat: Alan Freed and the Early Years of Rock & Roll* (London: Schirmer Trade Books, 1991); Brett Lashua, "In the Moondog's House: Alan Freed, Leo Mintz, and the 'Invention' of Rock 'n' Roll," in *Popular Music, Popular Myth and Cultural Heritage in Cleveland: The Moondog, The Buzzard, and the Battle for the Rock and Roll Hall of Fame* (Somerville, MA: Emerald Publishing, 2019), 37–47.

131. Alan Freed, "The Big Beat Has Arrived: Izzy Rowe's Notebook," *The Pittsburgh Courier*, 1955; Edith Evans Ashbury, "Rock 'n' Roll Teen-Agers Tie Up the Times Square Area," *The New York Times*, February 23, 1957.

132. Cantor, *Dewey and Elvis*, 140–141; Cantor, *Wheelin' on Beale*, 164.

133. Michael T. Bertrand, *Race, Rock and Elvis* (Champaign, IL: University of Illinois Press, 2000), 160; Theodore Irwin, "Rock 'n' Roll 'n' Alan," *Pageant*, July 1957, 61, The Alan Freed Collection, Box 1, Folder 55, The Rock and Roll Hall of Fame Library and Archives, Cleveland, OH.

134. Cantor, *Dewey and Elvis*, 227.

135. Franklin, interview with Milton Gabler, 57.

136. John Swenson, *Bill Haley: The Daddy of Rock and Roll* (New York: Stein and Day, 1982), 52.

137. Jesse Stone, "Shake, Rattle and Roll," Joe Turner, Atlantic, 1954; Jesse Stone, "Shake, Rattle and Roll," Bill Haley and His Comets, Decca, 1954; Chapple and Garofalo, *Rock 'n' Roll Is Here to Pay*, 234.

138. Charlie Gillett, *The Sound of the City: The Rise of Rock and Roll* (Cambridge, MA: Da Capo Press, 1996), 47.

139. Reebee Garofalo, "Crossing Over: From Black Rhythm & Blues to White Rock 'n' Roll," in *R&B, Rhythm and Business: The Political Economy of Black Music*, ed. Norman Kelley (New York: Akashic Books, 2005), 127; Chapple and Garofalo, *Rock 'n' Roll Is Here to Pay*, 29.

140. For more on the "Sh-Boom" crossover phenomenon, please see Ward, *Just My Soul Responding*, 1–2; 19–20. Ward parallels this record's crossover success with the *Brown v. Board of Education of Topeka* case, which ruled racially segregated schools to be illegal, and was decided two months after the song's original debut.

141. Ward, *Just My Soul Responding*, 1; *Billboard*, July 18, 1953–October 3, 1953; January 2–December 25, 1954; January 1–December 31, 1955. See also Chapple and Garofalo, *Rock 'n' Roll Is Here to Pay*, Gillett, *The Sound of the City*,

Shaw, *The Rockin' 50s*, Ennis, *The Seventh Stream*, Ward, *Just My Soul Responding*, and Albin Zak, *I Don't Sound Like Nobody: Remaking Music in 1950s America* (Ann Arbor, MI: University of Michigan Press, 2010).

142. Ennis, *The Seventh Stream*, 246; *Billboard*, July 9–November 5, 1955.

143. Shaw, *The Rockin' 50s*, 126.

144. *Billboard*, December 18, 1954–February 11, 1956.

145. *Billboard*, February 5–July 9, 1955; Arnold Shaw, *Honkers and Shouters: The Golden Years of Rhythm and Blues* (New York: Macmillan, 1978), 234.

146. Henry I., in discussion with the author; Rick T., in discussion with the author; Fran S., in discussion with the author; Bob S., in discussion with the author; Ron R., in discussion with the author; Bibb E., in discussion with the author.

147. Chapple and Garofalo, *Rock 'n' Roll Is Here to Pay*, 256.

148. "The Rolling Stone Interview: Phil Spector," *Rolling Stone*, November 1, 1969, Jerry Wexler Collection, Box 1, Folder 8, The Rock and Roll Hall of Fame Library and Archives, Cleveland, OH.

149. Ray Charles and David Ritz, *Brother Ray: Ray Charles' Own Story* (Cambridge MA: Da Capo Press, 2004), 72–73.

150. Edgar S. in discussion with the author, June 25, 2020; Cheryl J., in discussion with the author.

151. Ward, *Just My Soul Responding*, 3.

152. Tony T. in discussion with the author; Najee M. in discussion with the author; Edgar S., in discussion with the author.

153. Ralph Gleason, interview with Milt Gabler, 1974, 8–9, Milt Gabler Collection, Box 4, Folder 18, The Rock and Roll Hall of Fame Library and Archives, Cleveland, OH; 11; Ennis, *The Seventh Stream*, 221.

154. Haley's identity as the first real "rock and roll" star likely stemmed from the fact that he was identified as such by *Billboard* and other mainstream media outlets, especially after the 1955 re-release of "Rock Around the Clock." Although historians have consistently argued against this racialized mantle, noting that Black musicians like Fats Domino and Ike Turner released what are now considered "rock and roll" records well before Haley became popular on a national scale, the misnomer is still widely applied. His website, billhaley.com, is subtitled "The Father of Rock 'n' Roll," while Encyclopedia Britannica and IMDb both designate him as the first rock and roll star. Websites last accessed on June 14, 2018. Al Portch, "Manager of Bill Haley Defends the 'Real Thing,'" *Downbeat*, September 19, 1956, 43, Alan Freed Collection, Box 1, Folder 55, The Rock and Roll Hall of Fame Library and Archives, Cleveland, OH.

155. Shaw, *The Rockin' 50s*, 126; 136.

156. "Yeh-Heh-Heh-Hes, Baby," *Time*, June 18, 1956, 54.

157. Boone's first release, a cover of the Charms' "Two Hearts," hit number 16 on the Pop chart. But his follow-up record, a far more sedate version of Fats Domino's "Ain't That a Shame," took Domino's place on the Pop chart fairly quickly, spending several weeks at number 2, while the original topped out at number 16. *Billboard*, December 3, 1955–June 9, 1956; Zak, *I Don't Sound Like Nobody*, 130–131.

158. Franklin, interview with Milton Gabler, 57.

159. Alan Freed, "Wonderful World of Rock," *Pageant*, July 1957, 60, Alan Freed Collection, Box 1, Folder 55, The Rock and Roll Hall of Fame Library and Archives, Cleveland, OH. Freed may have been interviewed before May of 1957, seeing as Ricky Nelson's cover version of Domino's "I'm Walkin'" debuted on the *Billboard* Pop chart on May 6. Although Domino's original version held strong for two weeks, Nelson's cover pushed Domino off the Pop chart, peaking at number 4 by the following month.

160. Bundy, "Desegregation of Chart Categories Earmarks '56," 48; As previously stated, Pat Boone's cover version of Little Richard's "Tutti Frutti" appeared alongside the original. The only example of a racialized cover appearing on the Pop chart while the Black original remained on the R&B chart in 1956 is Boone's cover of the Flamingos' "I'll Be Home." Boone's record topped out at number 6, while the Flamingos' version reached number 10. Please see *Billboard* charts, January 7–December 29, 1956.

161. Clara A., in discussion with the author, May 29, 2020; Bill W., in discussion with the author.

162. *Billboard*, September 22–October 27, 1956.

163. *Billboard*, February 25–March 17, 1956; September 29–December 29, 1956.

164. Tony T., in discussion with the author; Cheryl J., in discussion with the author.

165. Fong-Torres, interview with Ray Charles.

166. Cantor, *Dewey and Elvis*, 138; Edgar S., in discussion with the author; Cosby, interview with B.B. King, 49.

167. Anthony Mattiaccio "Voice from the Heart of the Country," *Lifestyles*, May 13, 1979, A Folk Music Portrait of Elvis Presley, 879-19, 880, American Folklife Center, Library of Congress, Washington, DC; Irene Oppenheim, "Rocking the American Dream: Elvis Presley and Bruce Springsteen," *The Threepenny Review*, Winter, 1982, 22, Russell B. Nye Collection, Elvis Presley Clippings Folder, Michigan State University Archives, Lansing, MI; Cantor, *Dewey and Elvis*, 82–86; Kingsbury, *BMI 50th Anniversary*, 26; Peter Guralnick, *Last Train to Memphis: The Rise of Elvis Presley* (New York: Little, Brown and Co., 2012), 96.

168. Berry Gordy, *To Be Loved: The Music, the Magic, the Memories of Motown* (New York: Warner Books, 1994), 99.

169. Wexler, *Rhythm and the Blues*, 125.

170. Cantor, *Wheelin' On Beale*, 194–195.

171. Ennis, *The Seventh Stream*, 238.

172. Cosby, interview with B.B. King, 115.

173. Oppenheim, "Rocking the American Dream," 22.

174. Ed B., in discussion with the author, June 23, 2020; Chapple and Garofalo, *Rock 'n' Roll Is Here to Pay*, 246.

175. Hale, *A Nation of Outsiders*, 67.

176. Ed B., in discussion with the author.

Chapter 3

"A Teen Ager in Love," 1957–1960

In December, 1956, Gee Records released Frankie Lymon and the Teenagers' first and only full-length album. On the cover, the group's five members are captured walking down a semirural path as if headed to school. They are dressed identically, in a uniform of freshly pressed slacks and collegiate sweaters reminiscent of wholesome middle-class high school life, and their easy, casual postures portray the kinds of carefree attitudes that marketers often tried to insist were a mainstay of adolescent popularity.[1] The group's name was even chosen as a specific means of appealing directly to young people, who were beginning to assert themselves more directly, both as consumers and as individuals in a very particular stage of the life cycle. Although idealized images of 1950s teenagers were, and continue to be, coded as white and middle class, this group was comprised of Black and Latin kids from Harlem and the Bronx, most of whom grew up in more difficult socioeconomic conditions than their album cover suggests. Executives at Gee may have crafted these images in order to make the group seem more palatable to white parents and relatable to their children, particularly since the Teenagers had already achieved crossover success with many of the album's singles, including "Why Do Fools Fall in Love?" But this cover also reveals how Black kids were instrumental in helping to create and shape the new identity of the "Teen-Ager" during the late 1950s, and how teenage appeal helped to make interracial culture seem modern and fun.

The very concept of "teenagers" as separate from young adults is fairly new in American social history. Although adolescence was identified as a unique life period in the early twentieth century, the teenager, defined by Grace Palladino as "tied to the new high school world of dating, driving, music, and enjoyment," only emerged as a distinct identity because of the economic and social shifts that took place after World War II.[2] This demographic, which was "linked by national and generational, rather than local or class, bonds," relied on a mass media and consumer culture for identification, and reflected, according to Philip Ennis, "the culture of a leisure class."[3] Because of the affluent postwar economy, children were able to postpone adulthood for longer periods of time than their predecessors. Marketers, who were initially reluctant to sell to young people, realized that teenagers were no longer following adult guidelines when determining how to dress or what to listen to—they were creating their own cultural norms, which depended on peer, rather than parental, approval. The dollar amount attached to teenage desires increased into the billions, leading to an explosion of advertising both necessities and luxuries directly to young consumers.[4] The ability to remain in school well into their teens, and even beyond if attending college, to earn or receive disposable income to be spent on purchases for themselves rather than their households, and to interact with their peers in spaces apart from adult supervision, allowed middle-class youth the chance to fashion separate, more independent, selves that were influenced by mass media and consumer culture.

Black adolescents like Frankie Lymon and his groupmates were also routinely described as "teenagers" by their parents, by advertisements aiming to sell to their demographic, and, perhaps most importantly, by themselves. If the modern teenager was shaped by middle-class characteristics like full-time schooling and discretionary income, then Black adolescents, who were more likely to grow up in lower-income homes and to work or leave school early, would not be able to identify with this cultural shift. But many Black kids, especially those growing up in middle- or aspiring-class households, also participated in these idealized teenage activities, including shopping, studying, dating, and socializing with friends, even if the effects of institutionalized racism meant that their experiences would differ from those of their white peers. Sociologist Joseph Himes, for instance, noted in a 1961 report that kids from "high-prestige" Black families prized "moral conformity, good manners and taste, subordination of present gratifications to future achievements, and striving for social recognition and status," the same kinds of "respectable" qualities that were also highly valued by the white middle classes. As for their professional inclinations, "today's teen-agers want to be engineers, scientists, aviator technicians of all kinds, social workers, professional athletes, entertainers, radio and television workers, and so on." The only major difference that Himes identified between the behaviors and hopes of middle-class Black kids and their white peers is that Black teenagers were aware of the mitigating factors of racial discrimination.[5]

Popular music, especially rock and roll, which became a sort of signifier for teenage life during this period, was a major component of this interracial teenage culture. Many records, like those released by Frankie Lymon and the

Teenagers, continued to "cross over" between the Pop and the R&B charts on *Billboard*, so much so that, by the summer of 1958, the publication debuted the 'Hot 100' chart, which consolidated sales data from all genres, thereby "integrating" the buying habits of different demographic groups. The magazine continued to print separate charts for "Hot" R&B and C&W listings, but the Hot 100 became the publication's predominant chart guiding radio station playlists and distributor purchases. This new list was, at first, comprised of a solid mixture of white and Black musicians, most of whom defied separate categories, and were instead referred to as rock and roll artists.[6] Crossovers, a thing of the past for the time being, had effectively desegregated the *Billboard* charts, so much so that editor Paul Ackerman argued that popular music was "one aspect of America's cultural life . . . [where] integration has already taken place."[7]

This "desegregation" of the charts occurred merely one year after Central High School in Little Rock and the University of Alabama required federal intervention in order to protect Black students headed to previously all-white institutions from violent white resistance. These struggles drew such a definitive line between white supremacy and racial integration that listening to Black artists encouraged many white kids to start thinking about how their Black peers were treated unfairly. Although many people who grew up during this era affirm the connection between movement and music in this capacity, clear distinctions are again discernible among white and Black responses. White respondents often explain that they were more likely to see Black Americans as people who deserved equal rights after listening to their music, a perspective that aligns with their beliefs that integration was morally correct, and an assertion of the country's democratic principles. R&B artists' talents and industry successes also prompted white teenagers to believe that they had earned the right to be treated fairly, which correlates with desegregation movement rhetoric that Black children should be granted opportunities to better themselves by attending integrated schools. These perspectives are based on the notion that the American system of individual democratic rights is fundamentally sound, and simply needs to be expanded to include people from all racial groups.

Just as concepts of diversity and inclusion gained widespread approval among young whites, the belief that racial equality could be achieved by eradication of legal segregation in schools, and by a more inclusive teenage popular culture, also reinforced new, distorted versions of racism under the pretense that it could suddenly cease to exist. Civil rights organizers' decisions to focus on desegregation of public places and to use nonviolence and respectability politics as strategies may have worked too well in a sense, as many white kids came to view these tactics as the only acceptable means of working toward racial equality. Conversely, more aggressive policies that actually challenged white supremacist structures, like busing Black children to previously all-white schools, were often viewed as government overreach that could only lead to conflict. Even though the legal demise of school segregation did not lead to any sort of widespread or meaningful racial mixing in Southern classrooms, many white people who grew up during this period view even tacit support for integration as an ultimate achievement. These beliefs were reinforced by integration on the *Billboard* charts, and on radio and television airwaves, as rock and roll performers from both racial backgrounds saw incredible success with both Black and white teenage audiences. Part of being a teenager during this period, then, meant identifying with characteristics ostensibly shared by both Black and white youth, and accepting or even celebrating interracial elements, even if peaceful coexistence on actual school grounds remained uncommon.

Young consumer desires for music that espoused broader or diverse perspectives normalized the ideal of desegregation in public spaces, including the *Billboard* charts, but the assimilationist framework of this emerging ideology prevented any deeper criticism of racial hierarchies. As school segregation laws were declared unconstitutional, and some Southern districts began implementing plans to allow small numbers of Black students to attend better-funded white institutions, many Black kids who were eager to accept these educational opportunities found that they were instead left to deal with bullying, neglect, and outright violence without the support of community networks that existed in segregated Black schools and neighborhoods. Even though widespread Black support for school desegregation never wavered, the reality that many kids faced when they attempted to walk through the doors of majority-white institutions was a lot more harsh and complex than most of their white peers realized. Black kids may also have enjoyed this "integrated" music because it was popular and because it reflected many of their new realities as teenagers, high school students, and consumers. But they also looked to Black artists, and the opportunities that their successes indicated were available to people who looked like them, as role models as they dealt with some of the scarier aspects of confronting segregation firsthand.

In some ways, the integration of popular music through rock and roll mirrored the effects of desegregating school systems. Both, for instance, allowed for limited Black participation while simultaneously strengthening boundaries around white dominance. Most majority-white schools, for instance, did little to make Black students feel welcome, even if teachers and administrators supported the desegregation edict, which many, of course, did not. In some cases, Black kids thrived at their new schools, making friends, joining clubs, and even getting elected as class president or prom queen. In other cases, however, they were ignored and treated as inferior, with no support from others who could understand their concerns. Some had to deal with aggressive, and even violent, mobs that tried to prevent them from going to school in the first place. In order to succeed, or even to make it through the semester, many were forced to assimilate within their new school communities as much as possible, while hiding their true feelings beneath a supposedly carefree teenage façade. Rock and roll music, at least the kind that was distributed by major record labels, was similarly forced to assimilate within a white pop framework during this period. Even though Black artists continued to have a strong presence on the Pop and R&B charts, and on the Hot 100 after 1958, the years between 1957 and 1960 are generally regarded as a low point in the history of rock and roll. Little Richard gave up the devil's music when he found religion and became a minister; Elvis was drafted, sent to Germany, and (gasp) cut his hair; Jerry Lee Lewis merited widespread disgust by marrying his 13-year-old cousin; and Chuck Berry was arrested for attempting to transport a minor girl across state lines. Cover versions of Black R&B records no longer sold well among white teenage consumers, but record executives found that they could still exert control over the look and sound of popular music while retaining just enough of rock and roll's edge to make it profitable. Youth had become the most prominent marketing tool, so young white pop artists were recruited to perform new songs that retained the beat, instrumentation, and pace of R&B, while replacing most other elements from African-American traditions with softer percussion and inoffensive lyrics. While the charts were not entirely bombarded with these so-called "schlock rockers," major record companies did attempt to regain control over the charts while maintaining their white adolescent fan base. They heavily marketed these artists as though they came from the same traditions as Elvis Presley and Chuck Berry, even though a shift toward white pop aesthetics was clearly evident.

Since rock and roll became widely acknowledged as a distinct genre during this period, it is hardly surprising that major-label attempts to regain control over racialized aspects have led many critics and musicians to consider it little more than "whitened" R&B, renamed, Nelson George explains, "to camouflage its Black roots."[8] There is some contemporary standing for this claim: *Billboard* continued to refer to crossover hits as "a popularized form of r&b" as late as 1956, and in 1958, deejay Alan Freed declared that "Rock 'n' Roll is R&B and was called 'Race Music' because the Negroes originated the blues." By the late 1960s, journalist Michael Lydon described rock and roll as "blues with a beat," and even as Steve Chapple and Reebee Garofalo admit that "the differences between rock 'n' roll and r&b were real," they maintain that said differences "were motivated by the tastes of the music's new white audience."[9] Some white respondents had trouble distinguishing between these genre, as Bruce C. notes that "when they were playing, like, real rock and roll, it didn't sound to me like there was a lot of difference between that and R&B," while Larry R. points out that, when he was going to high school in Philadelphia, rock and roll music became the most popular genre, but "it was sort of a progression from rhythm and blues to rock and roll. . . . I didn't know any of this was Black music." Edgar S., who is Black, says that he immediately "saw rock and roll as more of a marketing term . . . because Chuck Berry and Little Richard have been playing that music, and I saw it as an acceptable term to white folk." He adds that "to me, that was just nomenclature [trying to become] more acceptable to a broader audience."[10] These impressions support Nick Tosches's argument that, by the late 1950s, the emergence of "whitefolk rock 'n' roll" merely meant that "what Black men had been doing since the mid-forties was now recast by a handful of young white boys who had spent their youth hearing those Black men, falling under the spell of their magic." This supposedly new music was dubbed "rock 'n' roll, the same phrase that Blacks had been using for more than a decade; but they let the white people who bought it think that they had invented the phrase, as they let them think they had invented the music."[11] This process led, Jack Hamilton argues, to rock and roll becoming a "whitened" genre by the 1960s, "in large part because of the stories people told themselves about it," which ultimately denied Black musicians recognition as progenitors of the genre.[12] Even though rock and roll was actually created by both Black and white musicians who combined pop, R&B, and country and western characteristics, among others, to form a genre that resonated with teenagers across racial lines, major-label efforts to dull the genre's rebellious edges and make it "respectable" in order to sell records to white audiences limited the music's ability to act as a template for interracial exchange.

These conceptions also reflect a profound unease with how Black musicians were exploited as rock and roll became associated with integration. Just as Black students in underfunded or desegregating schools often faced hardships that their white peers were protected from, Black artists were more financially and professionally vulnerable than white artists, even if they were more popular among teenage listeners. Frankie Lymon, for instance, enjoyed success among Black and white kids alike; Freed even noted how his young, mostly white listeners told him "We love Frankie Lymon and the Teenagers. . . . They're kids like ourselves and they understand us."[13] And yet, the limits of this interracial acceptance were made plain when Lymon appeared on Freed's nationally televised dance program, *The Big Beat*, in 1957, after he had decided to break from the group and embark on a solo career. Freed ensured that both Black and white dancers were allowed on the floor during filming, even though mixed-race couples were still forbidden from dancing with each other. Lymon eschewed this restriction, however, when he began dancing with a white girl during a break from his performance. ABC affiliates across the South almost immediately pulled the show off the air, and the network ultimately decided that the specter of social integration was just too risky. Freed lost his national broadcast, even though *The Big Beat* was picked up by the regional ABC affiliate in New York, where it ran until late 1959.[14] Despite many teenage fans professing not to care about segregation guidelines, Lymon's record sales began to dip, and he was never able to achieve the professional success he had reached at the outset of his career. Other Black artists met similar fates, as they were routinely unable to get the same representation or wages as their white counterparts, and were presented with fewer opportunities as major labels moved to sign more pop-inflected white artists.

The teenage aesthetics embraced by these Black artists could, however, help to challenge some of these racialized obstacles. Even as independent, Black-oriented label Specialty Records' official memoir states that "the early Frankie Avalon and Fabian records followed the Specialty formula, replete with sax section riffs, heavy eighth-note rhythm, and tunes with girls' names in the titles—the difference being that they were sung by those pretty boys in fluffy sweaters, pandering to middle-American pre-teen romantic fantasies," some Black artists like Lymon, Sam Cooke, and Chubby Checker became successful with interracial audiences using these exact formulas.[15] Marketing Black stars as wholesome teen idols, similar to the ways that their white "schlock rocker" counterparts were depicted, emphasized similarities among Black and white teenagers' experiences with school, dating, and rebellion, and reinforced the notion that teenage culture was nominally integrated. But their lived experiences often differed dramatically, even if they used the same label to define themselves, engaged in similar activities, and listened to the same records. Integrated schools and popular music alike were supposed to bring people from different races closer together, but in some ways they were pushed further apart as some racial injustices were ironically obscured by civil rights achievements.

ROCK AND ROLL AND TEENAGE CONSUMERISM

By 1957, even the term "crossover" had become seemingly obsolete, as the Pop and R&B charts looked more and more alike. These numbers reflected the fact that white and Black teenagers were increasingly listening to the same music, even if race was never completely eliminated as a signifier for each chart. Thirty-six records appeared on both charts, with only one racialized cover, Ricky Nelson's recording of Fats Domino's "I'm Walkin'," included in this number—and even then, Domino's original record also achieved crossover success. Records by 21 Black artists made the Pop chart, while 19 white artists made the R&B chart, an astonishing 217 percent increase over the previous year. Finally, 15 singles from seven different artists appeared on all three charts. Each of these artists was white, and all but one came from a country and western background, demonstrating the continuing cross-racial and demographic appeal of this supposedly guarded genre.[16] By 1958, the R&B-to-Pop crossover hits that had dominated most of the decade were accompanied more and more by white pop artists showing up on the R&B chart. Between January and July 1958, rock and roll icons like Elvis Presley, the Everly Brothers, and Jerry Lee Lewis continued to place on the R&B charts, but so did newer, more heavily commercialized "teen idol" acts like Ricky Nelson, Connie Francis, Danny and the Juniors, the Four Preps, and "David Seville," the *nom de plume* of Alvin and the Chipmunks creator Ross Bagdasarian.[17] At this point, the charts looked so similar that even *Billboard*'s managing editors decided to break down the divisions between them by creating the Hot 100 chart. The era of cover record dominance appeared to be over, and race seemed less likely than ever to dictate a record's popularity among different demographic groups.

The near-collapse of these separate marketing genres led to wider use of the term "rock and roll" to describe music that combined elements from pop, R&B, and country and western; appealed mostly to teenagers; and had a strong dance beat.[18] Even though Alan Freed (incorrectly) attested that he came up with the phrase in 1952, the term did not enter general parlance until the mid-1950s, and it continued to flummox those who did not understand its appeal. Any song recorded by Black artists and meant for wider white consumption could be categorized as such, exacerbating claims that the genre was nothing other than "whitefolk" R&B. A 1957 issue of *Pageant* magazine, for instance, could not seem able to accurately identify the genre. "Rock 'n' Roll has come a long way in a short time," the article read. "At this writing 46 of the top 60 tunes are 'Big Beat' numbers. More and more popular singers are turning to rhythm tunes."[19] It is unclear how the author determined which songs actually constituted rock and roll tunes when "Big Beat" was a term that had long been used to describe pop records, and "rhythm tunes" generally connoted R&B songs. If rock and roll consisted of both, then it is hardly surprising that so many of the most popular records could be classified as such. At the same time, Atlantic Records listed more traditional R&B artists Clyde McPhatter, Ruth Brown, Joe Turner, and Ivory Joe Hunter alongside newer sensations Ray Charles and the Drifters as the "six most prominent Rock & Roll artists" and noted that they "are basic inventory in this idiom and will be sales dynamite with the teenagers as long as there is any market for Rock & Roll at all."[20] In this case, Black artists with strong teenage followings were described as rock and roll acts, despite the fact that their musical styles varied widely, from the Drifters' doo-wop ditties, to Joe Turner's more traditional (and adult-oriented) R&B numbers. This confusion lasted well beyond the

1950s. Milt Gabler, for instance, struggled to explain these distinctions as late as 1974. "I had had rock and roll with Sammy Price—well, it goes back actually to the old blues—and Trixie Smith had that famous record, 'Rock Me Daddy with a Steady Roll,'" he said. "Al Freed started to call the music 'rock and roll'—I had . . . some blues singer [written in Albernie Jones, 'Hole in the Wall']—that had the phrase 'rock and roll' in the lyric, but it wasn't called that until Freed—Al was really the one who got everybody to call it rock and roll music. I believe he should get credit for that."[21] Despite the fact that Gabler, as vice president of Decca Records during the 1950s, was obviously aware of current trends and had an impressive knowledge of Black musical traditions, he still grappled with the concept of rock and roll, defining it mostly as Black music marketed to white audiences, even as he oversaw the release of many of the genre's early hits.

Despite the fact that it would take some time to determine the characteristics of the genre, rock and roll was identified as an integrated sound right from the start. The BMI official history describes Fats Domino, one of the first real rock and roll stars, as someone in whom "youngsters white and Black alike heard delicious echoes of the country and r&b fusion that was breaking loose all across the nation."[22] Here, Domino is described as both an R&B and a country singer; while he did, in fact, incorporate elements of both genres in his music, he was able to appeal to fans of both musics by allowing them to hear something familiar and something new at the same time. "Racial crossing proved highly unstable," Grace Elizabeth Hale argues. "Early rock and roll simultaneously assaulted the very idea that sounds could be segregated, that they could ever actually be Black or white."[23] Rock and roll, with its mixture of musics from different racial backgrounds, thus provided both white and Black teenagers with sounds that were combined by their favorite artists in new and exciting ways.

This form of marketing would become even more important as teenagers were increasingly recognized as a prominent consumer demographic. In the summer of 1959, for instance, *Life* magazine featured the profile of a supposedly average teenager, 17-year-old Suzie Slattery, daughter of a TV announcer in her Southern California hometown. The front page is graced with a picture of Slattery gleefully accepting a set of four matching suitcases from her father, a gift meant to complement her graduation present trip to Hawaii. "To some people the vision of a leggy adolescent happily squealing over the latest fancy present from Daddy is just another example of the way teen-agers are spoiled to death these days," the author notes. "But to a growing number of businessmen the picture spells out the profitable fact that the American teen-agers have emerged as a big-time consumer in the U.S. economy. They spend more and have more spent on them. And they have minds of their own about what they want." Indeed, the article, which is titled

"A New $10 Billion Power: the U.S. Teen-age Consumer," defines Slattery mostly in terms of her possessions, including a telephone—"white to match décor"—soda fountain, "frocks [and] furnishings for her room," and a remodeled bedroom, "which was recently done over for $1,300," in order to show readers the suddenly staggering power of teenage market consumption.[24]

Four months later, another teenage girl was profiled in *Ebony*, one of a small number of postwar general interest magazines targeted at Black audiences. Unlike Slattery, who was presented as an "average" teenage girl, Leslie Uggams, at 16 years old, was already a singing sensation after appearing on a host of televised musical and talent competition programs and signing a record deal with pop impresario Mitch Miller. The magazine's portrayal of Uggams, who is described as both a "teenage performer" and a regular high school student, is peppered with photographs of the singer on-set and on-stage, outfitted in glamorous dresses and enjoying a birthday party sponsored by Columbia Records, contrasted with pictures where she is seen "burning the midnight oil" at school, relaxing with her family, and hard at work in the recording studio. In many ways, the descriptions of Uggams's life bear many striking resemblances to Slattery's, particularly in the authors' assurances that both girls appreciate their material advantages, and that they are seriously planning for their futures. Slattery, the *Life* author is sure to mention, is not spoiled by her parents' "constant indulgence" and is preparing to attend college as a political science major later in the year. Uggams, meanwhile, "already earns through part-time singing more than many a veteran performer working full time," *Ebony*'s author proclaims, yet "the unspoiled girl is determined to let nothing interfere with her plans to enroll next year at New York University."[25] In each case, these girls' privileges are not celebrated for their own purposes, but as pathways to increasing independence and as preparation for even more promising futures.

Although these profiles of white and Black girls use similar language when describing their identities as teenagers, racialized distinctions among their experiences are not difficult to pinpoint. Slattery's access to material wealth, including indulging in biweekly beauty parlor visits and "wander[ing] with her mother through fashionable department stores," is meant to signal the importance of teen markets to *Life*'s readers, which the author points out are worth "a billion more than the total sales of GM."[26] Conversely, while the author of the Uggams profile is quick to note that she has earned over $100,000 performing over the past four years, one of the accompanying pictures is captioned: "Despite Leslie's excellent income, Uggams family lives in modest home." Another photograph reveals that her grandmother lives with her immediate family.[27] Pictures of their social lives also reveal the existence of racial fault lines. Both girls are described as popular, but Slattery's profile is awash in photographs where she is surrounded by friends or dancing with her boyfriend at a cookout around her parents' swimming pool, as her father serves up hot dogs and hamburgers while wearing a chef's hat, all presaging a happy marriage and leisurely social life.[28] Uggams is also photographed alongside friends, yet the settings—listening to records in her room or chatting in the school cafeteria—are far more mundane.[29] Within these publications, both of which boasted impressive readership numbers, being a teenager meant popularity among peers, indulging in teen fashion and culture, remaining humble amid previously unheard-of material wealth, and planning for the future. But the respective profiles of white and Black teenage girls also show how white adolescents had greater access to wealth and an ultimately more carefree lifestyle when compared to their Black counterparts, for whom hard work and education were inextricable from material comforts.

Some historians, notably Susan Cahn and Grace Palladino, have examined the cultures and social norms of both white and Black youth as emblematic of historic adolescence in the United States, and argued for the need to expand our descriptions of "teenager" in order to include experiences other than those of the white middle classes.[30] These similarities, however, do not negate the very real distinctions that shaped the ways that Black and white teenagers lived in and responded to a racially unjust world. But popular music during this period, particularly rock and roll, which quickly became a key signifier for late 1950s adolescence, offers a unique perspective on how both Black and white kids contributed to and identified with the role of "teenager." Matthew Delmont, for instance, has adroitly shown how white teenagers who grew up in Philadelphia during this period could enjoy the same music, dances, and television programs as their Black peers while remaining segregated from them, and even reinforcing unjust racist structures, while Brian Ward has explained how Black and white kids could have racially distinct responses to the same records.[31] "The conventions of middle-class youth were articulated as if they were everyone's," Wini Breines notes, even if Black and white teenagers "participated, if differentially, and were able to function as a group not only in market terms, but self-referentially as well."[32] The interracial characteristics of rock and roll would ultimately lead this new teenage culture to include tacit support for racial integration, even if the descriptors used in these records were largely reinforced by market decisions. Black and white adolescents could use this "teen-age" language about identity, school, romance, and rebellion to assume some of the role's characteristics, but racial injustice would continue to shape these meanings in fundamentally different ways.

Aside from its ability to encompass musical traits from both white and Black cultural backgrounds, rock and roll was defined by young audiences and the role it played in helping to shape the widening gap between adults and teenagers. John Sinclair asserted, "The rock 'n roll audience was mainly adolescent. It spoke in a language that adolescents could understand, and concerned itself with adolescent issues. Songs about romance, rebellion, dancing, and cars helped youngsters to break out of the rigid patterns of their parents."[33] Bill W. asserts that "the attraction" of rock and roll was that the artists "were closer to my age. It was no longer having to look at people who were 50 singing."[34] The genre so encompassed teenage culture that, as Larry R. explains, even though he was not a fan at first, he "had to get into rock and roll to some extent" at his high school "to fit in, to be invited to parties." At the time, Alan Freed stated that "Rock 'n' roll was discovered by the kids themselves. . . . They feel it's new; for their generation alone . . . when they encountered the powerful, affirmative jazz beat of rock 'n' roll, it was like making an amazing discovery."[35] Even though rock and roll music was shaped by racial traits that distinguished it from other genres, youth appeal was also integral. At first, producers assumed that only younger teenagers listened to this genre, which meant that the label was bestowed upon almost any song that was popular among high school kids. Not every single that sold well among young audiences could really be called "rock and roll," but the fact that most musicians and listeners were either teenagers or young adults ultimately helped to define rock and roll against other musical genres; more so, at times, than its actual musicological distinctions.

Many rock and roll groups, then, and the labels that represented them, used teenage idioms to appeal to young people across racial and class lines during this period. Record companies eagerly promoted "Hip Records" meant "Especially for the Teenagers," but, interestingly enough, the earliest musicians to actually use this term to brand themselves as young, hip, and fun were Black groups.[36] The first, and most successful, of these groups was Frankie Lymon and the Teenagers, whose epochal hit "Why Do Fools Fall In Love?" appeared on *Billboard*'s R&B chart in February of 1956, crossed over to the Pop chart the week after its release, and dominated both genres throughout spring and summer. Their follow-up record, "I Want You to Be My Girl," was also a crossover hit, appearing on both charts in May, and holding strong throughout most of the summer. Other Black teen groups also gained crossover attention by using this moniker. Later that year, the Teen Queens, comprised of sisters Betty and Rosie Collins, saw their only major hit, "Eddie, My Love," reach both the R&B and Pop charts throughout the spring months, while the Six Teens, a Los Angeles-based group of boys and girls ranging from ages 12 to 17, released two hit records, "A Casual Look" and "Teen Age Promise," in the summer after weeks of heavy promotion in *Billboard*'s pages.[37]

The use of this term in songs and group names was partly strategic. As cover records dwindled in popularity, some Black-oriented labels began recruiting artists and groups to record music specifically for white audiences.

Motown Records founder Berry Gordy decided to court "general [i.e. white] audiences" early on, partly because he was so disenchanted with record distribution systems that routinely discriminated against records by Black artists from independent labels that sold to mostly Black listeners.[38] Chuck Berry specifically wrote what Steve Chapple and Reebee Garofalo term "teen-directed" songs, maintaining traditional blues rhythms while changing the lyrics to reflect "the big beat, cars, and young love" that consumed teenage minds. "Why can't I do as Pat Boone does and play good music for the white people and sell as well there as I could in the neighborhood?" he asked.[39] Berry emerged as a particular favorite among teenagers of both races, both because of his background and his desire to profit from teenage consumer appeal. Although he grew up in segregated St. Louis, rock critic Michael Lydon explains that his father earned a good living as a contractor, and his neighborhood was marked by "small brick houses and tree-lined streets. His family were sober middle class, devout choir members at the toney Antioch Baptist Church." Although he went to an all-Black school, it still catered to the wealthiest African-American families in the city, and Berry remembered feeling ashamed of his middle-class status among fellow students who drove expensive cars and wore the latest fashions to class. Within a milieu that was so clearly marked by respectability politics, Berry grew up listening to white pop and country artists alongside blues and R&B musicians, all of which influenced his own songwriting and performances as he began his own musical career.[40]

Berry and his label, Chess Records, which signed him in 1955, plainly set out to court a young, white middle-class audience where he could earn the highest profits. Reebee Garofalo explains that this decision was in keeping with many civil rights goals during the 1950s. "The strategy of the early CRM was integrationist, and it was in this historical context that Berry pursued his career," he says. "While he never disowned his blackness, his goal was full acceptance in the white mainstream."[41] When Berry first met with the Chess brothers, for example, the label expressed interest in his remake of the blues and country standard, "Ida Red." The song, despite seemingly pleasant-sounding lyrics like "Light's in the parlor, fire's in the grate/Clock on the mantle says it's a' gettin' late/Curtains on the window, snowy white/ The parlor's pleasant on Sunday night," was generally interpreted as the story of a man in love with either a sex worker or a married woman who is nevertheless unfaithful to him.[42] Chess asked Berry to rejuvenate the song by writing new lyrics, and he was quick to oblige. The result was "Maybellene," a stunning mixture of old and new, Black and white, middle-class teenage propriety and working-class adult frivolity. Whereas the protagonist of "Ida Red" questions his promiscuous paramour in a seedy parlor, "Maybellene" evokes the "blues" of a young man whose girlfriend has cheated on him with a wealthier opponent. "As I was motivatin' over the hill/I saw Maybellene in a Coup de Ville/A Cadillac a-rollin' on the open road/Nothin' will outrun my V8 Ford."[43] All three characters in the song have cars, indicating that this story takes place in a modern, middle-class America where both Black and white teenagers come from fairly prosperous families. Listeners responded with overwhelming positivity across racial lines: "Maybellene" hit the top 5 on both the Pop and R&B charts in 1954, and even hit the Country and Western chart when covered by Marty Robbins the following year.[44]

Berry and his label knew where their profits were coming from and set about writing and recording songs that were explicitly directed toward middle-class teenagers. "Berry was writing for white adolescents out of a country bag, and his diction is unalloyed white middle America," Jerry Wexler asserted.[45] Cars and sex, the entwined teenage obsessions of the 1950s, as well as objection to authority, were explored in tones both bubbly and serious, leading white kids to believe that Berry's Blackness was fairly inconsequential. Indeed, Susan Cahn argues that "more than any other artist, Chuck Berry used his talents as a songwriter to recreate the experiences of teenage high school culture."[46] Although Berry ably courted a young white market, he never hid his racial identity, and, in fact, maintained the steady beat and blues basis in his songs. But he added lyrics that dealt with subjects all teens could identify with, like homework, crushes, and yearning for independence from parental authority. Black youth were included in his songs as well, not only in the acknowledgment that they were prone to enjoy the same activities and experience similar frustrations as their white counterparts, but in the structures of the songs, which echoed blues traditions. The similarities between Black and white adolescent desires in Berry's songs could chip away at the differences that both groups were taught existed between them. Alan Freed remarked in 1957 that "an old geezer, asked if he dug Chuck Berry could only tell you that all the berries he knew grew on vines. But you youngsters had heard Chuck sing *Maybellene* and *Too Much Monkey Business*. The words resounded over school lunchroom tables."[47] Here, Freed implied that age was more of a distinguishing factor among Berry's fans than race, as the voice of a Black man dominated high school hallways, some of which were undoubtedly segregated. White and Black teenagers did not have the same experiences in their day-to-day lives, but what Berry focused on were the similarities that did exist between these two groups.

Chuck Berry was not the only artist who set out to specifically appeal to teenagers during this period, thereby revealing cross-racial relatability and potential support for integration in the process. Mike Stoller and Jerry Leiber, two white songwriters from Baltimore, were hired by Atlantic Records in 1956 to write for young Black groups like the Coasters, the Platters, and the Drifters. "I was brought up in Baltimore in a mixed black-and-white neighborhood during World War II," Leiber noted. "I was exposed to a lot of country music and delta blues. . . . I decided I wanted to be a songwriter and naturally those sounds, the subject matter of blues material, jokes in the blues vein, the kind of backhanded social commentary in the blues were the elements of my work."[48] Many of their songs focused on the everyday experiences of Black teenagers. Leiber explained that, when he and Stoller were writing these songs, "we crawled inside the skins of our characters, we related to the guys in the singing groups, and the result was a cross-cultural phenomenon: a white kid's take on a black kid's take of white society. Color lines were blurred."[49] The writers, however, did not so much succeed at pretending to know what it was like to be Black in postwar American society as they did at showing that, despite deep, persistent racial inequality, Black and white teenagers shared many similarities. According to BMI's official history, "no one typified the new generation of songwriters more than the team of Jerry Leiber and Mike Stoller. Enthralled by black music, these white, middle-class teenagers wrote rhythm & blues songs that rang true for teenage listeners black and white alike."[50] Leiber and Stoller may not have been able to escape their white vantage points, even when writing songs for Black groups, but their words were nevertheless able to strike chords with teenagers across racial lines. "Even though we were white, we didn't play off a white sensibility," Leiber continued. "We identified with youth and rebellion and making mischief. We thumbed our nose at the adult world."[51] He may not have been wholly correct about so-called white sensibilities here, but it is interesting that he contrasted "white" with "youth." Youth was not necessarily signified as Black, but it did denote an identity that blurred the racial categories of white and Black and could possibly encompass both at the same time.

 The recording and marketing decisions that helped make gospel singer Sam Cooke a pop star in the late 1950s also show how teenage tastes included both white and Black performers, and how both major and independent Black-oriented labels aimed to appeal to this demographic group across racial lines. Cooke had sung with the Soul Stirrers for many years before he was tapped to record a solo album with Specialty Records. He had become somewhat disenchanted with his gospel performances, however, and so asked the label's owner, Art Rupe, if he could record more romanticized pop music instead. Rupe was intrigued, and plans were set for Cooke to record an album of pop standards, as well as a few original songs written by Cooke himself. This gamble paid off, as one of Cooke's original creations, "You Send Me," a dreamy romantic ballad with a distinctive urgency courtesy of the singer's gospel background hit number 1 on both the Pop and R&B charts in the fall of 1957.[52] The music hit a nerve with listeners, but Cooke's heartthrob looks also made him an immediate hit with teenage girls of both races. One promotional headshot from 1957 portrays his smiling visage resting gently on crossed arms, the same sweetly non-threatening pose favored by white teen idols.[53] The image was clearly meant to be hung on the bedroom walls of teenage girls across the country and to inspire scores of heart-encircled "Mrs. Cookes" on their notebooks. Cooke had always received his share of ecstatic female exhortations while performing with the Soul Stirrers, but Specialty's decision to market him as a teen pop idol to both white and Black teenage consumers, and in exactly the same way that a white musician would be portrayed, shows how the adolescent demographic had become somewhat cross-racial by this period.

Cooke's depiction as a potential love interest for both white and Black girls severely infringed on racial sexual norms, which aimed to prevent white girls from becoming romantically involved with Black boys. White Southern fear-mongering based on the image of a menacing "Black rapist" seems ridiculous when confronted with Cooke's non-threatening good looks and apparently gentle disposition, which girls from both racial backgrounds were quick to embrace. The decision to market Cooke as a teen pop idol was not only a business coup for Specialty, but it also reinforced support for small numbers of integrated rock and roll groups, especially the Del-Vikings, which an Alan Freed program described as consisting of "five handsome young men of the United States Air Force" without mentioning that three members were Black and two were white.[54] The group's biggest hit, "Come and Go With Me," was released in 1957, and hit both the Pop and R&B top 10 lists, to apparently little consternation. Some rock and roll fans of both races had seemingly begun to see white and Black rock and roll artists as equally representative of cultural expression among teenagers.

This form of integration had its limitations, though. By the late 1950s, white artists also started using the "Teen Age" label in their songs. "Teen Age Crush" by Tommy Sands, "A Teenager's Romance" by Ricky Nelson, "Teen Beat" by Sandy Nelson, and "A Teen Ager in Love" and "Lonely Teenager" by Dion and the Belmonts sold well among white adolescents but failed to cross over to the R&B chart, revealing how a descriptor that was initially used by Black kids had been more or less co-opted by young white artists. But young Black listeners continued to identify with this term. Chuck Berry's "Sweet Little Sixteen" crossed over from the Hot R&B to the Hot 100 chart in early 1958, while Black kids enjoyed the music of white teen idols like Nelson, Connie Francis, and Mark Dinning enough to send their respective singles to the R&B top 10 in 1957, and "Short Shorts" by the Royal Teens, a white novelty pop group, spent eight weeks each on the Pop and R&B charts in the spring of 1958. Teenage culture could look tacitly interracial in certain cases, like Freed's rock and roll shows featuring what *Billboard* columnist June Bundy described as "bright, good looking youngsters for the most part, and an integrated group."[55] This was music for a new generation that had supposedly learned to view racial barriers with suspicion, and which allowed young listeners a glimpse of what a happily integrated world might look like. "As regional politicians gathered their forces for legal battles and a strategy of 'massive resistance,' teenagers appeared on the surface to be moving in the opposite direction," Susan Cahn explains. "They had created an autonomous popular culture in which the lines of race were becoming more and more blurred as black and white performers shared stages and songs, the airwaves integrated black and white music, and adolescents embraced the music and dance of rock 'n' roll regardless of race."[56] Victor F., who is white and grew up in suburban New York, sums up this idea fairly succinctly: "The music was white and it was Black, the radio people were white and Black."[57] But even though the language of the "teen-ager" was used to sell records to young listeners across racial lines, the persistence of racial injustice meant that white and Black kids would interpret these songs in very different ways, especially as some of them would find themselves on the front lines of the movement to desegregate public schools.

SCHOOL DESEGREGATION MOVEMENTS AND THE BROWN RULING

Movements to desegregate public schools in the United States began as early as the mid-nineteenth century. Although most Black children received little to no formal schooling in the decades prior to the Civil War, many communities emphasized that education was the pathway to social status and economic stability, as well as increased self-sufficiency. Quality schools were therefore viewed as vital to segregated Black neighborhoods, even though most students received fewer years of instruction than their white peers and were overwhelmingly confined to a handful of poorly funded schools. Black communities poured donated resources into establishing private schools to offset this inequity, but Black children remained at a disadvantage, prompting intra-community disagreements over whether to fight for racially integrated classrooms or for stronger, better-funded segregated schools. Boston became the first city in the country to ban segregated public schools in 1855, but this bill was only passed after a failed lawsuit against the school board inspired the city's Black population to wage a five-year protest and boycott of separate schools. Activists in other Northern states were able to pressure some districts to pass legislation outlawing separate schools after maintaining two systems became too expensive. Still, integration supporters like George T. Downing in Providence, Rhode Island, and Fannie Richards in Detroit were able to garner strong networks of support that ultimately made it difficult for districts to continue operating separate school systems, even if legislation outlawing segregation remained vulnerable to continued white backlash.[58]

In the South, recently freed people were quick to support new schools implemented and organized by the Freedman's Bureau and were therefore devastated when most closed after federal support was removed. As in Northern cities, Southern Black communities sometimes established their own private schools, but most would come to rely on the poorly funded and segregated public institutions established under state Jim Crow laws in the early 1900s. In Atlanta, for example, Jay Driskell explains that, because of stricter legal codes and the pervasive fear of state-enforced violence, Black residents fought for better separate schools, even going so far as to organize the city's small number of voters in order to prevent passage of a 1919 bond issue unless a new Black high school was constructed, rather than trying to challenge segregation outright.[59] This focus on improved schools that remained segregated by law remained dangerous in regions where any form of advancement rendered Black residents susceptible to economic sanctions and violence, so demands for integrated schools would have been unimaginable no matter which ideologies protestors may have preferred. Many residents of Northern cities, however, also chose to fight for improved separate schools, even in areas where desegregation legislation was considered politically viable. Lawrence Grossman and David Gerber have both shown how Black residents in Rhode Island and Ohio, respectively, would not necessarily support school desegregation policies if they did not think that their communities would benefit. Most families simply wanted their children to receive the best education possible and to see their tax dollars supporting institutions that they could actually use. Supporters of separate schools often argued in favor of community control of Black institutions, while teachers rightly worried about getting fired if schools were desegregated. Integrationists, however, feared that any focus on skin color would diminish their own citizenship rights and their children's ability to be treated as equals within mainstream society. Ultimately, most parents and community members gave their support to whichever option seemed most likely to succeed in their area, revealing a more pragmatic component to supposedly ideological concerns.[60]

Debates over whether public schools should be forced to accept Black Americans extended into the twentieth century, as the NAACP began strategically filing suits at school boards across the country. However, "the NAACP was never committed to destroying school segregation because it was central to the system of racial subordination," Mark Tushnet explains. "Rather, school segregation was just one of many targets, and it became an increasingly attractive one," especially since concerns over educational issues united middle-class reformers and supporters of Black nationalism. But organizers, lawyers, community members, and parents were divided on how to achieve justice and equality for Black students. In the early part of the century, the organization mostly focused on ensuring that separate Black schools received equitable funding and that their physical facilities were roughly approximate to those in white schools. These campaigns worked within Southern segregationist frameworks and were less likely to invite white retaliation, but they also created jobs for Black teachers and principals and allowed them some degree of control over what students learned. Improving Black schools could also strengthen community ties, as children were able to learn and socialize without fear of white oversight, and to feel pride in their heritage. Indeed, most parents initially came to their local branches with potential lawsuits because they were concerned that their children's schools were underfunded or that teachers were paid less than their white counterparts in the same districts, not because they cared about desegregated classrooms. These concerns led the NAACP to focus its efforts on "equalization" suits that fought for equal salaries and physical facilities in segregated schools rather than abolishing segregation altogether, which did not seem feasible and had the potential to drain the organization's resources and political goodwill.[61]

Throughout the 1920s and 1930s, however, some members and lawyers began to speculate that consistent pressure to equalize would force cash-strapped school districts to desegregate simply because they lacked the financial support for two separate but equal educational systems.[62] Co-founder W. E. B. Du Bois disagreed with this mission, proclaiming in a 1934 *Crisis* editorial that segregation did not necessarily equate with racial discrimination, and advocating, Tushnet says, for Black people to "organize themselves and insist that public policy be non-discriminatory; but that did not entail the eradication of the color line for blacks and their community." He stressed that desegregation might actually be harmful for Black people, pointing to parents in Northern cities who are forced to send their kids to integrated schools where they are bullied by white classmates and overlooked by white teachers as examples.[63] But a growing contingent of staff members and lawyers who worked for the national branch disagreed with this logic. Thurgood Marshall, founder and director of the organization's Legal Defense and Educational Fund (and future United States Supreme Court Justice), disagreed, arguing that a so-called direct attack on segregated schools would include any concerns addressed in equalization suits, while simultaneously putting forth a clear, all-encompassing message that segregation was intolerable and unconstitutional. He feared, in fact, that continuing to wage equalization suits would reinforce the misconception that segregation in public life was acceptable in any way.[64]

Between 1945 and 1950, the latter strategy would prove triumphant. Tushnet explains that this shift is partially due to Marshall's fastidious work as both an attorney and organizer, as he carefully laid the foundations for

Supreme Court school desegregation cases that would actually have a chance of winning. At the same time, broader national and international political forces combined with organizational efforts to create a climate that allowed for more direct attacks on school segregation rather than piecemeal suits against particular school districts. President Harry Truman's postwar administration, first of all, seemed cautiously amenable to racial justice concerns. These concerns were also shared by some white Americans, who were awakened to these antidemocratic practices after fighting fascism during World War II. A renewed focus on the dignity of the individual and the foundational importance of equal citizenship meant that new strategies challenging segregation might stand a chance in the court of public opinion. Tushnet explains that NAACP lawyers began relying on sociological arguments that "separate schools induced a sense of superiority in whites and a sense of inferiority in blacks" which meant that "no matter what a state did to provide facilities that were equal in monetary or physical terms, an unconstitutional inequality in intangibles would remain."[65] This messaging was clearer, more forceful, and held solid appeal for whites in positions of power who were concerned about the state of their own democratic government, and how any inconsistencies might be used to Soviet advantage. Finally, Marshall and his supporters were urged to continue this path after the Supreme Court ruled that law schools in Oklahoma and Texas had to either admit qualified Black students or provide adequate separate facilities.[66] Although lawyers for these cases argued for desegregation because of an absence of alternatives for Black students, Marshall believed that the Court's readiness to support integration in these cases would extend to elementary and secondary schools, even in cases where similar facilities were available. By 1948, the NAACP's board of directors voted not to "participate in any case which has as its direct purpose the establishment of segregated public facilities," and by July 1950, crafted a resolution stating that cases would solely fight for "education on a non-segregated basis, and that no relief other than that will be acceptable."[67]

But even as the NAACP chose to focus on integration, Black Americans who lived in segregated areas still questioned whether this strategy would benefit their families. Most plaintiffs originally contacted their local branches because of equalization concerns and had to be convinced to file suits that directly challenged segregation in schools. Although the number of these suits increased between 1948 and 1951, many families continued to voice concerns that their children would face white backlash within desegregated schools, that teachers would not be invested in their education, and that they would lose the cultural and social benefits of going to an all-Black school. The NACCP had to cajole teachers and principals into supporting these suits as well, since white parents who otherwise supported integrated classrooms would still be averse to having their own children taught by Black educators, leading to widespread job loss. The sociological arguments advocated by the organization's mostly middle-class and New York-based lawyers may have appealed to potential white supporters who were ideologically concerned with supporting democratic rights, but they did not necessarily convince Black parents and educators that children would benefit by attending integrated schools. Although Tushnet argues that "NAACP lawyers simply could not win their lawsuits unless they represented the majority of the black community," many people's concerns were overwhelmed by an ideological argument meant to garner broader appeal.[68]

This tension became apparent by the time the NAACP filed the suit that would ultimately render racial segregation in public schools illegal. Black teachers and principals continued to voice their opposition to this strategy, but the national organization worked throughout the late 1940s to coordinate suits in four different states into one challenge against school segregation at the federal level. Two suits lost, and one, in Delaware, won "desegregation rather than equalization" at the state level. The case that the NAACP would bring to the Supreme Court, then, would be centered in Kansas, an upper-South state where, in many cases, "black schools [were] already reasonably equal to white," and where local lawsuits and boycotts had already been waged against many local school districts. One of these lawsuits was initiated in the Kansas City suburb of South Park by a white woman named Esther Brown, who was disturbed by the conditions of the segregated school in her neighborhood. After her arguments for improved facilities were ignored by the school board, she contacted the local NAACP branch about a possible desegregation suit. Branches in Wichita and Topeka were also consolidating cases from parents who were concerned about either the physical state of segregated schools in their areas or their locations. Oliver Brown, whose name would be listed first among 33 others, had initially approached his local branch because his six-year-old daughter, Linda, was forced to go to an all-Black school over 20 blocks away from their home, and he did not want her walking such a long distance when the family lived within the vicinity of a white school. When the NAACP brought these combined cases to the Supreme Court for review in November, 1951, however, the legal team led by Marshall decided to use the sociological argument to convince the Court that segregated schools fostered inferiority complexes among Black children, thus limiting their abilities to fully take advantage of economic opportunities. When the *Brown v. The Board of Education of Topeka* ruling was issued on May 17, 1954, Chief Justice Earl Warren's opinion that "the policy of separating the races is usually interpreted as denoting the inferiority of the negro group" and that "a sense of inferiority affects the motivation of a child to learn" displays how effective this argument was among liberal whites, who viewed segregation as intrinsically harmful to Black children's citizenship rights. Even though

Brown and the other parents did not decide to sue because they felt that their children's self-esteem was damaged, Marshall and his colleagues decided that, as Tushnet explains, "an equalization strategy would not have been compatible with the idea of equality that was successfully invoked in *Brown*." A strategy that would appeal to white liberal concerns about basic equality and citizenship rights in the early years of the Cold War, he says, would rely on "a vision of American society founded on competitive individualism," which "almost by definition denies the importance of collective action for mutual aid." This focus obscured some of the real concerns Black parents and educators had expressed for decades, but the Court's decision was simultaneously viewed as a true victory, and as a sign that the federal government would support some degree of civil rights action.[69]

After the *Brown* ruling, the NAACP and other civil rights organizations continued to focus on the legal desegregation of schools and public places not to ensure broad-based racial justice, but because it seemed like a winning plan. The Leadership Conference on Civil Rights, an umbrella group founded by the leaders of several civil rights groups and unions devoted to abolishing discrimination through legal means, listed school desegregation as the first point in its 1956 Civil Rights Plank, which was to be submitted to both the Republican and Democratic Conventions. "Racial segregation imposed by law is contrary to the principles on which democratic government is based," the platform read, urging each party to take on the task of "obtaining implementation of [the *Brown* decision] by the quickest possible elimination of all forms of state-imposed segregation."[70] Since these policies violated components of the Fourteenth Amendment, which supposedly ensured "equal protection under the law" for all American citizens, they were framed as violations of existing laws rather than requiring new ones in order to be eradicated. Amid Cold War concerns of communist infiltration, a focus on integration helped to protect civil rights activists from harassment by creating distance from labor and socialist movements.[71] These strategies could not completely prevent massive resistance from whites who lived in Southern districts that might be affected by this ruling, though. By 1956, 101 Congress members signed a "Southern Manifesto," describing the *Brown* ruling as an egregious form of federal overreach, and proclaiming that their states would not adhere to the decision. Some school districts in Southern states interpreted the Court's language that desegregation should be carried out "with all deliberate speed" to mean that they could mostly ignore the ruling while citing finances, transportation, recalcitrant parents, and a lack of suitable Black students as obstacles, while others chose to close for the year rather than adhere to the federal order.

School closures often backfired, however, as many white parents realized that they would prefer to accept the ruling and allow students to go back to school rather than making a stand and denying them their education, no matter how opposed they might be to racial integration. The father of a white student at Sturgis High School in Sturgis, Kentucky, for instance, announced that "my daughter is not going to lose her education because of some n*****," while a mother who had previously distributed White Citizens Council pamphlets urging parents to keep their children from attending integrated schools in her hometown of Louisville later changed her mind. "I don't like it, and no one I know likes it, but what can we do about it?" she asked. "I've just told my youngsters to stay as far away from them as possible." She had no regrets about her choice, admitting, "Actually it worked out pretty well. There wasn't any trouble, and as long as none of those n***** boys tries anything with the white girls, I don't suppose there will be any." Bob R., whose sister attended Central High School in Little Rock, remembers that "my parents' viewpoint was that the black students had a nice high school to go to (Horace Mann was the black high school and was only a couple of years old) so why should they go to the 'white' school?" But even though they voted for segregationist governor Orval Faubus in 1958, he explains, "they did not agree with Faubus closing the public high schools here for the 1958-59 school year in an attempt to avoid integration. I don't think they ever voted for him." Ultimately, a 1957 *New York Times* series that examined the effects of school desegregation in three Southern states similarly found that "white parents, faced with a situation they know is backed by the force of law, have found themselves in a position where integration is the least of the evils they can choose."[72]

This pronouncement was a bit sanguine given the alternative measures taken by politicians, educators, and parents, to ensure the perpetuation of white supremacist schooling in the South. White families who could afford to do so rushed to send their children to private schools, provoking anger among poorer white parents. Other school boards abided by the letter of the law, approving only a few Black students (usually those who were at the top of their classes) for admittance to previously all-white schools. A few schools, usually located in border states, made active attempts to create integrated schools that would help eradicate racial prejudice among their students. Whatever the outcome, one constant remained: the federal government almost always refused to intervene or to create any kind of standard guidelines to ensure that school boards would desegregate in a systematic manner or by a certain date. Unless violence broke out, or a high-profile demagogue publicly opposed the federal government and urged others to do so, as in the cases of Central High School or at the University of Alabama, the process of desegregation, and whether or not it would be pursued, was largely left up to individual school boards. When violence did break out, however, media coverage often presented these cases as morality plays, where respectable Black students had to battle overtly hateful white vitriol in order to attend school. In Little Rock, the school board cherry-picked nine high-achieving Black students to "integrate" a school with a population of almost 2,000 white students. Even though the school board clearly meant to carry out the ruling by only allowing token numbers of Black kids to attend otherwise all-white classes, Governor Faubus made a stand against even this capitulation, calling in the National Guard to prevent them from entering the building. This act of disobedience infuriated President Dwight Eisenhower enough to send in federal troops to protect the frightened Black children from the mobs of angry whites who had gathered to hurl stones and racial epithets. A photo by journalist Will Counts that captured the juxtaposition between 14-year-old Elizabeth Eckford's stoic expression as she walked into the school, and the angry, contorted face of white student Hazel Bryan was picked up by newspapers around the world, convincing many outside the South that school segregation could only be defended by the hateful. This image was safeguarded further with *Cooper v. Aaron* decision, which denied Faubus the right to close public schools rather than desegregate.

Two years later, Autherine Lucy's attempt to attend the University of Alabama was met with similar uproar. After she filed a suit with her local NAACP branch in 1956 for being denied entry to the library sciences program because of her race, the Supreme Court ordered her to be admitted since there was no separate program for Black students in the area. Even though photographic and video footage was not as ample as it was in Little Rock, people across the country were shocked by the violent harassment she received while simply trying to attend classes. After university trustees voted to suspend her "for her own safety," even though none of her attackers were arrested by order of Governor James Folsom, the NAACP tried to sue the university again, to no avail. Lucy was expelled for "conspiracy" and left Alabama in a state of exhaustion. Robert Caro argues that, although "some Alabama whites crowed that the riot had 'worked,'" that media coverage of her story "had stirred, and solidified, deep emotions," for "an entire nation had been reading about the injustice, had seen it all, stark and clear. Into the hearts of those willing to have their hearts opened had been brought home, with new vividness, the cruelty and inhumanity with which Black Americans were treated in the South."[73] Marshall's strategy seems to have succeeded in convincing liberal whites to support school integration as a democratic right. These cases represented landmark efforts in the fight for school desegregation, and activists often framed them as righteous struggles to show that Blacks were not inferior to whites. While this argument is undeniably true, it obscures the fact that, in each case, organizers, students, and parents were not necessarily looking to occupy the same spaces as whites; instead, they were fighting to receive proper educational opportunities, an aim that was often obscured by white Americans' focus on integration as an ultimate goal.

ON THE FRONT LINES IN DESEGREGATED CLASSROOMS

By the mid-1950s, an adolescence spent largely within the walls of high school surrounded by peers had become standard for white kids, despite being a relatively new historical phenomenon. Although higher education had traditionally been reserved for the elite, New Deal educational funding provided such widespread access that, by the 1950s, over 90 percent of youth between the ages of 14 and 17 would be enrolled in high school and roughly half of them would go on to graduate with a diploma.[74] But these NAACP battles for equal education, along with increased prosperity among the African-American middle classes, meant that more and more Black kids would be attending high school as well. Media outlets also encouraged Black kids to stay in school; *Ebony* clearly wanted readers to know how diligently Leslie Uggams approached her studies, while *Jet* ran a story featuring prominent Black teenage stars who "urge[d] their fans to remain in school and get an education," detailing their many reasons for remaining in high school themselves.[75] Even though the numbers continued to reveal inequitable educational opportunities, a 23-point difference between the two racial groups that persisted before World War II had decreased to merely 7 points by the postwar period.[76]

But the lack of educational opportunities in underfunded segregated schools that prompted the NAACP to file lawsuits inspired some Black kids to "desegregate" white schools, even if they did not necessarily wish to abandon the security of their old schools. Most white schools had better resources and more opportunities for college scholarships, prompting many Black kids to make the difficult decision to apply for admission. Joan Drake, for instance, wanted to attend Central High School because it "would mean an opportunity to obtain a better education. She feels she should not be denied these advantages because of her race."[77] Dolores Ann Poindexter, who applied to the school twice, felt "confident she can successfully compete with anyone at Central High, a school which offers more courses in speech and drama than Horace Mann," while Larry Collins wanted to attend because "it has more to offer and I want to be a Civil Engineer. They will train me at Central High." Gloria Ray, who gained admission to Central, said that she preferred to enroll because "I am a major in theoretical physics. It's my understanding they do not have a good program in physics at Horace Mann."[78] Indeed, most members of the so-called Little Rock Nine, who first integrated the school amid massive white resistance, cited the importance of educational opportunities that they could not get at their underfunded Black schools as the main reason they decided to transfer. In her memoir, *Warriors Don't Cry*, for instance, Melba Pattillo Beale recalls a childhood spent dreaming about a world where she could take advantage of the opportunities that awaited students who attended the gleaming, modern, well-funded white high school, while Ernest Green forced himself to keep attending because he felt the school's higher academic standards could help him get into a better university. The chance to prove that they were just as worthy as their white peers also encouraged some Black teens to make the difficult decision to transfer to majority-white schools; academic achievement, while prized among white families like Suzie Slattery's, could challenge racial stereotypes of Black teens as inferior students and workers, and provide them with the professional and financial opportunities that were historically denied to most African Americans. Carol Swann, who was chosen as one of only two 12-year-old girls to "integrate" Chandler Junior High in Richmond, Virginia, remembers how "little old black ladies—total strangers—would come up to me on the street and say, 'We're counting on you to show them that we're smart, that we're human.'"[79] Scott F.'s recollections were similar, even though he attended a private school in New Jersey, where Jim Crow laws did not exist, yet racial housing and economic divisions meant that he was one of the only Black students among an otherwise white majority. "One of the earliest things that I remember is my mom and my grandmother telling me and instilling in me is the fact that as a young Black man you have to be better than everybody else at what you do," he says. "Good isn't enough. You have to concentrate on being great. . . . They also made it clear that you had to work hard, that nothing was going to be given to you."[80]

Black teenagers and their parents were therefore often ambivalent about desegregating schools, even when they supported Black students' rights to attend these institutions. Respondents who grew up in the South often recall feeling comfortable in all-Black institutions, even though they were segregated by law, stressing the importance of receiving support and motivation from Black teachers and principals. Edgar S., who attended two segregated schools in Tennessee, explains how even though he and his classmates were denied new schoolbooks and other material resources that his white contemporaries had access to, "one of the things we had going for us were our teachers. We had some excellent teachers. They convinced us that we could learn, that the problem was not with us, the problem was with the system. So we took those old raggedy books and we learned from those, and we learned the fundamentals, and we learned how to appreciate learning." When he graduated, he says, "I felt as if I was capable of learning." Joseph J. explains how he was unable to attend the school that was closest to his home in New Orleans since it was a white school, and instead had to walk a mile to get to class. And yet, "it was great, it had some of the best teachers in the world." He says that his teachers' "focus was preparing us to go out into the world. . . . You learned, and the theory was, and we were told this, you're going to go into a world that is predominantly white, and you need to understand what this is."[81] Black parents were also often concerned that their cultural traditions would be lost if their children attended majority-white schools and that they would lose Black teachers and educators as role models.[82] Most Black adults and teenagers still supported school desegregation movements—a 1956 poll, for instance, found that Blacks "voted 90 per cent in favor of integration . . . no matter where [they] lived, or how much income or education they had."[83] After all, segregation had been enshrined in law in order to protect white supremacy, even if many Black Americans questioned just how much they would benefit once the barriers of Jim Crow were removed. But their concerns about how this process would be implemented, and how their own lives and the lives of their children would be affected, were often obscured by movement rhetoric promoting educational equality.

These concerns are echoed in the ambivalent responses from Black respondents regarding their thoughts on school desegregation. In the South, students could face very real physical danger by attempting to desegregate, and many were loath to leave the community institutions where they felt safe and supported. Joseph J. says that even though he was aware of these campaigns while growing up, he felt that "the likelihood of that changing your life was very remote. And so the focus [in school] was on making sure you got what you needed using what you had." Edgar S. was concerned that "[when] we integrated into the white schools . . . we didn't take the Black teachers. And we didn't take much of the Black community. It was forced. People didn't really want you there." Black kids who grew up outside of the South shared some of these concerns, even if many of them attended schools that were not strictly segregated themselves. Tyrone W., who grew up in Detroit, says that he "was opposed" to integration movements "since the issue of underfunding urban schools" was overlooked in favor of allowing a few Black students into white classrooms. Cheryl J. concurs, noting that "when Black people were fighting for integration, they were fighting because they wanted better schools, they wanted better housing, they wanted better lives." She further notes that even though "integration happened" and she herself attended an integrated school, "things divided in another kind of way. Schools started to be built. Little bullshit schools were built for African-American kids [while] wonderful learning institutions were built for white children." Najee M. made white friends at his school in New York, yet "didn't visit their homes, because I was never invited (although I invited them to where I lived) and because as a Black male you just didn't go to certain places; the geographic racial boundaries were clear." Rhonda E., who grew up in Detroit, does not recall these types of concerns, since "I just thought schools [in the city] were already integrated" and that "there were some Detroit Public Schools that were—had more whites than Blacks and vice-versa. But it wasn't because of any laws, it was just because of the make-up of the neighborhood at the time."[84] These responses differ widely based on region and on each respondent's personal experiences within segregated or integrated schools. And yet each reveals skepticism about the degree that desegregated schools would actually benefit Black students and communities, and concern that children and teachers would be forced to bear the brunt of this transition. Establishing integrated communities might be a nice thought, but it would not necessarily be created within desegregated classrooms, nor would it guarantee economic advancement and safety for Black students and their families.

Indeed, many kids who chose to desegregate white schools faced painful challenges, even if mass media outlets portrayed their stories as evidence of democracy in action. The torment that many white Southern kids unleashed on incoming Black students could have been taken straight from the playbooks of adult massive resisters. At Clinton High School in Clinton, Tennessee, where a scant 12 Black kids enrolled alongside 800 white students in the fall of 1956, the *New York Times* reported that "forty white students carried out the pestering of the Negro pupils." For a few days, Black students "boycotted the classrooms because of 'insults' and 'mean incidents' they were subjected to by some of the white students. These included name-calling, jostling in corridors and pouring ink over a Negro girl's books." The article notes, however, that "the school principal, D.J. Brittain Jr., had warned that white students would be expelled if they continued to molest the Negro children in the building," and the kids returned to their educations.[85] When Carlotta Walls was asked how she "enjoyed" her school year at Central High School, she responded, "how could I enjoy it with people throwing rocks at me. I would rather not think about it."[86] Carol Swann recalled a garden variety of abuse, including name-calling, spitting, tripping, and having white students flatten her tires, spray her with ink, or knock the books out of her arms. "Lunch was always very messy because they would throw all kinds of things," she said. "Afterward you frequently looked like you had swum through your lunch. If any adults saw it, they did nothing. The teachers didn't intervene. They didn't want us there." Furthermore, "gym was particularly horrible because we had to do sit-ups. The other students saw us as contaminate; no one wanted to hold down our feet or have any kind of physical contact." Afterward, "everyone was trying to get through a relatively narrow opening in the locker room at the same time. There was a lot of pushing and shoving. If someone accidentally touched Gloria [the other Black student at the school] or me, they'd start screaming, 'Help, help!' Then their friends would rush up and brush them off."[87] Swann persisted, however, as she, like many other Black students who helped integrate Southern schools, saw her experience as a chance for both individual and collective advancement.

These students' experiences revealed that, as many parents had feared, white teachers could also be a source of bullying and neglect. The *Times*, for instance, reported how "When a Negro girl was elected to the student council, one principal denied her the honor because of a 'rule' (invented by the principal) that new girls had to 'prove' themselves for two years.... In another school a teacher lining up her children for play exclaimed in the presence of other classes as well; 'Oh, these colored children! They're so slow, just like the colored people working for you at home.'"[88] Walter Blackwell recalled how he and other Black students at his high school in Virginia were upset "because [school administrators] were keeping the beauty contest lily-white; the queen had to be blue-eyed and blonde. And they couldn't get to be cheerleaders and so forth, and they were real angry about the whole bit." When both Black and white students got together to discuss the problem, however, they were met with obstacles. "The teachers' attitudes were problems," he asserted. This issue also plagued Black students who attended mixed-race schools in cities outside the South. "The kids that we encountered at the school were fine," Cheryl J. says of her Detroit-area school. "It was the teachers that had the negative, anti-, we-don't-want-you-here attitude . . . that was my first encounter with adverse feelings toward my skin color." Carol A., who also lived in Detroit, went to a mixed-race Catholic school where most of her classmates were white. She recalls how "there was racism in just little things. Like there was never a Black girl who crowned the Mother Mary on the beginning of May, for instance. And I was like, I wonder why. Or I remember really distinctly getting into trouble, you know, like talking or something in a class, and it was always that I would be the one who would be more disciplined than my white playmates."[89] The feeling of support and community that often existed in segregated Black schools was missing in a lot of these instances, even if respondents remember other aspects of school and friendships with fondness.

As hurtful as racist bullying could be, students at mixed-race schools also remember wrestling with feeling like they did not belong or out of place when white students ignored them. "There were a couple of white students who tried to be friendly, but they put themselves at risk," Carol Swann asserts. "When I was in junior high, there was one girl who was friendly when no one was around. But if she was talking with me and someone came down the hall, she would pretend she didn't know me." Even though Scott F. did befriend white classmates at his New Jersey private school, he cautions that "I never got to hang out with them because we weren't friends like that. Whereas, you know, my friends at home [in a Black neighborhood], we played basketball together, we played marbles together, we did all the things kids do together. I only saw my friends from school at school." Even though he does not recall being treated poorly at this school, and indeed, has positive memories of his time there, racial divisions continued to limit the extent of his social connections, ultimately creating a sense of discomfort. "I think because of the environment, one, with it being a private school, and two, with me being one of few Black students in the school, it didn't feel like a comfortable thing to have happen or a relatable thing for other kids in the class," he says.[90]

The challenges that Black students had to face at both desegregating and segregated schools reveal the fault lines of civil rights politics within classrooms across the country. And yet even though 1950s high school students are almost invariably presented as white in popular memory, Black students, who were at the forefront of school desegregation battles, were consistently depicted as teenagers in the press, adding a previously unidentified layer of political activism to this identity. The *New York Times* reporter Gertrude Samuels described some of the experiences of new Black students at a previously all-white school in Baltimore: "Several Negroes are members of the football and lacrosse teams," she wrote. "Most Negro students have been coached by their parents to ignore the name-calling and worse, to 'scratch it out like a wrong problem.' They are well aware of their role as pioneers." At another high school, where only 10 Black kids attended in a population of 1,900, "Negroes . . . mingle with other boys in sports, campus and social activities. They come with their dates to the monthly school dances."[91] And in one previously all-white school, the sixth-grade class elected a Black student as class president "because he was the smartest of us."[92] In each case, Black kids are described as partaking in high school activities just like their white peers, sometimes in spite of racist backlash, sometimes becoming friends with other students. These reports point out just how politicized regular school experiences like joining a sports team, going to a dance, or running a student president campaign became when they were held within desegregated schools. As one tenth-grade girl wrote in response to a 1956 poll on teenage experiences, "I am a Negro. I live in a white community and attend a white school. Many's the time when I think I've been graded unfairly but for the average teenager I don't have too many problems."[93]

Other Black respondents recall making white friends at school with little fuss, although this was a more common experience in Northern urban areas. Cheryl J. recalls that her school in Detroit "was a very close community. We spent the night at each other's houses. We did things together, Girl Scouts, you know, no big deal to have one of my white classmates spend the night with me." Miche B., who also grew up in Detroit, points out that she "just had all kinds of friends. I wasn't looking at anything for color. Even though the majority of the folks that I dealt with were Black people. But I didn't have a problem with anyone." White respondents who attended mixed-race schools echo her somewhat race-neutral sentiments when discussing their interracial friendships, though they tend to focus more on the fact that they failed to even notice racial differences, even if most attended majority-white schools. "We just knew each other as classmates," says Ron R., who started hanging out with both Black and white teammates when he started playing sports at his Indiana school. "We didn't pay any particular attention to the fact that some [had] a different skin color. So it wasn't something that we were forced to be conscious of as a distinction." John H. remembers having a friend named Bob when he was in the eighth grade at his Tucson school. One day, his teachers "handed out what we called a dream sheet, which was what classes you want to take when you enter the ninth grade," he recalls. "And in those days, they asked you for all of your personal information: Where does your dad work? What was your race? All that sort of thing." As he walked past Bob's desk, "I looked at his paper just out of curiosity, just to see what he had written down, and I noticed under race he had written 'Negro.' That's the first time in those years that it had ever occurred to me that he was any different than I was."[94] In some cases both Black and white respondents could claim that race was unimportant when it came to making friends at school, even if white respondents are more likely to emphasize how little they thought about race in the first place.

Other white respondents were more aware of racial differences among their friend groups, although in these cases respectability politics often played a role in the types of people they interacted with. Rose W., for instance, states that even though "there was a lot of not-racial-mixing" in her otherwise integrated New York schools, that two of her best friends from grade school were Black and that "we slept over at each other's houses. . . . We knew their famil[ies]. It was a very comfortable interaction." She points out that both girls came from wealthier, professional families, prompting one to move "off to better things," while the other stopped talking to her in high school when "the Black girls told her you cannot have white friends." In this case, the division worked against her, partially because Rose's school had a more equitable mix of Black and ethnic white students, but also perhaps because of a class disparity since she describes her own family as working class. Victor F. does not recall any Black kids living in his own neighborhood in New York, but he did socialize in some mixed-raced groups outside of school. "I never heard any one of them say a disparaging word," he says of his white friends' treatment of their Black pals. "They went to school with them and they played sports with them. They just, you know what, they were nice people raised in nice families. So they acted nice." Both respondents were aware of racial differences in their friend groups, but they emphasize their Black friends' respectability, whether by way of behavior, family background, or relative wealth. Even though both Black and white respondents could recall fond memories of friendships with people with different racial identities—some of which continued into adulthood—white respondents' propensity to stress either their own supposed "color blindness" or the ways that their friends disrupted racist class or behavior stereotypes reflect many of their views on the civil rights movement in general, and school desegregation specifically.

Interracial dating, unsurprisingly, was wracked with even more difficulty than friendship; after all, much opposition to school desegregation was stoked by racist white fears of interracial sex and marriage. Dating across racial lines was a step that many teenagers were unwilling to take during a period when interracial marriage was still illegal in many states. Emily W., who is white, remembers feeling pressured not to date a Black boy she met at her after-school job in St. Petersburg, Florida. "I told my mother I was going to bring him home, and she said 'Don't do that,'" she recalls. "We met clandestinely a few times, [but] he didn't want to bring me to his home either. It died for lack of being able to do things normally." She adds that her mother, who otherwise promoted racial tolerance, was worried "about the difficulty of relationships in the first place, and once you add a layer of big cultural differences, that the ramifications go on from there and it won't be easy." She recalls seeing very few interracial couples in her area growing up, and the ones that did manage to find ways to be together "were stared at. . . . It was totally radical to see something like that then, and invited a lot of staring, and probably ostracization." Further north, in Detroit, Marcia P. recalls talking to a Black boy she liked from school on the phone. "The first time he called, my mother answered the phone and she had pretty much a conniption fit," she recalls. "She could hardly even finish a sentence she was so upset. And she kept saying 'Get off the phone! Get off the phone.'"[95] And yet some relationships did develop as kids spent their days together and got to know one another on a more intimate basis. A writer for *Jet* magazine noted a preponderance of "mixed dating" at integrated schools, which often began at school dances. One white girl from Milwaukee stoked the fears of white protectors of "the Southern way of life" across the country when she admitted that "almost every white girl I know had a secret crush on one of the colored boys."[96] At a high school profiled by the *New York Times*, where only 10 Black kids existed in a population of 1,900, "Negroes . . . mingle with other boys in sports, campus and social activities. They come with their dates to the monthly school dances."[97] Although both news reports present these relationships in a neutral manner, they almost certainly glossed over the heightened emotions, parental fights, and risks of social ostracization that accompanied almost any teenage decision to date outside their race, no matter how tolerant their school environments might appear.

In the midst of these often uncomfortable and sometimes traumatizing environments, some Black students understandably chose to leave their mixed-race schools, especially if they were part of purposely half-hearted Southern desegregation efforts. But those who stayed could also come to feel accepted as part of a wider, integrated student body that ultimately benefited kids of both races. It was not just the promise of a better education and brighter future that drew these kids to integrated schools and convinced them to persevere amid humiliating circumstances, but the pride they could take in becoming part of a new future that sometimes seemed to augur more equal treatment. Gloria Ray, who attended Central, told a reporter "Yes, I made some friends. Some of them called me on the phone. We talked about the usual things girls talk about. And we talked about integration." The reporter added that "Gloria said her friends sympathized with her" as she attested that "sometimes we got letters from white people saying they understood."[98] Some Black students even used the same language of righteousness, common humanity, and democratic rights as white liberals when describing desegregation movement successes. One girl who attended an all-Black school in Baltimore proudly announced, "If white children came into my class, I would treat them as if they were members of our own race." When asked what she thought of school closings, Dolores Ann Poindexter, who applied to attend Central High School, sounded very much like her white counterparts, claiming "I do not like the idea. It retards the progress of everybody." She added that "she should not be denied the right to attend the school in her district just because she is a Negro." Sandra Johnson concurred, noting "I feel I should go. . . . I am in the vicinity. I am an American citizen. I know my constitutional rights." Jane Hill, who was not chosen to attend, even though Central was her "first choice," explained that "no one has the right not to let her go." Kay Francis Mort, whose father would not allow her to attend Central High because he feared she might fall victim to racist violence, claimed she was unconcerned about this threat because "I have faith in the people of my state," while Carolyn Ward, the only Black student to enroll at Hall, another Little Rock-area high school, said she did "not expect any trouble because the people in this district are rather intelligent." Other kids saw desegregation as an important step in a longer fight rather than a confirmation of equality in and of itself. When Joan Drake was interviewed about her decision to apply to Central High School, the reporter observed that "no bitterness is apparent in her outlook. She took a rather dim view of most whites until she made a trip to California, where she met some who were 'very nice.' Since then she accepts them for what they believe and hopes for the best." This girl's goals for her new desegregated school are not exactly framed by the same assurance of common humanity that many young whites extolled during this period. Yet her realization that some white classmates would treat her as equals encouraged her to prevail in her application.[99] Like their parents, Black kids could acknowledge the good that came out of desegregation movements, while continuing to fight for equity over equality, and opportunity over diversity. And yet all of this became much more difficult within a white-dominated culture that wrongly conflated integration with racial justice and equal treatment.

Despite the angry mobs that were captured protesting Black students entering white schools throughout the late 1950s and early 1960s, white teenagers mostly disagreed with racially segregated schools, and many supported integration within their own institutions. According to H. H. Remmers's March, 1954 poll of thousands of teenagers across the country, 54 percent of high school students agreed that "pupils of all races and nationalities should attend school together everywhere in this country." By October, five months after the *Brown* ruling, that statistic rose to 58 percent. School integration was overwhelmingly favored in both the East and West (74 and 80 percent, respectively), and received approval from a majority of students in the Midwest (58 percent), though only 27 percent agreed with this statement in the South. Still, in a region so fundamentally defined by Jim Crow, only 51 percent of Southern students fully disagreed with integration. Furthermore, when asked "How do you *personally* feel about attending the same school with pupils of different races?" 46 percent of teenage respondents across the country chose the option "I like it; definitely approve." Remmers further pointed out that "Easterners, Midwesterners and Westerners rarely chose the third alternative, 'Don't like it and would change it if I could,' even though 35 per cent of Southern teenagers checked this response." With regard to violent or aggressive anti-integration school demonstrations, a majority of students in the East, Midwest, and West (75, 64, and 78 percent) disapproved, but so did 48 percent of Southerners. Only 13 percent of Southern kids, however, said, "I approve, but I would not take part," while 20 percent chose the option "I approve, and I personally would take part in such actions." Almost half of Southern students also disagreed with these demonstrations on the whole. Overall, a vast majority of high school students across the country favored some degree of desegregation or integration, and, as Remmers points out, this percentage spiked significantly among middle-class students, especially those whose parents had received more than a secondary school education.[100]

These numbers, of course, belie the uneasy realities of attending school with people who have different racial identities, as respondents discussing their memories of interracial friendships and dating have already shown. White kids could support the concept of desegregation if they did not have to deal with any of the attendant difficulties personally or if they felt unthreatened as part of the white majority. But they could also continue to stress their belief in the theoretical ability for people to attend school wherever they wanted, regardless of racial identity, while finding it difficult to accept the realities of attending a desegregated or mixed-race school. Sometimes this was due to actual racial conflict. Rose W. recalls how some white parents got upset when her grade school began admitting Black students because they feared there would be fewer seats for their white children in competitive honors classes. She did not agree with this stance, but found it more difficult to deal with racial conflicts in junior high and high school, where white students were in the minority. "It was a rough school," she says of junior high in particular. "It was never any problem in the classes. Students got along fine. But it was dangerous out of class. I have many memories of, so we had to walk to the bus stop, which was like four long blocks away. And there would be, like, three white kids and 30 Black kids, and sometimes they would throw rocks." Sometimes she was so frightened that she would walk a mile and a half home in order to avoid the bus stop route. She also recalls volunteering in the library over lunch since the cafeteria and study hall areas were dangerous places to be avoided. Unsurprisingly, Rose notes that "by the time it was junior high, it was like things started to separate. Social circles were separating." Even though she stresses that her "comfort with racial issues, or with people who are different from me, it's just like, well, this is normal," her experiences clearly show that integration did not necessarily lead to comfortable interracial interactions.[101]

Fear of violence also intimidated Ann W., who admits that she was "scared" growing up in rural Alabama, since she "had no idea how desegregation might change our lives, and I was terribly scared of some of the tactics used in getting there. Watching Governor George Wallace and the National Guard barricade school entrances, seeing the pushing, shoving, shouting, and violent reactions of both races was frightening." Emily W. had a similar reaction when she entered high school in Florida, and students were bussed across the city to ensure integrated classrooms. This provoked a number of white parents, who started "picketing in front of the schools, and the schools became so overcrowded, and it was just the hot spot, and the National Guard got sent in because of the unrest at our high school." Beyond this chaos, she admits that her own fears of going to school with Black people after a lifetime of being kept separate played a role in why she ultimately left school early. "When I met Black people, they looked quite different," she says. "And I didn't meet any Black people until—I didn't really talk to them or sit with them or anything until maybe high school." She remembers being "afraid," partially of rumors "that they were going to corner the white girls in the bathroom and cut their hair," and partially that she might be one of the white students selected to desegregate a majority-Black school. "I think it was fear of the unknown," she says. "I never went to the school dances. I think the desegregation of the schools and what happened in the schools is part of why I pulled away. I did not socialize within the school at all. . . . And I think it was because of the turmoil at the school, it really made me pull away from that." She stresses, however, that "I didn't have any particular hatred, it was just scary. Because they were so separate."[102]

Beyond these uncomfortable or conflict-laden interactions, some white kids made it clear that they were against school desegregation in the first place, often through racist bullying and violence. A 1955 *New York Times* report on school desegregation in Baltimore, for instance, discovered "a class of 16-year-olds [who] reacted violently to the idea of Negro classmates." Their new Black classmates were "terrorized," subjugated to verbal abuse, and left out of school sports, even when their teachers tried to encourage peaceful coexistence.[103] Rick T. recalls "being jumped after a basketball game by five or six white guys" and seeing bathroom graffiti identifying him as an "N-lover" after he befriended one of the few Black kids admitted to his Virginia Beach middle school. "I was crucified for that," he recalls.[104] Others were less inclined to violence, yet still supported segregated schools. One white teenager from North Carolina responded to Remmers's October 1954 survey by stating, "My problem is segregation." Although he insisted that "it does not effect me [*sic*] directly," he declared that "when it comes, it will help neither race," citing a news report where Black and white students "firmly declared they did not want to go to school with each other. I don't believe the Negroes anywhere want to go to school with us anymore than we do with them."[105] The *Times* report featured white students who were opposed to segregation as well, stating that "if Negroes have their own schools, they should stay there," and "I can't see a minority pushing a majority around." One even added that "in three senior high schools, students who have had no contact with Negro students bridled at the mention of social or sports activities involving Negroes."[106] Lee Blackwell, an editor for the *Chicago Defender*, talked to three white students at Central High, all of whom "resented" the presence of Black classmates. They describe a girl in their class as "quiet" and a "teacher's pet," and note that "she would just sit quietly on the side" during gym class, giving little thought to how isolated she must have felt. One of the girls, Annette Jackson, was even more forthright, complaining that "last year the white kids were denied a lot of privileges because the Negroes were at Central high," including the cancellation of a minstrel show because "it might hurt the feelings of the Negras."[107]

Other white kids supported desegregation in their schools, although their support was often based on abstract moral values, without considering some of the conflicts that would likely occur. Segregation was clearly evil, and resolving this issue was simply the right thing to do. While Bibb E. admits that, "when I was small I accepted legal segregation without much thought," he also recalls instances that disturbed this easy acceptance. "At our local movie theatre the balcony was for 'coloreds only,'" he says. "But we all saw the same movie buying the same ticket for the same 25 cents; no problem. . . . I could take at face value 'separate but equal' for a while, [but] it became apparent that in fact we were separate and very unequal."[108] Remarks made by

William Ray, a white student from Mississippi who participated in a nationwide, interracial conference on school desegregation in 1956, reveal a similar focus on morality, even as he questioned just how quickly this goal might be achieved. According to the *New York Times*, Ray "declared that many young people in the South favored racial integration. But lines of bitterness between the races have hardened in the past year, he asserted, and it will take a great effort 'just to maintain interracial communication in a spirit of Christian love.'"[109] Another white high school student, when asked to write an essay on 'brotherhood,' mused that "To me, brotherhood means getting along with everyone, no matter what their religion, race, or nationality." The girl explained that many white kids and parents threatened to boycott her Laurel Hill, North Carolina school if it desegregated, but when her family moved to Baltimore, and she began attending a new, racially integrated school, "the colored girls have treated me just as nice as the white girls. I think that we all should get along."[110] In these cases, white teenagers viewed school segregation in fairly strict terms of good and evil, a perspective that was consistently enforced by Martin Luther King Jr., and other activists who worked within Black churches. It is perhaps unsurprising that some white respondents, like David S., link these responses to televised civil rights struggles that focused on nonviolent actions and depicted desegregation as a moral right. "I didn't know what that was about, just that it was happening," he says of the 1956–1957 school desegregation crisis in Little Rock. "But I didn't know why Black and white children couldn't go to school together."[111] The fact that so many white kids began to view desegregation as a moral good, and to see Black teenagers as potential classmates and friends despite the more difficult realities, shows how successful this strategy had become with white liberals.

Other white kids echoed rhetoric popular in the mass media and among certain politicians that described school segregation as unconstitutional and undemocratic. A California high school junior, for instance, responded to Remmers's survey by noting that "Another one of my dislikes is the segregation in the southern school. I think its stupid and very un-american. Our Constitution says that all men are created equal, but, the way thing are today, well it a discrace [*sic*]." The student continued to expand on the similarities among people of different races, explaining that "just because their skin is Black doesn't mean that thier different than the white. They want an education, home, job, just like anybody else [*sic*]."[112] Another white adolescent bravely addressed a Baltimore meeting of school board officials, teachers, parents, and students when she announced, "It's right to end segregation because we're all free and equal, and they [Black students] don't have a $6 million school like ours."[113] Bill W. explains that, when he was in junior high and high school, desegregation movements "opened my—at least my mind was open and my self was open to the idea that maybe this isn't all right.

Maybe this isn't playing out the way that we're all told we're all created equal."[114] These reflections on the hypocrisies allowed in a country that purported to treat everyone equally mirrored Cold War concerns about how the perpetuation of racial segregation would undermine American global power. They are also more indicative of Black student and parent concerns, which often focused on the basic contradictions between segregation and democracy, and the fact that many of these injustices were technically void under the Fourteenth Amendment. And yet white students rarely spoke out about the injustices that Black kids would have faced outside of the classroom. Instead, they depicted integration, even if that meant that only a handful of Black students would be allowed through the doors of white institutions, as an absolute moral good and constitutional right that would address a small imperfection within an otherwise fair and democratic system.

Some white respondents also frame school desegregation in terms of respectability politics. Victor F., for instance, remembers how many Black classmates at his private school on Long Island were "star athletes," but, because he went to a school that was "academically rigorous," they attended the school "not because they were athletes, but because they academically could do the work. It was, basically you were brought up that you're here because you earned it. And your parents sacrificed. They could send you to public school, but they're sending you here. It's very expensive." He recalls how if a Black player joined a team or was in a class, "nobody singled him out as a Black guy." Although he insists that "in my circle, there was no prejudice," he is also quick to claim that "these were kids who came from families who valued education more than anything else." So when he says that "race was not a factor, I liked everybody," it is difficult not to consider whether this lack of prejudice was linked to the "respectable" types of families who sent their kids to this school. Supposed color blindness could also cause white respondents, especially from Northern cities, to recall a lack of racial discrimination or conflict in their schools if they did not see it firsthand. Bruce S., for instance, remembers when his Queens junior high school began busing students between districts to create more integrated classrooms in 1961. "At first, I was a little apprehensive," he admits. "But as time went on, I think there was a good relationship at that school between the Blacks and whites." Even though he only recalls talking to Black classmates during school hours, he does not recall any resistance to busing in his neighborhood. "I never remember any fights or anything between Blacks and whites," he says. "I think it was a relatively harmonious situation." Bob S., who lived close by in Westchester County, says that he opposed busing, but his rationale is rooted in the same apparent color blindness and lack of recognition of how structural racism affected his Black classmates' experiences. "People couldn't go to the school down the street, they had to be bussed to another city," he says. "I thought that was dumb." His reaction is based on a notion of color blindness that was supposedly achieved by challenges to school segregation, but does not account for the very real distinctions among these schools that led families to fight for desegregation in the first place. He also explains how "most of it just seemed so foreign to us because of the area we lived in, you know up north. And most of it had to do with the South," a common perception among whites in Northern cities, who often viewed this struggle as separate from the supposedly race-neutral policies that existed in their own communities.[115]

This perception could take on almost ambivalent tones among white Northerners, many of whom either attended nominally integrated schools, or schools that were segregated by racist housing policies rather than Jim Crow laws. Walter S., who went to a mostly white school in New Jersey, describes it as "not segregated and not integrated" because "it was not segregated in that anybody could go to the school." Even though Marcia P. recalls only about 50 Black students attending her school of 4,000, she maintains that "it's not that it was a racist school. . . . I never remember hearing anybody say any bad words or anything, but it's because it was so—no one felt it was a problem because it was pretty much an all-white school." The fact that housing segregation would prevent most students of color from eligibility in the first place is not a consideration; rather, the lack of overt racism or segregation laws was enough to convince many white kids that racial discrimination was not a problem in their schools. This type of ambivalence could perpetuate racial inequities within classrooms just as easily as it could indicate white support for desegregation, since many kids were unable or unwilling to see how their Black classmates, or Black students who attended more segregated neighboring schools, continued to struggle with a lack of educational resources or supportive networks that would allow them to thrive. This was partially due to a sort of reverse color blindness, as many white kids failed to identify issues of race discrimination in such largely white environments, where they rarely saw evidence of overt racism firsthand. Ron R. admits that even though his Indiana school was "all white," he "wasn't particularly aware of the fact that all my classmates and schoolmates were white." And Andrew L. notes that "I know for sure we didn't have any Black people in our class" at his school in Ohio, but also that "we didn't have any computers either." Although this conflation of segregated school systems with a lack of technological resources shows the limited understanding many white students had of how their Black peers were affected by these discriminatory systems, he also adds that "I didn't know I was missing anything," further revealing how physical and psychological distance from Southern desegregation campaigns could reinforce white students' inability to identify racism in their own communities.[116]

This ability to view the movement from a distance, even when attending desegregating schools, is also clear among white teenagers in the South, although they were often more ambivalent about school integration. Lauren Lee, who was a senior at Central High the year that the Little Rock Nine attempted to desegregate the school, told the *New York Times* that "I am not an integrationist," but that she also did not agree with the district closing the schools rather than allowing admission to Black students. She told the reporter that she had "no objection to desegregation so long as school is not disrupted. However, she made no effort to make friends with the nine Negroes who attended Central." She admitted that, at first, she was afraid to do so for fear of retaliation from her friends, but later realized: "If nobody cared I still wouldn't be friendly. I wouldn't be friendly. I wouldn't be rude to them. I just don't care to be friends." The reporter notes that "her only explanation for her attitude is her Southern upbringing," but tradition only went so far. "The blame for the troubles of Little Rock," Lee told the paper, "lies with the parents."[117] Joyce Denny, who also attended Central, agreed, telling a reporter that she "preferred to go to segregated schools," yet proclaiming "Of course we're against them closing the schools. We want to go to school. But, if this is the way we have to do it to settle issues, then we can't say much." When asked what they thought of the desegregation ruling, one of Joyce's friends proclaimed "It had to be. Faubus can't stop the Federal government."[118] Even though their school had become fundamentally associated with the desegregation movement, these girls were still able to view the matter at an arm's length as an issue that did not really affect them much, and so ought to be left alone.

Some respondents who grew up in the South shared this ambivalence, although they recall being more open to the idea of racial integration so long as it did not disrupt their own lives. Bob C. says that, when he was in school, "I had no strong feelings . . . about trying to integrate schools, though I hated racism," a remark that is surprisingly close to Black concerns about desegregation, even if it stemmed more from lack of involvement than ideological differences.[119] Bob R. remembers that racial segregation of public places "seemed silly to me. I think I probably began to question school integration then too—my schools had no problem with black students (though we had very few black students) and neither did the white students, though it was only nominal integration. I have no idea what the black students' view of things were as I had no interaction with them. I suspect they felt very isolated."[120] Interestingly enough, both respondents were able to separate their disagreement with racism in general from their ambivalence toward school desegregation. Although it might make sense to assume that the former would necessitate the latter, the dictates of white privilege allowed these students to oppose racism in the abstract while ignoring the small racial changes in their own schools—as well as the Black kids themselves, who, consequently, often suffered from alienation and loneliness in desegregated classrooms. Even Rick T., who was brought up in a fervently antiracist household, and made efforts to reach out to new students, recalls feeling shocked and surprised when 200 of his white classmates were pulled from the school after it was forced to desegregate. "I'm thinking, what's the matter with y'all? What's the big deal?"[121] The fact that so many white kids could attend Southern schools *without caring* that they were sharing the same hallways with Black students is somewhat striking given the fact that Jim Crow was only able to prosper given its harsh and all-encompassing nature. Their responses show how a modern teenage identity necessitated at least tacit acceptance of school desegregation, even in the midst of massive resistance campaigns. But these kids' ambivalence also reveals the limits of many white people's investments in this struggle, presaging how they would mostly support efforts that demanded few personal sacrifices.

ROCK AND ROLL GOES TO HIGH SCHOOL

Just as schools could act as desegregated spaces where white and Black students would continue to have very different experiences, popular music in the late 1950s could be enjoyed across racial lines while provoking distinct racialized responses. Major labels were forced to accept rock and roll as a legitimate genre, especially as white cover artists failed to sell as many records as they had in the mid-1950s. But many executives got around this issue by "softening" the genre, promoting music that could appeal to teenagers while maintaining a gentler, more melodic sound. Young, personable, and inoffensive white artists were signed to major labels to sing songs that sounded suspiciously like earlier pop hits even if they were promoted as rock and roll. So-called schlock rockers like Fabian, Frankie Avalon, Bobby Rydell, Connie Francis, and Ricky Nelson achieved teen idol status not by covering records by Black musicians, but by singing and performing in a manner that significantly diluted the characteristics of early rock and roll. Specialty Records' official history explains how many television "network 'suits' encouraged the booking of these cuddly white boys, while considering artists like [Specialty head Art] Rupe's label roster of sweaty Black guys were too scary for teeny-bopper consumption."[122] The records made by these performers, which were directed specifically at a white teenage audience, often relied on a percussive beat and nearly always celebrated youth culture, just like early rock and roll records. But they were also drained of many of the African-American influences that had drawn white teenage listeners in the first place. Steve Chapple and Reebee Garofalo explain that while these artists "had no identifiable ties to any musical form (except the elusive notion of pop)" they also "had some semblance of rhythm and were young, [and so] they were marketed as rock 'n' roll singers. They effectively gave rock 'n' roll its final facelift of the fifties by whitening up the hit charts."[123]

Grace Elizabeth Hale places much of the blame for this transition on white supremacist attitudes and corporate apathy. "By the late 1950s the liberating force of the music seemed spent, buried under derivative product and the outpouring of criticism from politicians, ministers, and parents, as well as the growing force of the segregationists," she says.[124] Michael Lydon additionally faults the passage of time, neatly stating that "the first rock 'n' rollers were now voting adults, and the jet-setters were twisting at the Peppermint Lounge. What had been fresh in 1955 had become formula, and then simply repetition."[125] According to Jerry Wexler, all of these elements helped contribute to a seemingly fallow period for teenage popular music. "Ahmet [Ertegun] and I had begun moving in different directions back in the late fifties, early sixties," he recalled. "His success with Bobby Darin set him on a new track, introducing him to the California scene, where he would later discover a number of lucrative pop acts. As Ahmet grew older, he grew less judgmental and more interested in a wide range of commercial forms, particularly the exploding white rock 'n' roll. I stayed with what I knew and loved."[126] But whatever the reason, many rock and roll fans were left to struggle with the somewhat less dynamic acts they were expected to embrace.

The *Billboard* charts were not completely overwhelmed by white teen idols, though—a number of Black artists continued to place on the Pop and Hot 100 charts even as the music industry shifted, and Black and white teenagers continued to purchase the same records by performers of different races. And yet, as Bret Eynon explains, when compared to earlier rock and roll stars, most new teen idols "were white, where the originals had been black, were clean cut, where the originals had been wild and unpredictable, and most importantly were controlled by the major recording studios."[127] This strategy initially hooked many white teenage listeners. Ken A., for example, recalls how he initially began listening to music that he describes as "the non-threatening version of rock and roll" by new artists like Ricky Nelson "because he was a good singer and he was not shaking his hips, he was not threatening." Larry R. similarly recalls how, even though he did not care for these artists themselves, that "it was good music, you know, people enjoyed it, you could dance to it." Other respondents recall listening to this music even if they were somewhat dissatisfied with it. Marcia P. says that she liked Bobby Rydell best "because he was a little bit more of a greaser . . . he had this kind of ducktail, a haircut, a waterfall in the front. He was pretty cool, I liked him a lot," while Bruce C. recalls how "white disc jockeys coming out of New York" first played these artists on the radio. "They told us it was rock and roll," he says. "To me, it sounded a lot like the same music [i.e. pop]. . . . Some of what they played was really sappy."[128]

Even though the music and culture of 1950s adolescence was fundamentally shaped by African-American contributions, this shift to a more pop-inflected teen genre represented corporate attempts to cleanse teenage music and culture of any overtly Black characteristics. Just as schools allowed a few Black students into white spaces, the mainstream music industry "desegregated" by promoting relatively small numbers of Black artists who had proven popular with white listeners, while simultaneously strengthening the white-dominated boundaries of these institutions. But as much as late 1950s rock and roll and the image of the teenager both tacitly embraced the idea of integration, both were reconfigured as white during this period, forcing Black kids to assimilate rather than celebrate their own cultural identities. As Ken A. explains, popular music from this period "was palatable, it was accessible. It was not disturbing. This was not music that was going to make you think or be sad or anything. It was about what we were supposed to be striving for, having dates, riding in convertibles and going to drive-ins. . . . I thought, boy, this is what you were supposed to do when you were an American teenager."[129] These signifiers were clearly white and middle class, and yet they were depicted as though they belonged to everyone. This is how integration was conceived of by many sympathetic whites during this period, despite Black organizers' intentions. In some ways, this strategy may have worked too well, as schools and the *Billboard* Hot 100 chart alike were celebrated for racial inclusion when in reality they remained part of a white-dominated power structure that responded to varying degrees of Black acceptance by strengthening boundaries and demanding cultural assimilation. These processes neatly echo white Southern students' pronouncements that integration in schools was "no big deal" or that skin color should not affect access to opportunity in a country based on supposedly universal democratic principles.

These perspectives on desegregation also crop up in white respondents' increasingly negative reactions to these "schlock rockers." "The Paul Ankas and the Fabians of the day, you know, I mean, who wants to listen to that?" Bruce C. asserts. "Not me, that's for sure. Or Pat Boone. You know? Writing love letters in the sand." Singer-songwriter Janis Ian was put off by how "the singers looked manufactured, stamped out with cookie cutters by evil music-haters who just saw dollars signs instead of ways to change the world. The songs, too, sounded manufactured, with the same chord progressions and awful guitar parts. Fabian, Frankie Avalon—what was with these guys? Not to mention their hair."[130] This emphasis on a lack of authenticity hearkens back to teenagers' original complaints with white cover versions of Black originals. Listeners were not merely perturbed by the obvious corporate machinations that brought these artists to their radio stations and television screens, but by the lack of emotion, dynamism, and vulnerability in their performances, all of which remained African-American signifiers. Just as white teenage consumers began shopping for original recordings by Black artists a few years prior, some respondents say that their aversion to white schlock rockers pushed them to explore the more relatable music that many Black artists continued to release. Bill W. explains that he first started listening to Black artists in high school due to "originally hearing people like Frankie Avalon and Bobby Rydell and that kind of ilk, and okay, that's fine, whatever. But once I started to be exposed to vocalists like Clyde McPhatter, Jackie Wilson, those kinds, literally those singers that came out of the church and had these incredible voices that could, whether you realized it or not, move you even if you didn't want to be moved. The Frankie Avalons and that stuff just totally fell by the wayside." Even though Bill still listened to pop music on the radio, he says he noticed the racialized differences between these types of music right away: "the music that was resonating and moved me the most was the incredible music coming out of the Black community."[131]

Some of the biggest hit records of this period reveal how Black and white teenagers could share very similar experiences, yet understand them within radically different social contexts. Songs that specifically addressed high school challenges could help provide young Black listeners with guidance as they struggled to fit into desegregating spaces or to meet academic expectations, even if the lyrics otherwise attempted to capture a universal teenage experience. Chuck Berry, an experienced musician in his 20s, specialized in recording songs directed at teenage audiences throughout the 1950s, including "School Day," which reached number 1 on the R&B chart and number 3 on the Pop chart, and "Oh Baby Doll," which peaked at number 12 on the R&B chart. The lyrics of "School Day" use second-person narration to depict a day in the life of a typical student who has to wake up early and go to class, where students are "studyin' hard and hopin' to pass." This verse elucidates the academic side of high school and the pressure that many teenagers felt to succeed. And yet, the best part of the school day arrives at 3 o'clock when "you finally lay your burden down" by going to a "juke joint," dropping a "coin right into the slot," and dancing with a significant other. The record's popularity on both the Pop and R&B charts throughout the spring of 1957 shows that Berry's depiction resonated with teenagers across racial lines, all of whom faced academic challenges within the often restrictive walls of their educational institutions, and who eagerly awaited the end of the day when they could let loose and have fun.[132]

Although his follow-up single, "Oh Baby Doll," is not quite as iconic, Berry's first-person account of a teen reminiscing about his high school days is thematically similar to "School Day." The song begins by detailing a particular memory of the narrator and his love interest stopping on their way to school to listen to "the latest songs they sing," making it to class just "before the bells would ring." Again, school is the focal point of teenage life, and where students spend most of their time, but their major points of interest are romance, friendships, and music. Berry continues to relay this point, singing that when the teacher steps out of the classroom, "That's when we'd have a ball/We used to dance and play/All up and down the hall." As much as the kids in this school might sound like troublemakers who prefer dancing to studying, Berry assures his listeners that the students would fall in line once the teacher returned. These lyrics reflect the different roles that teenagers played during the day, noting that proper, serious students could easily transform into fun-loving social butterflies, and vice versa. Although "Oh Baby Doll" did not cross over to the Pop top 20 chart like "School Day" did, its subject matter is strikingly similar to white pop artist Ricky Nelson's "Waitin' in School," the B-side of his hit record "Stood Up," which graced the top of the Pop chart the following year. In this song, Nelson sings of his impatience during the school day, waiting for the moment he can "Throw my books on the table, pick up the telephone," and ask his girlfriend to go to the drugstore, "Throw a nickel in the jukebox, then we start to rock." The lyrical narrative here is almost identical to the one described by Berry in "School Day," and, like in "Oh Baby Doll," the academic side of high school is portrayed as a necessary obstacle to teenage enjoyment. Nelson's record crossed over to both the R&B and Country and Western charts for three weeks in February 1958, revealing, yet again, resonance for both Black and white teenagers across the country. Similar depictions in these songs highlight the fact that Black kids could relate to teenage identities as high school students, and that white kids could see their own lives mirrored in lyrics written by a Black artist like Berry. They did not address the isolation and harassment that Black kids faced in these schools, however, as Reebee Garofalo points out: "Berry's depiction of 'School Days' in 1957 did not describe the educational experience in Little Rock, Arkansas that same year. Berry conjured up the image of teachers teaching 'the golden rule' even as Eisenhower had to send federal troops to Little Rock to enforce the Supreme Court's school integration edict."[133]

If Berry's lyrics obscured this distinction in order to appeal to white teenage consumers, thereby overlooking the feelings of alienation and disenchantment that many Black kids felt when attending majority-white schools or underfunded schools in majority-Black neighborhoods, the Coasters' "Charlie Brown" and Sam Cooke's "Wonderful World" highlighted these experiences while acknowledging enough shared aspects of high school life that the records could still appeal to white teenagers. The Coasters were a Black vocal group who became famous singing songs like "Charlie Brown," written by Jerry Leiber and Mike Stoller. This record, which peaked at number 2 on the *Billboard* Hot 100 chart in May 1959, tells the story of a "clown" who smokes in the school auditorium, throws spitballs in the hall, and "calls the English teacher Daddy-O." Charlie Brown is clearly supposed to represent the troublemaker in a class of otherwise well-behaved students, a theme that was reflected in the group's live performance on *"Dick Clark's Saturday Night Beechnut Show."* Clark opens the show by stating "I think you'll find that, no matter where you go to school, there's always a fella who writes on the blackboard when he shouldn't, and maybe gives the teacher a little lip." On set, three of the Coasters are seated in desks in front of a chalkboard, dressed in the same kinds of school-appropriate sweaters and slacks worn by Frankie Lymon and the Teenagers on their album cover. As they begin lip synching along to the track, the singers stand and point to the fourth member, Cornell Gunter, who is being shamed by sitting alone on a stool in the corner, facing the wall. As the chorus nears its conclusion, however, Gunter spins around, bemoaning, "Why's everybody always picking on me?" while dabbing at his eyes with a handkerchief. As they complete the bridge, the three members rise from their seats, surround Gunter on his stool, and point accusingly at him. "Charlie Brown" does fight back by lightly slapping the other members in the face, but his behavior, and recurrent questioning of why he is being picked on, is somewhat perplexing. High school students everywhere could, as Clark noted in his introduction, identify a delinquent just like Brown in their own classrooms. But class clowns and juvenile delinquents were not necessarily known to be picked on by their classmates, especially not in the brooding manner evident in both Gunter's television performance and in his voice on the recording. Feeling alone and unfairly bullied, despite attempts to act cool on the outside, his depiction mirrored the experiences that many Black kids report having in desegregating schools where they felt isolated. Some of Charlie Brown's actions could reflect the mischievous antics of a delinquent teen, but his lonesome response to public humiliation speak more to the specific experiences of Black teenagers who chose to integrate white high schools or who felt that their opportunities were limited at majority-Black schools.[134]

Experiences specific to Black kids' experiences may also be identified within the more broadly relatable framework of Sam Cooke's "Wonderful World." On this 1960 recording, Cooke sings that he "Don't know much" about a variety of subjects, including history, biology, French, science, and a range of math topics. He even forthrightly states that he does not "claim to be an A-student," but that his unquestionable love for a presumed classmate encourages him to try harder in school. In this song, Cooke's focus on romantic love rather than academic skill recalls Berry's and Nelson's lyrics, and reiterates the prominence of dating in the mindsets of teenage listeners.

Figure 3.1   The Coasters Dress in Preppy Clothing on a Set Designed to Look Like a Middle-Class High School Classroom during a 1959 Performance on *Dick Clark's Saturday Night Beechnut Show*. ("The Coasters—Charlie Brown. *Dick Clark's Saturday Night Beechnut Show*, March 7, 1959, accessed at https://www.youtube.com/watch?v=Qpkn6SOy0l8.)

Figure 3.2   Lead singer Cornell Gunter, seen in the center modeling a dunce's cap, is portrayed as both a rebel and the victim of bullying in the song's lyrics. ("The Coasters—Charlie Brown. *Dick Clark's Saturday Night Beechnut Show*, March 7, 1959, accessed at https://www.youtube.com/watch?v=Qpkn6SOy0l8.)

The girl who has stolen his heart must care about academic progress, however, since Cooke croons that he could possibly win her love by becoming a high-achieving student. This girl is possibly a devoted student herself, or else she views strong academics as predicting professional success for a future husband. Cooke's record scored the second spot on *Billboard*'s "Hot R&B" chart, and number 12 on the Hot 100 chart, partially due to his looks and charm, but also because students from any racial group could identify with the struggle between studies and steadies. And yet the sense of striving apparent in both the narrator's attempts to better himself and in his beloved's emphasis on the importance of scholarly pursuits befits the mindset of middle-class Black teens, who knew they had to work particularly hard to take advantage of the few opportunities that were now open to them. After all, Cooke never says that he doesn't *care* about school; merely that he does not know anything about these academic subjects. Despite his hard work, he is having trouble actually *learning* which could indicate that, like many other Black kids, he attends a segregated school lacking in adequate educational resources or a desegregating school where his needs are neglected. The singer is clearly frustrated by his beloved's refusal to acknowledge him because of his poor grades, but he may also be chafing against the confines of a system that makes it difficult for him to succeed academically.[135]

Even though these songs take place within high school environments, and speak to academic and institutional stresses, they mostly focus on romantic relationships, the kind that inspire absolute devotion at the cost of almost everything else. Dating was an essential component of teenage daily life, but rules had changed so abruptly in the postwar period that parents became concerned about intense feelings between many young couples. Beth Bailey has written extensively about how teenagers' propensity for "going steady" with one partner for long periods of time disrupted their parents' romantic experiences in the 1920s and 1930s, which were largely based on dating many potential suitors. This shift caused widespread anxiety, not only because "going steady was widely accepted as a justification for greater physical intimacy," but also because it led to marriage at younger ages, reversing prewar trends of marrying older, which seemed more stable.[136] *Life* magazine may have gaily noted that these young marriages caused "major items like furniture and silver [to move] into the teen-age market," but a 1959 profile entitled "The Costly Hazard of Young Marriage" revealed a more ambivalent picture. Photos of 17-year-old Betty and Larry Fesmire, for instance, show the young couple sharing bathroom space with Betty's sisters after moving in with her family, and sitting alone in their high school cafeteria after friends expel them from their social groups. "A girl who is married, her interests change," Elizabeth Gullidge, president of the Girls Good Sports club at the Charlotte, North Carolina high school that the Fesmires attended, told the profile's author. "She doesn't have time for the service projects, parties, sock hops and we all do." The school's principal added that "a wedding ring provoked sympathy instead of congratulations," and each of the couples interviewed admitted that their parents had been adamantly opposed to their relationships, at least at first. Despite concerns among both adults and adolescents about the perils of early marriage, going steady remained the template for teenage relationships, with 57 percent of adolescents reporting fidelity to only one partner in a 1959 poll.[137]

Although images of white couples dancing at proms and standing in front of white picket-fenced houses tend to dominate historical memory of dating and early marriage in the 1950s, Black teenagers also partook in this shift, causing similar trepidation among their parents. After interviewing almost 300 students at a high school in a Southern city, Joseph Himes found that "with only minor local variations, the vogue is early and almost universal steady dating," with 84 percent of respondents stating their approval. And yet he warns that this practice "leads to early marriage, sexual laxities, venereal infections, and unplanned pregnancies."[138] White parents and authorities clearly worried about these consequences as well, even if they hid them beneath layers of concern for their children's futures. And yet a 1959 article in *Jet* entitled "Should Teen-Agers Have Steady Dates? Survey Reveals 'Going Steady' Is Increasing Among Teens" also echoed many of these worries by speaking to parental fears without directly mentioning pregnancy or disease. Similar to their white peers, Black "parents and authorities" issued "warnings" "of the dangers involved in such immature relationships," yet 82 percent of boys and 76 percent of girls who were interviewed responded that "they went steady because most of their friends did" and because of "loyalty and dependability." Or, in the case of a "southern belle" named Carlene Chevis, "I don't like a lot of fellows at the same time, because I might get mixed up."[139] The dating patterns that helped define white teenage life during this period were also practiced by Black kids, revealing teenage social norms that transcended racial boundaries, even in segregated high schools. Parents even voiced their concerns in similar ways by focusing on how these intense relationships would affect their children's educational and professional futures rather than directly referencing fears about premature sexual activity, even if stakes were usually higher for Black couples without the financial resources available to them if they married early.

These similar attitudes toward love and dating were reflected in popular records released by both Black and white artists. Many of these songs' lyrics show how both Black and white teenagers viewed true love as the pinnacle of human existence and that only one "steady" could fulfill their romantic longings, a severe shift from R&B's focus on bodily pleasures and casual flings. Breakups and unrequited love were therefore depicted as positively devastating. Lyrics to the Teenagers 1956 hit "Why Do Fools Fall in Love?" for instance, were inspired by love letters sent to a friend of the band. And yet they resonated with listeners befuddled by unreciprocated crushes, an ailment shared by all teenagers, regardless of race, who felt similarly "foolish" at being unable to obtain the objects of their affections. Similar themes were explored in "Eddie, My Love," which debuted the same year. In this song, the Teen Queens plead "Tell me your love is still only mine" after leaving them to "cry myself to sleep." Both groups were comprised of Black members, but records released by white artists tackled similar emotional terrain. Dion and the Belmonts, a pop vocal group of four young Italian-American New Yorkers, scored an iconic hit in the spring of 1959 with "A Teen Ager in Love," which detailed the narrator's anxious state of mind. After crooning about how lonely he feels when the object of his affections ignores him, lead singer Dion DiMucci confesses that "Each night I ask the stars up above/ Why must I be a teenager in love?" All three songs elevate the narrator's loved one to the status of nearly unobtainable soulmate who will drive their beloved crazy and leave them lonely forever if they fail to make a commitment. "Teen Ager in Love" reached number 5 on *Billboard*'s Hot 100 list without making an appearance on the Hot R&B chart, but both "Why Do Fools Fall in Love" and "Eddie, My Love" scored on the Pop and R&B charts, revealing how the records resonated with Black and white teenagers alike.[140]

Optimistic examples of monogamous relationships also existed in popular song lyrics; Sam Cooke, for instance, scored a number-one hit on both the Pop and R&B charts in the fall of 1957 with "You Send Me," a dreamy romantic ballad where the singer admits "At first I thought it was infatuation," but that he now wishes "To marry you and take you home." These words may have frightened parents who did not want their children to enter serious relationships so rapidly, but they also reflected the feelings of many teenagers who had made deeper commitments to their significant others. Cooke was Black, but yet again, the sentiments in his words paralleled those of romantic songs released by white artists. The lyrics to Ricky Nelson's 1957 hit record, for instance, describe "A Teenager's Romance" as "fickle or true" and "red hot or blue," echoing the intense ups and downs that seemed to accompany these steady relationships. The song also refers to parental disapproval, as Nelson bemoans that he and his girlfriend are told that they are too young and too different for their relationship to last. The song concludes just like Cooke's does, though, with faith in the lasting nature of this relationship. Nelson tells his girlfriend that if she keeps "saying you love me," they will have "A teenager's romance/That goes on and on." Falling in love with a steady partner, parental disapproval of an intense commitment, and devastation wrought by the breakup of what was considered a long-term partnership were experiences shared by both Black and white teenagers during this period and were ultimately reflected in popular songs by artists of both racial backgrounds.[141]

Not all 1950s teenagers were interested in academics or long-lasting school romances, though. The rebel or delinquent also depicted a particular image of postwar adolescence, one that caused even more concern for parents and authorities than "going steady." Sociologist Wini Breines describes fears of juvenile delinquency as "a major 1950s preoccupation," noting that supposedly rising crime rates among teenagers provided "evidence of social and familial disintegration," especially amid the dislocation of war, shifting gender roles, Cold War concerns about atomic warfare and social conformity, and rapid technological changes.[142] This anxiety was so pronounced that a special Senate subcommittee investigation into juvenile delinquency was established in 1954, despite numbers that show that "American juvenile delinquency was actually declining" during these years.[143] Nevertheless, so-called hoods and greasers modeled themselves after "inappropriate" movie star idols like James Dean and Marlon Brando, who wore Black leather and denim, and embraced a form of masculinity based on "alienation" and "defiance." Even though these celebrity rebels were white, teenage delinquents, or so-called "hoodlums," were often imagined to be Black, or at least inspired by African-American culture. Their aesthetic choices and supposed criminal behaviors elicited fears of trans-racial influence among many white middle-class authority figures. After all, as Breines says, "It is far from irrelevant that hoods and 'bad girls' were portrayed as wearing Black."[144]

And yet many Black families were also worried about the influence of the "juvenile delinquent" on their teenage children. Another *Jet* cover article, published in 1955, fretted "Are Teen-Agers Growing Up Too Fast?" and regaled its readers with tales of kids joy-riding and wrecking cars, "roam[ing] city streets at night, seeking out gang fights," and "addicting themselves to cigarettes, liquor, and crime." Although Black journalists did not racialize juvenile delinquency the way their white counterparts did, they described their actions and the supposed reasons for them in similar ways. The *Jet* article traced some of these behaviors to "the savagery of the new MGM movie Blackboard Jungle," a film featuring both white and Black street gangs, and agreed that "psychiatrists, sociologists and police point to many things" influencing the rise of juvenile delinquency, "most of them stemming from the lack of parental direction during World War II. Robbed of the influence and companionship of parents who worked overtime and graveyard shifts in war plants, many children were left to prepare their own meals, manage their own affairs, solve their own problems, come and go as they pleased." Whether youth crime rates were rising or not, Black teenage rebels engaged in many of the same activities as their white peers, causing similar outcry among their parents and authority figures.[145] Racial divisions were therefore blurred within the construction of both good and bad images of "the Teen Ager," despite the overall whiteness that came to be associated with the term.

This counter-image of the 1950s teenager was also portrayed in popular music, even though the image of the teen rebel was not yet glamorized as it would be by the early 1960s.[146] Instead, concerns about teenage delinquency were addressed in a light-hearted manner, suggesting that parents and authorities were getting worked up over nothing. The clearest example of this response is Mike Stoller and Jerry Leiber's "Jailhouse Rock," recorded by Elvis Presley to massive acclaim. This record, which debuted on all three *Billboard* charts simultaneously on October 14, 1957, hit number one on both the Pop and R&B charts a week later, and remained in the top 10 until early 1958, provides a tongue-in-cheek look at a "prison band" that seems more interested in having fun than committing crimes. In an institution where the "warden threw a party in the county jail," inmates are not faceless and violent figures, but rather identifiable members of a band with valuable musical skills. Instead of fighting with each other or defying the warden, as may be expected behind prison walls, "Everybody in the whole cell block was dancing to the jailhouse rock." The individuals themselves are hardly depicted as threatening; in one verse, the warden encourages "Sad Sack," who is "over in the corner weepin' all alone" to join the party, while in another, "Bugsy" refuses an offer to use the party as a distraction to make a break for freedom, instead claiming he wants to "stick around awhile and get my kicks." In this song, the so-called delinquents are portrayed not as dangerous criminals, but as people who simply want to dance and have fun, sending a not-so-subtle message to adults who worried that rock and roll would incite violent or rebellious behavior among teenage listeners.[147]

Stoller and Leiber reprised this theme in another hit song, "Yakety Yak," which was recorded by the Coasters, and hit number 1 on the R&B chart and number 2 on the Pop chart in the summer of 1958. This song is performed from a father's perspective as he commands his teenage son to finish a variety of chores without complaint, or else he will not be able to "go out Friday night" or "rock and roll no more." These behaviors may not have seemed overtly threatening to most parents, but the son's insistent chorus of "Yakety Yak," followed by the father's admonition, "Don't Talk Back," emphasizes the persistence of rebellious teenage attitudes toward their parents. In the last verse, the father informs his son to "tell your hoodlum friend outside/You ain't got time to take a ride," giving voice to parental concerns about car culture and their children falling in with the wrong crowds. Aimlessly driving around in cars and motorcycles was often linked to juvenile delinquency in the media, while use of the term "hoodlum" could imply someone who was involved in petty crime or belonged to a gang, whose members were often coded as Black or Latin. In this song, white songwriters created a humorous look at how parents of both racial backgrounds struggled to communicate with their rebellious kids for a Black group to perform to interracial audiences. And yet the song consistently winks at listeners, implying that the father, who unloads an inordinate number of chores on his son, and insists that "Your father's hip, he knows what cooks," is the actual problem in the relationship. Just because he implies that his son may be up to no good when he refuses to obey orders does not mean that he is actually causing trouble—the father may simply be unable to understand teenagers and their culture. In this case, Leiber and Stoller may have written a song that subtly mocked parental culture, but the Coasters' recording also showed audiences that Black kids were capable of partying and driving around with friends without necessarily committing criminal acts.[148]

This last part was particularly concerning for Black kids, who were far more likely to face grave consequences for petty crimes or acts of rebellion than their white counterparts. Whereas white teenagers were advised to stay in school and respect authorities in order to stave off any chances of falling prey to criminal behavior, Black kids were often presented as inherently susceptible to violent or rebellious behavior. In his examination of legal responses to juvenile delinquency in the 1950s, Jason Barnosky notes that "press reports of the period made the link between race and juvenile crime explicit," and that "a disproportionate number of African-American youth were caught in the juvenile justice system." At a time when the Black population comprised roughly 10 percent of Americans as a whole, roughly a fifth to a quarter of juvenile delinquency cases involved Black defendants, as well as up to 50 percent of the inhabitants of institutions for young offenders in larger urban areas. Some kids were questioned, arrested, or even assaulted by police for simply using public spaces. "When they said move off the corner, you moved off the corner," recalled Detroit resident Grant Friley, who would grow up to become a police officer himself. "And where do young Black men have but a corner? They don't have swimming pools, they don't have estates, they have corners in the cities. And they stand around, they harmonize, they clown, they have fun. But when the [police] said 'Give me that corner,' you gave them that corner, or else." And Regina Kunzel and Rickie Solinger have both written about how Black unwed teenage mothers were treated as immoral and possibly criminal at a time when white teenagers could be sent away to deliver their babies and give them up for adoption, returning to regular adolescent life cleansed of any sexual improprieties. As juvenile crime rates began to rise in white-dominated suburbs, many parents feared the perceived criminal impact of Black and Latin teenagers on their own children, leading to even more repression on behalf of authorities.[149]

Within this context, Black artists' attempts to make light of juvenile delinquency concerns take on meanings that may have been overlooked by white listeners. Frankie Lymon and the Teenagers' debut album, for instance, included a track entitled "I'm Not a Juvenile Delinquent." As the Teenagers croon "No, no, no," Lymon tells his young listeners that "It's easy to be good, it's hard to be bad/ Stay out of trouble, and you'll be glad." He presents himself, at the age of 13, as a role model on the subject, crooning "Take this tip from me, and you will see. . . . I know, because I'm not a juvenile delinquent." The group members even got a chance to present themselves as paragons of teen virtue on Alan Freed's *Big Beat* show, wearing the same matching sweaters they donned on their album cover as Lymon presses his palms together, as if in prayer, with his eyes raised to the heavens like an angel. Even though the song, written by professional songwriter George Goldner, was clearly meant to encourage young listeners to abstain from crime, the fact that Black kids were charged with relaying this message to white teenagers shows that they could also be considered wholesome role models, a direct rebuke to assumptions of Black criminality, and seemingly a sign of support for a more racially integrated teenage culture. But Black listeners may also have heard a warning in these lyrics not to stray from the straight and narrow path lest their lives be ruined by racist justice systems.[150]

Figure 3.3 Frankie Lymon, Front Center, Puts His Hands Together as If in Prayer While He and the Teenagers Perform "I'm Not a Juvenile Delinquent" in Matching Sweaters on The Big Beat, 1956. *Source*: Frankie Lymon and the Teenagers, "I'm Not a Juvenile Delinquent," The Big Beat, 1956, accessed at https://www.youtube.com/watch?v=ZsBSsdAhnxE.

ROCK AND ROLL AND RACE ON TELEVISION

Racialized tensions were also apparent in the teenage dance shows that became almost required viewing for American youth during the late 1950s. These shows, which featured young couples dancing to live performances, introduced new music to audiences across the country while also providing templates for how to look and act like a popular teenager. The most widely beloved of these shows, *American Bandstand*, actually started out as a local program aimed at teens in Philadelphia and its environs before achieving enormous success as a nationwide broadcast. Starting in 1952, WFIL-TV began airing the program, hosted by local deejay Bob Horn, who would play hit records as teenage couples performed the latest dance moves. Each show also featured lip-synced performances from musical guest stars, all of whom were white pop stars, at least at the outset. White kids began demanding to hear more of their favorite R&B and rock and roll hits by Black artists, but the racial makeup of the show's phenomenally popular teenage dancers remained white to a fault. Black teenagers protested this decision, but producers obstinately refused to allow them to even enter the studio where the show was filmed. Matthew Delmont explains that "*Bandstand*'s producers wanted to make the show's representations of Philadelphia teenagers safe for television advertisers and viewers in WFIL–adelphia," a demographic that extended beyond the borders of Maryland and Delaware, where Jim Crow-style segregation was often enforced, especially in school systems.[151] After all, Alan Freed's program, *The Big Beat*, which hit the airwaves in 1957, was already criticized for allowing Black and white couples on the same dance floor, and would ultimately be removed from Southern affiliate stations because of on-air interracial dancing. *The Big Beat* presented rock and roll and teenage culture alike as fundamentally racially integrated, but this conception remained controversial, and would have to be obscured in order to hold onto white audiences and sponsors.

Bandstand, however, became so popular that, by 1957, it was picked up by ABC and reformatted as a national broadcast. Horn, who had recently been arrested on a drunk driving charge, was jettisoned in favor of New York deejay Dick Clark, but only after pioneering R&B spinner Al Jarvis, who was white, declined the honor because of the network's reluctance to feature Black performers or dancers.[152] Clark became well known almost immediately for supposedly "integrating" the show by allowing Black performers and teenage dancers to be featured on the program. Years later, he promoted this myth himself, exclaiming that "Rock 'n' roll—and by extension *Bandstand*—owed its very existence to black people, their culture and their music. It would have been ridiculous, embarrassing *not* to integrate the show."[153] Although *Bandstand* featured many top-name Black performers like Frankie Lymon and the Teenagers, Chubby Checker, and the Shirelles, most of the teenage dancers were white, even when the show transitioned to a nationally aired program. Most respondents do not remember seeing many Black kids on the show, regardless of their own racial identity. "There were African-American performers of course, but the audience seemed to be largely white," Bruce C. asserts. He claims he was aware of this division even though he was very young when *Bandstand* first started broadcasting on ABC. "How could you not be?" he stresses. "I mean, if you see a group of African Americans performing, and all the people dancing to it are white."[154]

The program's popularity, however, skyrocketed across the country with teenagers across racial lines, a trend which had noticeable implications for the integrationist movement. Berry Gordy, whose first songwriting hit, "Reet Petite," debuted on the show in 1959 when singer Jackie Wilson took the stage, recalled being shocked at the sight of "Jackie's big booming voice blasting for millions all over the country, and all those white kids dancing up a storm to my song." Gordy's ambition had been to write and produce Black-oriented music that would also appeal to the supposedly deeper pocketbooks of white teenagers, and this broadcast seemed to show that his goal was supported by youth across the country.[155] Since the newly formatted *Bandstand* featured performers as diverse as Black pop singer Sam Cooke, white rockabilly star Buddy Holly, and white pop acts like Bobby Vee and Connie Francis, teenage viewers were able to see Black and white musicians performing in somewhat different genres (although always under the umbrella of rock and roll) who were treated in the same manner by the show's producers, shared the same stage, and inspired adulation from young fans across racial lines.[156] Many respondents recall, to this day, the impact of seeing some of their favorite artists on camera for the first time. "That's what made *American Bandstand* so fascinating to me," Bill W. claims. "To be able to see those guys for the first time, see what they look like, watch them perform, even though they weren't really singing . . . was the final piece of the puzzle." Scott F. concurs, stating that "what I love about those programs is not only did you get a chance to listen to the artist and see the artist perform, but there were also people having a good time and dancing while those artists were on. So it took their music to a different level." Ron R. says that he tuned in because "suddenly people could see how other kids danced to this music. It wasn't just a matter of passively listening to it, or maybe even trying to play it, but actually being able to get up and dance to it."[157]

One of the reasons that the ability to actually see artists perform was so meaningful and memorable is that viewers were often surprised by their race or otherwise forced to confront it in a way that was obstructed by simply listening over the airwaves. "You could see that they were Black guys singing versus white guys singing," says Michael P., who identifies as white. Victor

F., who also identifies as white, claims that "when I listened to the bass on certain records, I didn't know who they were. You know, until I saw them on television, or something. They were all these Black groups that were playing." Bibb E. recalls how, when he and his white friends started watching *Bandstand*, "Now we could see the musicians. We learned the names of the teen-age dancers on the show. My classmates talked about the clothes they wore, who was dancing with whom, and the latest dances. Sure, they were all Yankees with odd names, and few Negro couples danced on the floor as well; but nobody seemed to care."[158] Perhaps unsurprisingly, his assessment echoes those of white Southern students who did not understand why parents were so upset about nominal desegregation in schools. Both Black and white respondents claim that these visuals could help them feel like they were part of a larger, somewhat integrated, community of young people who were brought together by love for this music. Cheryl J., who identifies as Black, affirms Dick Clark's version of this story, saying that the host "brought the kids together. And that always made us happy. We sat and watched Dick Clark." Henry I., who identifies as white, and says that "we'd have *Bandstand* on all the time" in his Philadelphia home, recalls how "anybody who was doing Top 40, Black or white, was there. You know, I remember Chubby Checker there, and Dion and the Belmonts, Pat Boone. I mean, the whole gamut. Anybody who was making hits got on and lip-synched their number." Even the nominal integration on this program seemed meaningful to people like Victor F., who says that when he watched dancers with different racial identities on *Bandstand*, "you saw them dancing together, but you didn't know that they weren't allowed to dance with each other. I didn't know that. I only found that out [later in life]. Because I just watched those programs, and I saw Black people, who I didn't see in my neighborhood."[159]

Despite the fact that *Bandstand* in the late 1950s rarely included more than one Black couple, and Black dancers kept a careful distance from white dancers, many Black respondents say they were excited to see even this amount of Black representation on a fun, popular show for teenagers that aired across the country. "I would watch it every Saturday, I would watch it all the time, and saw all the artists," says Miche B. "It was so cool when a Black artist would finally come on." Rhonda E. similarly remembers how excited she and her entire family would get when Black artists performed on *Bandstand*. "We could be in our rooms playing and our dad would yell out, 'Terry, Rhonda, come here!' you know, and he would just be excited. I don't know if he would say a colored man is on TV, or, I don't think he said Black man. But he said either a colored man is on TV or a Negro is on TV. And we'd drop our toys and run in the living room and sit on the floor right in front of the TV. And, you know, whoever it was, we'd enjoy them." She remembers enjoying most Black artists, including Chubby Checker, Frankie Lymon, Little Anthony and the Imperials, and some of the early 1960s girl groups, as well as white performers like Bobby Darin and Bobby Rydell. "I probably didn't realize the change as it was taking place, just that, let's say before *American Bandstand*, Blacks on TV singing, it was probably a weekend or an evening show [and] we knew that wasn't the ordinary. We knew it was a deal. . . . But I guess by 1959, it wasn't, you know, an oddity, [but] it was still special." *Bandstand* therefore offered its legions of teenage fans a somewhat integrated adolescent fantasy when they flipped on their TVs every afternoon after school, even if representation of Black dancers remained limited. White teenagers could see a form of racial integration presented as natural, while Black teenagers were able to watch Black artists represented as popular, fashionable, fun, and scarcely different from their white contemporaries. And yet, limitations remained. Even though Scott F. remembers that "there were not necessarily just white acts, but there were white and Black acts," he also "noticed a lack of" Black representation, even among the performers chosen to grace the stage. He never saw some of his favorite Black R&B and rock and roll artists onscreen, even though "they're every bit as good as the records that are [featured on the show]." He admits that, even though he didn't really know how to process the limited, white-dominated forms of integration he saw on *Bandstand* that "that's how I deduced that, okay, there's a problem here."[160]

It is therefore unsurprising that *Bandstand* and its host and producers would be credited with facilitating acceptance of racial integration, at least in the abstract realm of television programming, but Matthew Delmont's qualms about the show bearing "little resemblance to the interracial makeup of Philadelphia's rock and roll scene," even as its popularity was based on the musical crossovers between R&B and pop, continued to haunt the program.[161] The show validated the contributions of Black individuals, showed that teenagers of both races listened and responded to the same kinds of music, dance, and clothing styles, and forced audiences to visually acknowledge the biracial nature of rock and roll in a way that radio could not. At a time when integrationist goals were paramount to civil rights activists, teen dance programs like *Bandstand* could provide viewers with the realization that young rock and roll fans were, in actuality, racially mixed. But even as the show presented a view of society that, like some desegregating schools, tacitly included Blacks and whites together in the same space, it did not depict any real sense of equality, despite Clark's pronouncements. Delmont argues that even aside from the limited number of Black dancers allowed onscreen and rules against interracial dance partners, which betrayed the fact that its intended audience was mainly white, white-dominated dance shows relied on diluted forms of African-American culture without acknowledging its roots. He says that a young white couple "awkwardly" performing "The Stroll" to Chuck Willis's "Betty and Dupree" on a local Iowa dance show, for instance, "did not need to know the history" of the song, which was inspired by a South Carolina folk legend. This form of appropriation on shows that either barred Black teenagers from the dance floor, or limited their presence to a single segregated couple, angered and frustrated many Black teenage viewers, even if they did allow Black performers a broader platform. After all, the music, dances, and performing artists on these shows were typically integrated, but the dancers who represented the teenage tastemakers upon which the entire enterprise was based were largely white—even Hazel Bryan appeared on Little Rock's local dance program, *Steve's Show*, within weeks of harassing Elizabeth Eckford as she tried to desegregate Central High School.[162]

Dance shows and desegregating schools therefore shared several characteristics that affected how Black and white teenagers understood and acted on their identities. Integration could be presented as a sign of modern life and a break from the past, at least in theory, even if Black individuals were unable to find much community in these new spaces. Black performers were lauded on shows like *Bandstand* and able to share their music with people across the country, but the few Black dancers allowed on camera paralleled the small numbers of students who were chosen to "desegregate" white institutions. Both spaces allowed Black and white teenagers to mingle in an era when any form of racial mixing signaled triumph for integrationist campaigns and challenges to Jim Crow restrictions. But at the same time, Delmont argues that these shows "asserted a racially segregated public culture" in the same way that school districts maintained, and even strengthened, white control by admitting small numbers of Black students and by neglecting their academic, cultural, and social needs once they attended class. Even though many Black kids continued to watch *Bandstand* and other similar shows, Delmont explains that they could also find solace in regional Black-oriented teen dance shows that hit the airwaves during this period. Shows like *The Mitch Thomas Show*, *Teenage Frolics*, and *Teenarama Dance Party* reached smaller audiences and featured lesser-known performers, but Delmont argues that watching dance floors filled with Black kids unafraid to celebrate their own talents and identities allowed viewers to feel fully seen and appreciated, rather than as token African Americans used to fulfill demographic needs. "If white teen shows sought to shore up the supremacy of whiteness in youth music culture," Delmont attests, "the black teen shows visualized black teens as equal participants in the production and consumption of music culture." Even though teen dance shows like *Bandstand* were promoted as integrated spaces that reached white and Black viewers alike, they were shaped by white visions of integration that reshaped African-American cultural characteristics so that they would become acceptable to majority-white populations, accepting small numbers of Black people while cutting them off from necessary forms of community with others who might understand their experiences.[163]

DESEGREGATION ON THE HOT 100 CHART

As the 1950s came to a close, rock and roll's original musical strands had melded together so well that the genre was allowed to stand on its own as a distinct category without its influences being constantly picked apart. By 1959, 57 records appeared on both the Hot 100 and Hot R&B charts, and 24 percent of artists on the Hot 100 chart were Black. This integrated listening continued to cross in both directions, as 28 percent of artists whose records made the R&B chart were white. The following year, 55 records showed up on the Hot 100 and Hot R&B charts, Black artists comprised 20 percent of those on the Hot 100 chart, and white artists made up 27 percent of those on the Hot R&B chart. Even amid this small decline, the *Billboard* charts revealed how integration in music, particularly within the genre of rock and roll, had become the norm. Major record labels were forced to embrace the terminology of rock and roll, some of the musicological aspects of R&B, and even a few Black artists who had proven so popular with young white listeners that profits would suffer if they were cast aside.

And yet this shift existed within a broader racial context that continued to deny Black culture its worth, and individuals their full citizenship rights. The creation of the Hot 100 chart may have signaled that top artists came from diverse backgrounds, and that race no longer predicted the types of records that consumers chose to purchase. But sales were still measured in major, majority-white areas, which meant that the numbers reflected the tastes of white consumers rather than their Black peers. No matter how similar the charts appeared on the surface, *Billboard* and its intended vendors still predicated most of their sales decisions on the actions of white listeners, which put smaller Black-owned labels at a disadvantage even as major labels began signing small numbers of Black artists. These shifts seemed to support the concept of integration on the surface, but the overarching power structures remained the same. Even the payola scandal of 1959–1960 has been interpreted as a means of cleansing the mainstream music industry of overtly Black characteristics. Numerous radio stations, deejays, and personalities, including Alan Freed and Dick Clark, were investigated for receiving illegal payments or gifts made in exchange for radio airplay.[164] Freed, who consistently acknowledged Black contributions to the rock and roll genre, hired numerous Black artists to appear on his live tours and television show, and refused to play cover songs, was ruined by this investigation. Clark, however, who tended to accept the racial status quo, and only allowed token Black participation on his show, was able to work with investigators to clear his name.[165]

Many music industry insiders believed that these investigations would sound the death knell for rock and roll, but *Billboard* noted that "Rock and roll's demise, like that of Mark Twain's, has been greatly exaggerated. For now, even after the payola scandals and the attempt to link all payola with rock and roll recordings, the music with a beat still dominates over 60 per cent of The Billboard's 'Hot 100' chart." This proclamation was not, however, meant to assert the triumph of an integrated musical genre over attempts to "re-whiten" the industry so much as it was an assertion that this "whitening" had already occurred. Indeed, the author goes on to note that "this is not to say that rock and roll isn't fading, or actually evolving into pop music," and included Frankie Avalon, Paul Anka, Fabian, and Bobby Rydell, alongside Lloyd Price, Joe Turner, Fats Domino, Bill Haley, and Ray Charles, among its list of popular "out-and-out rockers," as though no difference existed among these artists.[166] This failure to differentiate between crooning pop idols who were groomed by major record labels to sing trite love songs, and some of the hard-rocking progenitors of the genre whose gritty deliveries necessitated the need to be toned down in the first place, reflected the mainstream music industry's ability to absorb some of the Black or rebellious elements of rock and roll while still maintaining control over its production and dissemination. The mere fact that their music had a beat—however weak that beat might be—and that it was popular with teenagers meant that it could be identified as rock and roll. The genre was still viewed as an integrated form of music; the author of the *Billboard* article, for instance, saw no need to segregate their list of top performers into Black (or Black-inspired) and white artists.

But just as Black students struggled to succeed academically and to have teenage experiences that were similar to their white peers within the walls of desegregating schools, African-American musicians continued to face greater professional challenges than their white teen idol peers. Rock and roll came out of integrating musical traditions, and it appealed to both Black and white audiences alike more than ever before. But the white-dominated mainstream music industry, just like Southern schools that were forced to desegregate, proved flexible enough to encompass these racial mixtures and to force degrees of assimilation rather than allow change from within. Integration in schools and in the music industry did not necessarily provide Black Americans with the opportunities they sought, even if white liberals welcomed these supposedly mixed spaces as evidence of a truly modern democracy. The willingness of advertisers and record companies to use the term "Teen Ager" to sell to Black kids, and some shared experiences among Black and white teens at school, within peer groups, and in relation to authority, however, indicate a broader understanding of this label as somewhat multiracial. By proudly identifying as or performing for "Teen Agers," Black adolescents and musicians showed that they were instrumental in determining the defining characteristics of this demographic—and of rock and roll as a whole—for young people from all racial groups.

NOTES

1. Frankie Lymon, Herman Santiago, and Jimmy Merchant, "Why Do Fools Fall in Love," The Teenagers, featuring Frankie Lymon, Gee Records, 1956.
2. Grace Palladino, *Teenagers: An American History* (New York: Basic Books, 1996), 51.
3. Philip H. Ennis, *The Seventh Stream: The Emergence of Rocknroll in American Popular Music* (Middletown, CT: Wesleyan University Press, 1992), 286.
4. Marketing to teenagers was precipitated by Eugene Gilbert, who created Youth Marketing Co. in 1945. This company gathered research from actual teenagers and based strategies on their responses rather than trying to tell them what they should want. By the early 1950s, other companies began to emulate Gilbert's efforts. Lizabeth Cohen, *A Consumer's Economy: The Politics of Mass Consumption in Postwar America* (New York: Vintage, 2003), 319–320.
5. Joseph S. Himes, 1961, "Negro Teen-Age Culture," *The Annals of the American Academy of Political and Social Science* 338, no. 1 (1961), 93–99.
6. *Billboard*, August 4, 1958; Ennis, *The Seventh Stream*, 185. The Hot 100 differed from *Billboard*'s previous top 100 list, established in 1955, which was usually buried on a half-page in small print, while the Pop chart took precedence.
7. Peter Guralnick, *Last Train to Memphis: The Rise of Elvis Presley* (New York: Little, Brown and Company, 1994), 39–40.
8. Nelson George, *The Death of Rhythm and Blues* (New York: Penguin: 2003). Although George's book remains a pre-eminent examination of white theft of Black musical forms in the twentieth century, he is far from alone in his assertions that the term "rock and roll" refers to little more than R&B music performed by white artists. This argument is so widely accepted that even popular articles assert that "by the '50s, white folks repackaged the music as rock 'n' roll." Please see Nick Tosches, *Hellfire: The Jerry Lee Lewis Story* (New York: Grove Press, 1998), 86, and Jason King, "I'll Take You There: R&B From NPR Music," The Mix: NPR Music, February 10, 2014. Along the same lines, Peter Guralnick and Louis Cantor have both argued that rock and roll was "invented" by Memphis impresarios Sam Phillips and Dewey Phillips, both of whom were white. Cantor explains how Sam, who "understood the problems he faced in selling unknown Black performers to white teenagers," decided to visit Dewey, a popular local deejay, whose show, *Red, Hot and Blue*, "had become so popular that whites would be drawn to previously unheard black performers almost in spite of themselves." Here, Cantor depicts these white music lovers attempting to force Black music onto an unsuspecting young white populace, who just had to hear the music in order to be automatically drawn in. For more, please see Louie Cantor, *Dewey and Elvis: The Life and Times of a Rock 'n' Roll Deejay* (Champaign, IL: University of Illinois Press, 2010), 115 and Peter Guralnick, *Sam Phillips: The Man Who Invented Rock 'n' Roll* (Back Bay Books, 2016).
9. Anita Behrman, "What Alan Freed Really Thinks About Rock 'n' Roll," *People Today*, October 1958, 22, Alan Freed Collection, Box 1, Folder 56, The Rock and Roll Hall of Fame Library and Archives, Cleveland, OH; Michael Lydon, *Rock*

Folk: Portraits from the Rock 'n' Roll Pantheon (New York: Citadel Press, 1971), introduction; Steve Chapple and Reebee Garofalo, *Rock 'n' Roll Is Here to Pay: The History and Politics of the Music Industry* (Lanham, MD: Rowman & Littlefield, 1978), 231–234.

10. Bruce C., in discussion with the author, June 8, 2020. Larry R., in discussion with the author, October 4, 2019; Edgar S., in discussion with the author, June 25, 2020.

11. Tosches, *Hellfire*, 86–87.

12. Jack Hamilton, *Just Around Midnight* (Cambridge, MA: Harvard University Press, 2016), 6.

13. Alan Freed, "Wonderful World of Rock," The Alan Freed Collection, Box 1, Folder 55, The Rock and Roll Library and Archives, Cleveland, OH, 39.

14. Wayne Robins, *A Brief History of Rock, Off the Record* (London: Routledge, 2016), 5. For a video of Black and white teens sharing the dance floor during a 1959 broadcast of *The Big Beat* on WNEW-TV New York, please visit http://www.onlineshoes.com/Womens-steve-madden-rawlings-grey-suede-p_id310149?adtrack=tpart

15. Billy Vera, "Specialty Records 40th Anniversary 1946–1986: Celebrating Four Decades of Leadership in Rock, R&B, and Gospel Music," 38, Specialty Records Collection, Box-Folder OS1-OF6, The Rock and Roll Hall of Fame Library and Archives, Cleveland, OH.

16. Ennis, *The Seventh Stream*, 185. These seven artists included Elvis Presley, Jerry Lee Lewis, the Everly Brothers, Bill Justis, Bobby Helms, and Jimmie Rodgers. Jim Lowe was the sole white pop artist to achieve crossover appeal on both the R&B and Country and Western charts.

17. Ricky Nelson and the Four Preps each had two records cross directly from Pop to R&B in 1958: "Stood Up" in February and "Believe What You Say" in April, and "Twenty-Six Miles in March" and "Big Man" in June, respectively; otherwise, Connie Francis's "Who's Sorry Now" crossed over in March, David Seville's "Witch Doctor" in April, and Danny and the Juniors' "At the Hop" in December 1957, ultimately reaching number 1 on both charts.

18. Usage of this slang term for sexual activity has been traced to African-American communities as early as the 1920s.

19. Alan Freed, "Wonderful World of Rock," *Pageant*, July 1957, 60, Alan Freed Collection, Box 1, Folder 55, The Rock and Roll Hall of Fame Library and Archives, Cleveland, OH.

20. "Atlantic Long Playing Sales Fact Sheet: Atlantic Releases 6 Rock and Roll Long Plays by its 6 Top Artists. The Biggest Hits by the Biggest Names in the 'Big Beat' Idiom," Atlantic Recording Corporation Records, Box 1, Folder 5, The Rock and Roll Hall of Fame Library and Archives, Cleveland, OH.

21. Ralph Gleason, interview with Milt Gabler, 1974, 11, Milt Gabler Collection, Box 4, Folder 18, The Rock and Roll Hall of Fame Library and Archives, Cleveland, OH.

22. Paul Kingsbury, *BMI 50th Anniversary: The Explosion of American Music 1940–1990* (Nashville: The Country Music Foundation 1990), 29.

23. Grace Elizabeth Hale, *A Nation of Outsiders: How the White Middle Class Fell in Love with Rebellion in Postwar America* (New York: Oxford University Press, 2011), 51.

24. *Life*, "A New $10 Billion Power: the U.S. Teen-age Consumer," August 31, 1959, 78–84.

25. *Ebony*, "Child Star Grows Up," December 1959, 115–120.

26. *Life*, "A New $10 Billion Power: the U.S. Teen-age Consumer," 78–84.

27. *Ebony*, "Child Star Grows Up," 115–120.

28. *Life*, "A New $10 Billion Power: the U.S. Teen-age Consumer," 78–84.

29. *Ebony*, "Child Star Grows Up," 115–120.

30. Susan Cahn, *Sexual Reckonings: Southern Girls in a Troubling Age* (Cambridge, MA: Harvard University Press, 2007); Palladino, *Teenagers*.

31. Matthew F. Delmont, *The Nicest Kids in Town: American Bandstand, Rock 'n' Roll, and the Struggle for Civil Rights in 1950s Philadelphia* (Berkeley and Los Angeles: University of California Press, 2012); Brian Ward, *Just My Soul Responding: Rhythm and Blues, Black Consciousness, and Race Relations* (Berkeley and Los Angeles: University of California Press, 1998).

32. Wini Breines, *Young, White, and Miserable: Growing Up Female in the Fifties* (Boston, MA: Beacon Press, 1992), 136–137.

33. Bret Eynon, "John Sinclair: Hipster," November 21, 1977, 11, Michigan Historical Collections, Contemporary History Project Papers, Bentley Historical Library, Ann Arbor, MI.

34. Bill W., in discussion with the author, June 1–2, 2020.

35. Larry R., in discussion with the author, Theodore Irwin, "Rock 'n' Roll 'n' Alan," *Pageant*, July 1957, 59, Alan Freed Collection, Box 1, Folder 55, The Rock and Roll Hall of Fame Library and Archives, Cleveland, OH.

36. *Life*, "A New $10 Billion Power," 78–79.

37. *Billboard*, June 23, 1956.

38. Berry Gordy, *To Be Loved: The Music, the Magic, the Memories of Motown* (New York: Warner Books), 1994, 56.

39. Chapple and Garofalo, *Rock 'n' Roll Is Here to Pay*, 32; Reebee Garofalo, "Popular Music and the Civil Rights Movement," in *Rockin' the Boat: Mass Music and Mass Movement*, ed. Reebee Garofalo (Cambridge, MA: South End Press, 1999), 23.

40. Lydon, *Rock Folk*, 8; Ennis, *The Seventh Stream*, 227.

41. Garofalo, *Rockin' the Boat*, 23.

42. Lyrics taken from recording made by Bob Willis for Vocalion, 1938, though even this version included words "borrowed" from "Sunday Night," Frederick W. Root, 1878.

43. Chuck Berry, "Maybellene." Chess, 1955.

44. Kingsbury, *BMI 50th Anniversary*, 29.

45. Jerry Wexler and David Ritz, *Rhythm and the Blues: A Life in American Music* (New York: St. Martin's Press, 1994), 110.

46. Cahn, *Sexual Reckonings*, 254.

47. Freed, "Wonderful World of Rock," 39; 58.

48. Arnold Shaw, *The Rockin' 50s: The Decade That Transformed the Pop Music Scene* (New York: Hawthorn Books, 1973), 135.
49. Wexler and Ritz, *Rhythm and the Blues*, 134.
50. Kingsbury, *BMI 50th Anniversary*, 41.
51. Wexler and Ritz, *Rhythm and the Blues*, 134.
52. Kingsbury, *BMI 50th Anniversary*, 39.
53. Vera, "The Specialty Story."
54. "Alan Freed's Third Anniversary Show," Sieg Corporation, 1956, Alan Freed Collection, Box 2, Folder 4, The Rock and Roll Hall of Fame Library and Archives, Cleveland, OH.
55. June Bundy, "Road Show: Freed and Troupe Rock 'Today,'" *Billboard*, June 24, 1957, 7.
56. Cahn, *Sexual Reckonings*, 267.
57. Victor F., in discussion with the author, September 26, 2019.
58. Zebulon Vance Miletsky, "Before Busing: Boston's Long Movement for Civil Rights and the Legacy of Jim Crow in the 'Cradle of Liberty,'" *Journal of Urban History* 43, no. 2 (2017), 204–217; Lawrence Grossman, "George T. Downing and Desegregation of Rhode Island Public Schools, 1855–1866," *Rhode Island History* 36, no. 4 (1977), 99–105; John B. Reid, "'A Career to Build, a People to Serve, a Purpose to Accomplish': Race, Class, Gender, and Detroit's First Black Women Teachers, 1865–1916," *The Michigan Historical Review* (1992), 1–27; Linda G. Williams, "Fannie Richards and Gladys Roscoe: Repertoires of Two Early African American Teachers in Detroit" in *African American Women Educators: A Critical Examination of their Pedagogies, Educational Ideas, and Activism From the Nineteenth to the Mid-Twentieth Century* Vol. 2, ed. Karen A. Johnson, Abul Pitre, and Kenneth L. Johnson (R&L Education, 2014).
59. Hilary Green, *Educational Reconstruction: African American Schools in the Urban South, 1865–1890* (New York: Oxford University Press, 2016); Jay Winston Driskell Jr., *Schooling Jim Crow: The Fight for Atlanta's Booker T. Washington High School and the Roots of Black Protest Politics* (Charlottesville, VA: University of Virginia Press, 2014), 2–3.
60. Grossman, "George T. Downing"; Gerber, "Education, Expediency, and Ideology."
61. Mark V. Tushnet, *The NAACP's Legal Strategy Against Segregated Education, 1925–1950* (Chapel Hill, NC: University of North Carolina, 1987), 145; Driskell, *Schooling Jim Crow*, 244–245.
62. Tushnet, *The NAACP's Legal Strategy Against Segregated Education*, 13.
63. Tushnet, *The NAACP's Legal Strategy Against Segregated Education*, 8–10.
64. Tushnet, *The NAACP's Legal Strategy Against Segregated Education*, 9
65. Tushnet, *The NAACP's Legal Strategy Against Segregated Education*, 119–120.
66. Tushnet, *The NAACP's Legal Strategy Against Segregated Education*, 36; 106–131; Driskell, *Schooling Jim Crow*, 247.
67. Tushnet, *The NAACP's Legal Strategy Against Segregated Education*, 155; 136.

68. Tushnet, *The NAACP's Legal Strategy Against Segregated Education*, 111–148.

69. Tushnet, *The NAACP's Legal Strategy Against Segregated Education*, 139–143; 160–165; "Brown et al. v. Board of Education of Topeka et al.," in *The Eyes on the Prize Civil Rights Reader: Documents, Speeches, and Firsthand Accounts from the Black Freedom Struggle,* ed. Clayborne Carson, David J. Garrow, Gerald Gill, Vincent Harding, and Darlene Clark Hine (New York: Penguin Books, 1991).

70. Civil Rights Plank to be submitted to Republican and Democratic National Convention, July 19, 1956.
Leadership Conference on Civil Rights General Correspondence Box 1-1, Folder 3, The Library of Congress, Washington, DC.

71. For more on the ties between civil rights activism and labor/socialist movements, please see Jacquelyn Dowd Hall, "The Long Civil Rights Movement and the Political Uses of the Past," *The Journal of American History* 91, no. 4 (March 2005), 1233–1263, Glenda Elizabeth Gilmore, *Defying Dixie: The Radical Roots of Civil Rights, 1919–1950* (New York: W.W. Norton & Co., 2009), and Robin D.G. Kelley, *Hammer and Hoe: Alabama Communists During the Great Depression* (Chapel Hill, NC: The University of North Carolina Press, 1990).

72. Please see Matthew Lassiter, *The Silent Majority: Suburban Politics in the Sunbelt South* (Princeton, NJ: Princeton University Press, 2007), Chapters 2 and 3, and Mary Lee Muller, "New Orleans Public School Desegregation," *Louisiana History: The Journal of the Louisiana Historical Association* 17, no. 1 (Winter, 1976), 69–88 for more on Open Schools movements in Atlanta and New Orleans; Wayne Phillips, "Integration: A Pattern Emerges," *The New York Times Magazine*, September 29, 1957, 210; Bob R., in discussion with the author, December 31, 2011.

73. Mary Dudziak, *Cold War Civil Rights: Race and the Image of American Democracy* (Princeton, NJ: Princeton University Press, 2002), 113; 147; Robert A. Caro, "Autherine Lucy at the University of Alabama: How the Mob Won," *The Journal of Blacks in Higher Education* 37 (2002), 124.

74. Palladino, *Teenagers*, 39–45; 51–52.

75. *Ebony*, "Child Star Grows Up"; "Teen-Age Stars Who Prefer School to Dollars," *Jet*, November 1, 1962, 58–60.

76. Thomas D. Snyder, "120 Years of American Education: A Statistical Portrait," Center for Education Statistics, 1993.

77. Claude Sitton, "Troubled Actors in the Little Rock Drama," *The New York Times*, Oct. 5, 1958, SM11, 24.

78. James Forman, "Black Bourgeoise in Little Rock, September 15, 1958," James Forman Papers, Box 104, Folder 11, Little Rock AK School Integration Correspondence and Writings, September 1958, The Library of Congress, Washington, DC; Lee Blackwell, "Pupils, White, Negro Tell of Experiences at Central," *Chicago Defender*, James Forman Papers, Box 104, Folder 11, Little Rock AK School Integration Correspondence and Writings, September 1958, The Library of Congress, Washington, DC.

79. Melba Patillo Beals, *Warriors Don't Cry: A Searing Memoir of the Battle to Integrate Little Rock's Central High* (New York: Washington Square Press, 1994),

3; *Eyes on the Prize: Fighting Back: 1957–1962*, dir. Judith Vecchione (PBS Home Video, 1986); *My Soul Looks Back in Wonder: Voices of the Civil Rights Experience*, ed. Juan Williams (New York: Sterling: 2004), 65; 68.

80. Scott F., in discussion with the author, April 11, 2020.

81. Edgar S., in discussion with the author; Joseph J., in discussion with the author, January 30, 2020.

82. Matthew Delmont, "Dancing Around the 'Glaring Light of Television': Black Teen Dance Shows in the South," *Southern Spaces*, September 29, 2015, last accessed at https://southernspaces.org/2015/dancing-around-glaring-light-television-Black-teen-dance-shows-south/, on September 13, 2019.

83. Education Held Integration Key," *The New York Times*, May 20, 1956, 81.

84. Joseph J., in discussion with the author; Edgar S., in discussion with the author; Tyrone W., in discussion with the author, November 4, 2011; Cheryl J., in discussion with the author, January 9, 2020; Najee M., in discussion with the author, November 20, 2011; Rhonda E., in discussion with the author, February 26, 2020.

85. John N. Pophan, "Violence Shuts Clinton School," *The New York Times*, December 5, 1956, 44.

86. Blackwell, "Pupils, White, Negro Tell of Experiences at Central."

87. Williams, *My Soul Looks Back in Wonder*, 65.

88. Gertrude Samuels, "School Desegregation: A Case History," *The New York Times*, May 8, 1955, 69.

89. Ellen Fishman, interview with Walter Blackwell, July 17, 1978, 8–9, Contemporary History Project: The New Left in Ann Arbor, Bentley Historical Library, The University of Michigan, Ann Arbor, MI; Cheryl J., in discussion with the author; Carol A., in discussion with the author, February 24, 2020.

90. Williams, *My Soul Looks Back in Wonder*, 68; Scott F., in discussion with the author.

91. Samuels, "School Desegregation," 69.

92. Samuels, "School Desegregation," SM9; 69.

93. H.H. Remmers and D.H. Radler, *The American Teenager* (Newport, RI: Charter Books, 1957), 18.

94. Cheryl J., in discussion with the author; Miche B., in discussion with the author, April 5, 2020; Ron R., in discussion with the author, June 9, 2020; John H., in discussion with the author, September 20, 2019.

95. Emily W., in discussion with the author, June 30, 2020; Marcia P., in discussion with the author, December 6, 2019.

96. "White Girls Take Lead in Mixed Dating, Says Coed," *Jet*, November 27, 1958, 24.

97. Samuels, "Desegregation: A Case Study," 69.

98. Blackwell, "Pupils, White, Negro Tell of Experiences at Central."

99. Samuels, "School Desegregation: A Case History," 68; Forman, "Black Bourgeoise in Little Rock;" Sitton, "Troubled Actors in the Little Rock Drama," 24.

100. Remmers and Radler, *The American Teenager*, 202–205; 220–221. Although Remmers asserted that he interviewed teenagers from all racial and ethnic backgrounds, and did, indeed, include anecdotal evidence from some Black teenagers'

survey replies, these questions are framed as though they were only posed to white students. Since he did not provide a racial breakdown, it is uncertain how many Black responses he received, and how Black kids would have understood this question differently from their white peers.

101. Rose W., in discussion with the author, April 26, 2020.
102. Ann W., in discussion with the author, November 9, 2011; Emily W., in discussion with the author.
103. Samuels, "Desegregation: A Case Study," SM9.
104. Rick T., in discussion with the author, November 20, 2011.
105. Remmers and Radler, *The American Teenager*, 204.
106. Samuels, "School Desegregation: A Case Study," 69.
107. Blackwell, "Pupils, White, Negro Tell of Experiences at Central."
108. Bibb E., in discussion with the author, November 13, 2011.
109. Stanley Rowland, "Southern Youths Back Integration," *The New York Times*, January 1, 1956, 42.
110. Samuels, "School Desegregation: A Case Study," 69.
111. David S., in discussion with the author, September 16, 2019.
112. Remmers and Radler, *The American Teenager*, 203.
113. Samuels, "School Desegregation: A Case History," 68.
114. Bill W., in discussion with the author.
115. Victor F., in discussion with the author; Bruce S., in discussion with the author, September 24, 2019; Bob S., in discussion with the author, September 25, 2019.
116. Walter S., in discussion with the author, October 4, 2019; Marcia P., in discussion with the author; Ron R., in discussion with the author; Andrew L., in discussion with the author, April 8, 2020.
117. Sitton "Troubled Actors in the Little Rock Drama," 22.
118. Letter to James Forman from Lee Blackwell, Sept. 17, 1958, James Forman Papers, Box 104, Folder 11, Little Rock AK School Integration Correspondence and Writings, September, 1958, The Library of Congress, Washington, DC.
119. Bob C., in discussion with the author, December 13, 2011.
120. Bob R., in discussion with the author, December 31, 2011.
121. Rick T., in discussion with the author.
122. Vera, "The Specialty Story: 1944–1964," 38.
123. Chapple and Garofalo, *Rock 'n' Roll Is Here to Pay*, 247.
124. Hale, *A Nation of Outsiders*, 86.
125. Lydon, *Rock Folk*, 21.
126. Wexler and Ritz, *Rhythm and the Blues*, 161.
127. Eynon, "John Sinclair: Hipster," 12.
128. Ken A., in discussion with the author, November 22, 2011; Larry R., in discussion with the author; Marcia P., in discussion with the author; Bruce C., in discussion with the author.
129. Ken A., in discussion with the author.
130. Bruce C., in discussion with the author; Janis Ian, *Society's Child* (New York: Tarcher: 2008), 21.

131. Bill W., in discussion with the author.

132. *Billboard*, April 20–June 24, 1957; Chuck Berry, "School Day," Chess, 1957.

133. *Billboard*, January 7–March 3, 1958; Chuck Berry, "Oh Baby Doll," Chess, 1957; Johnny Burnette and Dorsey Burnette, "Waitin' in School," Imperial, 1957; Garofalo, *Rockin' the Boat*, 233.

134. *Billboard*, February 16–April 27, 1959; *Dick Clark's Saturday Night Beechnut Show*, March 7, 1959, last accessed at https://www.youtube.com/watch?v=Qpkn6SOy0l8, on November 4, 2018.

135. *Billboard*, June 6–July 25, 1960; Lou Adler, Herb Alpert, and Sam Cooke, "Wonderful World," Keen, 1959.

136. Beth Bailey, "Rebels Without a Cause? Teenagers in the 1950s," *History Today* 40 (2001), 25–31.

137. *Life*, "A New $10 Billion Power: the U.S. Teen-age Consumer," 83; "The Costly Hazard of Young Marriage," *Life*, April 13, 1959, 119–130. By 1951, the average age of marriage was 22.6 for men and 20.4 for women, down roughly 3 to 4 points from the 1930s and 1940s.

138. Himes, "Negro Teen-Age Culture," 94.

139. "Should Teen-Agers Have Steady Dates? Survey Reveals 'Going Steady' Is Increasing Among Teens," *Jet*, October 1, 1959, 24–26.

140. *Billboard*, February 16–June 9, 1956; Frankie Lymon, Herman Santiago, and Jimmy Merchant, "Why Do Fools Fall in Love?" Gee Records, 1956; Maxwell Davis, Aaron Collins Jr., and Sam Ling, "Eddie My Love," RPM, 1956; *Billboard*, May 4–July 6, 1959; Doc Pomus and Mort Shuman, "A Teenager in Love," Laurie, 1959.

141. *Billboard*, June 10, 1957–February 3, 1958; Sam Cooke, "You Send Me," Keen, 1957; David Gilliam, "A Teenager's Romance," Verve, 1957.

142. Breines, *Young, White, and Miserable*, 8–9.

143. John Springhall, *Youth, Popular Culture, and Moral Panics: Penny Gaffs to Gangsta-Rap, 1830–1996* (London: Palgrave-Macmillan, 1999), 130–131.

144. Breines, *Young, White, and Miserable*, 130–132; 148.

145. "Are Teen-Agers Growing Up Too Fast?" *Jet*, May 19, 1955, 24–27.

146. Examples include Gene Pitney, "He's a Rebel," Phillies, 1962, recorded by the Crystals, and George Morton, Jeff Barry, and Ellie Greenwich, "Leader of the Pack," Red Bird, 1964, recorded by the Shangri-Las.

147. Jerry Leiber and Mike Stoller, "Jailhouse Rock," RCA Victor, 1957; *Billboard*, October 14, 1957–February 24, 1958.

148. Jerry Leiber and Mike Stoller, "Yakety Yak," Atco, 1958; *Billboard*, June 9–30, 1958.

149. Jason Barnosky, "The Violent Years: Responses to Juvenile Crime in the 1950s," *Polity* 38, no. 3 (2006), 314–344; Sheila Curran Bernard and Sam Pollard, *"Eyes on the Prize" Two Societies: 1965–1968* (Blackside, 1990); Regina Kunzel, "Pulp Fictions and Problem Girls: Reading and Rewriting Single Pregnancy in the Postwar United States," *The American Historical Review*, 1995, 1465–1487; Rickie Solinger, *Wake Up Little Susie: Single Pregnancy and Race Before Roe v. Wade* (London: Routledge, 2013).

150. George Goldner, "I'm Not a Juvenile Delinquent," Gee, 1956; Frankie Lymon and the Teenagers, "I'm Not a Juvenile Delinquent," *The Big Beat*, 1956, last accessed at https://www.youtube.com/watch?v=ZsBSsdAhnxE on September 14, 2020.

151. Matthew Delmont *The Nicest Kids in Town*, 3; 34; 38; 41.

152. Chapple and Garofalo, *Rock 'n' Roll Is Here to Pay*, 247.

153. Ward, *Just My Soul Responding*, 168.

154. Bruce C., in discussion with the author.

155. Gordy, *To Be Loved*, 89.

156. Ennis, *The Seventh Stream*, 274.

157. Bill W., in discussion with the author; Scott F., in discussion with the author; Ron R. in discussion with the author.

158. Michael P., in discussion with the author, October 4, 2019; Victor F., in discussion with the author; Bibb E., in discussion with the author.

159. Cheryl J., in discussion with the author; Henry I., in discussion with the author, October 30, 2019; Victor F. in discussion with the author.

160. Miche B., in discussion with the author; Rhonda E. in discussion with the author; Scott F. in discussion with the author.

161. Delmont, *The Nicest Kids in Town*, 6.

162. Delmont, *The Nicest Kids in Town*, 6; Delmont, "Dancing Around the 'Glaring Light of Television.'"

163. Delmont, *The Nicest Kids in Town*, 6; Delmont, "Dancing Around the 'Glaring Light of Television.'"

164. For more, please see Ennis, *The Seventh Stream*, 260–268 and Kingsbury, *BMI 50th Anniversary*, 63.

165. Delmont, *The Nicest Kids in Town*.

166. "R&R Still Beams Plenty of Life," *The Billboard*, January 18, 1960, 6.

Chapter 4

"They'd All Be Dancing Together," 1961–1964

In April 1962, Chubby Checker, a Black pop singer signed to Philadelphia's Cameo-Parkway Records, released a duet with white pop star Bobby Rydell entitled "Teach Me How to Twist" to lukewarm critical and popular reviews. The record's cover, featuring Rydell with his hand on Checker's shoulder and both men dressed in similar pastel-colored button-down shirts with V-neck cardigans, instantly relayed a sense of interracial friendship and equality. Even the positioning of both men's names promoted a spirit of integration. Checker's name was spelled out in green letters and Rydell's in blue, but they were positioned to read "Chubby Rydell" over "Bobby Checker," indicating the almost interchangeable nature of their celebrity statuses. The lyrics to this record also engaged the listener in a non-threatening interracial exchange between two friends. Rydell, the supposedly clueless white singer, chants "Chubby, teach me to twist/For I don't know how/Look at all I miss," as Checker responds, "It's so easy to twist. . . . Bobby, I'll teach you to twist." Although the song may have reinforced stereotypes about "inherent" Black dance rhythms and insufficient white physicality, it also normalized an apparent friendship between Black and white pop stars. Since Rydell was able to pick up the steps to this "easy" dance by the end of the tune, the rhythm that is supposedly essential to Black culture was also depicted as easily accessible to anyone open enough to engage with it. By the end of the song, "The whole world is twistin'/Now everybody's doin' the twist."[1]

Checker, one of the biggest pop stars of the early 1960s, first gained popularity with a cover of Hank Ballard and the Midnighters' "The Twist," which took the top spot on both the *Billboard* Hot 100 and R&B charts. Despite his racial background, Steve Chapple and Reebee Garofalo dub Checker a member of "the second generation of schlock" who was "created by a corporate decision" and, like his white counterparts, became famous by covering a raucous R&B tune by a Black group. The authors admit that "the twist itself is ambiguous socially" since "it was first successful at a time when the Black liberation movement in the United States was surfacing," but ultimately determine that "its leading exponent was a harmless corporate controlled black man. It was essentially a frivolous fad welcomed by white audiences as a retreat from the worries of bomb shelters and missile gaps and an ever-imminent imagined war with Russia, but it released white bodies from their petrified stiffness, and anticipated more openly sexual dances."[2] As the Twist became omnipresent in dance clubs and at sock hops across the country, Black Power activist Eldridge Cleaver agreed that white listeners embraced the more dynamic dance patterns emblematic of working-class Black communities, but posited that this was a political shift rather than a "frivolous fad." "The Twist was a guided missile, launched from the ghetto into the very heart of suburbia," he famously argued in his 1965 memoir, *Soul on Ice*. "The Twist succeeded, as politics, religion, and law could never do, in writing in the heart and soul what the Supreme Court could only write on the books."[3]

The so-called integration of popular music, which became so pervasive in the early 1960s that *Billboard* stopped publishing a separate R&B chart in late 1963, meant that public spaces devoted to musical performances and dancing would also be shaped by degrees of interracial mixing. Black and white musicians alike played to increasingly mixed-race crowds, even if they were strictly segregated in certain areas, while dances in majority-white areas featured music from Black performers and sometimes even drew Black students from nearby schools and neighborhoods. At the same time, a new civil rights organization, the Student Nonviolent Coordinating Committee (SNCC), began staging direct action campaigns where predominantly younger Black activists forcibly integrated public spaces in Southern cities by "sitting in" and refusing to move until served or otherwise acknowledged as full and equal citizens. These campaigns, which were organized to gain as much media exposure as possible, were seen on TV news programs and in magazine photos across the country. Black and white kids alike were often inspired by the organization's use of moral and democratic rhetoric and its adherence to nonviolence. Their lived experiences, however, provoked distinct reactions that led to tensions over the necessity of these tactics, and the primacy of direct action and voting rights campaigns over other structural inequalities, particularly economic discrimination and institutionalized violence. These shifts in civil rights strategies contextualized how Black and white teenagers listened to music in public, interacted with people from other racial backgrounds, and viewed desegregation's potential to combat racial injustice. If direct action campaigns provided templates for what an integrated society might look like, musical venues allowed kids who were not involved with civil rights activism the chance to enter mixed-race spaces, potentially reinforcing support for desegregation overall.

But white and Black music lovers did not experience this type of integration in the same ways either, even if they were able to enjoy performances in the same venues. Indeed, their reactions often mirrored and reinforced distinctions among white and Black responses to nonviolent direct action campaigns for integration and voting rights. Most kids grew up in relatively racially homogenous neighborhoods, especially if they came from middle-class families, and had few close interactions with people from other racial backgrounds. Many white kids were therefore eager to see Black performers or dancers in traditionally white spaces and recall feeling like it was natural and normal to enter mixed-race areas, even if they rarely encountered people of color in majority-white neighborhoods and schools. But entering predominantly white spaces was more complex for Black teens and musicians, who could face threats of violence, exploitation, and exoticization. Even though many also believed that this music could lead to support for desegregation in other public spaces, they realized that this goal would not be quite so easy to achieve. Instead, most Black respondents prioritized representation and being treated with dignity over the ability to interact with white kids in the same venues. These distinctions meant that integration and equality would hold very different meanings for white and Black activists and music fans, even when they were sharing the same spaces and using similar moral and democratic language to describe their thoughts and experiences.

NEIGHBORHOOD SEGREGATION IN THE EARLY 1960S

Most middle-class teens who grew up in or near urban or metropolitan areas lived in racially homogenous areas, unlike working- or lower-income kids, who were more likely to live in spaces where people from different racial backgrounds had closer interactions with each other. Outside of the Jim Crow South, working-class and lower-income teenagers were more likely to go to school or work with people from different racial backgrounds, presenting opportunities for interracial friendships and relationships as well as feelings of hostility and competition. In middle-class neighborhoods, however, racial divisions were established and reinforced by federal, state, and local policies, as well as real estate codes, ensuring that most respondents experienced little diversity in their communities or transitioning neighborhoods as white flight to suburban areas accelerated throughout the late 1950s and early 1960s. This process was made clear to Black respondents who grew up in some of Detroit's more integrated communities during this period. Rhonda E., who says "we might have been the fourth [Black family] on the block," remembers seeing "'For Sale' signs go up. As soon as you moved in, you saw your white neighbors on both sides kind of hightail it out. But especially the families with children. They left first." When she asked one of her white friends why her family was moving from their block, her friend explained that her mom told her they never would have moved in the first place had they known so many Black families lived there. Carol A. also recalls becoming aware of how white residents began moving from her neighborhood, which she describes as "working-class integrated," in the early 1960s. "People got along well," she recalls. "I had lots of friends [from different families], although we knew that there were racial differences . . . sometimes I heard some racist comments made. And the kids sometimes would say it." When she became aware that her neighbors were starting to move away, however, "you couldn't believe how quickly it was white flight. Like, really fast." White flight affected Southern neighborhoods as well. Ed B. says that he "became a little bit more aware" of racial issues in his Memphis neighborhood "because there were a few white people who hadn't moved out yet. But it was only one or two homes there still occupied by whites. And one of my best friends was white. His name was Mick. And there were about three or four of them, and Mickey and I were the same age. And we would all always get together. . . . Climb trees, swing on vines, and just have a good childhood time." But just as his Northern contemporaries recall this type of integration as very brief, disappearing as whites fled to exclusionary suburbs throughout the 1950s and 1960s, Ed's friend's family would soon vacate his block, resulting in an all-Black neighborhood that he remembers thinking was "the norm."[4]

Some white respondents also recall seeing this process in their communities. In New York, Rose W. grew up in a neighborhood that "was essentially Italian, Jewish, and Black, but very separated." Despite this tentative form of integration, she also recalls that "a half mile from my neighborhood was one hundred percent white. Four blocks away, there was, like, one street that's kind of a mix. And then it's one hundred percent Black." Throughout the 1960s, however, blockbusting efforts began driving her parents and other white neighbors out of their homes. "There were realtors driving around the neighborhood with mega-horns saying, 'the n*****s are coming,'" she says. Henry I. remembers how his parents partook in these blockbusting efforts themselves on his Aldan, Pennsylvania, block. "A family who was new on our street was going to sell to a Black family," he explains. "And my folks and several—and you know, I could probably name half of them—the neighbors got together, they put in an amount of money. And for some reason two or three hundred dollars apiece sticks in my mind. . . . And they somehow bought off the realtor. Or bought off somebody to end this." Even though he notes that "they did prevent it," he adds that, a year later, "it was done again. And I think it was the same family. That sold." The white residents on his street did not welcome their new neighbors with open arms. "We woke up one morning, I remember, to the people who were selling. Their car had 'N***** Lover' written on the side, you know, that type of awful thing," he says. "I remember waking up to firecrackers being thrown on people's lawn. You know, just trying to disrupt the whole thing." Henry says that "they were lovely people—the father was a librarian at the University of Pennsylvania," but that they were never fully accepted on their street, and so "were there for a couple years and then moved on again. But . . . they were the first Black family in the town of Aldan."[5]

The results of these racist efforts and policies had become stunningly clear by the early 1960s. Most white respondents say they grew up in neighborhoods that were overwhelmingly, sometimes completely, populated by white families. "The neighborhood we grew up in was definitely white, all white," says Marcia P., who comes from the west side of Detroit. Patricia J. describes her Pittsburgh community as "white, middle class. It wasn't Levittown because my parents didn't own a house like everybody else's. But it was like the next closest thing . . . there were no Black people that I can remember at all." "It was homogenized," Walter S. asserts of his suburban New Jersey hometown. "The commonality was where we lived, and that's all we saw." Bruce S. describes the Regal Park section of Queens where he grew up as "very highly white Jewish" and "pretty insular . . . because the contact with people from different backgrounds was minimal." Jimmy F., who lived just north of the city in Westchester County, also comes from a primarily "Jewish, Italian, and Irish" neighborhood that was "middle-class, upper-middle class" and "didn't have a lot of minority people in it." Many respondents stress the safety and normalcy of these racially exclusive and class-based communities, echoing the marketing strategies that mortgage lenders, home builders, and real estate agents used to entice white families to purchase new suburban homes. "It was stable. Safe. Typical. Idyllic," Walter recalls. Victor F. succinctly notes that he "grew up in a typical Long Island neighborhood. Middle class." And John H., who lived in Federal Housing Administration (FHA) developments for veterans in Tucson, describes his "99 percent white" community as "about as middle America as you could get." Even though white respondents tend to critique how their all-white neighborhoods were orchestrated to keep others out, they simultaneously describe them as both normal and safe, therefore reinforcing the notion that racially homogenous and middle-class community spaces, while cruelly exclusionary, are the default and preferred way of life for many white Americans. Black respondents also use this language—Scott F., for instance, who grew up in an all-Black housing project near the New Jersey coast, describes his neighborhood as having "a very relaxed sort of atmosphere" and says that he and his friends "did all the things that normal kids would do. We would go to the beach. So it was, in a sense, a pretty normal upbringing." He still feels compelled, however, to note that "it wasn't like being in the projects in Harlem, for instance. I mean, even though it wasn't the best of worlds, it wasn't the worst by any stretch." Even though much of his description parallels those of respondents who grew up in suburban white neighborhoods, he nevertheless makes it clear that his upbringing did not adhere to racialized stereotypes of safe, family-friendly communities.[6]

When respondents who came from segregated or segregating neighborhoods did come into contact with people from other racial backgrounds, they often did so under very specific circumstances that reinforced the everyday politics of white supremacy. Some kids, like Scott F., attended schools where they were in the minority or where a degree of integration had occurred, yet remember feeling out of place in certain instances, or only hanging out with their school friends during the day. Even though many of Joseph J.'s neighbors were white, he remembers how he was excluded from public places more than he does any sort of meaningful integration with these kids. "There was a huge park about three blocks from our house, and we could never play in that park," he says. "And there was a swimming pool in the park, and I never swam in that pool." Even though they remember recognizing wealth distinctions among Black and white areas and feeling upset that they were unable to use supposedly public spaces and amenities, neither was incensed by living in mostly segregated spaces alone. "It was just a given," Joseph explains. "It was a part of life. You didn't know any different." He further notes that "fighting a white kid in the neighborhood was no different than fighting a bully at school."[7]

White kids could also recognize racial distinctions in mixed spaces, although they did so from a position of relative privilege that often prevented them from having to give the matter much thought. Bruce C., for instance, would play with Black friends when visiting family in Patterson, New Jersey, a city that was tentatively mixed during the early 1960s as Black residents moved onto previously all-white blocks. "They were surrounded by African-American poverty," he says of his grandmother's and aunt's houses. "And those were the kids that I played with growing up. And you know, even as a child, I was acutely aware of the distinctions between my life and theirs. Between the things I had, the things they didn't have." Despite the fact that the city was very close to his own suburban home and "all I had to do was go across the street for the world to change," he asserts that "I never really thought about it much, but it was almost as if there was, like, an invisible wall there." Ron R. explains how his family was forced to move to "what would be called across the tracks, toward the Black part of town" when they experienced financial hardships, even though many of the Black residents who already lived there had middle-class professional careers. Ron similarly befriended neighbor kids, some of whom he has kept in touch with throughout his life. "It wasn't like, you know, here's suddenly this is the line that you do not cross if you're white or something like that," he says. "So we palled around together simply because we were neighbors." Others realized that these divisions existed, but did not question them much, or attributed this division to factors other than racism. "There were never any definitions in our head beyond, oh, you live here," Walter S. says of how neighborhoods were divided in his suburban New Jersey hometown. "I would say that the demarcation lines were probably more economic than anything else," John H. says of growing up in Tucson, where white and Mexican-American communities were clearly separated from each other. "We had all the so-called advantages of an upper-middle-class white Anglo-Saxon background. We didn't tend to mix a lot with people from the other side of town. But I think that was more by mutual agreement than anything else." Andrew L. remembers seeing people of color at the park in his otherwise majority-white community in Ohio, and explains that "we were in the North. It was like they had already been accepting Black people for a long time by the '60s." Even though he notes that he "had friends who were Black," he also admits that "we didn't hang out" much and that "my mother never had friends that were Black that we went there to eat dinner or anything." As much as these divisions were fairly obvious, they were also easily explained away by economic differences or by the lack of overt Jim Crow segregation policies.[8]

Other white kids were introduced to Black people within specific frameworks of power, particularly hierarchical employment structures. Ellis B.'s father, for instance, was the principal at a majority-Black school in New York. "His assistant principal was African American," he says. "Although our community was mostly white, it was not unusual, if we had parties, to have African-American staff members, teachers, mostly." He adds that "these people did not generally live in our community. They lived in other communities, but they were part of my dad's staff. He frequently had staff meetings and parties over at our house." He and his family got along well with his dad's co-workers in their home, yet Ellis was consistently aware that they were visitors in this space rather than residents and neighbors. These interactions could be reversed as well. Jimmy F. recalls accompanying his father to work at his family's bread factory where "we had 450 employees, and they were basically all ethnic," mostly people who were African-American, Caribbean, and Puerto Rican. "That was very diverse," he says, "and probably my biggest personal exposure to that side of the ethnic thing." He says that he would "always" talk to some of the people working in the factory when he visited, and that the interactions "were great. I mean, you know, when I was just a little boy, people might drop me in a vat of wheat. Always very friendly. I always treated them as equals. They were sort of—I thought they were my friends. But I mean, they weren't my friends really, we didn't socialize outside of the work environment." Again, he remembers feeling comfortable with these interactions, but, similar to Ellis's family parties, they only occurred in spaces where he was in a position of privilege and where they did not impact his daily relationships. Not all interracial spaces operated this way, of course—Clara A. notes that she started thinking more critically about racial segregation when she started attending a church in Detroit with a "mixed congregation" since everyone entered and interacted with equal standing. But as much as white respondents recall these instances with degrees of either fondness or nonchalance, few recognized how mixed spaces that reinforced white power structures were far more dangerous for Black kids to enter. After he was beaten and harassed by Memphis police, for instance, Ed B. asserts that "most [Black people] didn't challenge white people. They did not challenge them at all. Whatever they said was true. We was always the one that may have been wrong."[9]

DESEGREGATED CHARTS, MOTOWN, AND THE BRITISH INVASION, 1961–1964

City and suburban spaces were overwhelmingly divided by race and signified by racial characteristics, but most kids growing up during this period would have been very familiar with rock and roll artists from different racial backgrounds. Popular music had desegregated to the point that *Billboard* stopped printing a separate chart for top-selling R&B hits by the end of 1963, Black and white musicians alike became celebrities among listeners across racial lines, and race was no longer an automatic signifier for specific genres. Even though *Billboard*'s "Hot R&B" and "Hot C&W" charts continued to list the best-selling discs in predominantly African-American communities and Southern and Southwestern regions, respectively, between 1961 and late 1963, the "Hot 100" chart compiled data from major markets across the country, displaying a mishmash of records that defied genre boundaries, with many simply categorized as rock and roll. "Sweeping generalizations are bound to be misleading," Bill Gavin, a contributing editor at the publication, wrote in an April 1964 issue. "There is no such thing as a musical color line. Negroes buy and enjoy many different kinds of music, while many rhythm and blues records are well received by whites."[10] Indeed, hit records from corporate pop artists like Checker and Rydell, as well as enormously popular Motown and British Invasion groups, appealed to young audiences during these years, regardless of race. Although the number of crossover hits between the Hot 100 and R&B charts decreased by almost 13 percent between 1960 and 1961, and the number of white artists represented on the R&B chart declined by almost a quarter, from 17 to 13, Black artists' success on the Hot 100 chart exploded, rising almost 60 percent to 30 from a mere 19. More experienced musicians like Ray Charles and Sam Cooke sold well enough to make the move, but these numbers also represent the rising popularity of Black "girl groups" signed by Berry Gordy and Phil Spector, as well as younger proto-soul performers like the Impressions and Ben E. King. By the following year, the number of Black artists who made the Hot 100 chart increased by only 7 percent, but crossover records skyrocketed to 63 from the previous year's paltry 48. The only number that continued to decline in 1962 was that of white artists who made the R&B chart, which fell by 15 percent. During the 11 months that *Billboard* continued to print a separate R&B chart in 1963, all three percentages increased, with the number of white artists crossing to R&B surpassing expectations at 23, representing a 109 percent growth in less than a year. Young, commercially successful pop artists, including Lesley Gore, Little Peggy March, and Jan and Dean, were selling well in Black neighborhoods, as were more established stars like Elvis Presley and Andy Williams, and edgier folk acts like Peter, Paul and Mary and the Rooftop Singers. But Black artists continued to prosper on the Hot 100 chart, and 77 records crossed over between the charts, each representing a growth of 22 percent from the previous year.[11]

The increasing number of crossover hits revealed that Black musicians were increasingly considered pop artists, hardly different from their white counterparts, and that they could expect just as many white listeners as Black when their records were released. It appeared that these "racial distinctions" were "weakening," David Brackett says, though he pointedly notes that white artists consistently maintained higher degrees of popularity on the Hot 100 chart. "The reason usually given in histories of the pop charts is that the large number of R&B tunes crossing over in 1963 obviated the need for a separate chart," he explains. "But observation of the 1963 charts does not support any rigid equation between heightened racial equality and increased integration of the Hot 100." He supports this claim by showing how only Black artists contributed to only six of the top 30 songs in the November 23, 1963, edition of the Hot 100. "The elimination of the chart had real effects on the R&B recording industry," he continues, noting that it became "more difficult for retailers and radio station program directors to pay attention to records made by African-American artists." This asymmetry is revealed the following year, when, he says, "this decrease in attention is mirrored by a decrease in the number of top-10 singles by African American artists in the Hot 100, a total that went from 37 in 1963 to 21 in 1964."[12] His argument brings up a number of important factors, yet the numbers do not necessarily reveal a decline in Black representation within the mainstream pop market. First of all, counting artists rather than the number of records released by Black musicians skews the results—after all, best-selling artists like Ray Charles, Sam Cooke, the

Impressions, and members of Berry Gordy's phenomenal Motown lineup scored more than one hit over the course of this year, revealing widespread white fandom and mainstream industry approval for specific Black performers. Second, expanding the data from the top 10 to 20 hits on the Hot 100 chart, which makes sense given the original Pop chart's designation of a top 20 chart, reveals more significant Black contributions to the mainstream field. Between November 30, 1963, and December 26, 1964, during which time *Billboard* did not print a proper R&B chart, 64 records by Black musicians placed on the Hot 100 chart, revealing only a small decrease from the number of crossovers the previous year. Brackett's numbers also do not take into account the immense popularity of the Beatles and other white British Invasion groups. The Beatles' unprecedented takeover of the Hot 100 chart in 1964 caused American record labels to panic as they bypassed the popularity of white stars as well as Black, providing a cultural phenomenon which again skews the numbers without necessarily representing a decline in popularity among Black rock and roll artists.[13]

And yet, Brackett is correct in his overall argument that *Billboard*'s decision to stop printing the R&B chart during this period ultimately harmed many Black artists and record labels, and even solidified some aspects of racial segregation within the music industry. The absence of this chart meant that *Billboard* was no longer specifically tracking purchases in majority-Black neighborhoods, thereby limiting the consumer power of Black store owners and listeners to shape the direction of popular music overall, or to introduce lesser-known artists to mainstream white audiences and major-label representatives. Bill Gavin even made this point at the time, noting how "radio programmers, while recognizing the importance of the Negro audience, are frequently at a loss in evaluating and selecting the best r.&b. material" because "total sales of a r.&b. hit may not be reflected in a sales survey. The r.&b. sales are frequently concentrated in a few specialty stores and will therefore not be reflected in the greater number of retail outlets whose reports are compared."[14] Black artists were still able to maintain a fairly steady representation on the Hot 100 chart as a whole, but they were mostly younger rock and roll artists whose music, lyrics, fashions, and performance styles were heavily influenced by trends that were popular across racial lines. They were also more likely to be signed to major record labels, with the exceptions of Berry Gordy's Motown and Phil Spector's Phillies, both of which explicitly marketed Black groups to white audiences. These performers, and the records they released, could be subsumed within the pop framework, which had already been altered by a shift in musical tastes toward rock and roll. But artists who performed in more traditional R&B or gospel styles did not adhere to popular youth fads, or who were signed to smaller, Black-oriented labels, remained segregated, both racially and musically, within the pages of *Billboard* and in the mainstream music industry overall.

By July, the publication began including a one-to-two-page R&B section that was similar to those featuring trends in the fields of country, folk, classical, and international music. Unlike the country section, however, which never stopped publishing a weekly list of "Hot Country Singles," and even began listing top-selling albums, this section was mostly comprised of brief reports from different deejays at Black-oriented radio stations across the country, market analyses of trends within the genre, and a handful of new record recommendations, most of which failed to cross over to the top 20 on the Hot 100 chart. Other than a few issues which listed top-selling singles that did achieve crossover success, like the Supremes' "Where Did Our Love Go," the Drifters' "Under the Boardwalk," and the Impressions' "Keep On Pushing," *Billboard* editors clearly viewed R&B as a separate Black-oriented genre with less import within the industry, even if specific Black rock and roll artists were able to gain mass, interracial appeal.[15] By September and October, a few issues promoted singles that were receiving "strong Pop play" while ads also made use of this language, touting R&B acts that were "Now Breaking Pop!" although none received enough of this "play" to break through to the top 20 on the Hot 100 chart.[16] Gavin defended this type of segregation, noting that some "recording artists, as well as certain musical sounds and subject matter, find a readier acceptance among Negroes than elsewhere," and that the difference between rock and roll and R&B is that the latter appeals "toward adults rather than children. When it is said of a record that it has 'soul,' the reference is to a deeply felt expression of a mature emotion, as opposed to a typical teen-age preoccupation with 'first love' and its attendant frustrations." In terms of music, he wrote, "an authentic blues performance exhibits a freedom of melodic improvisation, common enough in jazz, but completely foreign to the square and prescribed framework of the conventional 'rocker.'"[17] Genre differences existed, of course, but the continued overlap between records by Black artists that were destined for mainstream success and those released by smaller labels and lesser-known performers within this special section reveals how *Billboard* continued to view race as a signifier for the R&B genre. Rock and roll artists might be welcomed into the popular music fold if they were able to adhere to trends beloved by young white audiences and earn major profits for their mostly white-operated labels, a process that almost perfectly mirrors expectations that Black people assimilate to white-dominated norms within desegregating spaces. But even as Gavin advised that "wise program management will keep trying to understand and reflect the tastes of the Negroes in their audiences" since "musically, integration is already an established fact [and] It is time that some broadcasters stopped pretending otherwise," this integration was still driven and maintained by white editors, music executives, radio programmers, and audiences, while R&B artists who overwhelmingly appealed to Black audiences remained at a financial and professional disadvantage.[18]

Most respondents recall hearing records from both Black and white artists on the radio, since top stations would play hits mined from the integrated Hot 100 list. "There wasn't so much of a divide, you know," Jimmy F. says about the top 40 stations in the New York area. "They played it all, Motown, Beatles, all mixed together." Scott F. echoes this assertion, noting that "the New York radio market was a really interesting and pivotal place to be." He recalls how "the pop stations, because of ratings and popularity, were taking records that [Black-oriented] WWRL and WNJR would play. So again, you had this cross section of sounds that, again, I don't know you would have gotten in any other market." Even if New York's stations reflected these integrated sounds earlier than other cities, they soon spread to major urban markets across the country. In Detroit, for instance, Rhonda E. recalls how "CKLW was probably the station listened to most by, they probably had the largest integrated audience." And Lori B. sums it up nicely, claiming how "there was no silo of sound." Even though listeners were aware of racial distinctions among artists and genre types, most assert that they did not take race into account when choosing the songs they preferred. Walter S. says "I didn't think that way as a teenager. I thought about, did I like this song or not. That was it." This lack of concern was due partly, he says, because "in order for [racial discrimination] to have a bearing, I've later learned in life, you have to be taught it." Since his parents "would never say, 'Oh, that's a Black artist, that's a white artist,'" he explains, he rarely considered the race of the singer he liked unless it was identified by the disc jockey. Pat K. concurs, asserting that she "listened to everything, I loved everything. . . . I had a lot of favorites with Black groups, white groups, Black artists, white artists. It did not matter. I loved all of it."[19] These memories reflect the increasingly integrated nature of the Hot 100 chart, but they simultaneously erase racial differences in favor of the supposed "color blindness" that would shape many white people's views on race in the aftermath of the civil rights movement. This determination not to consider race when listening to music could lead to harmful results for Black artists, as shown by Brackett's argument.[20]

Still, listening to mixtures of Black and white performers would have an impact on the young people who could not get enough of the music that would come to define their generation. Despite the popularity of so-called schlock rockers like Checker and Rydell throughout the early 1960s, more dynamic tunes from white British acts who emulated Black rock and roll legends from the 1950s and Black musicians performing poppy, gospel-tinged earworms under Berry Gordy's phenomenally successful Motown label would rejuvenate popular music while simultaneously increasing the amount of integration on the charts. A rise in the popularity of white British Invasion artists did accompany a decline in Black musicians' sales, as Brackett noted, which decreased 20 percent between 1962 and 1966, but Black Motown artists made up for much of this discrepancy, sending 70 percent of their recordings to the Hot 100 list by 1967.[21] Both The Beatles and Motown made cultural impacts beyond the musical industry, of course, becoming signifiers for the 1960s in many people's memories. "In high school, you know, there were two sides of the music," Jimmy F. asserts. "There was the rock and roll side from the Beatles and all the white bands. And then there was the Motown side. And we were into all of that. We were into all of that music."[22] Both Black and white respondents recall their introduction to Motown and British Invasion artists as monumental events that would shape their views on music, generational divisions, and culture for the rest of their lives. Racial politics clearly influenced each of these genres, but again, most white respondents consciously try to minimize any distinctions, instead emphasizing the joys of a supposedly color-blind musical culture. Black respondents similarly recall loving both types of music during this period, but they are more likely to emphasize pride in the Black representation that resulted from Motown's immense popularity rather than any sort of hope for an integrated future where racial identity would become blurred.

Motown's origin story has been retold so often that it has become the stuff of cultural legend. Detroit businessman Berry Gordy recognized the financial potential of selling Black music to white customers early on, but his first attempt at opening a shop specializing in jazz and the blues had failed to prosper. His love of songwriting, however, would lead him to create his own independent label, and to release sounds that would reshape the sonic atmosphere of American popular music. When he wrote his first song, "You Are You," at the age of 20, he recalled already having "Doris Day in mind. She was America's girl next door." Nothing much came of this song, but Gordy insisted he was "thinking of general audiences even then," with the term "general" indicating mainstream white popularity.[23] His distinctive goal to sell Black pop music to moneyed white customers would come to fruition, however, by the late 1950s, as white teenagers continued to crave the dynamic sounds of R&B minus some of the genre's harsher or more dramatic musicological elements.[24] Although he thought he had cracked the code to selling Black music across racial lines, he realized he had made a mistake after writing the seemingly smash pop hit "Everyone Was There" for his brother Robert, who performed under the stage name "Bob Kayli." Even though Kayli performed the song to wide acclaim on *Dick Clark's Saturday Night Beechnut Show*, the record failed to make the charts. "The problem then became clear," he noted. "People were shocked. This white-sounding record did not go with his black face." When he used a small family loan to open Motown Records in

January 1959, he was determined to sell music to white audiences that would fulfill their desire for gospel- and R&B-tinged Black sounds, while dulling any of the more threatening or unfamiliar edges so that it would fit the contours of mass culture.[25]

The Motown label and its cadre of camera-ready young Black stars would soon dominate the airwaves. Gordy's first hit, "Come to Me," performed by Marv Johnson, appeared on the Hot R&B Sides chart in April 1959, but the label would really explode the following year, when Barrett Strong's "Money (That's What I Want)" remained on the chart between February and May 1960, and the Miracles' "Shop Around" took the number 1 spot while also crossing over to the Hot 100, culminating at number 2 in February 1961. Over the next three years, 35 of Gordy's records would make the top 20 on the Hot 100 chart, including number 1 hits like The Marvelettes' "Please Mr. Postman," Mary Wells' "You Beat Me to the Punch" and "My Guy," The Contours' "Do You Love Me?," Martha and the Vandellas' "Heatwave," The Temptations' "The Way You Do the Things You Do," and The Supremes' "Where Did Our Love Go."[26] Gordy recruited these groups and singers from Detroit clubs, high schools, and youth dances, signing Smokey Robinson, Diana Ross, Martha Reeves, and Stevie Wonder, among others, while they were still teenagers to perform, as Andrew Flory describes it, "music [that] embodied a tension between older, segregated forms of R&B and the emerging styles of Black pop positioned for crossover success."[27] Gordy's songwriting team provided these young artists with poppy tunes and lyrics that romanticized teenage affections, yet remained mostly devoid of overt sexuality. The melodies were heavily influenced by Black gospel music as well as more pop-inflected string arrangements meant to encourage crossover success. The "churchy feel" of gospel inspiration, such as the use of the tambourine and the repetition of words over the chorus, was utilized, Craig Werner asserts, "to set Motown apart from bland white pop."[28] Even so, Flory explains, girl groups were taught "choirgirl diction" and to sing in a pop-like style he describes as "unthreatening" in order to "sublimate their age and sexual character."[29] Dance routines were carefully choreographed with an eye toward television cameras, and Gordy's sisters Gwen and Anna famously dictated etiquette and fashion rules to Motown's female artists so that their Black bodies and cultural expressions would adhere to respectability politics.[30] "Motown often asserted black identity to serve its crossover agenda," Flory asserts in his study of how the label's music interacted with different markets and genres. "The company's artists used comportment, choreography, and image fabrication to depict an idealized black middle class."[31]

Gordy's marketing strategy turned his label into an extraordinary success among white teenagers. By the early 1960s, Motown singles were starting to appear on top 40 radio playlists, and white consumers were quick to purchase the label's records. "Everybody moved into Motown, obviously, we were all huge Motown fans," Henry I. recalls. Many white respondents were drawn to the gospel- and R&B-tinged "beat" that Gordy and his songwriters carefully cultivated in each record, and which invited people to dance when they heard the first few notes. "I memorized a lot of lyrics, but did I ever listen to what they really meant? Rarely," Ellis B. attests. "I guess I just liked the sound, the beat, the voices. You know, I think it's tough to describe what you like about a particular piece of music. But it's less so the content of the lyrics for me than just, that sounds great." Bruce S. agrees, noting, "they had good beats, I enjoyed the music." Bill W. goes even further, stating that "Motown really resonated with me" because "it was sort of like, two-, three-minute symphonies." Other respondents recall thinking that Motown seemed less intimidating than other forms of Black music, which was part of Gordy's plan in the first place. "Motown's lyrics weren't exactly changing the world, but the tone and the inflection and the style that they brought moved a city," Lori B. argues. She capitulates, however, that "the Motown sound was smoother, [a] more kind of Vegas sound. Like it was slick." Marcia P., who says that she "loved seeing Detroit performers" because "that really sort of started my pride in the city," recalls seeing the Temptations onscreen for the first time and liking "that they were all really dressed well and were so sharp.... I really liked just how coordinated they were, I thought that was really great." Bruce C. concurs, recalling how Motown minimized racial divisions in music, partly because the Black artists Gordy signed to his label were groomed to appeal to white audiences and to appear as non-threatening as possible. "Up until Motown . . . people stayed in their own worlds," he says. "Because Berry Gordy put the Supremes in evening gowns. With great coiffeurs. And put the Four Tops and the Temptations, put them into tuxedos and stuff. You know, he dressed them up. They weren't Little Richard, in his 50s version of a Zoot suit." He also insists that white listeners were less intimidated by Motown's earlier vocal acts since they were "not performing groups. Performance is threatening . . . a guy with an instrument is a threatening thing, you know, or can be threatening to your conservative white audience to see Chuck Berry doing all these gyrations with his guitar." Motown's carefully crafted vocal performances, however, "looked kind of like Vegas acts."[32]

Gordy's lineup of Black artists performing dynamic R&B-inflected pop specifically designed not to threaten or offend whites resulted in more cross-racial listening and record-purchasing than ever before. But his very specific aims further led some white respondents to claim that they enjoyed this music without caring about the race of the performer. "In high school, I mean, I remember specifically going to dances . . . and the Motown songs were playing and we were all dancing," Jimmy F. recalls. "Nobody really hated the Black artists, the Four Tops, the Temptations, the Supremes, Marvelettes.

Millions of artists, we all loved them." Carol B. admits that "I didn't really think about [the race of the performers]. I mean, obviously I knew that Diana Ross and the Supremes were Black, but . . . I wouldn't have listened to that to try and determine that at all." Victor F. recalls seeing groups like the Supremes on television and thinking "my God, they're beautiful. You never said, 'Oh, they're Black.'" Others say that their growing love for this music led them to accept Black performers as equals, and even to question some of the racial norms they were accustomed to. Carol B. says that "the beginning of butting up to my father's views on race" started when she purchased records by Motown performers, and he "yelled at me for buying Black people's music instead of white people's music."[33] Most white respondents describe their love for Motown in "color-blind" terms, emphasizing their implicit support for desegregation goals. And yet Gordy's efforts to commodify the music so that it reached the largest possible audience could simultaneously drain it of any direct link to racial justice movements. "I don't remember the civil rights movement having any influence on music at all until the late '60s," recalls David S. "Even Motown music didn't really touch on it . . . didn't talk about it. And then, the song, like, 'Sugar Pie, Honey Bunch.' You didn't have songs that really dealt with that."[34] Even though white Motown fans are quick to voice their admiration for Black performers, they do not necessarily view their success as racially transgressive, partially because most songs avoided overt political themes, at least prior to the mid-1960s.

Black stars performing in such a controlled, choreographed manner, singing songs about love and romance, and dressed in fashions that teenagers were already beginning to view as slightly old-fashioned allowed white kids a glimpse of what an integrated world might look like, where race could be used not to discriminate or separate, but to empower. Even the label's carefully chosen slogan, "The Sound of Young America," promoted the music as neither white nor Black, but as the voice of a new generation that had presumably learned to view racial barriers with suspicion. And yet widespread white consumption of Motown records did not necessarily lead to more tolerant attitudes toward Black people in general, or encourage white listeners to think critically about how racism is structured in American society. White listeners have long been able to enjoy output from Black entertainers without recognizing their humanity or rights as citizens, and this love for Motown could provoke similar reactions, even if the label was created and operated by a Black man who oversaw a largely Black workforce and specifically marketed records to interracial audiences. Gordy carefully curated the respectable, "non-threatening" performances mentioned by some respondents in order to appeal to white customers and to fit into the music industry's approved framework that would allow Motown records to make the Hot 100 chart, but this was only necessary because Black people and their cultural traditions were stereotyped as dangerous, crude, salacious, and vulgar. White respondents who loved Motown did not have to confront these prejudices when listening to records or watching performances on television because Gordy had already removed many of the obstacles that could prevent them from enjoying the music within their own cultural frameworks. This cross-racial appeal could also further support supposedly "color-blind" perspectives on race and racism, allowing white listeners to believe that race simply did not matter to them when it came to record choice, so it should not matter in other areas either. While this perspective technically supports racial equality in theory, there is no acknowledgment of racist harms that go any deeper than mere white acceptance. It may align with a belief that the goals of the civil rights movement were morally correct, but also that the work that was necessary to reach these goals was either unnecessary given these supposedly race-neutral views, or that it would violate their own rights within existing capitalist-democratic structures. Gordy's business strategy elevated the work of Black performers and songwriters, and amplified African-American cultural traditions within the white mainstream to an unprecedented extent. And yet these efforts could also minimize the importance of Black contributions and the people who were instrumental to its success. Jerry Wexler made a telling statement in this vein in 1969, admitting, "I don't consider Motown Black; I consider them half and half. Black people making white music."[35]

But even as Gordy consciously set out to gain the attention of white teenagers, the music he released simultaneously asserted the dignity and strength of African-American culture. "Music, particularly music created in Detroit's black community during the 1960s, could rarely, if ever, transcend the politically and racially charged environment in which it was produced," Suzanne Smith argues. "The sounds, music, and 'dancing' that emerged from the streets of black Detroit reflected and directly engaged with the challenges African Americans faced as they built their lives in that major industrial city." She goes on to argue that many of the narratives that depict Motown as successful only because of its appeal to white audiences ignores the music's distinct impact on and reflection of Black community concerns, which "teaches important lessons about how 'cultural politics' operated at the grass-roots level."[36] Lyrics to the Miracles' 1955 record, "Bad Girl," for instance, could conjure images of civil rights activists fighting for equal treatment at all costs, even though Smokey Robinson's crooning "They tell me that the river's too deep and it's much too wide/Boy you can't get over to the other side" could also be interpreted as romantic frustration at being unable to win over the girl he desires. Andrew Flory describes the 1960 hit "Money (That's What I Want)" as "unlike anything Gordy had ever released" because of its prominent, blues-based structure and vocal performance that was "raw and amateurish" with lyrics that he describes as "crude and direct, drawing on

African American vernacular tropes in a manner that Gordy's writing usually avoided." By 1965, the Miracles' hit "The Tracks of My Tears" harkened back to the Platters' sense of Black isolation in a white world and being forced to hide the pain caused by racism beneath an unruffled façade, even though the lyrics are ostensibly about how the narrator is unable to get over a breakup, as Smokey Robinson croons, "So take a good look at my face/ You know my smile looks out of place."[37] Even though Black Motown artists sang songs with teenage themes like domestic tranquility and romantic love that appealed to kids of all racial identities, they had a special resonance for Black listeners. Actress and comedian Whoopi Goldberg recalled how "most of us wanted to be Diana [Ross] or The Temptations. We wanted to be hip and cool and rich and happy—and some of us wanted to be white, but we got over that. Because that's what we saw, until Motown came along."[38] Miche B., who grew up to become a singer and musician, was similarly drawn to the familiar sounds that she connected back to music from church services. "The music, the heartbeat, the drumbeat, the bass. You know, all of it was together," she explains. "I figured out early on that certain music [had] patterns. And with hymns and certain gospel music, when I really started getting into the Blues, I said wait a minute, these are the same changes. These are kind of the same riffs that the blues people are doing. And they're doing them in church, you know. With the Motown sound . . . a lot of their music had that kind of danceability." She began comparing Motown songs to the gospel sounds she heard in church and noticed that "the lyrics had the same patterns and would fit very well into a gospel feel." The pride she felt in hearing these patterns woven through international pop hits extended to her hometown of Detroit. "Motown was less than a mile from my house. Every once in awhile you might see one of the stars," she says. "I think I was born in the best place in the world because there was so much music."[39]

This sense of pride could reconstitute majority-Black spaces in urban cities like Detroit as places where joy, creativity, innovation, and style could flourish during a period when high rates of white flight and government and corporate disinvestment were instead marking them as impoverished and crime-ridden. Motown's nationwide success, Smith argues, "reveals how the development of a strong black urban community created unique opportunities for the development of an independent black commercial culture, and how this independent commercial culture then participated in the larger struggle for racial equality."[40] Indeed, Scott F. recalls hearing Motown music played out of apartment windows in his home complex, out of passing cars, and at family events. "Everyone loved to dance, and they made music that allowed you to dance," he says. "So it wasn't just what was on the radio, it was situational as well." Cheryl J. recalls how "when people turned it up, whether it was in their car or in their house, they were turning it up to feel the music and not just hear it." And as much as Motown's appeal crossed racial boundaries, Black respondents recall how proud they felt knowing that the music was created by African-American artists and songwriters, and that the label was Black owned and operated. "I realized they had to have it together like that because they were an African-American company," Cheryl continues. "So they had all this competition out there, and everybody was either hoping, wishing, that maybe they're going to slip and fall because Motown did nothing but repeat itself year after year in rising to the top." Rhonda E., who also lived in Detroit, says she remembers "being really, really proud of when they . . . started playing the nightclubs," especially since two of her white friends did not share her affection for the music. "I remember playing a couple records for them over the phone," she recalls. "I forget what I played first, and they liked it. But I remember when I played 'Tracks of My Tears' [by Smokey Robinson and the Miracles], I could hear them yelling on the phone, 'Turn it off! Turn it off!' They hated it." The reason, she supposes, "is Motown was foreign in their home." Even though Gordy was intent on marketing his label's music across racial boundaries, it had special resonance for Black kids, who did not often see positive representations of themselves in mainstream pop culture. Larry R., who, as a white civil rights activist engaged in grassroots organizing in Southern states during this period, even notes how the Black residents he worked with enjoyed Motown because they "did not see Motown as ripping off their music because it was produced by Blacks . . . and all the performers were Black. And it was Black music in the mainstream."[41] As Smith asserts, "by recording black culture the company participated in a larger history of promoting racial equality through creative and educational endeavours."[42]

A number of these respondents, however, also report liking the music for many of the same reason as their white contemporaries. Cheryl J., who says she "liked almost everybody" on the Motown label, explains that "they were so professional. . . . I liked Motown for that reason. It was so structured and [they] had it so together." She enjoyed the label's love songs even though "I wasn't trying to be in love" because "they had a rhythm to them, you know? They weren't like mushy slow love songs." Aside from the lyrics, Motown "was the dance music," she continues. "Rhythm and blues, you spend more time listening, and possibly delving into some of your own life stories . . . as opposed to Motown, you don't really have to relate to anything. You're just singing happy music and dancing." Scott F. agrees, describing Motown as "happy music" and "the first records that I remember people turning them up loud because you can really dance to them." Rhonda E. recalls running out to buy new Motown records as soon as they were released on Mondays, after first hearing them on the radio over the weekends. "They were just *it*," she says emphatically. "The lyrics, Smokey, to this day, we talk about the poetry of his music. 'The Way You Do the Things You Do.' Your smile is so bright you could be a candle. If good looks [was] a minute, you could be an hour. That's pretty nice. . . . They wanted you to feel good about love. And happy in life, I guess." Like almost every other respondent, she also mentions the beat. "If a song pleases you in some way, it kind of burns an imprint on your brain. You know, you walk around, maybe humming it after the first or second time you heard it. But eventually, not long thereafter, you're singing it. A lot of times it's, well, it's the beat, the words. Just some of everything." Melodies that anyone could dance or sing along to, regardless of racial identity, set to dreamy pop lyrics that were impersonal enough for all to enjoy, resulted in a music style that, as Rhonda explains, "was more, I don't know if palatable is the right word. But it was kind of, I don't think middle of the road is even the right term. But even Berry Gordy talked about, you know, he was making his music for everybody." Cheryl uses the same word, asserting that "everybody listened to Motown. Oh yeah, if you found somebody that wasn't listening to Motown, then you probably backed away making the sign of the cross, because something wasn't right." Gordy's attempts to market Black pop music to interracial audiences were ultimately successful, and perhaps capable of providing a template for harmonious integration in certain spaces while simultaneously promoting Black pride and representation within mainstream culture. "Motown's music symbolized the possibility of amicable racial integration through popular culture," Smith asserts. "But as a company, Motown represented the possibilities of black economic independence."[43]

The other musical bombshell of the early to mid-1960s, the British Invasion, began, of course, with The Beatles. The origin story of the Liverpudlian quartet that would revolutionize music and style throughout the 1960s is, much like that of Berry Gordy and his Motown label, mythic at this point. John Lennon and Paul McCartney, both lower-middle-class white teenagers obsessed with skiffle, a British riff on country and blues from the American South, met while performing at a church festival in 1957. After impressing each other by performing hits by Little Richard and Gene Vincent, Lennon asked McCartney to join his band, the Quarrymen. McCartney would soon recommend his friend, an even-younger guitar virtuoso named George Harrison, and the foundations for the most influential band of the twentieth century were established, to be completed with the addition of drummer Ringo Starr three years later. Right from the beginning, Sam Lebovic explains, "The Beatles emerged as a direct result of the postwar hegemony of US pop culture. From their bedroom radio sets in Liverpool, they had thrilled to the sounds of American rock 'n' roll." They openly expressed their admiration for, and imitation of, early American rock and roll icons, both Black and white, including Elvis Presley, Little Richard, Chuck Berry, and Buddy Holly. Much of their early repertoire, well into the early 1960s, consisted of the kinds of cover songs that had mostly been rejected in the United States, yet thrilled listeners and audiences when they heard Berry's "Roll Over, Beethoven" and the Isley Brothers' "Twist and Shout" performed by these adorable, irreverent white British boys. Even as Lennon and McCartney began writing and recording their own songs, many, including major hits like "She Loves You" and "I Want to Hold Your Hand," drew directly from the words and stylings of Black girl groups, while Lennon admitted to mimicking Smokey Robinson's distinctive falsetto more than once. American exports had dominated the music trade up to this point, but the Beatles' ability to, as Lebovic puts it, "neatly reverse" the global impact of U.S. musicians, especially Black artists, combined with their media-friendly wit and good looks, led the group to overwhelm the Hot 100. The Beatles scored 15 spots in the top 20 throughout 1964, the year their first single was released in the United States, and rapidly slashed their own records, making music history every week from the moment that "I Want to Hold Your Hand" debuted at number 3 the week of January 25. The single quickly took the top spot the following week, where it remained for seven weeks. "She Loves You" took the second spot the week of February 22, and "Please Please Me" made it three in a row on March 14. The Beatles were able to take over the top 4 slots by March 28, as their cover of the Isley Brothers' "Twist and Shout" moved up the charts, then set a record that would not be broken for over 50 years (if at all) the following week, April 4, when "Can't Buy Me Love" debuted at number 1, resulting in the band holding the top 5 spots on the Hot 100 chart. American music executives' intense yet ambivalent reactions are evident within the pages of *Billboard* issues released during the spring of 1964. While pictures and stories about the band plastered the publication from front to back, advertisements for other British groups, purportedly the next to break through to American audiences, and promotions for other artists signed to Vee-Jay, which owned the original contract for the Beatles' first recordings, were printed side by side with anxious editorials about how the band has "Launched a New Redcoat Invasion" that could place American artists at a disadvantage.[44]

Aside from the Beatles' historic placement on the charts, their cultural impact, especially on American youth, was undeniable right from the start. Almost every respondent recalls the moment they first heard the Beatles, either on the radio or during the group's iconic appearance on the *Ed Sullivan Show* in February 1964. Although the band members ignited passionate feelings in white and Black fans alike, white respondents are more likely to identify their arrival on American shores as a monumental event in their own personal histories. Marcia P. recalls how, listening to the radio before school one morning, while "we're eating our cold cereal, and like, ehhhh, another day of school," the deejay began to play a new record called "I Want to Hold Your Hand." "Honestly, everything changed at that moment for me," she says. "It was like, gasp, I'll be okay. You know, I don't have to live in a beige world, there is something for me instead of just listening and being exactly what my parents want me to be. I can be this unique individual." Jimmy F. claims that "before the Beatles, I was just subliminally into music. I listened to the radio, I liked it a lot. But once the Beatles came, it almost became like part of our lifestyle." He says that one of the reasons they spoke to him so much is because the Beatles and other British Invasion groups "were actually bands who were creating the music. That's what, I think, how we perceived the differences.... I mean, in the '60s, you know, the Beatles were way more than just a band." Walter S. perfectly sums up these reactions, insisting that "the only album that I ever bought would have been a Beatles album."[45] The Fab Four had a crucial effect on youth culture, yet, when asked what they loved about the actual music, most white respondents use almost the same terms as they do when describing Motown's appeal, including the upbeat tempo, the ability to dance to the music, the high-quality song writing, and the simple, pop-influenced lyrics that focused on sweet, unthreatening, and vague conceptions of romantic love. "You'd be crazy not to love the Beatles, especially their first [album]," Mary R. asserts. "It was very fun and very danceable.... It was mostly upbeat. And, you know, mostly stupid. I mean, lyrics that were not anything that were supposed to challenge you in any way." Victor F. similarly liked that their music "had a bounce and a jump." He says that he "didn't like them at first, but they had a different sound.... We are all skeptics in New York, we don't believe in anything. But then I realized how good they were. And how good their writing was. And I liked them a lot. Particularly their singing and their harmony." And even though Marcia P. differentiates her love of the Beatles from other music by describing "the rebellion, the loudness, being able to hear everything and just feel it inside ... it's like a multi-sensory experience," the more concrete reasons for her devotion similarly recall depictions of Motown. "The Beatles said they wanted to hold my hand, you know? Like, they're talking to me. It was very sweet."[46] The fact that white kids heard something monumental in the Beatles, even when using the same terms to describe them as they did Black Motown artists, belies that there was something special in hearing these sounds coming from white people, especially since the Beatles' African-American influences were hardly kept secret. Victor F. recalls how the Beatles had a lot in common with Phil Spector-produced girl groups like the Ronettes, the Crystals, and the Chiffons, even if they "overshadowed everybody," while Bruce C. admits that "most of the white artists that I dug were doing old Black music." Marcia P. explains that she "really liked the sort of bluesy influence" in the Beatles music even though "I didn't know what the Black influence was back then."[47]

Even though the Beatles' first two albums released in America were comprised almost entirely of cover songs originally recorded by Black artists, including "Twist and Shout," "Please Mr. Postman," "Roll Over, Beethoven," and "Money (That's What I Want)," they were not received in the same fashion as earlier racialized cover artists like Pat Boone. The Beatles made no attempt to tone down the beats or lyrics of these songs—if anything, they quickened the tempos and leaned into R&B characteristics like infusing emotion into falsetto-laden screams and embracing imprecise diction. They also performed these songs because they had grown up loving and singing along to them, not because they were hired by record labels to provide white audiences with "acceptable" Black-inspired music. The Beatles were quick to give credit to their Black American influences, calling Chuck Berry a "rock poet" and Little Richard "the King" when they first met him, even offering him their coats in the rain because they did not want him to have to face the indignity of getting wet. This cross-racial idolization, which wreaked havoc with American mores, was seemingly less shocking across the Atlantic. Brian Ward argues that white youth in Britain were largely unaccustomed to American racial norms, at least prior to the mid-1960s. "What was missing—or much muted—in British opposition to rock and roll was the deep sense of racial transgression that dominated attacks on rock and roll in America, especially the South," he argues. Within a few years, however, as news coverage of civil rights campaigns began spanning the globe, "youngsters like John, Paul, George, and Ringo could easily accept the music's lower-class southern credentials, embracing them along with its perceived sexual abandon and disregard for other middle-class niceties as part of their own gestures of nonconformity, [but] they often found it less easy to ignore the continuing disregard for Black rights in the region." The Beatles would make their stances on racial injustices clear, for instance, by refusing to play any segregated venues on their first tour of the United States in 1964. Paul McCartney told CBS News, "I think it's silly to segregate people because, you know, colored people are no different, they're just the same as anyone else. There are some people that think that they're animals or something, but I just think it's stupid. You can't treat other human beings like animals. . . . There's never any segregation in concerts in England, and in fact if there was we probably wouldn't play them." Even though this remark glossed over the very real racial separations and violence that were plaguing England at the time (to say nothing of the lasting consequences of British imperialism around the world), the band's views that American racism was ridiculous, and that it clearly ought to be abolished, fell largely in line with those being espoused by more racially liberal white youth at the time.[48]

By the mid-1960s, other white British rock and roll groups like the Rolling Stones, the Animals, and the Kinks followed the Beatles across the Atlantic to American popularity by diffusing the works of earlier Black blues and rock and roll artists through a filter of either light English whimsy or more aggressive sexuality. Just like the Beatles, members of these groups refused to cover up the integrated nature of their music and their appreciation for the Black artists who provided inspiration. Eric Burdon, the lead singer of the Animals, even credited rock and roll with helping to eradicate racial prejudice in the United States, noting that "when rock and roll came along, so did integration . . . people didn't care whether the singers were Negro or white as far as the music went. The races were playing together." He went on to explain that rock and roll and R&B music, performed by Black musicians, led directly to his desire to learn more about African-American life and his decision to advocate on behalf of their civil rights struggles. "I've learned so much, not only about their music, but about life from people like Sonny Boy Williamson, B.B. King, John Lee Hooker, Nina Simone . . . and Chuck Berry," he said. "Through these associations I soon learned, however, that these people were being treated as something different from the rest of the population in their homeland because they were a different color. . . . I started collecting things—photographs, newspaper articles, magazine clippings—to find out why Negroes were being mistreated, often brutally so."[49] This transparency impressed some young Black listeners like Miche B. "I was a Beatle fanatic, I was more into them than Motown when they came out," she says. "I remember being so excited watching them on *Ed Sullivan*." She really loved their performance of "She Loves You" in particular. "I remember watching it and I'm screaming like I'm watching them in person. I loved the fact that they gave honor to the Black artists that they were influenced by. It didn't seem like the white artists in the States would give that credit, but the [British Invasion bands] always gave credit to the Black artists that they loved." She also recalls being drawn to the Beatles' representation of Black musical forms. "You can hear the African-American influence on all the music just about," she asserts. "There's no way in the world that they could try to say that they didn't get that. Yeah, they did 'Twist and Shout.' A whole bunch of [cover] songs. And they gave credit to a lot of the early [artists] like Muddy Waters and Chuck Berry."[50] As with Motown, the link between representation and affection for this music is clear here. Miche loved the Beatles, but what she remembers most is how they paid homage to their forebears and how she could hear respect for her own cultural traditions within their performances. Sometimes these links were less apparent. Historian Kitty Oliver, who grew up in an all-Black neighborhood in Florida, used to listen to "the 'White radio station' instead of just R&B before she went to bed at night, "for fun." When she and her best friend heard the Beatles on this station, they were immediately smitten, spending "hours in self-imposed isolation in the sanctity of the music room of her parents' split-level house singing along to 'Can't Buy Me Love,' dancing to 'Love Me Do'; fantasizing to 'This Boy.' We debated favorites—hers was Paul. Mine was Ringo." What she was drawn to, however, was not the knowledge that they were so heavily inspired by Black American artists, but their rebellious identities, "flaunting their difference in the way they looked and sounded," which clearly harkened back to the stage personas of R&B artists like Chuck Berry and Little Richard.[51]

White British musicians' willingness to share their admiration for earlier Black R&B and rock and roll artists could not mitigate the fact that they quickly became iconic figures in the music world while bypassing the musicians who had inspired them. Avant-garde jazz musician Albert Ayler made it known how displeased he was that the Beatles were profiting so handsomely off of his inspiration while he struggled to make ends meet with gigs at various clubs. And even though Little Richard met with the band before they exploded onto the world stage, helped them fine-tune their falsettos, and even described a close relationship with Paul McCartney, he would later tell interviewers that "the Beatles started with me" and that when they treated him like "the creator" of rock and roll, "I knew what they were saying was the truth."[52] Sometimes this public acknowledgment could inspire young white listeners to seek out recordings from the Beatles' Black predecessors. "After the near death (attempted murder) of rock and roll in the late '50s and early '60s we were very pleased to have our American music handed back to us by the Brits," Bibb E. asserts. "That brought about an introduction to many black artists to our generation we missed the first time around. We were older by then, and more adult themes made sense to us. So discovering old Muddy Waters, John Lee Hooker, and Louis Jordan records became the thing to do." Jimmy F. concurs, saying that "we found out that some of those [British Invasion] bands were basically emulating the Black artists. You know, and it became sort of obvious that, I think maybe some people might say they were ripping them off. For me, I would say that they weren't ripping them off. They were just popularizing them with a whole new group of people that weren't exposed to that."[53] The sincere appreciation that the Beatles showed to their Black forebears may have differentiated them from many earlier white musicians, but their raucous music remained more acceptable coming from these loveably irreverent white British boys than it did from its Black creators, which continued to rankle many Black respondents. Even though most remember liking the Beatles, the band was not as essential to their growth as musical individuals the way it was for almost all of the white respondents. They could enjoy the same attributes and characteristics of both the music and the cute boys who performed it as their white peers did, but Black listeners remain cognizant of how their popularity overshadowed Black artists who were just as talented. "Prior to going to a Motown Revue, I was one of the biggest Beatle fans," Rhonda E. recalls, explaining how she begged her mother to wait in line outside in the rain for hours to try and purchase concert tickets when the Fab Four came to Detroit. "But once I got to see this show live, it was like, I'm not screaming for a Beatle again. Look at all this." Miche B., who stresses how much she enjoyed hearing the influences of Black musicians in the Beatles' records, explains how "it's important to give credit. But to honor them. Don't let them die in poverty. If they have created this thing that has built on to what it has become now and you're not, and they're sitting up there trying to find some food to eat."[54]

The fact that white British Invasion groups proved more marketable than most of their older Black influences meant that Miche's prediction would ultimately come to pass, no matter how much praise these musicians heaped upon their African-American inspirations. Just like the Beatles, the music released by other white British Invasion groups was accepted by the white mainstream with greater degrees of tolerance despite the more aggressive and sexual personas of bands like the Rolling Stones. Even though this group's members were often portrayed as rock and roll's requisite "devils" in relation to the supposedly "angelic" Beatles, the criticisms lobbed at Mick Jagger and his bandmates were more contemptuous of the band's rough mannerisms, despite their upper-middle-class backgrounds and elite educations that distinguished them from the more working-class Beatles, and, even more so, of their androgynous looks that suggested resistance to traditional forms of masculinity. As the Stones descended on the United States for their first major tour in 1964, a Chicago reporter described them as wearing "tight trousers and haggard looks. All of them slouch. Each looks unkempt," while the *New York Times* London bureau snickered at their hair, which "cascades down their backs in a long bob of the type once favored by Miss Lauren Bacall. At the front, the fringe extends below the eye level, so that you have the feeling the boys should be using guide dogs as well as guitars." Black musicians like Little Richard and Chuck Berry had faced such criticisms when they first became popular too, but this resistance was shaped far more by racist fears of the aggressive sexuality and vulgarity so often attributed to Black men, even as they took pains to adjust somewhat to polite middle-class norms. The Rolling Stones, however, were more likely to be met with bewilderment or disdain rather than viewed as any sort of threat. "For the over-30s, it is hard to take the Stones and the Pretties [Pretty Things, another British Invasion band popular in the mid-1960s] seriously," the *New York Times* reporter added breezily. Jagger himself was able to decipher these criticisms adeptly, noting that "they seem to have a sort of personal anxiety because we are getting away with something they never dared to do. It's a sexual, personal, vain thing. They've always been taught that being masculine means looking clean, cropped and ugly." White desire for the types of freedoms often associated with Black people is evident in his comment, and yet the racialized fears of Black artists that led to unequal pay, airtime, and accusations of lewd behaviors are absent when directed toward white musicians. However controversial or bewildering their actions or aesthetics seemed to those outside their target audiences, British Invasion bands were widely seen as safe conduits for Black music; a 1965 *Time* article even wryly noted that "The Beatles . . . made it all right to be white."[55]

Despite these clear inequities, respondents recall an incredibly racially integrated popular music landscape throughout the early to mid-1960s, due in large part to the overwhelming and simultaneous popularity of the Beatles and Motown artists. "As I got older.... I listened to the Kinks, and the Beatles, and the Rolling Stones, and the Dave Clark Five as much as I listened to Marvin Gaye and Tammi Terrell and the Vandellas," says Scott F., who identifies as Black. "I was comfortable in both worlds. And I didn't realize how different that was. That was just how I grew up." Rhonda E. felt similarly, stating that, at her Detroit high school, everyone listened to both the rock station, CKLW, as well as the Black-oriented stations. "They played, bottom line, I'm going to say, the best Black and white music. They just played good, good music," she says. "They played the Stones. They played the Beatles. They played the Temptations. They played, you know, all of Motown." She set this station set in her car, she explains, "so if the Black station played something you didn't want to hear, and it's a commercial, you push CKLW and, nine times out of ten, you'd still be jamming." Cheryl J., who also grew up in Detroit, says that one of her favorite deejays, Frantic Ernie, "was more for Black Detroiters," playing "mostly Black music," including Motown artists, but would also air "a couple of other white rock groups that were very popular among Black teenagers." She and her friends would also listen to Wolfman Jack's show, even though she stresses that his audience was presumably mostly white. He "played mostly rock and roll, white rock and roll," she says. "But he would throw in Black musicians that were into rock." White listeners recall this shift as well. Ellis B. describes the radio stations he listened to growing up as "eclectic," explaining how they would play country music as well as British Invasion groups and R&B. "There was an awareness that this is a white group or this is an African-American group," he says. "But I liked all the music."[56] Black and white kids may not have been accustomed to, or comfortable with, moving through integrated physical spaces on a regular basis, but the music they listened to was more racially mixed than ever during the early 1960s, priming some of them to believe that integration could succeed in the real world just as easily as it did on the airwaves.

SNCC AND NONVIOLENT DIRECT ACTION CAMPAIGNS, 1960–1964

Radio airwaves seamlessly pumped out integrated playlists just as direct action campaigns that prioritized desegregation of public spaces began making headlines again in the early 1960s. Unlike earlier operations, which were organized by civil rights and Black church groups, led by professional organizers or other adults in good standing with the community, and focused on public facilities like schools and transportation, these protests were led by students and other young people, and held at restaurants, department stores, dime stores, and other retail establishments. These locations were chosen because they were public spaces that were easy to access, but also because they symbolized the twisted compromise that upwardly mobile Black Americans were expected to make in a society that remained fundamentally segregated. They were almost always welcome to spend their money at these establishments, especially in the major chains that were rapidly cropping up in downtown areas across the country. But Jim Crow laws in the South and bylaws in many cities across the North prevented these consumers from being treated with the respect granted to their white peers. In Southern states, Black shoppers often had to enter through a separate entrance, generally a back or side door, and were prevented from dining among white patrons, both reminiscent of how domestic servants were expected to behave in white homes. Ed B. remembers "going to the back of the stores 'cause the front was reserved for whites" while shopping with his mother in downtown Memphis. "The backside entrance was there for, they called us colored at the time."[57] Further south, in New Orleans, Joseph J. remembers lunch counters that "had a very long section for white people and . . . a short section for Black people. What would happen is that you would have all of these Black people standing behind one another trying to get food. Purchasing food. Because you'd go there hungry and it was a whole thing to go down and shop and eat, and it was a whole day. And what happened was, there were a number of [situations] when you . . . couldn't get your food."[58] These divisions were not usually enforced quite so strictly outside of the South, but consumer spaces often remained segregated in other parts of the country. Ellis B. recalls how, growing up in a largely white neighborhood in New York, "in the '60s, if you went into a shop or a restaurant in a largely white community and you saw an African-American family shopping there, you would do a double take. I think it was unusual to see that."[59] Although David S. recalls riding the bus alongside Black patrons going downtown in Detroit, he also asserts that "it wasn't segregated to that point. If you went downtown to the dime store and sat at the lunch counter, everybody sat there . . . and you dealt with it." And yet Carol B., who also grew up in Detroit, provides a different perspective on these uneasy instances where integration was necessary. "As a child with my mother, we would shop in Inkster," she recalls. "I can tell you that my mother was afraid to be there, but she went there anyways. Because there was a really nice dress shop."[60] The ability to consume was closely aligned with citizenship rights, and yet Black shoppers were persuaded to spend their hard-earned dollars in spaces where they received second-class, even hostile, treatment, and where they were consistently viewed with suspicion.

These consumption-based spaces were therefore chosen as sites for direct protest, partly to encourage companies to oppose Jim Crow laws if they did not want to lose Black customers, and partly because they invoked mass media coverage and degrees of white support. Housing, school, and economic desegregation might prove difficult within capitalist-democratic structures, but expecting to be treated with respect as a consumer was supposed to constitute a pillar of such a society. Furthermore, the students and young people who would fuel these campaigns captured the aspirational nature of many Black families who had managed to send their children to university and were on professional tracks, yet were still unable to enjoy all of the benefits of consumerism. Finally, Black kids had already been tacitly accepted into popular consumer culture by advertisers eager to sell music, fashion, and other teenage fad items to anyone with disposable income, and could therefore relate to using consumption as a means of fashioning identities for themselves that were separate from their parents. To be denied the ability to move freely and be treated with dignity in consumer spaces meant that these identities were not deemed as valid as their white counterparts, which incited many young people to fight for this particular type of access. Despite the distinctions that characterized direct action protest in the early 1960s, however, many campaigns continued to advocate for desegregation by appealing to the democratic, respectable, and nonviolent norms that could elicit white support in politics as well as music, even as activists increasingly understood the need to diversify the movement with more radical actions and goals.

Black activists have utilized direct action in urban public spaces since the early 1800s, but the first student-focused sit-ins at consumer sites occurred during World War II, organized by Howard University students in Washington, D.C.-area restaurants, and in Chicago by Congress of Racial Equality (CORE) members. Between 1953 and 1955, students at Morgan State University in Baltimore staged a similar sit-down strike at lunch counters in Read's drug store, forcing the company to desegregate its city branches, while a handful of Black teenagers and their minister, Douglas Moore, were arrested after sitting in booths reserved for white patrons at the Royal Ice Cream Parlor in Durham, North Carolina, in 1957. Other sit-ins were organized in Wichita, Kansas, in 1958, and in Oklahoma City in 1960. These campaigns were largely ignored by media outlets, and were often met with derision from both Black and white community members; Mary Clayburn, one of the teenagers who took part in a sit-in, even recalled how many Blacks were "madder than the white folks." Christina Greene recounts in her book, *Our Separate Ways*, how most civil rights and Black organizations, including the local National Association for the Advancement of

Colored People (NAACP) branch, refused to support this method of protest, or the people involved, mostly because of fears of white backlash and the chaos that might occur if campaigns were not soundly organized from the top down by established leaders. "Few blacks doubted that they had a clear right to deny patronage to a business or public service—they could spend their money as they pleased," Adam Fairclough notes. "But it was one thing to boycott segregated buses, quite another to 'sit in,' or otherwise physically intrude, at the premises of a private business. Such tactics involved breaking the law, courting arrest, and risking fines and incarceration." This method of action therefore remained mostly the purview of the young. "Arrest on a sit-in, a picket line, or a demonstration . . . invited economic disaster," Fairclough continues. "Apart from the cost of bail (usually exorbitant), legal fees (often considerable), and fines (frequently heavy), there was the real possibility of a spell in jail. Either way, fine or jail, arrestees faced the likelihood, often amounting to a near certainty, of losing their jobs." This would only change, he says, "in 1960, when black students entered the fray in large numbers."[61]

By February of that year, four members of the Greensboro, North Carolina NAACP youth council, Franklin McCain, Joseph McNeil, Ezell Blair Jr., and David Richmond, gathered in a dorm room at North Carolina A&T State University and started talking about how they were allowed to shop at their local Woolworth's branch, but had to dine on rickety picnic tables outside the store's back door rather than eat at the lunch counter, which was reserved for whites. Because of their experience in the NAACP, they were aware of many of the forms of protest used by civil rights activists, and were inspired by the concept of nonviolent direct action. They decided the next day to sit at that counter and refuse to leave unless they were served. Their decision to use nonviolence as a tactic, directly confronting the system of segregation and refusing to acquiesce to it, resounded locally and nationally in a way that prior sit-ins did not, revealing both young people's power to provoke change and the frustrations people had with the inability of established organizations to further the movement. A Black woman who worked behind the counter told them to leave, and that they were ruining things for all Black people, while a white customer quietly relayed her support. But, aside from the manager instructing the counter staff not to serve the students, they were more or less left alone. The next day, these four initial protestors were joined by more than 20 Black students, and the day after that, over 60 young people sat in at the counter, including some whites. Although the protestors were completely nonviolent, focusing their attention on their schoolwork as the store's entire staff continued to ignore them, white patrons began to heckle, and eventually harass them, yelling in their ears, throwing food at them, and even putting out cigarettes on their arms. Journalists streamed in to cover the story, and the store's business came to a halt, but the protestors were not arrested. The sit-in continued, and McCain recalled that "now it came to me all of a sudden.... Maybe they can't do anything to us. Maybe we can keep it up."[62]

Local advocates of white supremacy were not about to let the protest go on without a fight, though. When confronted with this direct action, many chose to avoid the store and the complications that came along with acknowledging the protest. By the fourth day, as over 300 Black and white students packed themselves into the increasingly crowded store, an angry white mob gathered outside screaming obscenities. The North Carolina A&T football team had to be recruited to protect the students as they left, but ultimately McCain's intuition proved correct—no one was arrested or seriously injured. Media coverage quickly spread beyond local and even state boundaries. Sit-in strikes in restaurants and shops would quickly spread to other college towns, first within North Carolina, then to Virginia, Atlanta, Nashville, and New Orleans, among several other locations. Student activists' enthusiasm was fueled by the fact that this protest method was fairly easy to organize, especially if church or youth groups already existed in the area. Protests could be quickly implemented, did not lead to high incidences of arrests or violence, and seemed to work, especially after Woolworth's announced the desegregation of lunch counters in most Southern stores in June. Many young middle-class white and Black kids found that they could identify with activists who were students like themselves. They might not have been able to see a place for themselves in the movement before, but now people of their own generation had carved out a niche on their own terms, showing the world that Jim Crow might be felled with youthful moral righteousness. Perceptions of civil rights activism, and who could participate, began to change.[63]

Since these younger activists were mainly affiliated with schools instead of churches, enacted plans without the help of an organization, and directly infiltrated white spaces instead of public areas, many civil rights leaders quickly realized that the movement was headed in a different direction. If they did not act quickly, their organizations could lose any control they might have over this momentum. Martin Luther King Jr. and Roy Wilkins attempted to corral these new activists into the Southern Christian Leadership Conference (SCLC) and NAACP, respectively, but Ella Baker, an established activist who had founded and led several political and social organizations in her lifetime, had a different idea. Instead of trying to lure young activists into established organizations in order to co-opt some of their ideas, she encouraged them to start their own group. In April, Baker invited interested students to Shaw University in Raleigh where, over the course of a weekend, the SNCC was created. Member James Bevel recalled how the organization was formed by different groups that had previously operated independently converging on the campus. "A large delegation from Atlanta came," he recalled.

An even larger delegation from Nashville came. At that time there was a great deal of pride and super pride among the different groups. One group would say, "We had 500 people on a picket line" and the other group would say, "Well, we only had 350" and a lot of little things like that. The Nashville group, because it was so large . . . just intimidated us because they had really been in the movement; by really been in the movement I meant they had achieved at that time, a degree of organization that other groups later achieved but didn't have at that time.[64]

Even though student activists made this trip in order to fuse their energies together, the organization was afflicted with some of the divisions Bevel mentioned right from the start. "It didn't really have any sense of direction" at first, asserted Ruby Doris Smith-Robinson, the administrative secretary who, despite her title, is largely known as the person who kept SNCC running amid several obstacles. "Its main object or main goal at that time was to try to coordinate the movement . . . the different protest movements that were springing up. . . . But there wasn't any depth, even in discussions. The main object was sit-ins and public accommodations. There wasn't any real feeling even of a movement."[65] She further explained how

> the national focus was on the protest movement, the sit-in protest movement, but it wasn't focused so much on the movement as a whole as it was on each individual group as it sprang up . . . when the sit-in movement began in Nashville, Tenn. there were pressmen from all over the country in Nashville. The same thing was happening in Greensboro and in Atlanta. And I think all the national magazine stories and national news coverage and stuff might have helped to create this kind of attitude because . . . everybody wanted their little group to get the most publicity.[66]

This organization was founded on principles of self-leadership; nonviolent, direct action taken at the grassroots level; and the establishment of a multiracial "beloved community"—as James Forman, who would become the group's executive secretary in 1961, explained in a letter that year, "Our basic goal is to work with protest groups in the South, initiate voter registration and direct action programs in the South, and to coordinate local protest groups where this is possible."[67] In a later interview, he explained that "we felt a direct action was necessary. The legalistic approach had been tried, that is, taking issues to the court and then getting these things adjudicated. And we certainly felt that direct action was important."[68] Even though he initially described the group as "a loosely-knit coordinating committee which only met occasionally," within its first year it "formed a staff" and established itself as "one unified organization" complete with centralized administration based in

Atlanta.[69] Despite the group's ideological divisions, nonviolent direct protest was chosen as its prime organizing method; as Forman recounted in a 1964 interview, "the agitators should make the society so uncomfortable that it is in itself would have to ameliorate certain basic things: the whole proposition of lunch-counters was absolutely absurd, and there was no reason why we could not have a law in the U.S. that would prohibit discrimination in lunch counter activity, but that the reason that we didn't have a law was that there was nobody agitating." He explained that, counter to those who doubted the power of nonviolence, "open street demonstrations would in fact lead to a building of militancy in people and also lead to an embarrassment to the government and would therefore lead to some solutions to the problems."[70]

During SNCC's early years, Clayborne Carson explains in his expansive account of the organization, members and supporters "reflected the almost unchallenged dominance within Afro-American political life of leaders who concentrated on eliminating overt southern racism by portraying it as anachronistic and irrational, contrary to the American creed, and damaging to the interests of the nation."[71] Many believed that the first step toward eradicating racial discrimination and injustice would be to use nonviolent direct action to convince white officials and voters to dismantle public segregation because it was immoral and antidemocratic. Constructing the organization around this goal earned sympathy from many Northern whites. This focus guided the organization's efforts in its earliest years, encouraging, Ruby Doris Smith-Robinson said, "students who had been successful in lunch-counter sit-ins to turn to the movies and have a stand-in and we asked people who had not been successful to go back again to their lunch-counters and attempt to re-mobilize their communities." A year later, as sit-in participants began to get arrested, SNCC activists decided to extend this method to the jails, advocating for individuals to serve out their sentences rather than being set free on bail as part of what Smith-Robinson described as "the nonviolent concept of jail, civil disobedience and without bail."[72] The result, as David Chalmers explains, was a new type of civil rights organization that explicitly "included young people and people of both races for the first time" and "transformed the cautious civil rights coalition of the late 1950s into a genuine social movement."[73] Indeed, SNCC's use of such tactics could challenge white supremacist accusations that they were nothing more than radical communist agitators, and instead encourage reporters to present protestors using direct action as inherently moral and law-abiding, in spirit if not in letter. *Time*, for instance, portrayed the initial sit-ins that led to the creation of SNCC as a classic tension between good and evil, as segregationist Nashville mayor Ben West was depicted telling a "well-behaved crowd: 'As God is my helper, the law is going to be enforced in Nashville.'" Savannah mayor Lee Mingledorff, who was obviously of a similar mindset, "asked the city council to pass an ordinance requiring licensing of pickets. 'I don't care if it's constitutional or not,' said he." In both cases, reporters showed how powerful white supremacists were explicitly opposed to the American ideals of freedom and constitutionality that respectable protestors were upholding with their illegal actions. The article went on to proclaim that "on both sides of Mason-Dixon, the sit-in campaign was gathering support from whites," while Black protestors were properly applauded for creating SNCC in the aftermath of the sit-ins, which "show[s] how far and wide the movement has spread without any help from whites."[74] The same sense of approval was evident in the *New York Times*. One article, titled "Campuses in North Back Southern Negro Students," approved of sit-in protestors, noting that "there is a quality of invention to their work. The students lack means and experience. They admit to uncertainty over what they can do. But money is being raised, meetings are being held and picket lines are forming in sympathy with Negroes who have protested segregation at chain-store lunch counters in the South."[75] The reporter's reference to protesting Southern segregation specifically, rather than a wider pattern of racial oppression across the nation, is key to understanding widespread acceptance of the sit-ins among mainstream media outlets, which SNCC organizers clearly understood from the outset.

SNCC's organizing methods and focus on nonviolent direct action campaigns and young people's concerns became so influential that they influenced and shaped protests staged by other civil rights organizations during the early 1960s. In 1961, CORE re-instituted the direct action campaign to desegregate interstate public transportation, which it had initiated in 1947. Despite the fact that the Journey of Reconciliation had resulted in a Supreme Court decision making segregation on interstate buses and in the terminals that serviced these routes illegal, the ruling was largely ignored once vehicles entered Southern states. During this five-week operation, Black and white volunteers rode side by side on these routes, refusing to follow Jim Crow guidelines, in an effort to force the federal government to intervene. White Southern governments labeled the students communist agitators, and local police were given permission to beat, arrest, and torture activists, while white crowds set their buses aflame. Attorney General Robert Kennedy ultimately ordered the Interstate Commerce Commission to remove any signage mandating segregation on interstate lines, which again revealed the power young activists had amassed through direct action, though they had to endure horrifying violence to get there. The following year, James Meredith, a Black student admitted to the previously all-white University of Mississippi, refused to retreat from the school's premises, even when faced with vicious massive resistance, to the point that President John F. Kennedy had to send federal troops in to ensure his safe access. A focus on students and school made the subjects of segregation and racism seem more urgent and understandable to young people of both races, while the use of nonviolent direct action ensured that journalists would cover the story, and that Meredith and his supporters would be viewed positively when juxtaposed with their violent opponents. Even Martin Luther King Jr.'s hallowed SCLC would use some of these tactics when descending on Birmingham, Alabama, in April 1963 for a well-publicized campaign involving sit-ins in the downtown business area, and organizing teenagers and children who were encouraged to "fill the jails" upon arrest.

The movement's shift to direct action tactics showed how segregation could be challenged with youthful moral righteousness. Perceptions of civil rights activism, and who could participate, began to change. And yet many Black kids who grew up during this period recall feeling somewhat distant from these struggles. Sometimes this was due to growing up outside of the South where, even when faced with persistent racial discrimination and injustice, younger people did not always see evidence of such blatant segregation firsthand. Cheryl J., who grew up in an integrated middle-class neighborhood in Detroit, explains that "coming from the environment I came from, there were a lot of things I just didn't think about. I didn't know Black people were being mistreated in the South, or wherever they were being mistreated. I just didn't understand any of that."[76] Similarly, Miche B., who also hails from Detroit, yet lived in what she describes as an "affluent Black neighborhood," says she mostly only heard about these campaigns in church. "They kept doing, like, the hoses on people that were just trying to get equal rights and everything," she says. "And it would be very sad."[77] But even in a Southern city like Memphis, Ed B. explains that he "wasn't that involved during the Civil Rights Movement. . . . I wasn't fully aware of the content of it. And what was the sole purpose of it, I guess." This was partly because, as he recalls, "I grew up thinking that [segregation] was the norm," and "I never looked at it as racism that much." But even if he never became explicitly involved in movement activities himself, Ed does remember what he describes as a "traumatizing" incident that occurred when he was a teenager, soon after the student sit-ins began in Memphis's downtown business area in March 1960. While working in a restaurant one night, he noticed a group of mostly Black young people headed toward the front doors. Even though closing time was still an hour away, his white manager ordered him to lock the doors. When he asked why, his manager proclaimed, "damn n*****, I told you to lock the door." "I looked at him," Ed recalls, "and I looked at the door, and I saw these people approaching. It was during the sit-ins. And I told him I wasn't going to lock the door, that if he wanted to lock the door, he had to lock it. I was so pissed off. I said, well, I'm finished. I threw my apron to the floor, went through the kitchen, out the back door. Walked around and caught the bus and went home. I never went back."[78] Even if Black kids were aware of these campaigns, many did not think that integration of public consumer areas would do much to affect or improve their daily lives. Others, however, were inspired by the actions of younger Black students, many not much older than themselves, which led to successful changes. Larry Hunter, who grew up in Ypsilanti, Michigan, remembered participating in a high school walkout where students, guided by their local NAACP branch, demanded that teachers acknowledge Black contributions to American history and that the school board hire more Black teachers. "We completely shut the place down, forcing a head-on confrontation with the board of education," he said. "We felt that not only should the textbooks be screened, but there should be a Black history course that would give Blacks as well as whites the opportunity to learn about Black history."[79] More broadly, Joseph J., who grew up in New Orleans, recalls learning about the sit-ins with his mother, who told him, "'I may not live to see the end of it, but things are going to be different.' And that was the paradigm shift. . . . You begin to say, no, I'm not going to settle for this."[80] The potential for change, then, seemed closer than ever, even if many kids remained uncertain of how integration in public spaces would affect their own lives in meaningful ways.

White kids who lived in Northern cities often used some of the same language as their Black counterparts when describing how little they thought about racial discrimination during this period, or how they failed to understand the violence meted out against activists. Much like the distinctions in responses to Motown and British Invasion groups, however, their recollections are shaped by an inability to identify with these issues based on their geographical and racial distance from Jim Crow segregation rather than ambivalence about the effects of desegregation on their own lives. David S., who notes that he rarely paid attention to civil rights struggles growing up in Detroit until he learned about the Greensboro sit-ins, says, "It was strange, you'd hear about civil rights on the radio, on television and in the news . . . and as a child you didn't have this frame of reference. You'd heard about it, but you didn't know what it was about. You didn't know what the context of it was, or just why this was happening." Ron R. notes how "even though it was not in our territory [Midwestern suburbs], we didn't have a problem with lunch counter segregation, for example, or stuff like that. You know, who gets to sit at the back of the bus. That sort of stuff, it was not an obvious presence for us." Bruce C., from suburban New Jersey, also highlights this sense of confusion, stating that "I saw, you know, all of the news reports. And it was always like, well, why are these people, why is this happening to these people? Why . . . are the white people doing this, what's going on here?" Victor F., who grew up on Long Island, New York, recalls how he "saw Black people down south getting the crap kicked out of them by cops and everything else. And I couldn't understand it. . . . You know, you live in your own safe little world, and then you see this stuff on television." "It made no sense to me," Marcia P., who grew up in Detroit, asserts. "I couldn't identify with them very well. It seemed like they were just happening in other places." John H., who is from Tucson, Arizona, echoes this feeling of watching events unfold from a safe distance, noting that he remembers thinking "I'm sure glad I don't live back there in Knoxville, Nashville, Birmingham, you know, places [where] they were burning down everything. And I could not understand why a policeman would have a firehose squirting down a bunch of Black people that were just holding signs. That never made sense to me at all." Bruce S., who watched the protests unfold on television from his home in Queens, New York, says he thought "it was unfortunate that discrimination [occurred] at that time, but we couldn't do anything about it. We could just kind of observe it."[81]

Many young observers were especially drawn to the fact that these sit-ins were overwhelmingly planned and implemented by college students not much older than themselves—indeed, one of SNCC's overarching missions was to harness younger people's ideas and energies to revitalize the movement. Ruby Doris Smith-Robinson noted, for instance, that college students' ability to leave school for a semester without the tethers of jobs or families allowed them to devote themselves entirely to civil rights campaigns and to identify with others who had made the same choice. "That's why people who've been to enlightened schools all apart of the southern system do this, to go downtown, to sit-in at lunch counters to possibly face violence," she explained.[82] The importance of student involvement and leadership could not be understated; in a 1964 position paper, for instance, James Forman proclaimed that "the Student Nonviolent Coordinating Committee owes its very existence to the college campuses and no matter how deep our roots may go into the people in the Black Belt, we started growing this little tree of protest in the college communities."[83] And yet, as the author of another position paper for the organization noted, the stakes were often quite high for Black students who signed up for direct action campaigns. "Most students at Southern Negro colleges are first-generation college students," they pointed out, "economically, their parents are either from the poor or lower middle-class. Thus the student, who usually has three or four sisters and brothers in high school, is considered the brains of the family. Hopes for upward mobility rest on him." These students may have had more leeway to engage in political campaigns than their parents would have, but they still lacked the resources of their white counterparts, who could more easily weather a few semesters away from school or a handful of arrests on their records. And yet they were aware that they were privileged in ways that remained rare in many poor and working-class Black families. "A formal education is respected and admired by people in the community and automatically gives the student a sense of status," the paper's author continued. "He feels a great deal of middle-class ambition and enjoys the anticipation of being able to earn four more times than his parents."[84] Many student activists, then, saw their work with SNCC as a means of giving back to their communities and ensuring that others would be able to have some of the advantages that they were able to enjoy.

Despite the aforementioned distance that some Black kids felt from these protests, increased publicization of younger activists engaged in freedom struggles encouraged them to relate to these campaigns, and even to participate themselves (or to try, at least). Carolyn Maull, whose family attended the same Birmingham church that became famous when four young girls were killed when a white supremacist bombed the building in September 1963, decided to join church rallies and protests even though she was only 14 at the time. "I never even thought about discussing it with my parents, though," she said. "I knew they'd worry about me. Plus I knew they were opposed to taking such a direct stand." She snuck out anyway and was hit by one of Police Chief Bull Connor's notorious fire hoses. "My parents took one look at my appearance—I was still wet, and my sweater was torn—and my father said, 'Where in the devil have you been?' I told him. I didn't really hear what they said to me, but I'm sure they were afraid for me and didn't want to show how much. My father told me I could not go back, that I could not be a part of the demonstrations." Their admonitions did not dissuade her, though. "I could go to church. And if I happened to be at the church and somebody happened to organize a demonstration, I could join it. He never connected the two."[85] These campaigns affected Black kids who lived outside of the South as well. Cheryl James grew up in Detroit, but she remembers how her sister tried to convince their parents to let her join a demonstration while they were all vacationing in Tennessee. "I didn't understand that conversation, but she wanted to get on the bus and they told her no," she recalls. "So I finally asked another family member, what are they fighting about? . . . And that's when I had it explained to me that they were going deeper into the South to fight for rights for Black America." Even though she was not yet a teenager herself, she tried to board a bus that was leaving from a college campus without her parents' permission. The activists on board told her that she was too young to come along, and her parents caught up with her before the bus left, but even today she stresses that "I wanted to get on. I wanted to go down. I wanted to see where they were going. I wanted to know what the problems were. Why didn't they like people further south? I wanted to know!"[86] Direct action protests led by student activists could therefore encourage action among other Black kids, even those who were more than a few years away from entering college themselves.

Some white kids were also inspired by these young activists, even if their motivations were based more on incredulity that this type of discrimination and violence existed rather than their ability to relate to the people who were affected. Students for a Democratic Society (SDS) co-founder Sharon Jeffrey recalled hearing from Black students, who had staged a sit-in at a segregated library, speak at a conference only a few weeks after the Greensboro campaign. "Well, if that didn't energize that conference!" she said. "The timing was incredible.... We flew them up, and, of course, everyone was interested, so a lot of people came and there was a lot of excitement.... After that, we in Ann Arbor organized supportive sit-ins for what was going on in the South."[87] Ken A. wrote letters to the editors of local newspapers in New York and supported political candidates with more progressive views on civil rights, while Ron R. recalls being "troubled" by "these little petty injustices—there were separate drinking fountains for 'colored' people. There was an entrance around the back of the restaurant for 'colored' only." Even though he lived outside of the South, learning about these demonstrations "stuck with me. It really chafed." When he got to college in 1962, these reactions caused him to participate in local marches and demonstrations. Other white kids were primed by their more politically engaged families to get involved, but the fact that students were shaping many of the movement's directions similarly inspired their determination to participate while they were still in school. Larry R., who grew up in a Leftist family in Philadelphia, had been working for civil rights and labor causes since he was a teenager, but ultimately dropped out of college to join SNCC, where he would become a prominent organizer. He explains that, at the time, the organizational structure was so informal that "I just showed up in Atlanta at the office when I was supposed to. And James Forman, the executive director, said you are going to go to Albany [Georgia, where SNCC organized a major sit-in campaign in 1962]. And I went. That was it." He recalls telling a news reporter that "I finally felt myself to be an American" after participating in the March on Washington, even though he and other SNCC members were originally skeptical about what it would achieve. Some became active at even younger ages—Bill W., for instance, joined SNCC during his senior year of high school in Washington, D.C. "There were a couple kids that were in it," he says. "And they knew that I was obviously interested in Black music, so they said to me, hey, there's this group that started for Black and white students. Sort of, you might be interested. So I ended up going to some of the meetings. Eventually I even had a little button of the Black hand and the white hand shaking hands."[88]

Activists decided to participate for a number of reasons, but, as Bill notes, the popular culture that embraced and reinforced this process throughout the 1950s and into the 1960s could affect white kids' views on civil rights demonstrations. "Time and time again, young middle-class whites in the sixties described hearing about southern student activism or meeting southern student activists (mostly African Americans but also some whites) as encounters that changed their lives," Grace Elizabeth Hale explains. "Their feelings about the civil rights movement in the South sparked the process through which they began to see themselves as outsiders too."[89] Indeed, student activist Arnie Bauchner recalled how he "used to have fantasies about going South" even if he never actually made the trip. He admitted that "a lot of my desire . . . was in terms of very romantic heroics."[90] Hale is rightfully critical of this form of identification, but its effects were often more limited, given that many white kids enjoyed Black artists and musical forms, yet neglected to become actively involved in protest demonstrations. Michael P. and Walter S., for instance, each remember learning about sit-in demonstrations while listening to Black-oriented radio stations. The deejays on his favorite New York stations, Walter explains, "would help diffuse the tension [and] would explain things to a kid like me," ultimately making it seem "accessible and manageable. Like we could understand it, it was explained to us." Victor F. explains that he "was learning about prejudice on television outside. And that's where the music was kind of the soundtrack of what was going on." Still, he admits that he "was having trouble grappling with it," often because opponents "tried to make you think that [activists] were troublemakers." He recalls "reading the John Birch Society stuff talking about Martin Luther King being a communist and a Russian this. . . . I didn't believe it. . . . But I just had a hard time sorting through all the stuff back then."[91]

Unlike the type of relation to activists that could spur young people to take action themselves, listening to Black music and learning about these demonstrations on television and the radio could inspire sympathy and support, but not necessarily direct participation. In the South, this disconnect was partially due to fears of social exclusion and even possible violence. Bob R. feared that he would be labeled a communist if he spoke out more directly, while Bibb E. explains that "Being called a 'n***** lover' (along with queer) was about the worst epithet that could be hurled about. . . . There seemed to be much incentive to keep such thoughts to one's self." He further notes that the threat of backlash in his Virginia home and community was simply too great for him to risk. "Even a small miscalculation could have led to me being kicked out of college and drafted, not something I wished for," he says. "I did not want to run the risk of (further) alienating my parents." Outside of the South, white respondents describe their sympathies as existing in the backgrounds of their lives out of a lack of direct relation rather than fear. "I'm sure it was in my periphery. . . . I guess whatever was on the news," Michael P. explains. "Was I active in it? No. Did it change my life around? No." Patricia J. recalls being a bit more affected than that, but "I didn't have time for sit ins. I had to make it to class. I had to get a good grade. I wanted to go to graduate school. I didn't look to the left; I didn't look to the right. But my heart was with them." She further admits that she "wasn't able to let all these sentiments turn into action until much later in life."[92] Many of these responses reveal a contrast in how Black and white kids viewed movement participation. While Black participants saw their involvement as a chance to ensure that the advantages they enjoyed as college students could be more readily available to others and their lack of job and family duties as allowing them to partake in protests with fewer lasting repercussions, white kids often viewed the movement from a distance. Like Patricia, some white respondents explain that they became more directly involved with civil rights as adults, but demonstrations otherwise existed mostly in the peripheries of lives devoted to school and other concerns.

Even though civil rights organizations communicated and worked with each other to an extent on overlapping goals, distinctions between the younger, more direct action-oriented SNCC and more established groups remained salient. "The bigger, better-organized civil rights organizations shudder at SNICK's [sic] bobtail operations," proclaimed a 1963 article in *Time*. And yet, the author notes, "for raw courage and persistence, SNICK wins grudging admiration even from its rivals."[93] The reality was a bit more nuanced, even if important distinctions—and conflicts—did persist among major organizations. "SNCC's relationship to other civil rights organizations and to local groups is not the same question," one of the organization's 1964 position papers cautioned. "Other civil rights organizations are inevitably rivals." And yet, at the same time, "rivals are not enemies. It is too easy to say, for example, 'What NAACP is doing in X situation will play into the hands of the establishment, therefore NAACP is part of the establishment and even worse because it pretends to be part of the movement.' We need to make our differences with NAACP, CORE, Urban League, SCLC, or anyone else clear, but not in such a way as to preclude working relationships with them."[94] SNCC staff members tried to work with members of the better-funded NAACP and SCLC to share their wealth, but were often turned down lest these organizations' more conservative donors object to SNCC's seemingly more radical campaigns. Differing group structures also interfered with some of the movement's shared goals. "SCLC operates on the principle of the messianic, charismatic leader" in direct contrast to SNCC's communal organization, James Forman said of Martin Luther King's group in a 1963 interview. He explained that "this has certain drawbacks" since some of their campaigns went forward "without the consultation with local people," a hallmark of SNCC's mission and organizing principles. He further criticized King's decision to allow children to face the wrath of Birmingham's racist and wrathful police chief, Bull Connor, when he himself would not be present for this particular campaign. "You just don't send down orders to people, especially when you're not around and you don't know what has happened," he asserted. "I became very disgusted because here kids were being beat with water hoses and so forth and the so-called spokesman of the Movement was sitting up in a comfortable room at the time that they were about to go to the slaughter."[95]

And yet even Forman had to admit that the Birmingham campaign was successful. The widely broadcast protests revealed that Connor's forces were willing to use extreme violence against children, horrifying people across the country, including President Kennedy, who made an emotional broadcast in June stating his intention to ask Congress to pass a civil rights bill that would render racial discrimination in public places and at voting booths illegal and increase the speed of school desegregation. He also offered his tacit support for the March on Washington for Jobs and Freedom later that summer, mainly organized by A. Philip Randolph and Bayard Rustin, although the six major civil rights organizations also contributed to its success. These major hallmarks of the civil rights movement legitimized desegregation goals among moderate Americans across age and racial divisions, and showed how direct activism stemming from young, multiracial groups continued to revitalize established organizations like the SCLC and NAACP. According to the *New York Times* correspondent Claude Sitton, who covered the Birmingham campaign, "Whites are now being forced to consider whether they are willing to pay the rising price of segregation. Is it worth herding children to jail by the hundreds, setting dogs upon adults or knocking them down with jets of water so powerful that they chip the bark off trees?" He referred to remarks made by SNCC member James Bevel, who is quoted as saying "Some punk who calls himself the President has the audacity to tell people to go slow. . . . I'm not prepared to be humiliated by white trash the rest of my life, including Mr. Kennedy," by noting that "the Bevels are the inevitable end product of the terror and hoodlumism employed by racists to deny the right of Negroes even to seek redress of grievances." Although Sitton made it clear that he did not condone Bevel's words, he implored readers to understand that they resulted from constant white violence and repression, and that the real threat laid within the political status quo rather than those who sought redress. Sitton ultimately upheld the moderate, reformist goals of the movement for his readers, noting that "although Negroes have seized the initiative, their leaders are still hopeful that whites will join them in the struggle before it is too late."[96] The implication here is that SNCC was still aiming for a "beloved community" of integrated white and Black Americans, but that whites would be tasked with determining whether that vision would be achieved.

The mainstreaming of values espoused by student activists, and successful attempts to gain support among Black youth, became even more apparent after 1963. Joseph J., who grew up in New Orleans, explains that, after the march, "you began to see the attitudes change in a lot of places . . . in terms of the way people talk to each other. White people talk to Black people."[97] Popular music also played a role in transmitting these values to Black kids, although unlike their white counterparts, Black listeners were more likely to respond to calls for direct participation. Shelley Stewart, a prominent Birmingham deejay in the 1950s and 1960s, says that he and other Southern platter spinners used the time between playing rock and roll and R&B hits to speak out against racial injustice. "I attempted to help persuade more members of the Black middle class to get involved in their own future by joining in demonstrations, and continued spotlighting inequities for minorities," he said. When Martin Luther King Jr. began planning Alabama campaigns, he contacted some of them and asked for assistance in gaining support. They complied by "using codes to help civil rights demonstrators outmaneuver Bull Connor's police department. It was common knowledge that the police employed informants among the civil rights demonstrators. One of our challenges was to distract the police so a phalanx of demonstrators could attempt to integrate lunch counters in the department stores like Woolworth's or Newberry's." Stewart and other area deejays worked out a plan where "an agreed-upon song would be played on a signal from a leader such as the Reverends King, N.H. Smith, and Andrew Young. It could be anything from 'Wade in the Water' to 'Yakety Yak.' Once a protest leader sent a messenger for [a deejay] to play the tune, people would walk from New Pilgrim Baptist on Southside to a downtown store."[98] The connection between the Birmingham campaign and rock and roll songs like the Coasters' "Yakety Yak" was therefore established for Black youth, who were alerted to this action by their favorite radio station personalities, and relied on them for vital information. In this case, rock and roll music was used as a tool to organize young Birmingham residents to participate in nonviolent direct actions. Civil rights leaders and deejays alike acted on the assumption that Black kids who listened to popular music programs mostly centered around rock and roll and R&B would want to support the campaign's goal of desegregating public spaces by participating in protests themselves.

TENSIONS OVER DESEGREGATION, VOTING RIGHTS, AND NONVIOLENCE, 1964–1965

Organizational decisions to work somewhat cooperatively toward desegregation in public places led to a major policy triumph in the summer of 1964. After President Kennedy's assassination, his successor, Lyndon Johnson, forced the Civil Rights Bill through Congress by reshaping it as a monument to Kennedy's legacy. Despite fervent opposition from Southern Congressmen in both parties, the 1964 Civil Rights Act was signed into law on July 2, rendering segregation in public places and other forms of racial, ethnic, and gender discrimination illegal with the stroke of a pen.[99] Loopholes and legal arguments, as well as blatant racial intimidation, provided continuing challenges, however, especially in Northern cities where extra-legal restrictions often proved more difficult to overcome. Passage of this act, however, meant that activists could rely on the federal government for at least nominal degrees of legal support with segregation complaints. And yet, as with the integrated Hot 100 chart, this Act could provide an obstacle to movement progress when many white, and even some Black, supporters began to view the struggle to desegregate as a *fait accompli*. If desegregation had been framed as the major civil rights issue since the late 1940s and was now technically considered illegal by the federal government, did it not then stand to reason that racial equality had been achieved? This line of thinking would prove difficult for civil rights groups like SNCC to address as they determined how to keep fighting for racial justice while maintaining that segregation had hardly been banished to the past, even if the federal government—and the pages of *Billboard*—had ostensibly rendered it obsolete.

This shift is evident when comparing young activists' descriptions of how segregation affected peoples' lives as the federal government began providing more support for this goal. During the 1961 Freedom Rides, for instance, Nashville student activist Catherine Burks told the driver who was tasked with bringing participants back to the Tennessee state line to prevent them from going forward with protests in Alabama that "for every reason he could give her for believing in segregation she could give him one why he didn't believe in segregation." When she asked him why he believed the races should be segregated and he responded that he didn't know, she responded that "you believe in God and all God's children are brothers and sisters. You would not harm your brothers, so why harm Negroes."[100] Burks's moral basis for her argument, and the stress she put on desegregation as the focal point of racial harm, is echoed in a 1962 memo written by Anne Braden, a white journalist from Alabama, who was deeply involved in civil rights organizations, including SNCC. "If the potential of this movement is to be developed in its full scope, drawing in both white and Negro Southerners acting together, we must effectively combat the widespread fear among many Southerners that the integration movement is or may be somewhat 'subversive,'" she wrote. "Many of us feel that if any basic change comes to the South it must come by Negro and white working together."[101] A year later, however, desegregation was more likely to be cited as one of a number of goals that were necessary to combat racist structures. A 1963 memo to the Conference on Religion and Race, for instance, described the March on Washington as a demonstration "for legislative measures to cope with the problems of discrimination in employment, public accommodations, education, voting, [and] the exercise of civil liberties," including "acts of brutality by police and die-hard segregationists without a single conviction for crimes."[102] A SNCC press release announcing an "Open City" campaign in Atlanta in early 1964 combined the fight for desegregated spaces with the need for job opportunities, declaring how "the new demonstrations . . . are aimed at integrating public and private eating places, hotels, and at securing more jobs of Negroes" while specifically stating how civil rights groups have "attempted to negotiate some integration but several members of the Negro community are dissatisfied with the slow pace of integration."[103] Even James Forman's description of a 1964 campaign, meant to pressure film studios to force desegregation on Southern movie theaters, in a letter to Joseph Strick, the president of the City Film Corporation, hinted at addressing economic issues. Although he explains that the American Broadcasting Company Television and Radio Network "could be placed in a position of great moral and direct pressure if their television advertisers were threatened by selective buying campaigns in the event the theaters were not desegregated," he also noted how the network's "top brass" should "be approached for a discussion of the ways in which truly democratic theater management should be practiced."[104]

Desegregation was never SNCC's only goal—as previously stated, many activists initially joined to work on voter registration, while other campaigns involved distributing food and clothing in impoverished rural Southern areas, working with labor groups to eradicate racial discrimination in employment, holding rallies and prayer vigils for people who had been injured or killed by racist violence or police brutality, and even buying stocks in companies so that they could influence corporate boards to adopt more equitable practices.[105] But activists began questioning just how much they should be working toward an integrated society in the aftermath of the Civil Rights Act's passage—especially after the Johnson administration proved that its support for the movement had reached its limit when the 1964 Democratic National Convention refused to seat SNCC's Mississippi Freedom Democratic Party delegation in favor of the state's traditional all-white representatives.[106] Ambivalence toward integration as a major civil rights goal became perfectly clear in many position papers delivered during the retreat that SNCC held in Waveland, Mississippi, in November 1964 for the organization to, as leader Bob Moses put it, "be rebuilt in order to stay afloat. It also has to stay afloat in order to be rebuilt."[107] "If SNCC were simply a protest group concerned with opening up a few local lunch counters, we would not need to maintain a file of newspaper articles and utilize a national clipping service," staff member Barbara Brandt argued. "We are, in some form or other, an organization aimed at bringing about changes in the political structure of the country. SNCC's intimate involvement with the [Mississippi Freedom Democratic Party], and our continued efforts to obtain Federal intervention and protection are just two examples of the importance of national politics and power to our organization."[108] Meanwhile, James Forman asked the rhetorical question "Why Do We Organize?" and responded by claiming that "obviously we are organizing because we feel that racial segregation is wrong." And yet his paper went on to explain how "we also organize because people who suffer from discrimination and segregation are denied a sense of dignity . . . a person working in Mississippi, a person earning $2–$3 a day, was being denied a sense of dignity, was being exploited economically and that this exploitation made it very difficult for him to hold his head high, to say to his family, 'I am a man.'"[109]

Other papers revealed deeper concerns about positioning desegregation as a primary goal. "Do we have the resources and the personnel to even begin to cope with the tremendous problems of rural decay[,] automation, unemployment?" the author of a working paper on class relations wondered. "We might ask ourselves where we would be in the Negro community today if we had to confront the economic issues head on and produce some tangible results. Instead, the issues of segregation, police brutality, injustice in the courts, and the vote have provided us with more immediately soluble problems around which we could organize."[110] Another paper's author reconsidered the tactic of using integrated groups to provide protection in hostile environments. "I do not know if I am willing to work in an integrated project simply to prove a point," they admitted. Although they simultaneously stress that "an integrated staff should be able to live and move together to do their job" and that "they should be able to move with a sense of rapport and oneness of purpose," they also claimed that "there are some areas (geographic) in which Blacks and whites cannot be productive as a team." Additionally, "there is a sort of 'ethnic relationship' among the [Black] staff and the community; I do not feel that this relationship can be entered into by whites." Ultimately the author proposed "that the relationship of whites to specific project areas must be decided for specific situations and that no generalities covering that relationship are possible."[111] Field Secretary Charles Sherrod also questioned whether this tactic would continue to be successful given new political realities. "For the past few years we have been using the symbols of what hundreds of bodies mean together with signs and blood in a common appeal on T.V., Radio, in newspaper, etc., on one side and the white man's guilt on the other," he wrote. "This has been effective. It has led to degrees of desegregation and levels of integration." And yet, he admitted, "there is a 'backlash' of the white man's conscience. There is a point at which the whites in our country are saying outside the NO's that have been present inside of them all the time, so you get this white boycott in Brooklyn and other places, you get the fight against housing . . . and finally you get [1964 Republican Presidential candidate Barry] Goldwater."[112] Although each author admitted that desegregation had offered student activists a clear goal capable of garnering outside support (including from the federal government), concerns that had existed since the organization's formation were more seriously considered after the Civil Rights Act was written into law. "Blacks didn't necessarily want to be integrated," SNCC organizer Larry R. says, looking back on this period. "They didn't equate that with freedom at all. They wanted to be Black and have the same rights as everybody else."[113]

Campaigns to register Black voters, who were routinely denied the ability to cast their ballots in the South, remained integral to SNCC members and to student activists from other civil rights organizations. Their efforts were bolstered after President Kennedy announced his support for the Civil Rights Bill. As a means of both recruiting voters for the Democratic Party and (supposedly) quelling violent protests and arrests in Southern states by transferring activists' energies away from direct action, the Kennedy administration instead pledged support for registration campaigns. James Forman recalls how "this was a big debate in the student movement and in the U.S. government" because "there were some people who were objecting to this concept of going into voter registration as that would be a capitulation and an ending of the direct-action campaigns." Although he admits that he "didn't think that the distinctions were very real," he admits that the government's push in this direction was "about how to get people out of direct action and how to get the student movement to stop protesting."[114] Proponents argued that widespread voting rights were the most effective means of ensuring that Black people could force government officials to address structural racism, economic disparities, and racial violence rather than relying on desegregation as the first step toward eradicating these inequities. And yet a focus on voting rights was similarly rooted in existing democratic values that most Americans held dear rather than the more revolutionary changes that were gaining popularity by the mid-1960s.

When SNCC members first met with Amzie Moore, head of the local NAACP branch in the Mississippi Delta, he "made clear that his main concern was voter registration rather than desegregation," Charles Payne explains. "He suggested that SNCC send students to Mississippi to assist in a voter registration drive that could ultimately result in the overthrow of the segregationist regime in that state."[115] These drives began as early as 1961, when SNCC activists headed to McComb, Mississippi, "to help local Negroes register to vote [who] have been beaten, jailed, and threatened with death," as well as open voter registration schools to help train citizens how to challenge the racist and unconstitutional barriers that kept them from the ballot, and to prepare them for the violent and legal repercussions that they would almost definitely face for trying to exercise this right. The organization also supported nine high school students who had been arrested for staging sit-ins.

In their defense, the students used democratic rhetoric that made plain the indignities of being denied the right to vote using appeals to Christian morals. "In the schools we are taught democracy, but the rights offered by democracy have been denied to us by our oppressors," a SNCC flyer advocating their plight read. "We have not had a balanced school system; we have not had an opportunity to participate in any of the branches of our local, state, and federal government; however, we are children of God who makes our fellow men to love rather than hate, to build rather than tear down, to bind our nation with love and justice without regard to race, color, or creed."[116] This combination of democratic and moral rhetoric, which civil rights activists had used to draw support to their causes since World War II, continued to shape narratives around SNCC's voter registration campaigns as well as sit-in protests.

SNCC continued sending student activists to rural counties throughout 1962 and 1963, partnering them with local residents and training them, member Howard Zinn writes, "to register people to vote, to protest against racism, [and] to build up courage against violence."[117] When participants began complaining about increased violence and a lack of media attention that would help keep them safer, SNCC collaborated with the NAACP, SCLC, CORE, and other groups under the umbrella organization Council of Federated Organizations (COFO) to organize the Freedom Summer project, to be carried out over the summer of 1964. White and Black college students were recruited to travel to Mississippi to canvas, teach citizenship rights and African-American history in Freedom Schools, and, most of all, help disenfranchised voters register at hostile polling stations. As Sara Evans, who participated in this campaign, explains, "The urban sit-ins had been in many ways attempts by middle-class blacks to gain access to the social rights and privileges of the white middle-class by integrating public facilities. Voter registration, on the other hand, required reaching out to the impoverished masses of rural Southern blacks and experiencing sustained violence and the constant threat of death from local whites."[118] Voter registration could also turn the sympathy that direct action protestors were able to drum up into concrete political action that could benefit Black citizens. In a 1963 tract entitled "Race and Law," for instance, theologian D. Elton Trueblood claimed that "a powerful moral thrust" was responsible for increased movement support, "but this thrust, powerful as it is, cannot succeed without enactment and enforcement of laws." Activists who focused on direct action alone were making "a serious mistake to suggest what the lawmakers are doing in such a connection is trivial. What they do is not trivial because the entire power of the state can, by their action, be placed behind the man who has been treated unjustly. His neighbors may still resent his presence next door, but they cannot, with impunity, break his windows."[119] This line of thought informed SNCC's Freedom Summer project, as Larry R. explains. "White Southern racists were the chairs of the House and Senate," he says. "And the reason they were in Congress for so long is that, in many cases, the majority of their own constituents were not allowed to vote. Could not exercise the right to vote. So, you know, we reason that if Black people in the South got the right to vote, they would vote these people out and vote in people who would be progressive." When he made his first trip to the South as a member of SNCC, he says he "went down with this political analysis in my mind, you know, about [how to get] people to vote and vote out these bad guys." When he got there, however, he "learned that the job was making sure that Mrs. Jones had a car, you know, had a way to get to the mass meeting." Although much of his work involved knocking on people's doors or recruiting them to come to mass meetings where they could get help registering to vote, he cautions that these efforts were "very dangerous" for poor Black residents and that "we couldn't sugarcoat that."[120]

Appealing to the country's democratic values for support, particularly from the federal government, was not a new tactic, of course. SNCC made use of this rhetoric in earlier campaigns as well, whether it was focused directly on voter registration or simply invoking Black Americans' citizenship rights during direct action protests or after unfair arrests. "The Federal Government is committed to a policy of voting rights for all and to support Supreme Court decisions against segregation," read a 1962 SNCC memo urging the Justice Department to free members, including Charles McDew and Bob Zellner, from prison in Baton Rouge, Louisiana. "But laws guaranteeing voting rights and court decisions against segregation will be translated into life only by people working in the South. This is precisely what these students have been doing." Attorney General Robert Kennedy's office was not living up to its stated credo, however, as the memo's author states that "we feel that the Federal Government, if it is truly committed to these things, cannot afford to sit idle while the people who provide the grass-roots leadership for implementing them are harassed in this manner." The student activists were only imprisoned because "state officials are using an unconstitutional law, unconstitutionally applied, to cripple the people who are trying to implement Federal law," and so SNCC demands "that the U.S. Department of Justice step in *now*" in order to "serve notice that embattled defenders of the U.S. Constitution have the full and active backing of the Federal Government."[121] That same year, Anne Braden explained in another memo how such rhetoric, beyond shaming federal agencies into actually enforcing laws that were already on the books, could offer SNCC some protection against accusations that members were radicals or communists. "The best weapon that *we* have for combatting [these accusations] is the U.S. Constitution," she wrote. "The First Amendment guarantees the right of every citizen to speak his views, print them, assemble with others to promote them, etc. . . . In a society where the First Amendment truly prevailed

... no *idea* could be stifled by labelling it 'subversive.' People could feel free to promote any idea as long as they did not engage in acts that are illegal under our Constitution." She further described SNCC's campaigns as distinctly situated within American values systems, stating that "the future of the integration movement in the South is tied inevitably to what happens in the country generally—whether we continue on the path of stifling ideas or whether we are true to our democratic tradition in which protest is honored and active citizen-participation in movements toward change are seen as the lifeblood of our society."[122] Finally, this rhetoric was also used to recruit new members to the cause. "This is a call to every red blooded American; to every decent person; to every Christian person; to everyone who believes in democracy," reads a 1963 flyer advertising a rally featuring comedian and activist Dick Gregory. The event was organized to urge participants to "Learn Facts About Voter Registration in the South" and to fight "for FREE ELECTIONS in the South Now—the right of every American to vote."[123] This rally was held at a Tabernacle Baptist Church in Chicago, which would have had a predominantly Black congregation. Appealing to existing democratic values for voter registration support was therefore viewed as an effective tactic within Black circles too, not just as a means of gaining attention and sympathy from white outsiders and federal officials.

Even if democratic rhetoric could be used to entice support across racial lines, it was particularly important for Freedom Summer organizers to recruit white participants. Some activists believed that the success of this project, like that of Black musicians within the mainstream music industry, would be contingent on white support. But middle- and upper-middle-class white university students were not directly affected by racial injustice themselves, and, because of housing and school segregation, may not have even been exposed to racist discrimination firsthand, so SNCC instead constructed the problem as an affront to American democracy as a whole. This tactic drew about one thousand white college students to Mississippi for the summer, but it also encouraged broader support among white youth in general, who often expressed shock over what they saw as an inherent mismatch between the country's democratic standards and treatment of Black activists. "Seeing kids have dogs sicced on them and hoses sprayed, that kind of thing, was absolutely horrifying," Bill W., who grew up in Washington, D.C., asserts. "Seeing people beaten because they were marching for free rights and whatever was absolutely horrifying." Larry R. explains that he was less surprised by this treatment, having grown up in a family of communist sympathizers where civil rights activism and unfair treatment by the authorities were regular topics of conversation. But he does remember friends who would "say something like, 'oh, you know at school we were brought up to believe that everybody in America is equal,' and that, you know, the land of the free. And then I watched on television Bull Connor in

Birmingham turning firehoses on people just trying to register to vote. And I was shocked." Indeed, many white respondents use the language of capitalist-democratic frameworks or moral righteousness to explain their sympathy for Black Southerners who were denied basic rights of assembly. Pat K. says "there were just a lot of things that I knew in my mind weren't right" when recalling her growing support for direct action campaigns. "I just thought voter registration was the right thing to do. Sometimes you just get a feeling that there are the right things to do." Mary R. points out that, in her liberal Seattle home, racial discrimination "was always presented as if this was fundamentally un-American. And you would never have any part of it." Ken A. remembers supporting passage of the Civil Rights and Voting Rights Acts even though he previously would have thought "somehow it interferes with individual choice." By 1964, however, "I became more sympathetic to civil rights and anti-war [movements] and I saw how much of that was considered the best part of America, this whole myth of this entirely middle-class country driving Chevrolets all over the place was very much a myth, that there were people whose rights were being trampled on."[124]

Each of these responses reveals a fundamental belief in the inevitability of course correction, that the United States would surely live up to its stated ideals once the evils of Southern segregation were made plain to the rest of the nation. Even if their wording about how movement actions did not really affect their daily lives parallels how many Black respondents recall this era, white respondents do not display the same ambivalence about how or whether desegregation in public spaces would affect the trajectory of racial citizenship in the country. Indeed, many white respondents recall feeling hopeful that these protests would usher in a new era of peaceful interactions among individuals of different races. Bruce C., for instance, recalls "feeling this great sense of the possibility that something was going to change. That here we have all these people, and it's Black and white together, you know, that's something, something's going on here. I had this sense of the moment that this was an important thing that we were taking place in."[125] This hope that an emotional connection across racial lines would bring people together to challenge segregation and discrimination laid the foundation for many white kids to support SNCC.

Interracial participation and white recruitment were viewed as essential to the Freedom Summer project for tactical and safety reasons, however, rather than ideological hopes of enacting an integrated "beloved community" in Mississippi. COFO organizers ensured that Black activists would be paired with white participants when they went into the field on the pretense that journalists would follow white college students to rural Southern areas to file their stories. Their presence would provide both visibility and protection against the harsh realities of white massive resistance. But yet again, a mostly tactical decision was often publicized as what Grace Elizabeth Hale describes as "a version of an integrated world" which she argues was too romanticized to ever come to fruition.[126] Freedom Summer organizers were aware of this disconnect; as SNCC field secretary Jesse Morris wrote to James Forman in a 1963 letter, "An enormous amount of rhetoric is being used in the civil rights movement for equal rights and equal opportunity. One might even say too much rhetoric is being used. It is used in an attempt to arouse the masses, reach the consciences of the men of good will, castigate the opponents of the civil rights movement and inform the entire nation of the consequences that stem from racial injustice." Despite the fact that this rhetoric was "so effective as a means of arousing the masses and a means of castigating racists and bigots," he cautioned that "as a means of informing the nation of the consequences that stem from racial injustices, it leaves much to be desired."[127] Larry R. adds that the program's reliance on white participation "was naïve too. Because, you know, Black people were experiencing this [oppression and discrimination] as Black people. . . . They considered that kind of, that I was being opportunistic. Or that we were being opportunistic. That we were taking advantage of the movement."[128]

Even if the presence of white students from often-prominent families ensured that journalists and Justice Department officials also made the trip to Mississippi during the summer of 1964, the almost immediate murders of activists James Chaney, Andrew Goodman, and Michael Schwerner at the hands of the local Ku Klux Klan revealed that Freedom Summer participants could expect little protection from white supremacist violence. Many were arrested, beaten, shot at, or otherwise harassed throughout the campaign's duration; meeting places were bombed or set aflame; and local Black participants experienced economic threats, including loss of jobs, homes, bank loans, and access to electricity and water. Although political pressure forced FBI officials to the region to search for the bodies of the three murdered activists, they ultimately proved unwilling to offer protection to the activists who continued working on this campaign despite constant threats of violence. As a SNCC news release makes clear: "No American of good conscience can rest until the murderer or murderers are apprehended and brought to justice for this barbarous act." The copy further asserted that "The federal government can no longer afford to remain aloof while unprotected students and local citizens try to ensure constitutional rights that should never have been denied. America is burning its own cross on the graves of its children because it has not taken the responsibility for enforcing the democratic way of life."[129] The rhetoric that civil rights activists had used since World War II to make Americans realize that Black citizens were unconstitutionally deprived of their basic rights continued to anger and inspire white supporters, even if they were more likely to romanticize the interracial community aspect of campaigns like Freedom Summer. This support, along with horrified reactions to broadcasts of SNCC chairman John Lewis and other activists being brutally beaten by police during an SCLC-sponsored march for voter rights in Selma, Alabama, ultimately forced President Johnson to sign the 1965 Voting Rights Act, which "abolished literacy tests and poll taxes designed to disenfranchise African American voters and gave the federal government the authority to take over voter registration in counties with a pattern of persistent discrimination."[130] The percentage of eligible Black voters registering in counties across the South skyrocketed over the following five years, including a whopping 857 percent increase in Mississippi.[131] Civil rights activists, including those in SNCC, had achieved their goal of getting the federal government to enforce voting rights for all citizens (for the time being, at least), but more than a little blood had to be shed in order for these fundamental democratic values to be upheld for Black voters.

The violence meted out against these young activists remained in keeping with SNCC's tactic of nonviolent protest. Just as Martin Luther King Jr. stressed during the Montgomery Bus Boycott and other major campaigns in the 1950s and early 1960s, nonviolent direct action was meant to elicit sympathy and support from outsiders when they saw white supremacist opposition attacking activists who refused to inflict harm. Even when members advocated for the moral superiority of nonviolence, organizers continued to stress the rational outcomes of these actions. Tactical nonviolence, then, meant that students sitting in at lunch counters allowed themselves to be assaulted by angry onlookers without budging from their seats, Birmingham locals took to the streets planning to be attacked by Bull Connor's police force because of its reputation for being among the most violent in the South, and Freedom Summer workers were put through extensive training on a college campus in Ohio to ensure that they would not fight back in the face of harm once they reached Mississippi. "Segregation is something that they wanted to maintain, and so they were willing to kill people and they apparently killed pretty much who they wanted," James Forman attested in a 1996 interview. He explained how SNCC organizers were careful to explain to volunteers that "they could be killed, they may not come back alive. But we wanted them also to know that we were not asking them to do anything that we had not done, that we didn't do."[132] Some activists clearly revealed how nonviolence was used as a tactic to draw media attention and support by intertwining it with the respectability politics that had been used in civil rights protests since the late nineteenth century. Ruby Doris Smith-Robinson recalled, for instance, that when SNCC first started holding meetings "people came with their suits and ties on and high heel shoes; it was a very sophisticated type of operation."[133] Rhonda E. also attests to the power of "sophisticated" clothing, noting that when one of her friends attended marches "she can describe what she wore:

A dress that you would wear to church and patent leather shoes and socks."[134] Clothing that conveyed middle-class respectability could also be used to inform onlookers that protestors did not intend to engage in violence, and that any form of brutality was initiated by white supremacist hatred rather than activist action. This intersection clearly had a positive impact on the *New York Times*, where journalist Claude Sitton described Freedom Riders as "young Negroes in sport shirts, Ivy League suits and print dresses" and noted how most white participants were students at elite institutions like Wesleyan, Duke, and Yale.[135] But the moral appeal of nonviolence continued to be stressed, as a 1962 SNCC memo arguing for the release of student activists from prison confirms: Their charges of violence against the state are described as "fantastic" since "these students are followers of the philosophy of nonviolence. . . . In fact, the movements these students lead are the very hope of a nonviolent solution to the tense crisis facing the South."[136]

Use of nonviolent action and respectability politics was originally meant to recruit Black proponents, but by the mid-1960s this conception was not quite as enticing as it once was. Although some prominent SNCC members, like Paul Brooks and Catherine Burk, for instance "[do] not believe in war" and "are trying to redeem the South," claiming that "we are not going there full of hatred," many Black activists and supporters admitted that they had doubts about the efficacy of this tactic, felt that it involved too many capitulations to middle-class white norms, and were tired and traumatized after seeing Black activists constantly being beaten on the news.[137] "People were just getting killed," Walter Blackwell reiterated. "And people who were going down [South], the only thing they wanted to do was just demonstrate. They weren't going down to do any harm. But they were getting killed." Even protestors in his city, Ann Arbor, Michigan, "were afraid of getting waylaid by local hoodlums."[138] Carolyn Maull, who participated in the Birmingham campaign, noted how she struggled with her decision not to engage in other direct action protests. "I felt guilty, like I was wimping out by not joining in," she explained. "I'd rationalize it by saying, 'Well, it ain't going to do any good for me to get beat up.' I suppose in some ways I was just a chicken. It bothered me that I wasn't out there."[139] These concerns were increasingly echoed by SNCC members across racial lines, especially after white supremacist violence failed to subside even after the federal government passed pivotal civil rights legislation. "We were supposed to be nonviolent, and we were, we were nonviolent because the local people protected us with their rifles," Larry R. asserts. "They stayed up at night and protected us. Well, I carried around a shotgun. I never used it. At all. But what I did is I stuck it out the window, just to show them that I had something."[140] SDS member Barbara Haber mused that many activists expected "to make speeches in front of the Washington Monument" when really "you get the feeling that in order to really do the things you want, you're going to have a bloody revolution, and that's scary."[141] One Waveland conference paper made plain its authors' views on the subject, proclaiming "Allright—let us love everybody—but does it have to be so much of a spectacle?" while the steering committee was concerned with the "question of whether we are a social service agency or a band of revolutionaries."[142]

Not every SNCC member felt this way, though—indeed, the division between adherents of the philosophy of nonviolence and those who felt that they could no longer assent to sending Black activists into protests knowing they would be beaten would inform the organization's shift toward Black Power ideologies in 1966. But during the tumultuous year of 1964, some members maintained that nonviolence was still key to achieving SNCC's goals. "We of the Student Nonviolent Coordinating Committee recognize the necessity to be consistent with principles of morality and not bow to the pressures of political expediency," John Lewis declared in an April press release. "We are committed in our practice to the use of any tactic or strategy which is nonviolent, and which will dramatize the plight of numbers of Negroes in the ghettoes of the North and in the South, so long as these actions do not endanger innocent lives nor cause the gratuitous destruction of property."[143] Although Lewis confirmed the organization's support for nonviolence in ideological terms, his use of the term "dramatize" in a release meant for major publications also shows how members continued to use this type of protest as a means of gaining sympathy and support from the outside. Indeed, in a less public conversation that year, James Forman warned that what "we cannot forget is that a nonviolent movement must dramatize the evils in some way," focusing here on convincing outsiders to care rather than the movement's inherent moral superiority.[144] Other members considered how nonviolence could be used to further the group's goals beyond desegregation and voting rights in the aftermath of landmark civil rights legislation passing. At the Waveland conference, Howard Zinn, when considering whether "we maintain nonviolence or do we buy guns and declare the revolution?" made a tactical argument when he affirmed that "SNCC needs to begin using the tactic it made famous: nonviolent direct action, to tackle problems outside of lunch counters and outside of voting, in relation to issues like food, shelter, clothing, medical care, jobs, justice in the courts in 'ordinary criminal' cases, right of free expression in press, radio, television, etc." And yet, in the same document, Charles Sherrod relied on moral ideology to proclaim that "there can be no place for race hatred among us, SNCC that is, we Blacks must recognize the needs of the whites are not so different from our own as regards recognition, fulfillment, status in our group, and so forth."[145]

Continued focus on nonviolence as a morally superior tactic resonated with white liberals, including those with access to resources and power structures, as summed up neatly in a letter Dr. Florence LaFontaine Randall wrote to Amzie Moore in the aftermath of the Birmingham campaign and President Kennedy's address on the Civil Rights Bill. "Now that enough realization has captured the imagination of the public I feel things will get better for you all," she proclaimed. "DO NOT RELENT keep forging ahead as much as possible with the Non Violence theme. I have an honor from Gandhi before he died." She shaped this admonishment in distinctly moral terms, noting that "I only know before God we are all his children, in heaven there is no color line," and admitting that "my people have sinned against yours horribly."[146] This heavily emotional response to what white supporters often viewed as a simple battle between right and wrong had a major influence on many white kids. Bob R., for instance, explains how he came to see that "SNCC was simply the more liberal of the groups involved. Not radical at all. John Lewis is a hero to me." Despite widespread opposition against the group in his hometown of Little Rock, he says that one of the reasons he came to support the movement is that "people involved weren't even necessarily 'activists.' I saw that immediately since the Little Rock Nine were just local black teenagers trying to go to a high school they thought was better than the black high school. The Montgomery bus boycott was a boycott by 'regular' people."[147] Andrew L. similarly focuses on a moment when he was personally able to connect with a woman whom he saw protesting at a segregated movie theater in Florida. "As with any event that you see in person versus watching it, even watching it on TV is not the same thing, you do not pick up the emotion," he says. "And when you see this person who's walking down the sidewalk, and you just incorporate her pain, to think, why is she being excluded? I mean, what a silly thing. I mean, you could exclude somebody because they were throwing things inside the movie theatre or creating a commotion. But just because she was Black? I couldn't get my head around that." This ability to relate to Black protestors, which is reminiscent of how white narrators responded to music by Black artists, relied on a link that was more emotional than political, and which necessarily eschewed the use of violence. This connection could, as Lewis and Forman clearly hoped, inspire some of these kids to join movement organizations themselves. Mary R. joined the Friends of SNCC chapter at her college in Washington State in 1964, where students "picketed places. We marched. We had meetings" and tutored Black children in local schools, while Bruce C. was moved to join SDS and the Young Lords the same year, which "seemed to be, like, it was a no-brainer. The idea of political action was very important to me." Although Ellis B. notes that "I can't say that I was involved in sit-ins or went to the national, you know, civil rights marches or demonstrations," he was still "supportive of liberal politics, liberal politicians," and got involved by "passing out leaflets at the train station for candidates."[148] This seeming disbelief that people could be arrested or subject to brutal violence just for demanding that they be treated as equal citizens without resorting to violence clearly resonated with white respondents who were then inspired to get involved in political organizing themselves. But because so many white kids focused on their emotional responses to the violence directed against nonviolent protestors, they often missed the fact that it was used tactically, and that Black activists may have had different aims in mind that they may not have fully agreed with. When young activists both within SNCC and in other organizations began to disavow nonviolence, their actions could more readily be viewed as hostile, unreasonable, and fearsome, strengthening harmful stereotypes about Black people rather than showing how different forms of protest were necessary if the movement was to prevail.

DESEGREGATION OF MUSIC AND SPACE DURING ROCK AND ROLL PERFORMANCES

The distinctions between Black and white kids' views on the effectiveness and desirability of nonviolent direct action campaigns to end segregation were also present in spaces where people gathered to hear music in groups. These segregated or tacitly integrated areas could potentially encourage young listeners to reevaluate the ways that racial discrimination affected their own lives, and to react against these divisions. Since popular music was one area that was already considered to be "integrated" by the early 1960s, spaces devoted to this music, such as school dances and record hops, club performances, and major concerts, drew audiences from all racial backgrounds, providing opportunities for young people to think more critically about the boundaries that existed in their own communities. In many cases, Black and white respondents alike claim that they were aware that attending these events constituted a shift from their normal lives spent in more segregated spaces. Paralleling their views on direct action protests, however, white respondents are more likely to describe these experiences as exciting, yet nothing to be concerned about, almost as a means of revealing how comfortable they felt in mixed-race spaces even if they would have been unfamiliar at the time. Black respondents, however, are more circumspect about their expectations for any changes to extend beyond the confines of these spaces. Black musicians performing at white high school dances or in white dance clubs did not necessarily challenge local racial norms, even in Jim Crow states, as white audiences had long enjoyed these types of performances as a form of exoticized entertainment.[149] Ed B., for instance, does not recall any type of treatment that challenged racial norms when performing as part of a singing group at clubs and school dances in Memphis, Arkansas, and Mississippi. "I don't remember too much discrimination," he says. "The only difference that

I noted was that they [white venues] were better clubs." Overall, "we was treated nice and basically we was kids. Our ages were like 15 through 17, something like that. So they didn't treat us that bad. . . . Didn't feed us, didn't drink us, but they enjoyed our meeting. And that's what we was there for anyways." Even though he stresses that "they would come up, pat us on the backs, and say ya'll come back, man, we had a ball," he also says that "when it came to white venues, it didn't matter. They just loved the music."[150] In these cases, his experiences differed little from those of Black jazz performers who had provided exoticized entertainment to white audiences throughout the early to mid-twentieth centuries. White audience members may have treated him and his bandmates with politeness, but part of this treatment was contingent on their youth, and they were in no way invited to feel like they were on an equal footing with the people who had come to watch their show. In this case, music and dance could be separated from the people who created and performed in these traditions.

By the mid- to late 1950s, rock and roll shows, which appealed to both Black and white teenage concertgoers, featured large rosters of integrated musicians performing on the same stage. Unlike earlier blues and jazz shows, race was not mentioned in the advertisements for these shows, and performers were usually listed according to name recognition rather than race. Sometimes white acts would open for Black performers, a clear reversal of expected racial hierarchies, and few complaints were raised.[151] Deejay and impresario Alan Freed explained that, at one of his famous Rock 'n' Roll Revues, "no stage or band pit separated them from the performers. The boys and girls danced on camera with me. They shared the screen with Ivory Joe Hunter. When LaVern Baker came out with *Jim Dandy Got Married,* the audience joined right in on the refrain and kept time with their hands and feet." Even though many of Freed's shows were integrated, the majority of the audience was white, which meant that they were invited to ignore any perceived boundaries to dance and sing with Black performers. Freed's emphasis on the lack of division between the audience and musicians is also telling. "Nowhere in show business will you find a more democratic relationship between entertainers and audience," he reiterated, neatly incorporating the democratic rhetoric that was so important in civil rights communications.[152]

The program given out at a 1957 Freed concert made a similar statement by presenting the show as a safe space for young people who felt out of place in their social groups. "There's no fear of being a failure as a Rock 'n' Roll fan," the copy crowed. "The heavy beat engulfs everyone in the crowd. IF you can clap your hands and move your feet you're *in.* The dancing is good exercise for everybody. As a guy you *might* make the varsity team. As a gal you *might* win a beauty contest while your girl friends placed way down the list, but *everyone* comes out on top with Rock 'n' Roll music. Everyone can dance and enjoy the beat."[153] The term "everyone" here included both the Black and white concertgoers who routinely filled the seats at Freed's shows. Teenage fans were very much aware that when they purchased a ticket to one of Freed's revues they would be entering a more open public space where socializing with musicians and other audience members across racial lines may occur. Even if many of Freed's shows encouraged white kids to cheer and scream for Black musicians, just like their jazz- and blues-loving forebears, the racially mixed performers and audiences at many concerts complicated this dynamic by focusing on a unified love of music that crossed racial divisions rather than white exoticization of African-American art forms.

Spaces marked by race were supposed to influence how people moved through them, how they acted and presented themselves, and who they communicated with. In some cases, however, young people violated social expectations when they crossed into mixed-race spaces, or areas that were dominated by another race, revealing that they were comfortable with varying degrees of integration in public areas, and that they did not support racial division of public spaces. Whites always had more power to enter Black spaces, particularly if they were doing so as part of a "slumming" exercise that only served to emphasize their social and political dominance. These spaces were still widely considered to be dangerous, though, and white kids who crossed into Black neighborhoods were aware that just being in these areas could harm their reputations and mark them personally as dirty, criminal, or transgressive. Conversely, white spaces, which were depicted as clean and safe to their inhabitants, were marked as unsafe for Blacks, who risked violence, harassment, and arrest if they crossed these boundaries. Racial divisions were not absolute in either case; many factors influenced the ways that people negotiated racialized spaces to fit their own lives and needs so that Blacks and whites were never completely cut off from one another, even in terms of geographical space. Nevertheless, spaces were clearly marked with racial signifiers in ways that perpetuated systems of inequality and politicized the transgression of boundaries, even if an individual was not engaged in overtly political activities. But by the early 1960s, forms of resistance within segregated and desegregated music venues revealed increasing public objections to unequal racial laws or customs. Young concertgoers often resisted these divisions in ways that could echo or parallel the methods of SNCC protestors, who directly confronted racist laws by filling public spaces with integrated bodies and forcing authorities to act rather than passively acquiescing with unjust laws. Unlike civil rights activists, concertgoers usually did not set out to protest racial dictates, and when they did, they mostly resulted from spontaneous anger or frustration over rules that prevented them from choosing where they could sit or dance, or whom they could talk to. And yet when they entered these spaces, young listeners were invited to evaluate the ways that racial discrimination affected their own lives, and to react against many of these divisions. When teenagers enjoyed rock and roll music in public spaces, or when this music prompted them to cross into areas outside their usually limited neighborhoods and communities, their actions could therefore reflect support for desegregation movements. But just like their responses to SNCC's tactics and goals, these experiences varied based on the race of the attendee and the type of space they entered in order to hear these musical performances.

Concert venues could act as physical spaces that encouraged this type of racial boundary crossing, even though the amount of racial mixing differed based on region, venue, and performing artists. Southern venues were officially segregated until at least 1964, with certain areas restricted to either Black or white audiences. By the late 1950s, as rock and roll shows proved profitable, more and more venue operators realized that they were losing money by not allowing patrons of all races to purchase tickets. Black kids had increasing amounts of disposable income to spend on tickets to shows featuring white entertainers or integrated acts, and larger numbers of white kids were trying to see African-American performers in Black clubs. In some cases, the same acts were booked for two separate shows, one for Black audiences and another for white audiences, so that racial mixing was prevented from the outset, and venue operators did not have to worry about being charged for violating segregation orders. In November 1956, Bluefield Auditorium in Bluefield, West Virginia, featured a "Colored Rock 'N' Roll Dance" with all Black acts, including The Coasters, The Tune Weavers, and Ernie Freeman's Orchestra. The Coasters and Ernie Freeman stayed in town to perform at a show held for white patrons five days later, where ticket prices were 50 cents cheaper, but little else about the events seemed to differ. Posters for the two events look exactly the same, using the same colors, font for the lettering, and even the same pictures of the musical acts performing at both shows.[154] Even though the organizers were careful to plan two shows to keep Black and white fans separate, the posters did not need to be altered to appeal to different tastes—they attracted the same kind of teenage music fans, regardless of race. By utilizing their power as potential consumers who were not afraid to cross-racial boundaries, young music fans were helping to reshape the limits of segregated spaces.

Many venue operators realized it would be inefficient to hold completely different shows, though, so they compromised by imposing some form of race-based division on the space. Some responded to increasing white interest by allowing "white spectators" to purchase tickets to all-Black shows. These tickets cost less than the normal price of admission, but relegated patrons to the backs of theaters, often without chairs, and prevented them from using the dance floor.[155] Posters advertising all-Black rock and roll shows held at

Bluefield Auditorium between 1956 and 1957, for instance, betrayed little racial tension amid their Technicolor designs and the bright, punchy look of their graphics other than the fact that separate ticket prices were listed for "admission" and "white spectators."[156] Again, there was no difference in how the posters attempted to draw both white and Black kids to the shows; the assumption was that patrons from both groups would respond positively to the same acts, designs, and slogans. As much as this setup allowed concertgoers of both races to attend the same shows, it also presented a consistent reminder of the indignities of segregation. Gladys Knight and her brother Merald explained that it "hurt" to "sing for our brothers and sisters in the basement of these auditoriums, and sing for the whites with the nice cushioned seats and everything on top."[157] Edgar S. also recalls the tactile differences in segregated theaters in Mississippi, where Black patrons had to sit "upstairs with those hard seats" while "whites were downstairs, and we took different routes to go into the theater." If all else failed, smaller venues would divide dance floors with a rope down the middle so that kids would be deterred from dancing with, or even talking to, people of different races. Ultimately, many venues were so committed to abiding by state segregation laws that, as Edgar recalls, "either whites would be up in the balcony, or there would be some type of rope. Or they would go at a different time."[158]

Young concertgoers did not necessarily abide by these rules, though. Chuck Berry remembered how, at a concert he performed in Mobile, Alabama, in the 1950s, "over a dozen patrolmen were lined up forming a path for the show people to walk through [separating Black band members from white fans]. . . . The isolation ignited ill feelings in the fans as well as the artists."[159] In some cases, these "ill feelings" inspired actions that could echo or parallel the methods used by direct action protestors. Ralph Bass, an A&R representative for Chess records, explained that even when white patrons were forced to sit in roped-off "spectator" sections, "pretty soon they started jumping over the rope to dance" among Black concertgoers. In other instances, white Southern kids would drive to all-Black clubs on the outskirts of their towns and try to check out the musical performances inside. "The promoter would be at the door with a gun in his belt for protection," he said. "Kids came in and he'd say, 'You kids can't come in here. You know it's against the law.' They said, 'Look out. We're coming in.'"[160] Early rock and roll legend Ike Turner remembered similar occurrences while playing for young, integrated audiences. "The police would raid the club on Sunday evenings," he said. "This club was only for teens and there were no wrongdoings going on, but the police didn't like these kids mixing with blacks. So they loaded up the truck with the white kids, took them to the police station and called their parents to come and pick them up. They'd tell the parents that their kids were hanging round blacks and so they'd been brought in before they got into trouble."[161]

The privilege of having white skin in the South clearly allowed these young concertgoers to break the rules, even if they might wind up at the mercy of local law enforcement. Sometimes officers would stop performances and lead white patrons out, or, as Turner recounted, call their parents, but these instances did not prevent white kids from continuing to find room for themselves in Black spaces. Venue operators, Bass said, "had to keep enlarging [white areas] anyway, 'cause they just couldn't keep the white kids out, and by the early fifties they'd have white nights sometimes."[162] These areas grew so rapidly that, in some cases, roles were reversed, and dance floors were limited to white patrons with special sections for "colored spectators," even at shows with Black headliners.[163] This sense of entitlement was clearly borne from the white privilege that assured these kids of their (relative) safety even when they were breaking the law and asserting their rights to infiltrate Black spaces. And yet their actions are almost always described as more spontaneous types of sit-ins, as though these kids were actively challenging segregation laws rather than asserting that they cared more about seeing their favorite performers than they did about upholding Jim Crow laws. In cases where venues were segregated by rope, Bass recalled, it was common to see "the blacks on one side, whites on the other, digging how the blacks were dancing and copying them. Then, hell, the rope would come down, and they'd all be dancing together."[164] As early as 1956, rock and roll fans in Houston, Texas, forcefully desegregated concert venues on three separate occasions in ways that precipitated the use of direct action tactics by civil rights activists. In June, *Jet* magazine described a concert "where the cops got an unscheduled workout trying to stop white girls from dancing with Negro men. They broke up a first floor session only to have other mixed couples start rug-cutting in the second and third balconies."[165] In this instance, police officers chose to let the matter go. Two months later, when Carl Perkins invited white teens, who made up roughly 60 percent of his audience, to join Black kids on the dance floor, police also declined to intervene. When white teenagers attempted the same feat at a Record Stars show featuring Fats Domino one week later, however, the results were different. When police stopped the music to tell Black attendees to go back to their seats so that white kids could dance separately, Domino refused to play. Hundreds of concertgoers ran to the box office to demand refunds, and police panicked, ended the show, and escorted the promoters out of the facility. Promoter R. J. Rausaw was offended, telling a journalist at the *Pittsburgh Courier* that "he did not give Negro or white dances and all were invited to come. Since all the talk about desegregation, white teenagers are no longer content to come to dances featuring Negro artists and sit and listen while Negroes dance." The *Courier* concurred, noting, "white teenagers are getting their first taste of discrimination and they don't like it."[166] The week after this incident, Houston police chief Carl Sheptnine told promoters they would be denied the use of concert venues if they did not ensure that the races were kept separate during shows. In response, the *Courier* noted, "there has not been a single interracial incident at the Houston dances in question. All the incidents have been touched off by police insisting on strict segregation and white teen-agers determined to dance."[167]

Teenage dancers mingling or sharing the floor with each other, regardless of race, was not uncommon, even when obstacles tried to ensure segregation. As one of Little Richard's band members, H. B. Barnum, recalled, "When I first went on the road there were many segregated audiences. With Richard, although they still had the audiences segregated in the building, they were there together. And most times, before the end of the night, they would all be mixed together."[168] These actions had the potential to be viewed as political statements against segregation at a time when young civil rights activists were forcibly desegregating lunch counters and department stores. From the distance of the stage, many performers and producers believed that they saw this connection firsthand. "You know, it was a revolution," Ralph Bass asserted. "We did it as much with our music as the civil rights acts and all of the marches, for breaking the race thing down."[169] Chuck Berry recalled how several such incidents affected him while on tour. In one city, "the white people there mixed with the blacks who were black as well as those who appeared white, leaving no black blacks or white whites feeling uncomfortable." At another show, "twice as many young whites as blacks rushed toward the stage, climbed on, and began socializing with us. We knew the authorities were blazing angry with them for rushing on stage and at us for welcoming them, but they could only stand there and watch young public opinion exercise its reaction to the boundaries they were up against." Even at the Apollo Theater, the cultural heart of Harlem's Black community, "white folks mingled and conversed as black as colored folks, if you know what I mean. [Blacks and whites] jived between each other. All were artists, playing foolish, having fights, and making love as if the rest of the world had no racial problems whatsoever."[170] Looking back on this period, Shirley Reeves, a member of the Shirelles, a top-selling Black girl group, claimed "I'm just amazed at it now everyone got along so well and this was a time of real high prejudice, you know. But in New York there was . . . you never saw it."[171] "We felt like that our music could bring these people together," Gladys and Merald Knight asserted. "We can bring everybody together—race doesn't matter."[172] When an interviewer asked Apollo Theater promoter Hal Jackson if he had been able to "build bridges between black and white people" during this period, he responded with an unequivocal "Oh yes." Black groups like the Temptations were such a popular draw, he said, that "young people, were coming out more and more after hearing it on the radio, they were coming out to see these groups." Once they were there, the interviewer continued, "You didn't play the race card. You integrated your show. You had black musicians and white musicians on the radio. You were interested in brotherhood." Again, Jackson assented: "Yes. That's the whole thing."[173]

Many concertgoers' actions, including occupying cross-racial spaces, tearing down ropes and other divisions, mingling with people across racial lines, and publicly acting on cross-racial crushes, paralleled actions that civil rights and student groups organized to overturn Jim Crow laws. This is perhaps unsurprising given that SNCC's direct action campaigns were heavily covered by journalists, and most kids would have been familiar with images of sit-ins and other methods of direct action. Actions taken by Southern teenagers in mixed-race concert venues were not planned in advance, though, and they did not intend to attack the political system as a whole. As Grace Elizabeth Hale has cautioned, attending mixed-race concerts "did not require [white attendees] to confront their racist or worried parents and friends or to face being beaten, gassed, kicked, arrested, and even killed. Singing together enabled people to feel the music. Deep in the heart, singing was not an argument or an ideology. It was a feeling. It was the tap of the foot and the leap of faith. While some people were inspired to go south and work, all a person had to do to 'feel' like part of the movement was to sing along."[174] White teenagers like Bob R., who grew up in Little Rock, Arkansas, could make light of efforts to segregate concert venues, recalling that "somehow they divided the auditorium in half with Black people on one side and the white people on the other. I think they ran a rope down the middle of the auditorium as the divider. How silly was that."[175] But this derision did not generally translate into meaningful interactions that might actually help bridge racial chasms and create determination to challenge racist structures, despite what musicians and producers might proclaim about the power of music to bring people together. Although Bob C. says that he and his friends thought that "integration was fine" at the concerts they attended in Virginia Beach, and even notes how some audience members mingled across racial lines "and it did not raise any concerns," he does not recall ever having done so himself.[176] Jeff T. says that, although most concerts he went to in Atlanta were not legally segregated, "the races didn't mix much."[177] Stan W. cannot recall any problems among concertgoers of different races but adds that most shows he went to in Alabama were either majority white or majority Black, which minimized the chance for any real cross-racial interaction.[178] Rick T., who often attended majority-Black concerts in Virginia where he was one of the only white attendees, explains that most people did not attempt to communicate across racial boundaries. "In retrospect, [Black concertgoers] were just as, I don't want to say the word afraid, but they were just as cautious as I was. Because it was a new thing for both of us."[179] And Bruce C., who remembers seeing shows at the Apollo Theater in New York in the early 1960s where he was among "maybe three or four of us that constituted the white faces," enjoyed his experiences in majority-Black audiences, yet does not remember any mingling whatsoever. "They stayed where they were supposed to," Edgar S., who is Black, says of the segregated audiences at shows in his home state of Mississippi. "That's the way it was. I expected that. That was the norm, unfortunately."[180]

Sometimes Black concertgoers were able to feel the type of interracial camaraderie that white respondents spoke of when they entered these spaces. Kitty Oliver, for instance, described how she was affected by the interracial audience she found herself a part of when she attended a desegregated Beatles concert in Jacksonville, Florida, in 1964. "The room chilled as I walked into a sea of White faces," she recalled. "I sat in silence with elbows drawn in tight to make sure I did not accidentally brush an arm and spark an outburst." And yet, when the band came on and the music started, "the crowd rose, thunderous, in unison. . . . Then, tunnel vision set in: Eyes glued to the front, I sang along to 'She loves me, yeah, yeah, yeah . . .' full-voiced, just as loudly as everyone, all of us lost in the sound." In a later interview for the Ron Howard film *Eight Days a Week*, she noted how she "still can feel, to this day, that there were all these white people around, but everyone was standing up with everybody and then just yelling as loud as I could and singing along."[181] Most Black music fans recall whether concerts they attended were mixed race or segregated, but, as with their responses to direct action campaigns, they did not seem terribly relevant to their own lives. Edgar S. remembers going to theaters and concert venues that were segregated by race but asserts that "I really didn't pay too much attention. I was focusing on the performer." Respondents who grew up in Detroit remember attending Motown Revues in the early 1960s, which featured a bevy of groups and performers signed to the local label. Even though most of the musicians were Black, audiences were often interracial and rarely segregated by design—as Cheryl J. attests, "Everybody was into Motown." But even in these venues, mingling across racial lines remained rare. Rhonda E. states: "I'm sure there had to be some white people there, but they didn't stick out. I didn't see them and think, 'Oh, look.'" But her focus was similarly on the performers and not on the racial mix of the audience. When asked about whether these shows were segregated, she instead explains the ease with which she was able to access these venues. "I never remember or even heard of a segregated anything Detroit," she says. "I never went into a theater and [had] not been able to sit where I wanted." Similarly, Miche B. was more inspired by the fact that local Black kids had become national celebrities than she was by any interracial appeal when she went to these concerts. "It was the most wonderful thing to see them and to know that they were from Detroit, or if they weren't from Detroit, they were based in Detroit for the music," she says. As with their views on direct action campaigns, many Black respondents were more interested in strong portrayals of young African-American role models and with how their actions might make it easier for them to move freely through public and consumer spaces rather than the potentials of sharing a room with white contemporaries.

Some white respondents, however, recall their attendance in mixed-race concert venues as a sign that the country's values were changing and that civil rights struggles had triumphed, while simultaneously implying that integration in these arenas was not worth the massive opposition they saw on television. "Those were integrated shows," Bob S. says of concerts he attended in New York. "Not forcefully. Just how everybody went and had a good time." Michael P. similarly attended shows in New York where "the top stars of the era would perform. And that was pretty much an integrated act also." The audiences too were "mixed," he says, especially a Sam and Dave performance which "was a Hispanic, Black, white crowd for sure." Jeff T. recalls how he and his friends were among the only white attendees at many shows in Atlanta, including a Ray Charles concert, but that "we always were treated very courteously," while Ron R. is completely dismissive of the KKK "dumbasses with their hoods and their confederate flags" who protested a Beatles concert he attended in Washington, D.C. for refusing to play segregated venues. "It was really irritating because here we were trying to be more diverse, more accepting," he says. "These bastards were trying to preserve their sense of what the status quo should be."[182] White respondents do not display the same heightened enthusiasm when recalling their own participation in desegregated spaces as they do when discussing their responses to sit-ins. Their almost nonchalant reflections instead reveal that while they supported desegregation in public spaces, they did not necessarily understand the opposition forged by white massive resistance or the violence and discrimination that Black kids often encountered when they entered majority-white or mixed-race spaces. Their responses also reflect beliefs that desegregation would be key to ending racial injustice overall by encouraging interracial interactions and mutual identification rather than acting as a crucial first step toward granting full citizenship and mobility rights to Black Americans, as civil rights activists had originally intended.

Other white respondents remember attending shows in Black neighborhoods where they were among the only white audience members. Even though most recall some feelings of awkwardness, they also focus on how warmly they were received or how exciting they found the performances in contrast to shows put on by white artists. When Rick T. attended his first concert at a majority-Black venue in Richmond, Virginia, at the age of 12 in 1961, for example, he remembers being shocked by the friendly treatment he received. "People that you knew in your neighborhood and people that you knew in church and in school, and the things that you saw on television were always portraying Black people in a negative light," he says. "Well my experience with that was 180 degrees opposite of that. So that had tremendous impact on my life. And I noticed when I'd go to shows the Black artists would take their time to speak to me, to talk to me, would treat me like I was one of them. And when I went to white shows, I didn't get that treatment at all."[183] Bruce C., who grew up in New Jersey, had somewhat similar experiences attending R&B and blues shows in Harlem and Chicago. "There would be some other whites who were totally into the music because they themselves were musicians . . . but it was predominantly African-American audiences," he says. "I never felt threatened. But yeah, I mean, sometimes people would look at us with a quizzical look, and sometimes people would just welcome you with completely open arms." He shares Rick's experience of noting the difference between majority-Black and majority-white shows, though, explaining how when he and his friends would visit record stores in Black neighborhoods, "There would always be a crowd of African Americans around the record stores on the sidewalk dancing [to the music played by the shop's loudspeaker]. We'd just go up there and we'd love it because, you know, this is not something white people did." This sense of unfamiliar excitement also drew Bill W. to majority-Black shows at the Howard Theater in Washington, D.C., when he was as young as 14 years old. "There were very, very few white people, so sometimes I was the only white person in the theater," he says. "I never had any problems. I mean, there might have been a couple times when it was, what are you doing here, white boy? kind of stuff. But it never got nasty, I was never threatened or things like that." In return, he was able to see the Motown Revue, James Brown, and other major stars where "all of a sudden, you find yourself in a crowd, and the African Americans next to you are jumping up and down and screaming . . . as loud as you're jumping up and down and screaming." Common love for these performers led, he says, to a feeling of interracial unity. "Instead of it being us and them, we are now all us," he claims. "There is no us and them."[184]

These experiences clearly show how white concertgoers felt excited to be present in majority-Black spaces, and may have even relished their status as one of the few white people in the crowd. They may have led white attendees to support desegregation based on their own positive experiences, but they are also reminiscent of how earlier white jazz and blues aficionados were drawn to Black music because they found it mysterious and exotic, and helped them to escape the confines of their own whiteness for the span of the performance. Black R&B and rock and roll musicians often did deliver more dynamic and emotional performances that would inspire dancing and enthusiasm within the audience, but these characteristics could also be used to justify harmful racial stereotypes when contrasted with relatively sedate, supposedly more respectable, performances by white artists. These respondents clearly preferred attending majority-Black concerts, which could encourage them to view integration as new, intriguing, exciting, and, ultimately, not much of an issue, especially since they were often treated so kindly by other attendees. But integration often meant something entirely different to Black concertgoers, many of whom may have felt as though they had to treat white people with politeness if they did not want to face legal consequences or violence. They would likely not have felt quite so safe or welcome in majority-white spaces either, since engaging in integrated areas could result in very different experiences for Black and white music fans.

White attendees are also more likely to insist that race was not much of a consideration when they entered integrated music venues, again paralleling their views on desegregation as a whole. Ron R. remembers attending record hops in his Ohio hometown where local deejays often played a mixture of records by Black and white artists which, he says, "brought people of different races together and different dance skills." Because deejay collections were often limited to what they were able to play at their home stations, he began volunteering his own records, which he special-ordered from Randy Woods' storied music shop in Gallatin, Tennessee. "The kids were impressed because they got music that they liked and they could dance to and they had a chance to hear it," he says, unlike the more conventional pop music playing on most local stations. Ultimately, even though he lived in a largely white area, Ron explains that Black kids from a neighboring community began attending these record hops. "We were intermixed all the time," he says. "That's where a lot of white people became aware of the merit of music as a way of bringing people together who might not otherwise be together." And yet the way he describes some of these interactions is reminiscent of how white respondents try to minimize their own acknowledgments of racial distinctions as they simultaneously voice support for desegregation in public places. He describes some Black acquaintances as "the guys who would later get into trouble with drugs and drinking. Burglary and stuff like that. . . . Frankly, not the best citizens of the world. But they would go over to those dances because they appreciated and respected the music and the dancing. So they would go for the music. Even though they weren't active participants, so to speak. They were at least respectful of it. They respected the people who could do it." He similarly explains how his white friends who were less than physically gifted were able to admit "well, I can't do that, but I can recognize talent when I see it." Even as Ron notes the social possibilities of an integrated dance playlist drawing attendees from different racial backgrounds to the same venue, he tries to minimize the very real racial distinctions in his story by focusing on how dance abilities could garner respect among these teenagers, regardless of race. He even stresses that "it wasn't a racial thing. For those who made it a race thing, I think, that's another matter, I guess. I just . . . didn't really care about that aspect of it. I was already past that. Or never had it in the first place."[185] This means of downplaying racial difference also shapes white respondents' memories of sharing residential or school spaces with Black musicians. Andrew L., for instance, played in a high school band with a guitarist who was Black. He explains that, while the band often practiced at the guitarist's house, and that his house was the only Black residence he recalls ever entering as a kid in Ohio, that these instances did not shape his thoughts on civil rights campaigns either way. Stan W., who also played in a high school band in rural Alabama, concurs, noting how "several times a Black blues group from my high school came over to my house to jam with us." He explains that "I enjoyed that a lot, but we did not discuss civil rights."[186] Attending integrated dances or playing in integrated bands did not challenge established perspectives, then, so much as they could reinforce white kids' beliefs that integration in certain areas did not bother them and that race could (possibly) be ignored in favor of individual ability. These perspectives lined up with the missions of SNCC's direct action campaigns, but they could also obscure the need for deeper structural changes, and prevent many white people from acknowledging the racism that persisted after segregation in public spaces was made illegal.

Black and white kids who grew up during this period may have supported the efforts of sit-in activists, but their distinct responses when listening to music in segregated and desegregated venues would shape the contours of post-civil rights racial liberalism in the decades to come. Black kids supported direct action and voting rights as means of accessing consumer spaces and demanding full citizenship rights and dignified treatment, but were not necessarily convinced of the virtues of integration alone. White kids, however, expressed more shock at what they saw on their television screens, often using democratic or moral language to explain why they supported desegregation as a means of ensuring equal racial treatment, and why nonviolence was the most acceptable method of fighting for integration. Their responses reflect young music fans' reactions to entering desegregated or otherwise mixed-race musical venues, as Black respondents focus more on representation and accessibility, while white respondents are more intent on showing that they were completely fine with entering these areas, even when they were in the minority, and therefore could not understand the racist opposition leveled against them. Many continue to support this narrative about music acting as a bridge between white and Black fans during the civil rights movement, even if, as Bill W. asserts, "there were lots of people that could segregate in their mind, that they loved these Black artists. That this guy over here was still the 'N' word. The kids over here were still the 'N' word. Those guys in DC, they steal, they rob, they're ignorant, that kind of thing. Even though they are loving the music here. I couldn't do that, it just didn't match up for me. But there were plenty of people that were able to separate those things as if they weren't related."[187] This type of overt racism was not necessarily overcome by a love of Black music or musicians, but white kids more often came to believe that integration should be a guaranteed aspect of citizenship within the framework of loving rock and roll and attending concerts at increasingly mixed-race venues. Since they rarely had to interact with actual Black people, or face the systemic discrimination they continued to experience, however, many of the continued challenges of the following decades would be obscured and negated by post-civil rights liberal beliefs that overt racism had already ceased to exist.

NOTES

1. Kal Mann and Dave Appell, "Teach Me How to Twist," Cameo-Parkway Records, 1962.

2. Steve Chapple and Reebee Garofalo, *Rock 'n' Roll is Here to Pay: The History and Politics of the Music Industry* (Lanham, MD: Rowman & Littlefield Publishers, 1978), 247–248.

3. Eldridge Cleaver, *Soul on Ice* (New York: Delta Trade Paperbacks, 1999), 197.

4. Rhonda E., in discussion with the author, February 26, 2020; Carol A., in discussion with the author, February 24, 2020; Ed B., in discussion with the author, June 23, 2020.

5. Rose W., in discussion with the author, April 26, 2020; Henry I., in discussion with the author, October 30, 2019.

6. Marcia P., in discussion with the author, December 6, 2019; Patricia J., in discussion with the author, March 9, 2020; Walter S., in discussion with the author, October 4, 2019; Bruce S., in discussion with the author, September 24, 2019; Jimmy F., in discussion with the author, September 25, 2019; Victor F., in discussion with the author, September 30, 2019; John H., in discussion with the author, September 20, 2019; Scott F., in discussion with the author, April 20, 2020.

7. Scott F., in discussion with the author; Joseph J., in discussion with the author, January 30, 2020.

8. Bruce C., in discussion with the author, June 8, 2020; Ron R., in discussion with the author, June 9, 2020; Walter S., in discussion with the author, John H., in discussion with the author; Andrew L., in discussion with the author, April 8, 2020.

9. Ellis B., in discussion with the author, September 26, 2019; Jimmy F., in discussion with the author; Clara A., in discussion with the author, May 29, 2020; Ed B., in discussion with the author.

10. Bill Gavin, "No Musical Color Line," *Billboard*, April 25, 1964, 46.

11. *Billboard*, January 9, 1961–November 23, 1963.

12. David Brackett, "The Politics and Practice of 'Crossover' in American Popular Music, 1963 to 1965," *The Musical Quarterly* 78, no. 4 (1994), 778–779.

13. *Billboard*, November 30, 1963–December 26, 1964; Jack Mahler, "No Mercy From Mersey? Beatles Have Launched a New Redcoat Invasion," *Billboard*, April 25, 1964, 12.

14. Gavin, "No Musical Color Line," 46.

15. *Billboard*, July 25, 1964, August 8–22, 1964.

16. *Billboard*, September 19, 1964, 18; October 3, 1964, 12.

17. Gavin, "No Musical Color Line," 46.

18. Gavin, "No Musical Color Line," 46.

19. Jimmy F., in discussion with the author; Scott F., in discussion with the author; Rhonda E., in discussion with the author; Lori B., in discussion with the author, January 7, 2020; Walter S., in discussion with the author; Pat K in discussion with the author, November 19, 2019.

20. Brackett, "The Politics and Practice of 'Crossover,'" 779.

21. Reebee Garofalo, *Rockin' the Boat: Music and Mass Movements* (Cambridge, MA: South End Press, 1992), 249; Paul Kingsbury, *BMI 50th Anniversary: The Explosion of American Music 1940–1990* (Nashville: The Country Music Foundation, 1990), 59; Brackett, "The Politics and Practice of 'Crossover,'" 795.

22. Jimmy F., in discussion with the author.

23. Andrew Flory, *I Hear a Symphony: Motown and Crossover R&B* (Ann Arbor, MI: University of Michigan Press, 2017), 24; Berry Gordy, *To Be Loved: The Music, the Magic, the Memories of Motown* (New York: Warner Books, 1994), 56.

24. Gordy, *To Be Loved*, 89.

25. Gordy, *To Be Loved*, 99; Suzanne E. Smith, *Dancing In The Street: Motown and The Cultural Politics of Detroit* (Cambridge, MA: Harvard University Press, 2009), 6.

26. *Billboard,* April 1959; February-May 1960; December 1960–December 26, 1964; Smith, *Dancing In The Street*, 6.

27. Grace Palladino, *Teenagers: An American History* (New York: Basic Books, 1996), 140–145; Smith, *Dancing In The Street*, 6; Flory, *I Hear a Symphony*, 35.

28. Craig Werner, *A Change is Gonna Come: Music, Race and the Soul of America* (New York: Penguin Putnam, 1998). 19.

29. Flory, *I Hear a Symphony*, 35; 53.

30. Gordy, *To Be Loved*, 182–183.

31. Flory, *I Hear a Symphony*, 5.

32. Henry I., in discussion with the author; Ellis B., in discussion with the author; Bruce S., in discussion with the author; Bill W., in discussion with the author, June 1–2, 2020; Lori B., in discussion with the author; Marcia P., in discussion with the author; Bruce C., in discussion with the author.

33. Jimmy F., in discussion with the author; Carol B., in discussion with the author, October 2, 2019; Victor F., in discussion with the author.

34. David S., in discussion with the author, September 16, 2019.

35. "The Rolling Stone Interview: Phil Spector," *Rolling Stone*, November 1, 1969, Jerry Wexler Collection, Box 1, Folder 8, The Rock and Roll Hall of Fame Library and Archives, Cleveland, OH.

36. Smith, *Dancing in the Street*, 2; 8.

37. Flory, *I Hear a Symphony*, 28; Smokey Robinson and Berry Gordy, "Bad Girl," Chess/Motown, 1959; Janie Bradford and Berry Gordy, "Money (That's What I Want)," Tamla, 1959; Smokey Robinson, Pete Moore, and Marv Tarplin, "The Tracks of My Tears," Tamla, 1965.

38. Timothy Carlson, "Soul Providers: A TV Special Celebrates the Cultural Contributions of Black Artists," *TV Guide*, November 24, 1990, 25, Russell B. Nye Collection, Special Collections, Michigan State University Libraries, Lansing, MI.

39. Miche B., in discussion with the author, April 25, 2020.

40. Smith, *Dancing in the Street*, 9.

41. Scott F., in discussion with the author; Cheryl J., in discussion with the author, January 9, 2020; Rhonda E., in discussion with the author; Larry R., in discussion with the author, October 4, 2019.

42. Smith, *Dancing in the Street*, 16.

43. Cheryl J., in discussion with the author; Scott F., in discussion with the author; Rhonda E., in discussion with the author; Smith, *Dancing in the Street*, 18.

44. Sam Lebovic, "'Here, There and Everywhere': The Beatles, America, and Cultural Globalization, 1964–1968," *Journal of American Studies* 51, no. 1 (2017), 44; 48–49; 52; Steve Turner, *A Hard Day's Write: The Stories Behind Every Beatles Song* (London: Carlton Books, 1994), 27–38; *Billboard*, January 25–December 26, 1964; Mahler, "No Mercy From Mersey?", 12. *Billboard* announced that rapper Drake had taken seven of the top 10 slots in the Hot 100 the week of July 14, 2018, a feat that supposedly broke the Beatles' long-standing record. The announcement was almost immediately met with skepticism, however, since the methods used by *Billboard* to calculate chart positions have changed dramatically since 1964. Please see Gary Trust, "Chart Beat," *Billboard*, July 9, 2018, last accessed at https://www.billboard.com/articles/columns/chart-beat/8464454/drake-hot-100-record-nice-for-what-scorpion, on June 8, 2021.

45. Marcia P., in discussion with the author; Jimmy F., in discussion with the author; Walter S., in discussion with the author.

46. Mary R., in discussion with the author, May 11, 2020; Victor F., in discussion with the author; Marcia P., in discussion with the author.

47. Victor F., in discussion with the author; Bruce C., in discussion with the author; Marcia P., in discussion with the author.

48. Bob Spitz, *The Beatles: The Biography* (New York: Little, Brown and Co., 2012), 446; Merv Griffin, interview with Little Richard, *The Merv Griffin Show*, October 18, 1971, last accessed at https://www.youtube.com/watch?v=qyPHSs-w7tiQ, on March 15, 2021; Brian Ward, "By Elvis and All the Saints," in *Britain and the American South: From Colonialism to Rock and Roll*, ed. Joseph P. Ward (Jackson, MS: University Press of Mississippi, 2003); "The Beatles Encounter a Segregated America in 1964," CBS News, last accessed at http://www.cbsnews.com/videos/the-beatles-encounter-a-segregated-america-in-1964/, on May 21, 2014.

49. Eric Burdon, "An 'Animal' Views America," *Ebony*, December 1966, 162; 166; 168.

50. Miche B., in discussion with the author.

51. Kitty Oliver, "The Beatles, Race and Segregation," The Beatles Story, February 1, 2018, last accessed at www.beatlesstory.com on April 7, 2021.

52. Amy Abugo Ongiri, *Spectacular Blackness: The Cultural Politics of the Black Power Movement and the Search for a Black Aesthetic* (Charlottesville, VA: University of Virginia Press, 2009), 134; Ed Bradley, interview with Little Richard, *60 Minutes*, 1985, last accessed at https://www.youtube.com/watch?v=JmdpmM6mhBg on March 15, 2021; Griffin, interview with Little Richard.

53. Bibb E., in discussion with the author, November 13, 2011; Jimmy F., in discussion with the author.

54. Rhonda E., in discussion with the author; Miche B., in discussion with the author.

55. Louise Hutchinson, "Barber Gives Scare to Five Fuzzy Singers: Rolling Stones Roll Out of His Way," *Chicago Tribune*, June 12, 1964, 20; Anthony Carthew, "Shaggy Englishman Story: British Long-Hairs Are Proud of Setting a New Tonsorial Style—But the Barbers are Crying," *The New York Times*, September 6, 1964, SM18; Gloria Emerson, "British 'His and Her' Hairdos Blur 'Him-Her' Line," *The New York Times*, July 23, 1964, 29; "Rock 'n' Roll: The Sound of the Sixties," *Time*, May 25, 1965.

56. Scott F., in discussion with the author; Rhonda E., in discussion with the author; Cheryl J., in discussion with the author; Ellis B., in discussion with the author.

57. Ed B., in discussion with the author.

58. Joseph J., in discussion with the author.

59. Ellis B., in discussion with the author.

60. David S., in discussion with the author; Carol B., in discussion with the author.

61. Robert E. Weems and Robert E. Weems Jr., *Desegregating the Dollar: African American Consumerism in the Twentieth Century* (New York: New York University Press, 1998), 63; Glenda Elizabeth Gilmore, *Defying Dixie: The Radical Roots of Civil Rights* (New York: W.W. Norton & Co., 2008); Michael R. Winston, "Opinion: Sit-Ins in the District in the 1940s," *The Washington Post*, November 14, 2011; Sean Robinson, "Revitalizing Northwood: Morgan State University's Role in Economic and Community Development," in *Re-envisioning Higher Education's Public Mission*, ed. A. Papadimitriou and M. Boboc (New York: Palgrave Macmillan, 2021); Christina Greene, *Our Separate Ways: Women and the Black Freedom Movement in Durham, North Carolina* (Chapel Hill, NC: University of North Carolina Press, 2005), 65–67; Adam Fairclough, *To Redeem the Soul of America: The Southern Christian Leadership Conference & Martin Luther King, Jr.* (Athens, GA: The University of Georgia Press, 1987), 53–54.

62. Clayborne Carson, *In Struggle: SNCC and the Black Awakening of the 1960s* (Cambridge, MA: Harvard University Press, 1995), 10.

63. "Student Nonviolent Coordinating Committee (SNCC) Actions, 1960–1970," Mapping American Social Movements Project, University of Washington, last accessed at http://depts.washington.edu/moves/SNCC_map-events.shtml, on December 8, 2020; "Greensboro Sit-Ins: The Sit-Ins Spread," The Greensboro Sit-Ins, last accessed at https://greensborositinsalegacy.wordpress.com/2017/04/06/the-sit-in-spreads/, on December 9, 2020.

64. James Forman, interview with James Bevel, "Forman—A History," 41–42, James Forman Papers, Box 55, Folder 6, The Library of Congress, Washington, DC.

65. James Forman, interview with Ruby Doris Smith-Robinson, "Forman—A History," 55, James Forman Papers, Box 55, Folder 6, The Library of Congress, Washington, DC.

66. Forman, interview with Ruby Doris Smith-Robinson.

67. Letter from James Forman, November 20, 1961, James Forman Papers, Box 16, Folder 8, The Library of Congress, Washington, DC.

68. Victoria Valentine, interview with James Forman, *Emerge* 7, no. 6 (April 1996), James Forman Papers, Box 92, Folder 1, The Library of Congress, Washington, DC.

69. Herb Boyd, interview with James Forman, November 17, 1985, 3–4, James Forman Papers, Box 92, Folder 1, The Library of Congress, Washington, DC.

70. James Forman, "What is SNCC?" transcript, October 21, 1964, James Forman Papers, Box 35, Folder 15, The Library of Congress, Washington, DC.

71. Carson, *In Struggle*, 14.

72. Forman, interview with Ruby Doris Smith-Robinson, 64–67. For more on SNCC's decision to "sit-in" jail cells and the effectiveness of mass arrests as protest, please see Zoe A. Colley, *Ain't Scared of Your Jail: Arrest, Imprisonment, and the Civil Rights Movement* (Gainesville, FL: University Press of Florida, 2012).

73. David Chalmers, *And the Crooked Places Made Straight: The Struggle for Social Change in the 1960s* (Baltimore, MD: The Johns Hopkins University Press, 1996), 22.

74. "The South: A Universal Effort," *Time*, May 2, 1960.

75. McCandlish Phillips, "Campuses in North Back Southern Negro Students," *The New York Times*, March 20, 1960, 1.

76. Cheryl J., in discussion with the author.

77. Miche B., in discussion with the author.

78. Ed B., in discussion with the author.

79. Bret Eynon, interview with Larry Hunter, September 9, 1979, 15–16, Contemporary History Project: The New Left in Ann Arbor, Bentley Historical Library, The University of Michigan, Ann Arbor, MI.

80. Joseph J., in discussion with the author.

81. David S., in discussion with the author; Ron R., in discussion with the author; Bruce C., in discussion with the author; Victor F., in discussion with the author; John H., in discussion with the author; Marcia P., in discussion with the author; Bruce S., in discussion with the author.

82. Forman, interview with Ruby Doris Smith-Robinson, 59–63.

83. James Forman, "What is the Student Nonviolent Coordinating Committee," James Forman Papers, Box 54, Folder 4, Staff Retreat, 1964, The Library of Congress, Washington, DC.

84. "What is SNCC? What Should Be Done to Accomplish its Goals?" November 1964, Mary King Papers, Box 1, Folder 18, Wisconsin Historical Society Library, Archives, and Museum Collections, Madison, WI.

85. "Carolyn Maull," in *My Soul Looks Back in Wonder: Voices of the Civil Rights Experience*, ed. Juan Williams (New York: Sterling Publishing, 2005), 78.

86. Cheryl J., in discussion with the author.

87. Bret Eynon, interview with Sharon Jeffrey, October 1978, 3, Contemporary History Project: The New Left in Ann Arbor, Bentley Historical Library, The University of Michigan, Ann Arbor, MI.

88. Ken A., in discussion with the author, November 22, 2011; Ron R., in discussion with the author; Larry R., in discussion with the author; Bill W., in discussion with the author.

89. Grace Elizabeth Hale, *A Nation of Outsiders: How the White Middle Class Fell in Love with Rebellion in Postwar America* (New York: Oxford University Press, 2011), 164.

90. Bret Eynon, interview with Arnie Bauchner, December 1978, 4, Contemporary History Project: The New Left in Ann Arbor, Bentley Historical Library, The University of Michigan, Ann Arbor, MI.

91. Michael P., in discussion with the author, October 4, 2019; Walter S., in discussion with the author; Victor F., in discussion with the author.

92. Bob R., in discussion with the author, December 31, 2011; Bibb E., in discussion with the author; Michael P., in discussion with the author; Patricia J., in discussion with the author.

93. "Nation: The Big Five in Civil Rights," *Time*, June 28, 1963.

94. "What Is the Relationship of SNCC to Other Civil Rights Groups and to Local Groups," SNCC, James Forman Papers, Box 54, Folder 1, 1962–1968, Staff General, The Library of Congress, Washington, DC.

95. Interview with James Forman, December 15, 1963, 73–81, SNCC, James Forman Papers, Box 55, Folder 6, The Library of Congress, Washington, DC.

96. Claude Sitton, "Not Token Freedom, Full Freedom," *The New York Times*, June 9, 1963, 219.

97. Joseph J., in discussion with the author.

98. Shelley Stewart with Nathan Hale Turner, *The Road South: A Memoir* (New York: Grand Central Publishing, 2002), 243; 247–248.

99. The Civil Rights Act of 1964, Office of the Assistant Secretary for Administration and Management, U.S. Department of Labor, last accessed at https://www.dol.gov/agencies/oasam/civil-rights-center/statutes/civil-rights-act-of-1964, on May 25, 2021.

100. Letter from James Forman, June 5, 1961, James Forman Diaries, Correspondence 1961–1962, James Forman Papers, Box 1, Folder 2, The Library of Congress, Washington, DC.

101. Anne Braden, Memo to Jim Forman, 1962, SNCC Committee Files, 1950–2003, James Forman Papers, Box 16, Folder 19, The Library of Congress, Washington, DC.

102. Galen R. Weaver, "Memo to Conference on Religion and Race: Communication on Civil Rights Bill," October 22, 1963, Leadership Conference on Civil Rights General Correspondence, 1956–1960, Box 1-1 September–October 1963 Folder 6, The Library of Congress, Washington, DC.

103. "Atlanta 'Open City' Drive Begins," January 11, 1964, Mary King Papers, Box 1, Folder 11, SNCC Press Releases, Wisconsin Historical Society Library, Archives, and Museum Collections, Madison, WI.

104. James Forman, Letter to Joseph Strick, January 8, 1964, SNCC Committee Files, 1950–2003, James Forman Papers, Box 16, Folder 14, The Library of Congress, Washington, DC.

105. Memos from James Forman to Charles McDew and Dr. W.G. Anderson, 1962, SNCC Committee Files, 1950–2003, James Forman Papers, Box 16, Folder 9, The Library of Congress, Washington, DC; Letter from Charles Cobb to Wiley A. Branton, March 4, 1963, SNCC Committee Files, 1950–2003, James Forman Papers, Box 16, Folder 9, The Library of Congress, Washington, DC.

106. For more on the creation of the Mississippi Freedom Democratic Party and how the 1964 Democratic National Convention led many activists to break with the Democratic Party, please see Chapters 11 and 12 of Charles M. Payne, *I've Got the Light of Freedom: The Organizing Tradition and the Mississippi Freedom Struggle* (Berkeley and Los Angeles: University of California Press, 2007), 317–362.

107. "November 1964: SNCC's Waveland Conference," SNCC Digital Gateway, last accessed at https://snccdigital.org/events/snccs-waveland-conference/, on May 25, 2021.

108. Barbara Brandt, "All Those Little Newspaper Articles . . . ." October 21, 1964, SNCC, Research General, James Forman Papers, Box 51, Folder 1, The Library of Congress, Washington, DC.

109. James Forman, "What is the Student Nonviolent Coordinating Committee," SNCC, James Forman Papers, Box 54, Folder 4, Staff Retreat, 1964, The Library of Congress, Washington, DC.

110. "Working Paper: Poor Whites and the Movement," SNCC, James Forman Papers, Box 54, Folder 5 SNCC Retreat November 6, 1964, The Library of Congress, Washington, DC.

111. "Proposed Outline of Study Institute," Gulfside Methodist Assembly, Waveland, Mississippi, November 1964, Mary King Papers, Box 1, Folder 18 SNCC Position Papers, Waveland MS Meeting, November 1964, Historical Society of Wisconsin Library, Archives, and Museum Collections, Madison, WI.

112. Sherrod Brown, "Some Basic Considerations for the Staff Retreat," Mary King Papers, Box 1, Folder 18 SNCC Position Papers, Waveland, MS Meeting, November 1964, Historical Society of Wisconsin Library, Archives, and Museum Collections, Madison, WI.

113. Larry R., in discussion with the author.

114. Boyd, "An Interview with James Forman."

115. Payne, *I've Got the Light of Freedom*, 26.

116. "Students Face Mississippi Violence for You!" 1961, SNCC Committee Files, 1950–2003, James Forman Papers, Box 16, Folder 8 Letters, The Library of Congress, Washington, DC.

117. Howard Zinn, *A People's History of the United States, 1492-Present* (New York: Harper Perennial Modern Classics, 2005), 455.

118. Sara Evans, *Personal Politics: The Roots of Women's Liberation in the Civil Rights Movement and the New Left* (New York: Vintage Books, 1980), 41.

119. D. Elton Trueblood, "Race and Law," Plain Speech, *New Series* No. 23, November 1963, Leadership Conference on Civil Rights General Correspondence, Box 1-1 January–August 1963 Folder 5, The Library of Congress, Washington, DC.

120. Larry R., in discussion with the author.

121. "Students Facing Possible 10 Years in Prison in Baton Rouge, La.," 1962, SNCC Committee Files, 1950–2003, James Forman Papers, Box 16, Folder 19, The Library of Congress, Washington, DC.

122. Braeden, Memo to Jim Forman.

123. Flyer, Dick Gregory at the Tabernacle Baptist Church, Chicago, May 1, 1963, Correspondence, James Forman Papers, Box 6 Folder 20, The Library of Congress, Washington, DC.

124. Bill W., in discussion with the author; Larry R., in discussion with the author; Pat K., in discussion with the author; Mary R., in discussion with the author; Ken A., in discussion with the author.

125. Bruce C., in discussion with the author.

126. Hale, *A Nation of Outsiders*, 194.

127. Jesse Morris, Letter to James Forman, October 20, 1963, SNCC Committee Files, 1950–2003, James Forman Papers, Box 16, Folder 11, The Library of Congress, Washington, DC.

128. Larry R., in discussion with the author.

129. News Release on the Murder of Freedom Summer Workers, Mary King Collection, Box 1, Folder 11.

130. Voting Rights Act of 1965, August 6, 1965, The Martin Luther King Jr. Research and Education Institute, Stanford University, last accessed at https://kinginstitute.stanford.edu/encyclopedia/voting-rights-act-1965, on June 2, 2021; Robert Caro, *The Passage of Power: The Years of Lyndon Johnson* (New York: Knopf/Doubleday Publishing Group, 2012), xv; 600–601.

131. James C. Cobb, "The Voting Rights Act at 50: How it Changed the World," *Time*, August 6, 2015.

132. Valentine, Interview with James Forman, 26–27.

133. Forman, interview with Ruby Doris Smith-Robinson, 57.

134. Rhonda E., in discussion with the author.

135. Claude Sitton, "Group Maps Plans on Freedom Rides," *The New York Times*, June 1, 1961, 25.

136. "Students Facing Possible 10 Years in Prison in Baton Rouge, La."

137. James Forman Diaries, June 5, 1961, James Forman Papers, Correspondence 1961–1962, Box 1, Folder 2, The Library of Congress, Washington, DC.

138. Ellen Fishman, interview with Walter Blackwell, July 17, 1978, 6–7, Contemporary History Project: The New Left in Ann Arbor, Bentley Historical Library, The University of Michigan, Ann Arbor, MI.

139. "Carolyn Maull," *My Soul Looks Back in Wonder*, 79.

140. Larry R., in discussion with the author.

141. Bret Eynon, interview with Barbara Haber, September 1978, 28, Contemporary History Project: The New Left in Ann Arbor, Bentley Historical Library, The University of Michigan, Ann Arbor, MI.

142. "SNCC's Goals and Bourgeoisie Sentimentality," November 6, 1964, James Forman Papers, Box 54 Folder 5 SNCC Retreat, The Library of Congress, Washington, DC; SNCC Steering Committee Meeting Minutes, November 7, 1964, SNCC Committee Files, 1950–2003, James Forman Papers, Box 35, Folder 16, The Library of Congress, Washington, DC.

143. John Lewis, "Proposed 'Stall-In' of Motor Vehicles on Road to World's Fair," April 17, 1964, Mary King Papers, Box 1, Folder 11, Wisconsin Historical Society Library, Archives, and Museum Collections, Madison, WI.

144. Forman—Conversation, 1964, SNCC, James Forman Papers, Box 55 Folder 7, The Library of Congress, Washington, DC.

145. Betty Garman, Howard Zinn and Charles Sharrod, "Some Basic Considerations for the Staff Retreat," November 7, 1964, Mary King Papers, Box 1, Folder 11, Wisconsin Historical Society Library, Archives, and Museum Collections, Madison, WI.

146. Dr. Florence LaFontaine Randall, letter to Amzie Moore, June 20, 1963, Amzie Moore Papers, Box 1, Folder 5, Wisconsin Historical Society Library, Archives, and Museum Collections, Madison, WI.

147. Bob R., in discussion with the author.

148. Mary R., in discussion with the author; Bruce C., in discussion with the author; Ellis B., in discussion with the author.

149. In the early decades of the twentieth century, small numbers of whites became attracted to the blues and jazz, often because the qualities of primitivism and sexuality that were supposedly inherent in these musics were shunned in their own culture. They therefore responded to Black cultural stereotypes that comprised repressed elements in mainstream society. By the 1920s, jazz clubs became especially popular among urban white sophisticates who were drawn to the trendiness and sense of rebellion involved in venturing up to Harlem and other majority-Black neighborhoods to see Black performers. For more, please see Charley Gerard, *Jazz in Black and White: Race, Culture, and Identity in the Jazz Community* (Westport CT: Praeger Publishers, 1998).

150. Ed B., in discussion with the author.

151. For examples of these posters, programs, or playbills, please see the Programs boxes in the Alan Freed Collection and the Bluefield Auditorium Posters at The Rock and Roll Hall of Fame Library and Archives, Cleveland, OH.

152. Alan Freed, "Wonderful World of Rock," *Pageant*, July 1957, 36, Alan Freed Collection, Box 1, Folder 55, The Rock and Roll Hall of Fame Library and Archives, Cleveland, OH.

153. Freed, "Wonderful World of Rock," 39–58.

154. Bluefield Auditorium Posters, FF. 1.2.3., The Rock and Roll Hall of Fame Library and Archives, Cleveland, OH.

155. *Reader, Chicago's Free Weekly*, Friday May 17, 1991, 39, Ralph Bass Papers, Box 1, Folder 1, The Rock and Roll Hall of Fame Library and Archives, Cleveland, OH.

156. Bluefield Auditorium Posters, FF. 1.2.3.

157. Brent Edwards, interview with Gladys and Merald "Bubba" Knight, New York, NY, January 9, 2011, 1, 35-1-36, The Apollo Theater Oral History Project, Columbia University Rare Book and Manuscript Library, New York, NY.

158. Edgar S., in discussion with the author, June 25, 2020.

159. Chuck Berry, *Chuck Berry: The Autobiography* (New York: Harmony Books, 1987), 126.

160. *Reader, Chicago's Free Weekly*, 39.

161. Ike Turner and Nigel Cawthorne, *Takin' Back My Name: The Confessions of Ike Turner* (London: Virgin Books, 1999), 69.

162. Michael Lydon, *Rock Folk: Portraits from the Rock 'n' Roll Pantheon* (New York: Citadel Press, 1990), 9–10.

163. Bluefield Auditorium poster, May 6, 1957.

164. Michael Lydon and Ralph Bass, "Ralph Bass," in *Boogie Lightning* (New York: The Dial Press), 92.

165. Dan Burley, "People Are Talking About," *Jet*, June 14, 1956, 43.

166. Cliff Richardson, "Police Attempt to Halt Rock 'n' Rollers Fails: Integrated Houston Dance Draws 4,000," *The Pittsburgh Courier*, August 25, 1956, 21.

167. Richardson, "Police Attempt to Halt Rock 'n' Rollers Fails," 20.

168. Charles White, *The Life and Times of Little Richard: The Quasar of Rock* (New York: Da Capo Press, 1994), 69.

169. Lydon, "Ralph Bass," *Boogie Lightning*, 92.

170. Berry, *Chuck Berry: The Autobiography*, 124; 135; 116.

171. Morgan Neville, "The Hitmakers: The Teens Who Stole Pop Music," Peter Jones Productions, 2001.

172. Edwards, interview with Gladys and Merald Knight, 1–36.

173. Steve Rowland, interview with Hal Jackson, New York, NY, November 12, 2008, 1–22; 1-45-1-46, The Apollo Theater Oral History Project, Columbia University Rare Book and Manuscript Library, New York, NY.

174. Hale, *A Nation of Outsiders*, 115.

175. Bob R., in discussion with the author.

176. Bob C., in discussion with the author, December 13, 2011.

177. Jeff T., in discussion with the author, November 5, 2011.

178. Stan W., in discussion with the author, December 20, 2011.

179. Rick T., in discussion with the author, November 20, 2011.

180. Bruce C., in discussion with the author; Edgar S., in discussion with the author.

181. Oliver, "The Beatles, Race and Segregation"; Ron Howard, *The Beatles: Eight Days a Week, The Touring Years*, Imagine Entertainment, 2016.

182. Bob S., in discussion with the author; Michael P., in discussion with the author; Jeff T., in discussion with the author; Ron R., in discussion with the author.

183. Rick T., in discussion with the author.

184. Rick T., in discussion with the author; Bruce C., in discussion with the author; Bill W., in discussion with the author.

185. Ron R., in discussion with the author.

186. Andrew L., in discussion with the author; Stan W. in discussion with the author.

187. Bill W., in discussion with the author.

Chapter 5

"A Drummer with a Totally Different Beat," The Post-Civil Rights Era

In 1965, *Time* magazine ran a 10-page article proclaiming rock and roll music "The Sound of the Sixties." This title seemingly indicated a resounding triumph on the part of a genre that had previously been maligned in the mainstream press for either its excessive (and heavily racialized) sexuality or its supposedly mind-numbing capabilities. "The big beat is everywhere," the article's author proclaimed. "It has become, in fact, the international anthem of a new and restless generation, the pulse beat for new modes of dress, dance, language, art and morality."[1] The major labels and dominant forces within the music industry had therefore succeeded at turning a genre that was heavily shaped by Black artists and African-American cultural traditions into the leading form of popular music, acceptable to white audiences, and profitable within existing economic power structures. Furthermore, it had attained a degree of respectability, which would have seemed unthinkable less than 10 years earlier. "The big boost for big-beat music has come, amazingly enough, from the adult world," the article stated. "Where knock-the-rock was once the conditioned reflex of the older generation . . . a surprisingly large segment of 20-to-40-year-olds are now facing up to the music and, what is more, liking it." The author went on to list some of the "5,000 discotheques [that] have cropped up in the U.S.," many in chic sections of New York, Los Angeles, Aspen, and even Paris, where socialites mingled with liberal yet staid politicians like Bobby and Ethel Kennedy and Jacob Javits, noting that "no debutante cotillion or country-club dance is complete these days without a heavy dose of rock 'n' roll." As adult appeal grew, the article insinuated, the genre's ability to reinforce rebellion of any sort among young people seemed to diminish. "Everywhere the couples go-going on the dance floor are like, well, old," the author continued. "Moans one teenager: 'Nothing is sacred any more. I mean, we no sooner develop a new dance or something and our parents are doing it.'"[2]

Similarly, the struggle for desegregation had become largely accepted within liberal and moderate white circles by the mid- to late 1960s. Passage of the Civil Rights and Voting Rights Acts had made desegregation the law of the land, at least in theory, leading most white Southerners to acquiesce to some degree, even if they personally opposed any sort of racial equity.[3] Although school districts continued to challenge the law by desegregating at incredibly slow rates, Title VII of the Civil Rights Act, which made it "illegal to discriminate against someone on the basis of race, color, religion, national origin, or sex," meant that people would be working with colleagues from different racial backgrounds in workplaces across the country, especially in the government sector, while the very public spaces that sit-in activists had fought so hard to desegregate had, to an extent, become more diverse.[4] The Supreme Court struck down state-level interracial marriage bans with the 1967 *Loving v. Virginia* case, paving the way for a roughly 3,900 percent increase in the number of such unions across the country between 1960 and 2015, a shift that one-fifth of white respondents (yet no Black respondents) interviewed after 2016 point to when gauging the success of the civil rights movement.[5] Advertisers began to recognize that they should have been following the advice given in "The Forgotten 15,000,000" all along, and began targeting Black Americans as an increasingly important market demographic for almost every consumer product or service imaginable.[6] Increased Black voter turnout, combined with white flight to the suburbs that had continued unabated since the late 1940s, led to more African-American politicians elected to local- and state-level positions since the Reconstruction era. And as much as Martin Luther King Jr. was still viewed unfavorably by a majority of white Americans upon his death in 1968, he nevertheless remained the respectable face of the civil rights movement, earning the Nobel Peace Prize in 1964, and standing at President Lyndon Johnson's side as the Voting Rights Act was written into law. Indeed, upon his assassination, Student Nonviolent Coordinating Committee (SNCC) chairman Stokely Carmichael declared that "white America made its biggest mistake" because King was "the only man of our race . . . of the older generation who the militants and the revolutionaries and the masses of black people would still listen to," presumably to subdue their more radical impulses using the philosophy of nonviolence.[7] Just like rock and roll, the more moderate goals and tactics of the movement, including struggles for desegregation and voting rights using nonviolent protest, were subsumed, to an extent, into the country's existing capitalist-democratic framework, while economic discrimination, racial violence, and other deeply rooted forms of racism went largely unaddressed outside of activist circles. Many real and important changes resulted from campaigns staged during the integrationist period of the civil rights movement, which spanned the late 1940s into the mid-1960s, even if the structural components of racial discrimination, which most organizers had identified all along, were largely disregarded by mainstream narratives in favor of the new framework of post-civil rights racial liberalism.

Disdain for racialized attributes that lay outside the boundaries of post-civil rights racial liberalism, including perceived vulgarity, overt sexuality and emotional expression, propensity for violence, and any form of racial separatism, would continue to shape racial narratives in this country. Despite the integrated nature of popular music and its growing acceptance from many segments of society, the *Time* author continued to treat the genre with levels of suspicion and condescension reminiscent of alarmist descriptions from the 1950s, subtly bemoaning "The sudden public acceptance of rock 'n' roll by so many people who supposedly should know better" (i.e., adults), and even engaging in the same coded race-baiting that had plagued cultural commenters a decade earlier. The author ensured that readers knew that rock and roll was originally "played by Negroes for Negroes," and that "cured in misery, it was a lonesome, soul-sad music, full of cries and gospel wails, punctuated by a heavy, regular beat." Yet again, the concept of "the beat" was Africanized as "relentless" and "perhaps the most kinetic sound since the tom-tom or the jungle drum." Teenagers who screamed were "orgiastic," referencing both the sexuality in the genre and stereotypes associating Blackness with sexual promiscuity, while those who expressed themselves openly engaged in "some of the most wildly creative dancing ever seen by modern or primitive man." The old concept of teenagers lulled into trances by so-called primitive beats was seemingly alive and well in "discotheque[s], where the sound is so loud that conversation is impossible, the hypnotic beat works a strange magic. Many dancers become literally transported. They drift away from their partners; inhibitions flake away, eyes glaze over, until suddenly they are seemingly swimming alone in a sea of sound."[8]

It is perhaps surprising that rock and roll continued to be depicted in such an overtly racialized and demeaning fashion even after pivotal civil rights goals had been achieved and mainstream liberalism had expanded to include concepts of racial equality and democratic rights for all. The language used here shows that, despite widespread support for desegregation and voting rights, the structural racism that integrationist campaigns were unable to fully address continued to shape cultural narratives. Rock and roll may have become the prototype for popular music among teenagers, and even many adults, within a mere decade, but it still represented a form of racial mixing that remained controversial. The author, however, was somewhat aware that they were fighting a losing battle. "Some of it, in fact, is very good, far better than the adenoidal lamentations of a few years ago," they admitted. "Some of it is still awful, as might be expected in an industry that grinds out more than 300 new records each week. But for the first time rock 'n' roll can boast a host of singers who can actually sing. The music, once limited to four chords, is now more sophisticated, replete with counterrhythms, advanced harmonics, and multivoiced choirs." These admissions, combined with examinations of such respected personages as the Duke and Duchess of Windsor and Walter Cronkite doing the Twist and the Frug, betrayed a grudging acknowledgment that the world had changed, and that rock and roll, as much as it continued to espouse cross-racial elements, had become widely accepted, much like moderate civil rights goals.[9]

BLACK POWER, POST-CIVIL RIGHTS POLITICS, AND SOUL

By the mid-1960s, Black Nationalist philosophies, which had always informed strains of movement thought and action, were revitalized by young activists who did not necessarily agree with a major focus on desegregation or with tactical nonviolence. When Stokely Carmichael, the new chairman of SNCC, declared in his legendary 1966 speech at the University of California at Berkeley that "we maintain the use of the words Black Power" and "we are not going to wait for white people to sanction Black Power," he gave name to the concerns many Black people had about the uses and effects of integrationist campaigns. Calling integration "irrelevant" and "a thalidomide drug of integration," he maintained that "sitting next to white people . . . does not begin to solve the problem. We didn't go to Mississippi to sit next to Ross Barnett [former governor of Mississippi], we did not go to sit next to Jim Clark [sheriff of Selma, Alabama], we went to get them out of our way. People ought to understand that; we were never fighting for the right to integrate, we were fighting against white supremacy." Although his incendiary words prompted backlash from moderates, and even Martin Luther King Jr., who feared that many of the alliances he had cultivated with political officials would be broken, they clearly resonated with Black Americans who felt that tactical decisions had been mistaken for overall goals, and that their own humanity and identity would never be fully appreciated unless they were willing to assimilate into white-approved society. Even the federal policies that were lauded by Black and white supporters alike were called into question, as Carmichael asserted that "every civil rights bill in this country was passed for white people, not for black people. For example, I am black. I know that. I also know that while I am black I am a human being. Therefore I have the right to go into any public place. White people don't know that. Every time I tried to go into a public place they stopped me. So some boys had to write a bill to tell that white man, 'He's a human being; don't stop him.'" Here, Carmichael displays the fallacy at the heart of the racist American policies that oppressed Black people for roughly 80 years, but also within the strategies and celebrations surrounding integrationist work that, he argues, was never real for Black Americans in the first place. Black people already had their rights, as both humans and political subjects, he says, and never needed to change anything in the first place—the only thing that needed changing was white reaction.[10] Even though none of the Black respondents for this project undermined the integrationist movement quite this severely, their reservations about its successes are far more understandable when viewed through this lens. This is a perspective that does not allow for going slowly, appreciating incremental growth, or aiming for diversity, and therefore does not have a place in the post-civil rights racial liberalism that has shaped the worldviews of many white moderates.

By the mid-1960s, Black Power exerted an increasingly strong influence on movement politics and culture, calling for unapologetic pride in Black identity, traditions, and self-sufficiency. White members were expelled from SNCC shortly after Carmichael's speech, in which he plainly stated that "white America cannot condemn herself for her criminal acts against black America," leaving many who had dedicated years of their lives to the cause particularly heartbroken.[11] Carmichael had, however, tapped into the need to separate from an integrationist movement which had more or less reached its end point for many people. Indeed, the previous SNCC chairman, John Lewis, who had largely been supportive of integrationist policies, had issued a statement to the organization the previous year claiming that "too many of us are too busy telling white people that we are now ready to be integrated into their society. When we make appeals for active, moral, and financial support they have been geared toward the white community and for the most part not at all toward the black community." Contrary to SNCC's initial aims of achieving a society where people could learn to live together peacefully, regardless of race, Lewis claimed that "most whites still hold to a master-slave mentality" and even overtly criticized the racial liberalism of "good liberals in the North, who believe that somehow Negroes (North and South) will gradually and quietly 'fit in' to white society, exactly as it is, with its power structure, its affluent economy, its political machine, and the values of its middle class suburban folkways." Instead, he asserted, "the Negro hears a drummer with a totally different beat, one which the white man is not yet capable of understanding," and "if the movement and SNCC are going to be effective in attempting to liberate the black masses, the civil rights movement must be black-controlled, dominated, and led." The tensions cropping up in major civil rights organizations like SNCC were therefore widely apparent even before Carmichael's speech, making his words that much more resonant to people who were tired of expectations that they behave according to norms acceptable to white Americans just to win the right to walk among them. "Much as it may anger some die-hard whites," Lewis proclaimed, "the fact that a Negro sits down next to a white woman at a lunch counter and orders a Coke and a hamburger is still short of revolution."[12]

A revolution was exactly what many Black activists had in mind, but since this goal did not fall neatly within the parameters of accepted racial liberalism, they would ultimately face angry opposition from federal officials and white moderates who had been considered allies only a few years earlier. The same year that Carmichael gave his momentous speech, Oakland, California, college students Huey P. Newton and Bobby Seale formed the Black Panther Party, which put the Black Power ideology into action by fighting back against white oppression, supporting mindful Black separation, and aiming to help Black communities become self-functioning with schools, daycare centers, and poverty-reducing initiatives created and implemented by the people who would use them. Sensing a threat to the entire system, one that actually targeted structural inequities and aimed to solve them with grassroots solutions that challenged government and corporate power, the FBI's Counter Intelligence Program began tracking and harassing members of what were dubbed "Black hate organizations," while the mainstream media focused more on the Panther Party's militaristic language and dress than the group's community activism.[13] Culturally, Black Power advocates embraced the slogan "Black is Beautiful," promoting hair, clothing, and jewelry styles that celebrated Blackness and African heritage that visually set them apart from their white peers rather than trying to emulate the same trends. Most white Americans, and some Black Americans, especially members of the middle class and others who felt that they could still benefit from the politics of integration, felt alienated by this shift, but Black respondents who grew up during this period recall more nuanced responses. "I knew two girls in high school who donned the Panthers [black leather] jackets and the look and that kind of thing, and I thought that was cool but I thought that was a little scary," Carol A. recalls. "Because the Panthers were calling for armed resistance. And while I knew that they did things like . . . the breakfast club kind of stuff, I was also aware that they were being killed." Her support, then, was tempered by a fear not of what the Panthers might do themselves, but of the violent response the FBI had waged against them. Still, she remembers getting detention for wearing an African piece of clothing over her Catholic school uniform even though she says she was not explicitly supportive of the Black Panthers. "I was aware that they were being, really massacred," she recalls. "I was really aware of what it meant to protest against the government." Miche B. has more assuredly positive memories of this shift in the movement, claiming that Black Power advocates "were making sense to me.

They were making too much sense." She remembers being explicitly drawn to "the look and the music" stemming from this ideology, particularly Nina Simone's "African hairstyle" and explicitly political anthems, both of which she emulated. Scott F. remembers being affected by both the Black Panthers and SNCC because they "brought subject matter to places where it might not have otherwise reached because they positioned themselves in a way where you at least had to pay attention to the issue. So it's less for me about right or wrong and more about the fact that they have assumed a platform to get people to pay attention." Elements of the Black Power ideology that fell outside the scope of widely accepted post-civil rights racial liberalism, and which went largely unacknowledged (at least publicly) by major integrationist organizations, clearly appealed to these respondents, even if they stopped short of fully endorsing the Black Panthers as a group.[14]

This political shift was, again, echoed in the musical realm, as the highly "integrated" *Billboard* charts and popular music scene began to "separate" once again. The publication began listing 40 "Top Selling R&B Singles," and even including a chart of best-selling LPs, in the same manner as country and other genres like classical, folk, and easy listening, which would intermittently grace these pages whenever they experienced a surge of popularity. This apparent "re-segregation" of the charts indicates that different racial demographics were again starting to purchase and listen to different kinds of music, although David Brackett also argues that it resulted from a "difference in value" that put Black musicians and Black-oriented labels at a sales disadvantage. Even though he explains that integrated playlists and staff at both white- and Black-oriented radio stations became more common during the mid- to late 1960s, the reintroduction of the R&B chart clearly connoted another shift in how "popular" music was again becoming racialized, and Black artists and listeners viewed as separate and less important than major releases by white performers, aimed at white audiences.[15] This music, as typified by British groups like the Rolling Stones, the Who, and Led Zeppelin, all of whom were heavily influenced by earlier Black American artists, would come to be known as "rock," and ultimately took the place on the Hot 100 previously reserved for artists and groups with more interracial appeal. As the genre became dominated by white performers and audiences, Jack Hamilton argues, "a racial imagination of rock music" was created "that was quickly rendering blackness invisible." He argues that as the genre shifted from a "teen-driven dance music of the 1950s and early 1960s" to "something distinctly more high-minded" from the mid-1960s onward, that it also "purged itself of (visible) blackness" while also "foreclosing not simply African American performers but an entire young tradition of interracial fluidity." Hamilton cautions, however, against conflating music and politics to the extent that Black artists' attempts at "self-segregation" align with the growing impact of Black Power politics since some musicians, like James Brown, espoused more conservative ideals as private citizens.[16]

But artists like Brown were moving in new directions by the mid- to late 1960s, building on R&B and rock and roll traditions to create soul, a new genre that spoke more directly to post-civil rights political and cultural concerns largely shaped by Black Power. While soul grew out of the rock and roll tradition, and therefore retained pop characteristics such as the use of a repeated chorus and melodic refrains, it was clearly meant to appeal to Black audiences, drawing heavily on blues and gospel traditions. Andrew Flory explains that, while "there were never prescriptive attributes for a soul style," recordings in this genre "often avoided large-scale arrangements featuring strings, varied orchestration drawing from Western classical traditions, overt use of reverberation, and signs of overdubbing," all of which were associated with white-dominated pop music, "in favor of an approach that valued earthiness and spontaneity." When performing, artists "often showed signs of physical exertion, danced ecstatically, and loosened formal clothing as performances escalated and energy levels rose," evoking the emotional dynamism of early R&B that initially drew white teenage listeners out of their segregated musical zones, while simultaneously declaring pride in their own traditions and a refusal to adhere to white performance expectations. Furthermore, as Flory notes, soul often specifically referred to Black cultural traditions, including "vernacularisms, references to food, and messages of uplift." The difference between soul records like Marvin Gaye's "What's Going On" and James Brown's "Say It Loud—I'm Black and I'm Proud" and earlier forms of popular and sacred Black music is that these soul recordings explicitly addressed political concerns in a way that celebrated Blackness as a worthy and desired trait.[17] The genre was so influential that *Billboard* editors abruptly changed the name of its R&B chart to "Best-Selling Soul Singles" the week of August 23, 1969, stating that they were "motivated by the fact that the term 'soul' more properly embraces the broad range of song and instrumental material which derives from the musical genius of the black American."[18]

The genre retained a fairly sizable number of white fans—indeed, five white respondents talk about seeing James Brown in concert when they were young, and each describes the experience in almost transcendent terms. Rick T., who got front-row tickets when Brown came to Virginia Beach in 1968, was called onstage to dance with Brown after he "looks dead to me and points his finger and says 'Brother!' and I said 'Yes Sir!' and he says 'Get up here.'" Bill W. says that the concert he attended at the Howard Theater in Washington, D.C., was "mind blowing. It was inconceivable to see 500 people all rise to their seats, screaming, dancing, yelling, reciting, singing the words with James Brown." Bruce C. simply remarks that "James Brown was just . . . the be all and end all" after seeing him perform at the Apollo Theater in New York. Their reactions and the language they use to describe their experiences are similar to that of Scott F.'s experience seeing James Brown in concert. "Amazing. He was unbelievable," says Scott, who identifies as Black. And yet he is also able to make connections to Brown's clear use of Black cultural traditions, explaining how "the most prevalent thing that I remember about going to see him was the emotion in that room . . . that emotion paralleled the emotions [that I felt] in the church."[19] Even if white kids could appreciate soul music, it clearly resonated with Black listeners by incorporating elements of pride in Black identity and tradition. Bibb E, who identifies as white, actually notes that he felt "a bit of sadness" over the fact "that race was being overtly interject[ed] into the music" since "music, which had brought some of us together, was now becoming a vehicle for expressing difference."[20] This difference could offer a welcome change for Black kids, though, who may have tired of having to adhere to white norms and hide parts of their own identities and histories in order to feel like they belonged in post-Jim Crow America. But this shift would also be decidedly unwelcome to many white Americans who had embraced the integrationist ideology advocated by civil rights groups since the postwar period, and who would come to view Black-advocated separatism as regressive, unhelpful, and possibly dangerous.

White fear of Black people who were not appeased by federal desegregation laws, and who refused to be hemmed in by the respectability norms that civil rights organizations used to gain outside attention and support, increased dramatically between 1964 and 1968, as urban uprisings broke out in majority-Black neighborhoods in over 100 cities. Persistent economic discrimination, police violence, and urban development plans that devastated Black communities continued to plague many cities outside of the South, but little media attention was given to the racial discrimination that operated outside of Southern Jim Crow laws. Misconceptions were immediate, as many white moderates and liberals wondered why Black residents would fight back just as important civil rights legislation was being passed, while some Black onlookers condemned those participants for making Black Americans look bad just as powerful whites were starting to listen to their cause. Support for desegregation movements and nonviolent tactics had already begun to twist into immediate condemnation of any type of protest that existed beyond this framework, misinterpreting the aims of most civil rights organizations. The results of these uprisings also persist in many white respondents' memories, causing them to look back with varying levels of sadness and bewilderment even when they understand why they broke out in the first place. Pat K., who explains that the 1966 uprising in Dayton, Ohio, "changed my perspective on things" and allowed her "to become sympathetic" to the plight of "people being oppressed," nevertheless explains how scared and angry she became after the classroom she was teaching in had been destroyed. "That movement, I understood it, but I didn't agree with it," she says. "It bothered me because I was sympathetic to [civil rights concerns] when I was very young, and I think when you're young, and 22 or 23 years old, you don't have the background to deal with that stuff. We were not prepared."[21] Even though white flight to the suburbs had accelerated throughout the 1950s and 1960s, the historical narrative was altered so that these uprisings would be blamed for driving terrified white residents from their urban homes and creating a pervasive sense of fear and violence in most cities. These fears proved fruitful for Republican presidential candidate Richard Nixon, who won the 1968 presidential election on a platform advocating "Law and Order" in the streets, promising to take a tough stance on those who engaged in destructive activities without acknowledging the root problems that caused them. Scores of mostly white voters responded, refusing to understand or care about the structural issues that resulted in extreme income, housing, and educational inequality, or the depletion of urban resources without which suburban neighborhoods would be unable to function.

Nixon's presidency would also represent a shift in politics that both adhered to and sought to undermine widespread acceptance of post-civil rights racial liberalism. If the Democratic Party had positioned itself as the voice of moderate racial equality under the law, the Republican Party depended on a "Southern" strategy to gain votes from disenchanted whites by supporting policies that would roll back civil rights achievements using the "coded" language of color-blind meritocracy and individual rights.[22] The entire political system systematically moved further to the Right, as formerly Democratic states shifted allegiance, one by one, to the Republican Party, and Democratic politicians lent their support to "moderate" policies that often chipped away at the gains created by federal civil rights acts. In the following decades, the civil rights movement would be depicted as almost hallowed historical ground, a pivotal, isolated moment when Black people, mostly in the South, fought for, and received, equality under the law, with little opposition other than from hardcore racists like Bull Connor and Jim Clark, the likes of whom have subsequently disappeared, time out of mind. As most of the radical politics that informed the movement were wiped clean from official histories, and time and historical inaccuracies created comfortable distance for white proponents, Martin Luther King Jr.'s birthday was transformed into a national holiday in the 1980s (even segregationist senator Strom Thurmond supported the bill), and conservative pundit Glenn Beck argued for conservatives to "reclaim the civil rights movement," while increased backlash against progressive gains encouraged passage of many racist policies. Widespread acceptance of post-civil rights racial liberalism, even across political parties, may have allowed white Americans to pass the blame for centuries of racial oppression onto villains of the past, and to assume that the most virulent forms of discrimination were abolished by federal policies that now work to support diversity practices across many different arenas. And yet, in many ways, the gains sought by integrationist civil rights groups have fallen in on themselves as any attempts to address systemic racism may be muted by opponents by simply rendering them invisible.[23]

BLM, THE TRUMP ADMINISTRATION, AND SHIFTING RACIAL POLITICS, 2012–2020

Black activists have been challenging this type of racial liberalism ever since the height of the civil rights movement, perhaps most famously by Martin Luther King Jr.'s admonishment "that the Negro's great stumbling block in the stride toward freedom is not the White Citizens' 'Councilor' or the Ku Klux Klanner, but the white moderate" in his 1963 Letter from a Birmingham Jail.[24] But the damages caused by this type of ideology were centered more than ever by the mid-2010s, as younger organizers responded to police killings of Black citizens, reorienting the goals of a new movement in an age when legalized segregation had been abolished, and diversity and equality were supposed to be championed within mainstream culture. Widespread white refusal to acknowledge the systemic effects of racial injustice, however, too often obscured the violence that younger Black boys and men in particular have faced at the hands of police, even after laws had been altered to allow for ostensible equality. Even though many activists, including John Lewis and James Forman, were severely beaten by police officers during demonstrations, most civil rights organizations in the 1950s and 1960s focused on the safer and more persuasive claims that segregation presented an affront to American democracy. After all, anti-lynching campaigns, organized in the early part of the twentieth century as Black Americans were terrorized by extra-legal violence across the South, failed to convince Congress to pass anti-lynching legislation time and time again until the House of Representatives finally voted to consider lynching a hate crime in early 2020.[25] But by the time that Barack Obama had assumed the presidency, an overwhelming percentage of the American population carried smart phones outfitted with cameras and had access to social media platforms that could broadcast their posts around the globe in seconds, effectively transforming anyone who witnessed or experienced this violence into a potential activist. Just as Martin Luther King Jr. and other civil rights organizers structured their campaigns so that journalists would ensure that their stories would be heard and people would support the gross injustices they saw on their television screens and in their daily newspapers, these younger activists broke the protective seal of racial liberalism by showing white Americans how Black people were really treated at the hands of authorities. Between 2012 and 2014, the tragic murders of Trayvon Martin and Michael Brown were broadcast throughout the country, revealing how Black children and teenagers could be killed by a haughty vigilante while walking to the store, or shot in the back while running away from a police officer. The slogan "Black Lives Matter," born out of ensuing outrage, was first used on social media in 2013 after George Zimmerman was acquitted of Martin's murder, then during the protests and uprisings in the summer of 2014 in Brown's hometown of Ferguson, Missouri, mere days after his death was reported. By 2015, activists Alicia Garza, Patrisse Cullors, and Opal Tometi organized distinct campaigns across the country into the Black Lives Matter (BLM) movement, aiming to protest police violence against people of color. This goal, which had been identified by prior civil rights organizations, yet never informed major campaigns, was now at the forefront of a major national movement. And yet the tenets of racial liberalism ultimately allowed many whites to assume the same stance of massive resistance that existed in the 1950s and 1960s, only this time under the guise that BLM represented some sort of threat to the country's capitalist-democratic framework. The term "All Lives Matter" became part of this opposition almost immediately after the movement began, sometimes used to directly defend police officers accused of violent acts against Black citizens, but also by those who had come to believe that desegregation and supposed color blindness had mostly solved the problem of racism in America, and who simply could not comprehend that Black Americans continue to face disproportionate harm within this system.

Widespread assumption of the triumph of post-civil rights racial liberalism would be largely shattered by the election of Donald Trump, who almost gleefully threw out the script for using coded racism to lure white voters that Republicans had adhered to since Richard Nixon's election, as president of the United States in 2016. Instead, his speeches and debates were rife with the kind of overt racism that most adherents to racial liberalism had believed was long relegated to the fringes of society. "Racial issues aren't just sparking the occasional flashpoint in this campaign cycle," CNN journalist Nia-Malika Henderson warned, "they are a constant and troubling feature of the contest." Even before his presidential run, Trump "faced federal charges of racial discrimination" in his business dealings, and led a campaign to de-legitimize Obama's presidency by claiming that the first Black president was not born in the United States. On the campaign trail, he referred to BLM activists as "thugs," accused a Mexican-American judge of bias based on his ethnicity alone, made false statements about the number of whites killed by Black Americans each year, and famously proclaimed that "when Mexico sends its people, they're not sending their best. They're sending people that have lots of problems. . . . They're bringing drugs. They're bringing crime. They're rapists. And some, I assume, are good people." In the closing months of his campaign, he told a majority-Black audience in the Metro Detroit area that "you're living in poverty, your schools are no good, you have no jobs, 58% of your youth is unemployed—what the hell do you have to lose?" When Neo-Nazi and former Grand Wizard of the Ku Klux Klan David Duke voiced his support for Trump's campaign in the summer of 2015, Trump hedged questions about whether or not he would "repudiate" this endorsement. When he finally did, his response was "sure . . . if it made you feel better." His actions and remarks so rejected the tenets of post-civil rights racial liberalism that a survey taken just before his election revealed that a majority of voters, including a third of Republicans, believed that "the way Trump talks appeals to bigotry." Upon his election, the Brookings Institute found that "while some observers have explained Trump's success as a result of economic anxiety, the data demonstrate that anti-immigrant sentiment, racism, and sexism are much more strongly related to support for Trump," and that "he did especially well with white people who express sexist views about women and who deny racism exists." These findings very succinctly reveal the flaws with post-civil rights racial liberalism, which aims to deny the continued existence of racism with a few individual exceptions rather than identifying and uprooting its causes. This type of overt racism may have become largely unsavory in the decades after federal policies supporting civil rights mandates were passed, as Americans were urged to relegate racial discrimination and injustice to an uncomfortable past and to celebrate how far we have come rather than focusing on how they continue to shape our institutions regardless of desegregation laws. For many white people, the virulence of existing racism therefore remained hidden, lying in wait for someone like Trump to stoke people's anxieties and allow them to voice and act on racist beliefs without feeling ashamed.[26]

Any expectations that a reliance on racial liberalism would be upheld under Trump's presidency crumbled almost immediately, as one of his first executive orders severely restricted citizens from Muslim-majority countries Iran, Iraq, Libya, Somalia, Sudan, Syria, and Yemen from entering the United States, threatening the livelihoods of many permanent residents, and conflating religion and national citizenship with terrorist threat. The FBI found that, between 2016 and 2019, "there has been an anomalous spike in hate crimes concentrated in counties where Trump won larger margins" and that "it was the second-largest uptick in hate crimes in the 25 years for which data were available, second only to the spike after September 11, 2001."[27] Indeed, several of the most publicized mass shootings during this period, including those that took place in Olathe, Kansas, in 2017; Pittsburgh and

Parkland, Florida, in 2018; and El Paso in 2019, were motivated by racial hatred. One of the turning points in the Trump presidency came after a "Unite the Right" rally took place in Charlottesville, Virginia, on August 11, 2017, ostensibly to protest the removal of a statue of Confederate General Robert E. Lee. Hundreds of white supremacists marched the streets, some bearing swastikas, Confederate flags, and other racist regalia, others simply dressed in Hawaiian shirts and khakis, their unassuming gear accessorized only by burning torches, chanting "Jews will not replace us! You will not replace us!" and other racist slogans. The next day, counter-protestor Heather Heyer was murdered by a member of a fascist organization who intentionally drove his car into a crowd of activists. Rather than condemning these acts of overt racism and domestic terrorism, Trump emboldened alt-Right participants, declaring that acts of hatred had occurred "on both sides" and mentioning the "very fine people on both sides," even adding that "you had a lot of people in that group that were there to innocently protest and very legally protest," and that alt-Left activists were supposedly just as responsible for meting out violence. His comments were met with an almost immediate uproar, as news analysis for the *New York Times* proclaimed that "President Trump buoyed the white nationalist movement on Tuesday as no president has done in generations—equating activists protesting racism with the neo-Nazis and white supremacists who rampaged in Charlottesville, Va., over the weekend." The piece made note of how the president eschewed the coded racism that had been used for decades to appeal to white voters, and which remained generally unacceptable within a racially liberal framework which espoused overt mentions of race, in favor of more overt bigotry. "Since the 1960s, Republican politicians have made muscular appeals to white voters, especially those in the South, on broad cultural grounds," the authors argue. "But as a rule, they have taken a hard line on the party's racist, nativist and anti-Semitic fringe. Presidents Ronald Reagan, George Bush and George W. Bush roundly condemned white supremacists. . . . But Mr. Trump, who has repeatedly said he is not prejudiced, has been equivocal in his public or private statements against white nationalists and other racist organizations." After receiving intense backlash, Trump did relent somewhat, stating that "racism is evil" and that "those who cause violence in its name are criminals and thugs, including the K.K.K., white supremacists and other hate groups," both of which seem to support Eduardo Bonilla-Silva's assertion that the language of racism is still considered widely unacceptable, even when the speaker's transparent beliefs say otherwise. But he also continued to rail about how he was treated unfairly, and "expressed sympathy with nonviolent protesters who he said were defending their 'heritage.'" David Duke, Richard B. Spencer, who had participated in the Charlottesville rally, and other advocates of white nationalism praised the president's response, while many white Americans came to realize that the racism they had largely viewed as a relic of the past had never actually been abolished by the civil rights movement as they had been taught. Desegregated public spaces and popular music may have made the United States look like it was fairly racially equitable, but these positive shifts had also allowed much of the country to avoid acknowledging the persistence of racial injustice, which was now given the chance to fully emerge, unashamed and unapologetic.[28]

But even as white supremacists were emboldened by Trump's actions during his presidency, antiracist activists organized on a scale not seen since the mid-1960s. BLM protested throughout the Trump administration, but George Floyd's murder at the hands of four Minneapolis police officers in May 2020 sparked the catalyst for a global movement that rallied people of all racial identities to demand police accountability and reform, or the eradication of police forces altogether. When Breonna Taylor was shot to death while asleep in her bedroom because Louisville, Kentucky, police officers forced their way into her home thinking it was the address of a suspected drug dealer, BLM protests only gained momentum. Both Floyd and Taylor were murdered when they posed no threat to the officers who committed violence against them: Taylor because she was unconscious when police burst through her door, and Floyd because he was thoroughly subdued by officer Derek Chauvin, who kneeled on his neck for almost 9 minutes, despite cries from several onlookers to let him go. Many Americans were horrified by the impunity granted to most police officers who killed Black victims, and took this anger to the streets in the tens of thousands, in cities across the country and around the world, throughout the summer of 2020. The majority of protests were nonviolent, but even though opponents (including members of the Trump administration) tried to divert focus to instances where activists broke windows, looted stores, or, in Minneapolis, set fire to businesses and a local police precinct, the movement retained support among large numbers of Black and white Americans alike, as well as from major media outlets, all of whom were forced to confront the realities of how systemic racism continue to threaten Black lives. Comparisons between the BLM protests of 2020 and desegregation campaigns in the 1950s and 1960s were unavoidable, as both used nonviolent methods like street protests and boycotts to draw media attention and support for the cause, urged the government to take action, and gained interracial support. If post-civil rights racial liberalism had convinced Americans that the civil rights movement had effectively negated racial injustice as a real problem, Floyd's and Taylor's murders at the hands of the state, among countless others, revealed the lie at the heart of this theory, which many found unacceptable. The United States was supposed to uphold democratic rights for all citizens, regardless of race, and if the country was still not living up to the promise, even after the tumult and the supposed successes of the 1950s and 1960s, then supporters would demand this rectification. And yet this time, organizers were less concerned with respectability, even as they urged activists not to partake in acts of destruction since Black protestors were more likely to draw ire from presiding police. The movement's focus on bodily integrity and racist policing was also more radical than the earlier drive for desegregation, since even the acknowledgment of this problem reveals a structural flaw within the American political system, while any real solution would involve systemic changes that no one would be able to remain unaffected by, unlike the results of desegregation policies.

The evolution of civil rights struggles between the purported "end" of the movement in the late 1960s and the BLM marches that dominated the summer of 2020 reveals the extent to which C. W. Mills's conception of post-civil rights racial liberalism has largely come to dominate political culture, even across party lines. As widespread assumptions of fundamental legal equalities prevail, what Mills calls a "race-evading and calculatedly amnesiac" perspective obscures how "the atrocities of the past" have yet to be fully grappled with on a broader scale. Once the federal government abolished the practice of overt racism in the political sphere and rendered racist behaviors "an embarrassment," he says that "they must be denied, minimized, or conceptually bypassed." Voter suppression bills passed in the wake of the Supreme Court's 2013 decision to allow states with histories of discrimination against Black voters to make changes to voting laws without federal approval reflect this perspective; even though many of these policies clearly aim to limit Black voter participation by limiting poll openings to particular days and times and closing polling stations in African-American communities, Chief Justice John Roberts's opinion instead used the minimizing language that Mills refers to as emblematic of post-civil rights racially liberal thought. "The Voting Rights Act of 1965 employed extraordinary measures to address an extraordinary problem," he wrote before attempting to reveal the Court's sympathies to racial injustice enacted long ago and fortify its supposedly undeniable commitment to racial equality by admitting that "this was strong medicine, but Congress determined it was needed to address entrenched racial discrimination in voting." The Act's success, as evidenced by a 2009 report that Roberts used to show how the racial voting gap had virtually ceased to exist, therefore provided assurance that racist voting policies had been "fixed," and that they no longer needed to be addressed when this type of overt racism had ostensibly disappeared. "There is no denying," Roberts wrote, "that the conditions that originally justified these measures no longer characterize voting in the covered jurisdictions." Here, Roberts deftly reveals a thought process shared by many white Americans, that the civil rights movement had so successfully eradicated racial injustice that structural policies meant to address racial inequities are, at best, unnecessary, and could possibly border on offensive. His opinion also betrays a belief, or desire to believe in, Mills's description of color blindness, which allows white people to abstain from their responsibilities to confront racial injustice because "in a perfectly just society, race would not exist." Pretending that this erasure has already occurred means that "we do not . . . have to concern ourselves with matters of racial justice in our own society where it does exist." Justice Ruth Bader Ginsbrg famously tried to explain how this ideology would harm Black people by weakening federal power to enforce the Voting Rights Act, claiming in her dissenting opinion that "throwing out preclearance when it has worked and is continuing to work to stop discriminatory changes is like throwing away your umbrella in a rainstorm because you are not getting wet." And yet, adhering to the philosophy of post-civil rights racial liberalism allows white Americans to, as Mills attests, "insist that the surest way of bringing about a raceless society is to ignore race and that those (largely people of color) who still claim to see race themselves are the real racists."[29]

Many white respondents also invoke this desire to view post-civil rights America through a color-blind lens, often by maintaining that they do not "see" race, or that having friends or family members from different racial backgrounds has allowed them to transcend these types of boundaries. John H., for instance, relays how he was unaware of the effects of racial discrimination, even though one of his best friends growing up was Black. "Years later, Bob, my Black friend, told me about some discrimination events that happened when he had his first job," he explains. "And that seemed really weird to me because I had never seen or experienced that when I was a kid. Even when I was with him when the two of us went out together, horsing around, and stuff." John admits that he may have missed these instances "because I didn't look for problems," but he also uses color-blind or race-neutral language when describing both his experiences with his childhood friend and how he has navigated racial differences as an adult. He describes Bob as "a regular guy who happened to have different skin color than me, but otherwise we were two peas in a pod." Later on in his life, when he began dating a Black woman, he recounts how "it never occurred to me how much animosity was directed my way because people knew that I was dating a Black girl. To me, she was just a girlfriend." Ultimately, he claims that "I've never been uncomfortable [when interacting with people of color]. I treat them like people, they treat me like people. And everything is cool." Here, John's account of his experiences completely supports Mills's description of post-civil rights color blindness by linking his ability to avoid acknowledging racial difference with ease in interracial communications and relationships. Victor F. also uses this language, explaining how "race was not a factor. I liked everybody" in his New York high school. "I had a 50th reunion, everybody was hugging and everything. It just wasn't an issue." Even though he admits that "as we grew older, we became more and more aware of [racial discrimination], redlining in neighborhoods, all the stuff that whites did to Blacks," he similarly argues that one of the key solutions is for individuals to stop seeing each other in terms of color. "If we stay with the basic stuff, the way Jesus taught us to live, we'll be all right, we won't have racism." Here, both John and Victor reveal the very beliefs that informed Justice Roberts's decision, even as they simultaneously excoriate instances of overt racism. "I try to see through people's color," Andrew L. says, echoing the belief that recognizing race is ultimately what allows for the persistence of racial injustice. Since his interview took place in the months before the 2020 presidential election, he even added that one of the reasons he was "hopeful" that Joe Biden would be elected president is because "he doesn't see color either. Ask [South Carolina Congressman] James Clyburn and the people from South Carolina who turned around his whole campaign."[30]

Other white respondents also adhere to this concept, linking acknowledgment of racial difference and racist beliefs together, and implicitly arguing for a society dominated by this aspect of racial liberalism, even if they do not explicitly define themselves as color blind. Marcia P., who has lived in a majority-Black neighborhood in Detroit since the late 1960s, says that she "got along with everybody" and that "I treat everybody the same." Here, Marcia is not pretending she cannot see race, but she does claim that treating everyone equally may transcend it in ways that similarly overlook the structural injustices that shape the lives of Black people in the United States. Others explain that, because they raised their children to see beyond race, and because of the effects of the civil rights movement, those children have grown up to become color blind themselves. "I certainly don't have any kind of prejudice. I didn't raise my kids that way. Even though, you know, they were raised in basically an all-white neighborhood," Jimmy F. explains. "But we were always open to all kinds of cultures." The link between color blindness and distance or, as Mills describes it, "amnesia," is clearer here, as Jimmy's family was taught to treat everyone equally, even if they rarely interacted with people of color in their daily lives. Conversely, Victor F. says that neither of his daughters "has any racism in her. They just don't. And I'm glad, but they got it not from me, they got it from the circle that they're in." Walter S. expands on this importance of a post-civil rights society, stating that his kids became color blind because integrationist movement gains meant that they had many Black teachers and classmates and that they "grew up largely knowing that the President of the United States happened to be Black." The consequence, he says, is that "my children don't think that way. They have to think a moment about whether or not somebody they know, what race they are. . . . And therefore they are far less conscious of race because it doesn't seem to be an issue." Again, his assertions that "that's a success" and "from my point of view, that's the beginning of true victory" support Mills's argument that systemic racism will continue to endure if this color blindness, which "is really a blindness to the historical and enduring whiteness of liberalism," is consistently clung to as a solution for deeply rooted political, social, and economic inequities.[31]

This ideology also shapes many white respondents' reactions to both President Donald Trump and BLM protests. Almost every white respondent who agreed to an oral history interview after the 2016 presidential election voiced their dissatisfaction with the Trump administration, and acknowledged that racism remained a major issue in the United States. The similarities in these responses stem partially from the selection bias which occurred when prospective narrators reached out to be interviewed, since the subject matter of this study was clear in all advertising materials and largely appealed to those who identify as liberal, progressive, or politically moderate. Many interviews also took place during the summer of 2020, in the midst of BLM protests, which undoubtedly prompted respondents to think about the effects of racism in different ways and on a more regular basis since they were covered on television and online in such great detail. One theme that comes up consistently is how President Trump's racist rhetoric and policies have emboldened white supremacists. "I do think that certain practices of President Trump have been what I would consider troubling. I don't know if I want to say flat-out racist, but certainly disgraceful, if not racist. And that troubles me," Ellis B. asserts. Jimmy F. responds in a similar fashion, dubbing the president a "redneck" and stating that he is "fanning the flames of, not just racism, Black versus white, but anything that is outside of [the white mainstream]." Still, like Ellis, he qualifies his description, saying that "it's sort of a horrible term to use, that's discriminatory in a certain way itself. But I think there is still a lot of ethnic animosity among certain people in America." Even though both respondents convey concern over the Trump administration's impact, they still hesitate to actually use the term "racist," revealing how the word itself has come to be viewed as more distasteful than actual racist actions.[32]

But even respondents who are more comfortable using this identifier reserve it for individuals like Trump, who upset the careful balance supposedly preserved by color blindness, rather than the political and social structures that allowed him to rise to the highest rank in the nation. Ron R., for instance, cites "the fact that we have an overt racist as a president" as a major reason for the rise in white supremacist activity. "I think it's absolutely atrocious what's going on," says Henry I. "I loved the last guy. Most of us did around [my neighborhood]. What's happened in the last three years is absolutely atrocious. I think he has taken everything he could do to look at some of the advances that people of color have made and tried to throw it in the toilet." Marcia P. echoes much of the extreme emotion in Henry's response, stating she was "shocked when Trump got in. And I thought, oh gosh, talk about going to hell in a handbasket. He is just bringing us down." She is careful, however, to single the president out as an anomaly within a political society that is far more tolerant than his election would suggest. "I always explained, we don't all like him," she argues. "He might not have gotten voted in; he just might have [had] a couple of little tricks that were played. And don't think we've changed that much since Obama. We're not all of a sudden racist like [Trump] is." Here, respondents' views of Trump as an individual instigator rather than part of the same system that has undermined acknowledgment of racist discrimination since the Nixon administration reveals a fundamental belief in an otherwise fair and racially neutral color-blind system that has unfortunately been disturbed. Since the former president did not play by the rules dictated by post-civil rights racial liberalism, he is therefore understood as an outlier with the power to rile people with fringe beliefs, which is understandably infuriating when viewed through this lens. "Racial tensions are much higher now," Michael P. concedes. "I think our tolerance has changed dramatically because of who we have in the lead [Trump]." He admits, however, that "I'm sure all of these things have been present for a long time, but we were much more civil about it."[33]

Even though most white respondents express some degree of support for BLM protests, or at least an understanding of why they are necessary, they are far more likely to qualify this stance than their Black peers, partly because of an attachment to a supposedly color-blind post-civil rights America. "Now you have Black Lives Matter, and the cops are Blue Lives Matter, and you're a group that's looking just to create trouble," says Victor F. "I mean, a lot of cops are Black. So what do they call, Black and Blue Lives Matter? Lives Matter. It's silly." Even though he gets caught up in linguistics attempting to ease some of these tensions and insist on a calmer reality where racial distinctions are mostly irrelevant, he still agrees with the reasoning behind the movement. "Some Black people were manhandled by police and died. Okay, Black Lives Matter, treat us with respect," he says. Henry I. displays similar levels of ambivalence in his response, stating that "well, [Black Lives] do matter. But, you know, all lives matter too. And I'm not negative towards it at all. They have reasons for that, and there's reasons that there are Black kids that are getting shot that shouldn't be getting shot in big cities by white cops. I understand why it's cropped up." Yet he adds that "I have to say I'm neutral, because I have no problem with the movement." His reasons for equivocating are unclear when he explicitly states his understanding of the underlying problem, but BLM's unapologetic racial distinction may seem jarring when so many civil rights organizers took pains to minimize racial differences when fighting for desegregation. Ellis B.'s qualifications are stated more clearly but still reflect some discomfort, despite his overall support for the movement's goals. "I am shocked like many Americans by the incidents of violence against Black people, primarily, who I believe have not been threatening, but have been seen by police in certain instances as threatening. And I can understand, in those communities, why they would be shocked by a policeman getting off scot-free when the video we can see kind of demonstrates the perpetrator was not threatening." He adds, however, that "I try to be open-minded about it though, because you're not in that situation. You want to make sure that police are protecting us. And they may be in certain circumstances where it's unclear whether the perpetrator is carrying a gun, or whatever. But there have been so many instances which appear to be shocking from a distance." His concern here seems to stem from a need to uphold public safety, but he still tries to understand the opposing point of view in a way that few Black respondents have the privilege of doing since the risk of facing police violence is not an abstract concern. Andrew L. concurs, explaining how he "definitely related to the concerns of both parties" since "I flat-out guarantee you that there are a lot of police officers that have a chip on their shoulder, and they've accumulated these incidents that they've had with their interfacing with the Black culture. They see all the worst of the Black people. And so it registers. It's so much easier to register prejudice when it's the other." Still, he claims that "the people that don't think Black Lives Matter is a movement that is really deserving of its time, the ones that say Blue Lives Matter, and White Lives Matter and all that, they don't get it. They don't understand. This is a culture that has been oppressed ever since they were slaves." In this case, he tries to merge individual blame with the systemic injustices that shape these actions, causing some level of dissonance in his response. Ron R. also grapples with these tensions, gravitating between stating that "we shouldn't be just saying Black Lives Matter, you know, because indeed all lives matter, so stop belittling one to the advantage of the other" and condemning "the lunatic fringe [that] came up with All Lives Matter. And you know, of course all lives matter. But now, unfortunately, your privileged white ass seems to matter to you more than Black lives." These vacillations only make sense when considering just how much white respondents have believed in some of the tenets of color-blind racial liberalism. When directly faced with evidence that this theory never really reflected realities in the United States for Black citizens, many white respondents have struggled to adjust their worldviews, even if they cannot justify what they have learned from this new movement. Ron actually gestures toward this realization, and the need for continued action, when he notes that "the George Floyd murder in particular has really galvanized a lot of people who maybe didn't even think about it before. They assumed, maybe incorrectly, oh, I thought we've already taken care of this. But in fact, we haven't."[34]

Black respondents, unsurprisingly, do not uphold the virtues of color blindness as their white peers are apt to do, even if they use some of the same language to describe current racial politics. Miche B., for example, attests that "we are all humans. Got the same blood, got the same hearts, everything." But this basic truth is used not to promote a future where everyone's racial differences fade away, but to shape her own pained questions about the persistent nature of white supremacy half a century after major civil rights successes. "I cannot understand why we are still at this point," she says. "I don't get it. You know, I don't like feeling like I'm not wanted somewhere, or not allowed to be somewhere because of this. It makes no damn sense." She goes on to explain how persistent racial hatred makes it difficult for her to engage with people without racial differences intervening. "I love people. You know, I don't give a damn what color, what creed, what religion, whatever it is, I just love people," she asserts. "But it's so hard to do when people are just being so negative." Although she similarly notes that "as a people we were just so proud to finally have a Black president," she continues to use the language of color blindness when claiming that "the thing that still bothers me is when they make an announcement that this is the first Black person to do such and such." But this is not because she thinks racial identity should be avoided, but rather because such achievements point out the lack of civil rights progress in many areas. "This is 2020, why are we still doing the first Black [achievement]?" she asks.[35]

Black respondents are also more forthright in their support for BLM than their white peers, even if they remain influenced by color-blind racial liberalism when explaining their perspectives. Trump is also regarded as the symptom of a much deeper problem rather than the cause of increased racist agitation. Miche explains how "with Trump in office, he's giving [white supremacists] license to feel and do what it is they want. And to me it really started getting bad when Obama was in office." Even though she makes note of Trump's more overt racism, she also references a broader culture of racial liberalism when explaining why she believes that BLM is necessary. "It's only because [Black people] were being killed unnecessarily," she says. "People would get upset about it and say 'All Lives Matter.' We know that. But for some reason, people tend to forget when it comes to Black or Brown people, the Mexicans, the Hispanic people." Joseph J. also makes note of the tension within these slogans, explaining that "it's not that you are saying that Black lives are more important than other lives. . . . It's saying that, based upon what has happened, we need to pay attention and say, yep, these people matter. Because you know, all lives matter in so far as that goes." Cheryl J. uses this language herself while simultaneously stressing the need for a movement focused on specific Black concerns. "I'm one of those people that believe all lives matter," she says. "But I understand why Black lives really have to matter. You have to stop gunning people down in the street." Rhonda E. adds that "Black lives do, you know, matter. And you have to say that because Black lives don't matter to so many people in so many instances. . . . They don't matter equally to Americans, and to the world in general. And it's by design." She says that the level of racism in the country right now is "probably worse now than ever. Not than ever, but worse than it's been in my lifetime." And the reason for this is that "for all the good that the civil rights movement did, it proved one thing, that you can't legislate love or hate." Furthermore, "we never really dealt with racism for what it was. Okay, it's bad, we shouldn't have had, you know, kidnapped, raped, murdered. That shouldn't have been legal in this country, but it was. So just to say it's wrong, and we're going to do A, B, and C, and it's over." Instead, "you've got people who think, who have thought even before Donald Trump, that the playing field was level" when, she stresses, this was clearly not the case.[36] Black respondents, then, attempt to rationalize the language of "All Lives Matter" in ways that support the expectations of racial liberalism even though it is so often used as a means of shutting down any productive conversations about racial violence. But they are also quick to explain how and why their lived experiences reveal the need for a movement that shows how Black people are routinely dehumanized and denied the ability to simply move through the world with relative safely.

Even though Black and white respondents clearly conceive of color blindness and its effects on society in distinct ways, almost all of the people interviewed for this study are steadfast in their belief that everyone is fundamentally equal regardless of skin color, and that the world would be a better place if they were consistently treated as such. But white respondents are more likely to infer that most already abide by these dictates, or at least they did until bad actors like Trump or racist police officers upset this balance. Black respondents, however, do not have the luxury of distance that allows them to believe in a color-blind society, even if they may extol some of its virtues in theory. This is why white respondents are so much more likely to describe President Trump in such hostile terms while hesitating to describe his policies and personal behaviors as definitively racist. But what accounts for such widespread embrace of this ideology? Post-civil rights racial liberalism allows whites to forfeit any real responsibility for eradicating racial injustice so long as they do not actually harm people themselves. But the fact that almost all respondents identify as politically liberal or progressive, and many whites assert that they are learning about the lasting effects of structural racism, begs the following question: What explains the enduring appeal of color-blind racial liberalism, especially as the rise in white supremacist actions and policies has revealed that it never really existed in the first place?

There is no simple answer to this question, of course, but many white respondents were seemingly primed by both rock and roll music and the civil rights movements of the 1950s and 1960s to accept this form of liberalism as the one true antidote to racial injustice. Since popular music "desegregated" at the same time that civil rights activists were fighting for desegregated public spaces, many are keen to identify connections between listening to rock and roll and changing racial politics. This fairly linear understanding meant that listening to music across racial lines and identifying with Black artists could ostensibly make white listeners more aware of racial inequities, and therefore more sympathetic to civil rights causes. "With more exposure to their music and culture, I questioned even more the unfairness of segregation," says Ann W. "Exposure through music caused people to stop, watch, and question if they had perhaps been wrong." Patricia J. claims that she only began asking questions about racism after her high school boyfriend introduced her to the Motown artists he was listening to, although she admits that she does not have "any rational thought on how that triggered civil rights interest." And Michael P. says "I think the whole Black experience which you certainly would hear on the radio was a growth from [the connection between music and movement politics]. Because otherwise that would never have happened." In each case, respondents explicitly describe how their experiences listening to Black artists prepared them to accept the changes that civil rights activists were able to achieve. Bill W., who began working for social justice efforts in college, even claims that "as I look back, this all, this whole thread, and sort of where I placed my life and the things that I've done, resonates way, way back, and I have to say, it starts because of the music." Even though his parents were not "crazily racist," they were also not involved in the progressive politics he would come to engage in himself. "I felt for a long, long time that there were lots of reasons why the civil rights movement became so important, but I honestly have felt that, for the white side, that what led more whites into the civil rights movement [more] than anything else was the music." While he describes a connection based on relatability that other white respondents also evoke, he is aware that it represented a first step toward greater awareness and accountability rather than an eradication of most forms of racism. "For my generation, these incredible performers and musicians and personalities sort of, I think more unconsciously than consciously . . . led a whole generation like me into realizing that maybe the way this is all set up, and what we've been taught, is not quite the whole story," he says. "And I think music is the thing that broke those barriers down, much more subtly. And I think probably much more completely than preaching at people, arguing with them, lectures, whatever, all that stuff. And I'm not saying that stuff isn't important, or isn't part of it, but I think it's the music that sort of found a place to bring these groups together."³⁷

This connection, however, can also provide a foundation for "color blindness" by assuming that race matters less than emotional and artistic connections. "Just to have had the experience of listening to artists, appreciating what they're doing, I think [the] linkage was that simple," Patricia J. asserts. "How does my brain make a correlation, or a linkage, I should say, between listening to R&B a lot and liking it, and any kind of civil rights thing? And I think it was the familiarity thing. . . . I think the seeds were planted, because I went to university at a time when they were occupying the university, and there were big student uprisings." Victor F. makes a similar argument, saying that he thinks that rock and roll music is "really where the civil rights movement started. Because people were hanging out with Black people, and they really thought they were the same. And then they saw people getting the shit kicked out of them in the South, and we just really didn't understand it up here." Bob S. explains that "the music had a lot to do with [the success of the civil rights movement], especially with teenagers at the time, young people like myself. It wasn't the color of the artist, it was the song. Look at when the Supremes came out, and all those Motown artists. They were all famous. Well, I think that a lot of it is that Black people were more accepted." He even invokes the concept of color blindness to explain how "rock and roll had a big influence on bringing people together of all races," claiming that "a good song is a good song. And it didn't make any difference if it was a Black person or a Black group [that] did it or a white group." Bob R. concurs, noting that "the more familiar someone is with something, I think the more accepting they are of it, since it becomes a 'known' rather than an 'unknown.' I can see how familiarity with Black music and Black singers and liking them, could generate more positive feelings from white people toward civil rights for Blacks."³⁸ These respondents' assertions that they began to see Black people as "regular" or "the same" as white people while listening to rock and roll music reveal how white kids' perspectives on desegregation and on the destructive nature of racism in general were in flux during this period. And yet simple assertions that they were able to recognize Black people's humanity could also neatly obstruct the need to uproot and challenge the many levels of institutional racism. If Blacks and whites were the same, regardless of the racial injustices or privileges that shaped their daily lives, then any continuing inequities could be blamed on Black people's choices or shortcomings rather than institutionalized racism, and white people would otherwise be excused from having to face the ways that they continue to reproduce the structures of white supremacy. Ending racism is therefore reconstituted as an easy individual fix, rather than as a political and economic commitment that requires societal sacrifice and deeper reflection than merely accepting that Black and white Americans can relate to each other on personal levels.

These limits become even more apparent in accounts of white rock and roll fans who remained steadfastly opposed to any type of racial justice. As early as 1966, Eric Burdon, the lead singer for the Animals, a British Invasion group, told an *Ebony* journalist that, as much as his own interest in American racial politics had been shaped by his love of R&B and early rock and roll, he had also met a Southern girl who claimed that Otis Redding was one of her favorite people in the world while simultaneously denouncing Black people in general with a pejorative term. Similarly, Bibb E. recalls how his college roommate was "well known for extreme racism. . . . He dropped the 'n' word every now and then, to my discomfort, but with no real malice in his voice. He seemed perfectly normal for the time and place, except that he was obsessed with James Brown. . . . He had all the records, played them all the time." In these cases, Madison Foster, who is Black, explained, white fans could love rock and roll while retaining views on racial inequality because "the counter-culture took the guts of what it is to be black, and stayed white. . . . They've been socialized to feel that it's theirs. They don't understand that rock music has a particular relationship to black music." Other white respondents, including some who became active in civil rights activities themselves, also question any connection between their own listening habits and their views on desegregation and the civil rights movement. "I certainly loved the Supremes, Four Tops, etc. as music, but did not integrate them into any racial view," Bob C. proclaims. Bruce C. is even more explicit, stating "I don't see music as having accomplished a whole heck of a lot," and explaining how "the majority of rock and roll, the majority of pop music, it was just merely background clatter. It was background noise, you know?" He admits that "it changed those people who were already either leaning there, or had been there," but otherwise, "I don't think it made any converts." And former Students for a Democratic Society (SDS) president Todd Gitlin very explicitly stated that "I liked rock and roll in the fifties . . . but, one could not delude oneself any further, even if it meant anything for political change." Still, Larry R., who was actively involved in many social justice organizations, is a bit more circumspect when considering how these connections may have worked. "The general wisdom is that rock and roll was Black music, and it attracted white kids," he says. "White kids came to like it, and therefore it helped break down barriers between whites and Blacks. Well, that might be true, I'm not saying it's not. But it was not my experience."[39]

From an activist standpoint, then, the emotional connections that had supposedly revealed the lie of racial differences to white listeners were not enough to truly overcome personal biases, let alone expose the depths of racial injustice in every aspect of society. This belief correlates somewhat with responses from Black narrators, though the importance of hearing Black voices on the radio and seeing Black faces on television, even if they were usually at the behest of a white-dominated music industry, inspired some to see these connections as a source of cultural and political pride. "This became part of my fabric and the fabric of the people who were around me, [the] music that we were listening to," Joseph J. recalls. As much as performers like James Brown and Marvin Gaye strengthened feelings of Black pride, he adds that he and his friends also listened to more overtly political white artists like Bob Dylan and Crosby, Stills, Nash, and Young, "so when those things begin to merge, you end up being a very, very different person." Even though Joseph mostly remembers being drawn to positive representations of Black experiences, these artists' mainstream successes also contributed to an environment where he also became interested in white folk and rock music, creating a more integrated listening environment just as public spaces were becoming desegregated. Scott F. does not comment on this connection explicitly, but he does note that music can intersect with political movements in very powerful ways. "As a music lover, I'm hoping that, on the heels of [the Black Lives Matter movement] there is going to be a wave of music that's a lot more insightful and honest and heartfelt," he says. But this time, he adds, it will have to be more complicated than artists from different racial backgrounds singing about unrequited crushes and long days at school: "What we have gone through from a societal standpoint is so tragic and gut-wrenching that happy-go-lucky just doesn't feel right." Music may be able to affect or reflect people's political views, he implies, but that relationship is not quite as simple as many listeners would like to believe.[40]

These responses to rock and roll music cast light on the ways that people gauge the successes of the civil rights movement overall, and desegregation and diversity efforts in particular. Many Black respondents implicitly invoke Mills's argument that post-civil rights racial liberalism advocates for equal citizenship in theory, while deep-rooted discrimination continues to disadvantage Black citizens under the guise of complete equality. Rhonda E., for instance, outlines what she sees as the movement's shortcomings by asking "Was it lasting? Was it complete? Was it thorough? Were people staying awake at night trying to figure out ways to make sure it didn't work?" And yet she still describes it as "definitely successful" by explaining how passage of the Civil Rights Act affected her personally. "Around [the age of] 10, I think, doors that I probably never knew were shut were opened," she says. "There was no place I couldn't go that I wanted to go. . . . I just never felt excluded because I was Black, at least from anything I wanted to do. And the Baby Boomers were probably the first generation to feel that way."[41] Her definition dovetails with former Student Nonviolent Coordinating Committee (SNCC) executive director James Forman's response when he was asked the same question in a 1996 interview. "I think it was a fantastic success," he asserted. "It helped to end segregation."[42] Desegregation at the federal level had many important consequences, as Ta-Nehisi Coates details in his seminal 2014 article on why Black citizens deserve reparations. "The lives of black Americans are better than they were half a century ago," he points out. "The humiliation of WHITES ONLY signs are gone. Rates of black poverty have decreased. Black teen pregnancy rates are at record lows—and the gap between black and white teen-pregnancy rates has shrunk significantly."[43] And yet other Black respondents specify awareness as the movement's greatest success, rather than any actual gains within Black communities. When asked whether the movement was successful or not, Scott F. claims that "a flat 'no' is probably too strong of an answer, and it probably does not do the movement the justice it deserves," since activists "made leaps and bounds for my people. I think they brought the attention that the cause deserved to the forefront." Ed B. agrees, noting "I think it awakened a lot of people. I don't think it was that successful, but it was an eye opener." And Edgar S. provides an almost identical response, stating that "it was successful in bringing folks' attention to things that really needed to be changed." He stipulates, however, that "there were some changes, but there was very little transformation." These more cautious assessments reflect the dominance of a post-civil rights racial liberalism that values the appearance of racial equality over representation, acknowledgment of racist harms, and working toward lasting solutions.[44]

White narrators' responses to the question of whether or not the civil rights movement was successful are more varied, yet they similarly reveal how aspects of post-civil rights racial liberalism have shaped the country's racial and historical narratives. Some echo Black respondents' focus on awareness over concrete changes. "We did get more people aware of the inequality," Ron R. states. "We have less tolerance for overt racial discrimination. But it's really difficult because a lot of the discrimination is so subtle." Henry I. concurs, noting how "we've made a lot of progress" because integration is "much more, obviously, accepted than it was 50 years ago," even if "we have a long way to go." But, as Mills points out in his article, this awareness can act as a double-edged sword. "Now, most people would say this about the civil rights movement," Larry R. explains. "Rosa Parks sat down, Martin Luther King got up with his dream, and problem solved." Even though he acknowledges that these individuals and the major events commonly associated with the major civil rights narrative did represent "a turning point," the fact that so many people believe that racial justice was achieved via a few short, disconnected protests elides the very real struggles that existed at the time, and which continue into the present. And yet he also identifies specific policies that were passed due to movement activism. "I believed that the movement was successful in changing the legal structure," Larry continues. "You know, sitting together at a lunch counter was no longer illegal. Segregation was no longer the law. And they had to come up with something better than the literacy test to deny people their right to vote." Major successes in terms of policies, as specified by both Black and white respondents, fall within the realm of voting rights and desegregation in public spaces, both vitally important aspects of citizenship, yet confined to a fairly narrow realm of actions that can be overseen by the federal government.[45]

Even if much of the language they use is similar to that of their Black peers, most white respondents seem more certain regarding the successes of the movement, even if they are somewhat aware of its limitations. Although Rose W. admits that "race was, remains, the American tragedy," she also notes that today "you can buy a house. Will it be as easy for you to get a mortgage as it is for a white person? No. But, you know, if you're middle class, you probably can get a house. You couldn't [before the movement], it was just impossible." Here, she identifies a shift made possible by the Civil Rights Act of 1968, which declared redlining illegal, while simultaneously relying on a facet of racial liberalism, which is that socioeconomic class is responsible for certain types of oppression rather than race. Other respondents describe the projected "arc of justice" that Martin Luther King first described, and former president Barack Obama heeded, in terms that make it clear that racial justice does not affect them personally, even if they are concerned about the issue. David S., for instance, thinks that the movement was successful because it "forced there to be a change," but he also believes that "racism is probably so ingrained in our culture, in our society, that it will never really go away." Conversely, Victor F. cautions that "change takes time, unfortunately. Positive change takes time. Are we a better nation now than we were then? Absolutely. Do we have a long way to go? Absolutely." Although these responses may seem diametrically opposed to each other, they both display a distance from the types of oppression and discrimination that compel Black Americans to work towards a more equitable future.[46] And finally, the tendency to focus on distinctions between life before and after the movement, emphasizing how much better and more equal the country is now than it was even if it is not entirely equal, is summed up by Mary R.'s response. "It irritates the hell out of me when people say, well, no, it was a complete failure. It made a lot of difference [even] if there's still a lot of difference to be made," she says.

> The Civil Rights Act of 1964 ended segregation. *De jure* segregation. There is still *de facto* segregation. The [Voting Rights] Act of 1965 opened voting to everyone. Is it abused by Republicans all over the fricken country? Yes. But can you register to vote in Mississippi without having to go through a constitutional

questionnaire? Yes. Because, you know, I think the critique of the civil rights movement is often the whole issue of letting the desire for the perfect denigrate the good. And there has been a lot of good. . . . I mean, can Blacks get jobs at higher levels? Is there Black Studies at universities? Are Blacks included in textbooks now? Do students know about Frederick Douglass? Can people assume they will be able to register to vote? Yes![47]

Although Mary also notes that "massive racism" still exists, using the 2020 murder of Ahmaud Arbery at the hands of white supremacists while he was jogging in his Georgia neighborhood as an example, her insistence regarding the amount of change, and the desire to focus on the "good" rather than the "perfect," is almost completely absent in responses from Black narrators. These types of responses are indicative of post-civil rights liberal views. Even if each respondent is quick to note that racism continues to persist in all levels of American society, their arguments that even slow and unequal changes should be lauded support the concept of a democratic framework that is ultimately sustainable, and can accommodate alterations without having to be fundamentally altered in order to root out systemic oppression. Just like "integrated" rock and roll music, civil rights movement goals have been widely deemed acceptable only if they adhere to culturally expected norms, and if "respectable" white people find them appealing. Focusing on these aspects in isolation, however, could automatically denigrate other types of protests, civil rights goals, and music that did not necessarily aim for integrated audiences within mainstream narratives, and would ultimately lead to white backlash against burgeoning Black Power movements and the cultural creations that promoted unapologetic Black pride.

Most respondents, regardless of race, identify increased diversity and desegregation in many aspects of public life, made possible by the organizations and activists who identified and worked toward these goals, and passage of the Civil Rights and Voting Rights Acts, as the movement's most successful legacies. "Yes, I sure do," Ed B., who is Black, responds when asked whether he thinks that desegregation is an effective means of working toward racial justice. "I think that when people see each other in a different light they get to know each other, they get to hear their stories. And they get to hear our stories. And the only way that's going to happen is through integration of just about all levels." David P., who is white, echoes Ed's response fairly closely: "I think it does always help when there is diversity and people are exposed to each other and actually see people face to face and talk to them," he says. "We become real to each other, and we are not a caricature of some kind." Similarly, Carol B. claims that she and her husband would not have purchased their house were it not for the Black neighbors living next door. "If you're not around Black people or gay people, or if you never have a chance, you know, how are you ever going to see that these people are just like you?" she asks. The difference here is that David and Carol equate exposure to people of different races in a way that Ed does not by assuming that Black people may also need to acknowledge the humanity of their white peers, despite the uneven power structures that have denied Black Americans the right to be treated as full citizens. Other white respondents identify some of the changes which led to more diverse public spaces, schools, and workplaces, increases in interracial relationships, and more diverse representation in popular culture as major civil rights movement successes. Emily W. states that desegregation was a "big step, a hard step for a lot of people. So that kind of thing was very helpful [even though] I'm sure that was low-hanging fruit, kind of obvious stuff." Because of these policies, Ellis B. says that he has seen growing "acceptance" of integrated spaces in the intervening decades, explaining how he interacted with few people of color when he was young, "but as I grew up and in the workplace I [have] had a lot of African-American, Hispanic, and Asian-American colleagues. And they're great people, you know. And we were friends wherever I worked. We partied together. . . . I didn't have any Black friends growing up, I have a lot of Black friends now." Henry I. points out that his grandchildren live and attend school in a racially integrated district, and that "we liked the fact that our family has been able to interact with all kinds of folks," while Rose W. brings up "TV shows that are pretty good on diversity" as well as "Black faculty, Black guidance counselors" in schools, and "the ease with which students interact with each other across racial boundaries." Ultimately, she says, "The whole nation is more integrated than it was."[48]

Some white respondents talk about how fewer instances of overt segregation reflect the movement's overwhelming success. Even though Jimmy F. admits that "there are still rednecks out there," he also professes that "I don't see, didn't see, any kind of discrimination or anything like that. The restaurants are all interracial, multiracial." Walter S. concurs, noting how racial difference is "not an issue" for his kids because "there are just blessedly no boundaries now, in terms of the real world. There's no boundaries in their school, in their society, in their anything. And therefore they don't see it." And Victor F. expands on this notion more broadly, claiming that "most Americans are nice, no matter what their political views. There are some extremists. But most of them are nice. Most of them would not treat other people the way a racist would treat somebody. Some may have some racist things that come out, [but] they don't mean it to. It could be humor. But they're not hateful. It's a learning thing." Each of these respondents, all of whom grew up and currently live in the area surrounding New York City, base their belief that color blindness has helped to create a more equal society on the fact that they rarely encounter instances of discrimination themselves. Although the movement was undoubtedly successful in getting the government to remove Jim Crow signs and desegregate public spaces, the lack of visual cues has made it harder for white individuals, especially those living in more cosmopolitan areas, to notice the persistence of racial discrimination when they do not see it in their daily lives. Many, then, conclude that it has mostly ceased to exist, or, like Jimmy and Victor, attribute the persistence of racism to individual fringe "racists" and "rednecks" rather than the structures that define every aspect of American life, many of which were never adequately addressed, as means of reproducing racial injustice.[49]

It is perhaps unsurprising that so many people would talk about desegregation of public areas as one of the civil rights movement's major successes when activists and organizations clearly identified this goal as media-friendly and likely to garner widespread support between the late 1940s and mid-1960s. At the same time, the rock and roll music that quickly overtook the music industry during this period presented white listeners with a template for interracial mixing that was fun and devoid of any painful sacrifices—for many, its success seemed to prove that integration was the natural order of things, requiring mere acceptance rather than political struggle. Since white respondents grew up during a period when this genre suggested that integration had seemingly already occurred, peacefully and joyously, within popular music, it is perhaps to be expected that their support for desegregation in public spaces would go unquestioned, and that they would be shocked by any fringe elements that might present any opposition. Larry R., who has worked on civil rights campaigns throughout his life, says that even though "today everybody is talking about diversity" that this "was a hard one, maverick, to gain." And yet, he allows that "now, it's accepted. You don't have to act white; you can act however you want to." Although he is careful to specify that "a lot of [Black] people say, 'We don't want to be integrated, we want to have a separate Black this and a separate Black that,'" he also claims that "I do think that integration is in fact the natural way of things" and that "when people live together, it's gonna happen. Neighbors are going to be with neighbors, and there's going to be marriage." Ultimately, he says, "There's more integration today than there was ten years ago, just by the nature of things. But one of the reasons I do think that there's more integration is that people have a choice, basically."[50]

Larry is more circumspect than other respondents about the effectiveness of desegregation, but many others second his assertion of a "natural" way of living that can only make people's lives better, albeit in fairly vague ways. Mary R. explains how engaging with diverse groups of people "enriches us. It enriches everything we study. It enriches how we live with people." Ultimately, she says, "I think it's hard to argue that . . . it's better to have a segregated or integrated or predominantly one ethnic group society than a more diverse society." Ellis B. applauds "laws or good policies" enacted by companies that "have been encouraged to integrate their workforce. Damn good. That's the way it should have been done. And that can only ease, lessen, racial tensions. . . . When you work alongside someone, when you get to know someone. Yeah, it's better for our society. There's no question about that." Victor F. explains that if one of his children decides to date someone outside their own race, "that's normal . . . we wouldn't have seen it in my day. But you look on Long Island, you go shopping [and you see] tons of interracial couples." In these cases, respondents discuss the changes brought about by degrees of integration in certain areas, but are somewhat unclear about how or why they consider them to be positive steps toward actual racial justice. This lack of clarity and specificity, mirrored in Mills's description of racial liberalism, reflects the positioning of desegregation as an absolute good and as a movement end goal without delving more deeply into why it is so important in the first place. "I don't know what the goal is," claims Walter S., whose answer reflects the same oddly certain sense of ambiguity about this issue. "I don't know what the successful result is. I know that I'm living in a much more diverse world every day. And that it's positive."[51]

Other white respondents are more direct about how their own positive experiences in integrated spaces reveal that desegregation has created better and more equitable treatment for everyone. Marcia P. recounts a field trip to Stratford, Ontario, she took in the late 1960s, when "there was a big push for Detroit Public Schools, or at least my school, to get Black and white students together." She enjoyed getting to know her seatmate, recalling how "it was the longest conversation I had ever had with a Black person," and yet "we never saw each other again. That was it." Experiences like this led her to "think that sort of 'working together,' you know, 'we're stronger together' mentality, always hit home for me." She continues to live in a majority-Black neighborhood today because "I never want to feel like I have something in common with the people around me just because we look the same." Patricia J. concurs, noting how "I like to see more people of color everywhere. In the news, on my bus, everywhere," while Clara A. voices her displeasure over continued segregation in major cities, noting "that's my belief, that people have to live together." Both Patricia and Clara caution, however, that living or working in integrated spaces may cause discomfort at first. "I have sat out experiences where I'm a little uncomfortable sometimes, but. . . . I don't know of any better way to integrate than that. And reduce the fear," Patricia says. Clara adds that "you have to accept your neighbors that they are louder, they play their music, it's different music than what you want."

But not everyone mentions the types of compromises people need to make or expect when attempting to desegregate. Bob S. says that he was unaware of any problems working with a diverse group of employees at the postal service for 20 years. "There was never any talk of racial inequalities, or anything like that. Everybody got along," he says. "I never heard of any racial problems. I never saw any on my shift." In this case, his assertion that people got along with each other seemed to prove that a desegregated workplace led to positive experiences for all employees when the reality is that white people would not necessarily be able to identify racial discrimination if they do not encounter it personally. The fact that he equates a lack of discussion of racial issues with a successful diversification of his workplace also relates back to Mills's argument that post-civil rights racial liberalism requires people to pretend that racism no longer has a major impact on society, and that anyone who talks about it is actually perpetrating racial harm.[52]

Even though Black respondents tend to support desegregation in theory or, like their activist predecessors, as a crucial step in a broader and more difficult fight for full citizenship rights, they are also more likely to question whether desegregation of public places has actually led to positive changes in their lives or within Black communities in general. "I thought it was important," Carol A. says of integration goals and yet "I held, I think, maybe two beliefs. I thought it was important to have equality, like equal access. But I really thought that Black Pride was important, and access to who we are and learning a little bit more about our history and our background." Even though she applauds increased access to jobs and education, "it seems to have weakened the cohesion of Black neighborhoods" at the same time. Before spaces were desegregated by law, and before urban renewal programs that built highways through economically viable Black communities, these neighborhoods provided opportunity and support for the people who lived there. But now "we're not as solidified. So you asked about desegregation, and that's something that seemingly was lost." Edgar S. voices concerns that "integration" has, in some instances, merely meant "assimilation" and that it is not an intrinsic good if Black people are expected to alter their identities in order to fit into supposedly diverse spaces. "I'm thinking there should be integration if both parties want to integrate," he explains. "It's not a melting pot. America is like a vegetable salad. You bring all your ingredients, right? The carrot is not a tomato, is not a cucumber, it's not a lettuce, but they all make that salad." Integration can work if different cultures are equally respected, he says, but "the issue is, if you've got to treat that carrot and that bell pepper as part of the salad, an integral part of the salad, but you don't have to change it. You don't try to make it something else. That's how I feel about integration." Cheryl J., who wonders whether "maybe integration was not a good thing," points out similar concerns about how such policies are not necessarily beneficial if

Black people are still denied full citizenship rights. "When integration was, I don't want to use the word 'forced' on everybody, but when integration came about, it was unequal," she explains. "It still was not equal. You all fought for this integration, but what did it do for you?" Rhonda E. similarly doubts how well integration alone can address aspects of racial injustice, stating that "I think there's a lot of work to do before you even do that. You know, we talk about healing. But healing from what? You really need to understand the depths of what the sickness is." Scott F. concurs, noting how "I continue to see people of color being treated and excluded. And until we get to the core of that problem, all of the other stuff is window dressing." He explains that:

> I think it depends on what the goal is. I think, you know, you have to look at what is trying to be accomplished within the framework of diversity and inclusion. And in the framework of integration. Because if you are going to do harm to people, that has to be considered. And what I've found and what I've noticed is that people throw around diversity and inclusion and integration without the extra level of thought as to what that means. What the repercussions are. Who is being impacted over what period of time? Why? Who stands to benefit? How much? So I'm not moved by words as much as I am the backdrop to all of that.[53]

Indeed, despite the many accolades that white respondents give integrated workplaces and communities, Black respondents' far more detailed and nuanced experiences reveal the flaws inherent in pretending all is equal simply because these spaces are technically open to people with different racial identities. Joseph J., for instance, recalls a time when he visited the dean of the law school where he was a student. "In the middle of the conversation, this man paused and looked at me and said, 'Why did you come here?'" he recounts. "And I said, I want to be a lawyer. He said, 'Is your mother a lawyer?' And I said no, she works in the cafeteria at an elementary school." The dean continued to harangue Joseph about whether any other members of his family were lawyers until "proudly I said, well, I have an aunt who is a professor at Marshall College. 'But nobody in your family is a lawyer' [the dean continued]. And I said no. And he just went on to another subject." Even though the law school was integrated, Joseph asserts that "my past [growing up in segregated New Orleans] thoroughly prepared me for these moments," since he was clearly made to feel like he did not belong because of his race and family background. "If the playing field is leveled, and everybody is moving towards the same goal, it's great," he says of desegregation in general. "If it's not, then it's highly problematic." Similarly, Ed B. relays a story that provides a sharp rebuke to the many concerns voiced about unqualified applicants getting jobs solely based on race under affirmative action policies meant to diversify workplaces. Although he worked in integrated settings in the military for 37 years, he was well aware that people of color were often bypassed for promotions. Still, by the time he applied for a supervisory position in the late 1970s or early 1980s, his coworkers assured him that he was next in line, and that he had all of the qualifications for the position. After several interviews, however, "they picked a guy who I was supervising... I said, what a slap in the face." When he talked to his supervisor about his dissatisfaction, referring to his experience and expertise, the supervisor simply replied that he "chose the guy who [he] thought was best." Even when Ed told his supervisor that he thought race had played a role in the decision, his supervisor said nothing more than "That's my prerogative, or some corny old statement. Then he said, 'I'm the supervisor and I can do what I want.'" Even though Ed remained in his position, he says he "was kind of heart broken. And the only reason he could give me was that he thought he picked the best man. He was white and the guy he picked was white." Ed's supervisors were not always unfair to him—in another instance, when he told a supervisor that a subordinate had refused to listen to him because he "ain't never took orders from a n***** before," he says that the guy was let go before he ever saw him again and that he "shortened his Air Force career real short." But ultimately, working in a diverse atmosphere was not as easy, natural, or beneficial as many white respondents made it out to be. "Being Black, [in] my experience, you go through life, you always have to fight for what's rightfully yours," he explains. "It's a never-ending cycle."[54]

The more recent issue of gentrification also reveals how integration alone does not necessarily benefit Black people. "I almost hate to say it, because we had businesses and everything in the area, and I think that once we started spreading out, the power left," says Miche B. of her hometown neighborhood in Detroit. Now, when she visits from her current residence in New York, "it feels like I'm a stranger in my home." Even though the majority-Black city has publicized the population's recent increase in younger white professionals as a sign that it is moving in a more prosperous direction, Miche says that all she can think about is how "they have pushed everybody out. . . . I would just love to see the old Detroit. I would love to see the Detroit that held onto everybody. Right now, I can say it, I'm scared to come home." She says that a similar process has occurred in her current neighborhood of Fort Greene in Brooklyn, a community with a strong African-American history, home to celebrities like Spike Lee and Chris Rock. But now, "if I see any Black folks over there, they are going through to get to the store and go back to their neighborhood." The pain, frustration, and even fear that these respondents report feeling in these integrated spaces hardly lines up with the experiences detailed by their white peers. When adhering to a philosophy of racial liberalism encourages people to distance themselves from any racial issues, and to accept integration as an absolute good, the very real traumas and lack of opportunities that Black Americans still experience go unnoticed and unacknowledged, even as American culture is simultaneously celebrated for embracing diversity.[55]

Most Black respondents, however, also expressed hope that the BLM movement would pick up where the last one left off, and that Americans will begin to actually engage in productive discussions about how to deal with the country's traumatic racist foundations. "That's been happening all along, but nowadays you can see it. You're seeing things with the video, with the camera," Edgar S. says of instances of where police violence has been recorded and shared online for the world to see. "So I think they have their value. I'm too old to [protest], but. . . . I love the diversity of the groups, white, Black." Ed B. also has higher hopes for this movement, stating that "I think now, this is the first time in my lifespan that I see the other races getting involved, truly involved, in discriminatory practice here in the United States. I've never seen what I see now on TV. And that's a whole different look, perspective, we're having, when you see a multitude of ethnicities out there walking and protesting for the same thing." His assertion that interracial participation is essential for the movement to succeed neatly coincides with SNCC's call for white participation during Freedom Summer in 1964, while also reinforcing the widespread belief that racial diversity is inherently good for American society—except, in this case, it is in the service of promoting bodily rights for Black citizens rather than trying to get them to assimilate into white-dominated spaces. "It hit home, more people are listening now, and not looking at [protesting] as a fad due to the police killings," he says. "They were so brutal and so inhumane [that] Black Lives Matter has gotten a big push."[56]

Indeed, some white narrators talked about how the recent movement has challenged them to reconsider their views on how racism operates in the United States, and what it might take to actually resist racist injustice. Michael P., for instance, supports BLM because "I think it's a change that has to come about for us to live civilly here in America." Patricia J. explains how important this movement is even if the methods do not necessarily align with what she was used to back in the 1960s. "If it's not in your face, you do forget about it," she stresses. "People are worried about paying their mortgage and making sure their kids go to school. So some of that stuff has got to be in your face even though it may make us uncomfortable from time to time. I'm okay. I look forward to being uncomfortable sometimes. That's a good thing." And Emily W., who admits that she struggles to understand how racism continues to affect society since she does not experience it herself, is still able to detail what she has learned about white privilege and racial violence, and how the Trayvon Martin case has specifically affected her perspective. "I raised three boys, and it broke my heart the way people looked at them sometimes, just, what are you doing, you're up to no good, just because you're walking down the street," she says. "Now that is 10 times worse, I'm sure, for a Black mother to be so worried about their own sons just minding their own business, just going down to the store to pick up a pack of gum, and people looking at them with suspicion and maybe approaching them accusatorily, taking them totally off guard." She acknowledges that having to always consider whether it is safe to walk through a neighborhood clashes with the privilege she enjoys as a white person, since "it just is not my experience. Mine was I [went] wherever I wanted, and could do whatever I wanted, and if a police officer pulled me over, I would bat my eyelashes and say, 'I'm so sorry, Officer,' and he would say, 'That's okay, go on your way.' So yes, we have a lot more to be done, just with that."[57]

Other white respondents report less shock over these revelations while simultaneously stressing the importance of BLM in combating racist violence. "Obviously I think a lot of the white community is shocked by the level of anger and what's happening, and it's kind of like, really?" Bill W. questions. "This is shocking to you? Did we really miss the boat by that much? And honestly, I have to say, I—we—missed the boat by that much. And the consequences are now." Even though Marcia P. qualifies her answer by stating that "you know, to me, all lives matter. Of course Black Lives Matter," she shares Bill's concerns and overall support for the movement, stating that "it's so horrible that we have to get to this point where you have to show everyone statistically that more Black people are being harassed by the police, or in jail, or whatever the reason is. But until we get to the point where you can say that and not everybody cringes, I think it's important." And Bruce C. takes on the opposition directly, noting how "the moment Black Lives Matter came about, you know, people started saying, oh, no, no, no. All Lives Matter. And they just didn't get the point. By creating the anti-thesis, they completely negated the idea of what Black Lives Matter was about."[58] Unlike some of their fellow white respondents, these people, all of whom either participated in civil rights campaigns themselves, or live in majority-Black neighborhoods, are aware of the structural damage caused by racial injustice that was not adequately addressed in the wake of the civil rights movement, and are therefore unsurprised by a movement like BLM that, in some ways, operates outside of the limits of racial liberalism.

When respondents are asked to consider how effective civil rights campaigns in the 1950s and 1960s have been in promoting racial equality and challenging different types of racial discrimination more than half a century later, many clearly state that the movement is not yet over, and that, as Bruce C. professes, "there's a lot of work that still has to be done." He explains how he has seen "gradual progress, you know, in the jobs—you certainly have Blacks getting better jobs than you did 50 years ago. There's more social integration among Blacks and whites." But at the same time, even though he stresses "I think it did help integrate schools," he points out that "as a result of that we end up with things like school busing which drives people further apart. It just created more hostility." Desegregation of public spaces did not eliminate racial economic gaps which, in fact, have started growing again after narrowing in the years after the civil rights movement. Bill W. adroitly points out that "there are no more Jim Crow laws that are formally on the books" but that "doesn't mean Jim Crow doesn't still exist." He points to the issues of desegregated schools that have been "re-segregated based on people that have money being able to pull their kids out and forcing certain groups to stay." Even though segregation "doesn't exist legitimately" anymore, "the personal level" has led schools in many districts to remain racially divided and, most often, unequal with regard to resources and opportunities.

"For the longest time, I would have said government is the answer," Bill continues. "You desegregate, the forced desegregation, take away the laws that don't allow people to live in certain [places]. But obviously, government isn't the answer. I guess it's sort of like you can lead a horse to water, but you can't make it drink. The government can pass laws and lead us to a certain place, but we have not found a way to work on the personal level to get people to really understand and change." These respondents are ultimately more ambivalent about the successes of the civil rights movement, particularly with regard to desegregation. "Racism in America is so ingrained in our fabric, it is so ingrained in our social fiber," Bruce C. proclaims. "It is so institutionalized; it is so deeply rooted in every single thing that we do. How do you legislate? You can't legislate that. Doesn't work like that. Yeah, there has to be integration. But how?" The focus, still, seems to be on how to better implement desegregation policies rather than any real consideration of how effectively they eradicate discrimination in the first place. Bill does, however, address some of the issues that Black respondents have run into in integrated spaces, as well as their concern that these types of policies can only work if everyone is treated equally to begin with. "Mixing [white people] into [Black political movements] does not work, doesn't help them," he says. "The whites that were into this, what we need to do is listen to what the Blacks are saying and then find ways to come back to the white community. And make the change within the white community so when the Black community [is] back, ready to re-engage, hopefully the white community [is] ready to re-engage with them."[59]

And yet, some respondents voice hope that the actions waged by civil rights protestors in the past will continue to inspire new activism that directly addresses the issues that are so often explained away by nonracial causes under this new form of racial liberalism. Some are even involved in these types of efforts themselves; Larry R., an early and prominent SNCC organizer, continues this work with other activists on the SNCC Legacy Project which, he explains, has been working with BLM organizers to develop successful programs. Clara A. runs a peace center and gallery that is dedicated to bringing people together from different backgrounds to create art and work on social justice issues. Edgar S. oversees the Mississippi Blues Commission's Blues Musicians Benevolent Fund, which offers financial and medical assistance to artists, some of whom live in impoverished circumstances that have not been ameliorated by the interracial appeal of their music. And Cheryl J., who bemoans the fact that "I just grew up in a diverse environment where everybody got along and everybody liked each other, and we shared everything, and our experiences, and our fun, and our sicknesses, and people can't do that anymore," has tried to compensate by managing a podcast that broadcasts from the Charles Wright Museum of African-American History in Detroit. She describes these events as truly integrated, where participants are able to bond across racial lines and really recognize each other as people. But she challenges the dictates of post-civil rights racial liberalism by stressing the importance of racial identity within these spaces rather than minimizing the distinctions. "People are so freaking amazed when they get there," she says. "My white friends are amazed because they see so many white people. My Black friends are amazed because they see such a diverse crowd. And we have so much fun telling stories. We give them stories, we give them entertainment. And everybody walks out just ecstatic." These events allow people from different racial backgrounds to come together in a truly integrated space and interact on a human level, something that Cheryl explains has been missing in other avenues of daily life. "Once a month I just feel so good when I look out in that audience and see all of those different, diverse people out there having a ball," she says. "Everybody is hugging each other, laughing and talking together. I mean, it's just amazing.... We bring people together."[60]

Billboard continues to publish a weekly Hot 100 chart to this day, listing best-selling (and streaming!) releases regardless of the racial background of the artists recording these singles or the listeners who purchase them. The data for this chart, however, is gathered in completely different ways. Chart editors no longer rely on subjective lists cobbled together by sample record stores across the country to determine best-selling singles. In 1991, *Billboard* began using Nielsen SoundScan, a system that tabulates sales via in-store scanners, to count album sales and pinpoint the most popular records in the country with greater accuracy. What music executives discovered was that supposedly fringe genres like hip-hop and heavy metal were selling surprisingly well, once again forcing major labels and radio stations to follow the desires of audiences rather than the other way around. Chart editors began incorporating digital sales in 2005, streaming numbers in 2012, and currently use TikTok, Spotify, and other platforms to create listings based on percentages that include sales, streaming, and radio play. Even though the mainstream music industry was slow to embrace rap for many of the same racist reasons that prompted the brief rise of racialized cover records in the mid- to late 1950s, Nielsen declared the genre to be the most popular in the country in 2018. These advances in charting technologies have been hailed as more democratic, placing greater power in the hands of listeners to decide which artists and genres should receive more promotion and airtime. And yet genres continue to be signified by race. More specific sales numbers led chart editors to begin listing top records in a number of different genres, including Dance/Electronic, Latin, Christian/Gospel, and "Rock" alongside the established Pop, Country, and (renamed, yet again) R&B/Hip-Hop charts. Since genre is no longer determined by the location where records are selling, different methods are used to decide which list they should appear on. The Latin list, for instance, is partially derived from Spanish radio station airplay, but *Billboard* initially charts most releases based on the genre tags provided by artists and their representation. After a record is released, editors also take note of which playlists it appears on, which can help determine how listeners categorize music according to genre. This system seemingly grants more control to musicians and listeners and how they see themselves rather than making automatic assumptions based on their racial identities. And yet music industry executives and *Billboard* editors still use race to determine genre in ways that are in keeping with post-civil rights racially liberal norms. This process became clear when Lil Nas X's explosive 2018 single "Old Town Road," recorded with country music legend Billy Ray Cyrus, first appeared on *Billboard*'s Hot Country chart, as per the artist's request, but was removed after only a few weeks. Even though the single topped both the Hot 100 and R&B/Hip-Hop charts, *Billboard* was accused of removing the song simply because it was released by a Black artist.[61]

The success of rock and roll music as an integrated genre encouraged positive images of integration in other areas, helping to reinforce moderate movement goals and reshape how the nation thinks about race. Geographer David Harvey explains that "when you change the language, you can change the way people think and their mental conceptions. And when that changes, you can start to push in new politics."[62] Not everything has changed for the better, though. As Ta-Nehisi Coates attests, living in the contemporary United States, "It is as though we have run up a credit-card bill and, having pledged to charge no more, remain befuddled that the balance does not disappear. The effects of that balance, interest accruing daily, are all around us."[63] Before those issues can be tackled, it is first integral to stop making new purchases. This, in essence, is the legacy left to us by the civil rights movement and reinforced by rock and roll music, as crucial steps were taken toward eliminating racial discrimination and promoting tolerance and cross-racial identification. These efforts were preliminary, but they were essential in precipitating a much more prolonged struggle to address the wrongs of the past, and to create a truly just and equitable society for all.

NOTES

1. "Rock 'n' Roll: The Sound of the Sixties," *Time*, May 21, 1965.
2. "Rock 'n' Roll: The Sound of the Sixties."
3. Jason Sokol, *There Goes My Everything: White Southerners in the Age of Civil Rights, 1945–1975* (New York: Vintage, 2008).
4. Equal Employment Opportunity: Title VII of the Civil Rights Act of 1964, last accessed at https://www.usda.gov/oascr/civil-right-laws-authorities, on June 16, 2021; Nancy MacLean, *Freedom Is Not Enough: The Opening of the American Work Place* (Cambridge, MA: Harvard University Press, 2006).
5. "Intermarriage Across the U.S. by Metro Area," Pew Research Center, May 18, 2017. Last accessed at https://www.pewresearch.org/social-trends/interactives/intermarriage-across-the-u-s-by-metro-area/, on June 16, 2021.
6. Lizabeth Cohen, *A Consumers' Republic: The Politics of Mass Consumption in Postwar America* (Cambridge, MA: Harvard University Press, 2006), 292–398.
7. James C. Cobb, "Even Though He Is Revered Today, MLK Was Widely Disliked by the American Public When He Was Killed," *Smithsonian* Magazine, April 4, 2018. Last accessed at https://www.smithsonianmag.com/history/why-martin-luther-king-had-75-percent-disapproval-rating-year-he-died-180968664/, on June 16, 2021.
8. "Rock 'n' Roll: The Sound of the Sixties."
9. "Rock 'n' Roll: The Sound of the Sixties."
10. Stokely Carmichael, "Black Power," Berkeley, California, October 29, 1966, last accessed at https://www.blackpast.org/african-american-history/speeches-african-american-history/1966-stokely-carmichael-black-power/, on June 17, 2021.
11. Carmichael, "Black Power."
12. John Lewis, Statement, SNCC Staff Meeting, February 1965, Mary King Papers, Box 1, Folder 20, Wisconsin Historical Society Library, Archives, and Museum Collections, Madison, WI.
13. One of the most famous Black Panther images, for instance, is that of Newton, Seale, and other California Black Panther Party members standing on the steps of the State House in Sacramento in full military garb, armed with rifles. The narrative that most people got from newspapers and television news was that angry Black Panthers were trying to violently take over the State House building. In reality, they were staging a highly theatrical protest in response to the proposed Mulford Act, which would make it illegal to carry firearms in public places. The Panthers, who were scrupulous in their adherence to legalities when it came to owning and using firearms, rightly interpreted the Act as an attempt to limit their power. The protest on the steps of the State House was therefore meant to show that Panther members knew their rights, but backfired because their message was obscured by politicians and journalists who engaged in fear mongering in order to limit the Party's

power. Please see Peniel Joseph's account of this event in *Waiting 'Til the Midnight Hour: A Narrative History of Black Power in America* (London: Macmillan, 2007), 205–240.

14. Carol A., in discussion with the author, February 24, 2020; Miche B., in discussion with the author, April 5, 2020; Scott F., in discussion with the author, April 20, 2020.

15. David Brackett, "The Politics and Practice of 'Crossover' in American Popular Music, 1963 to 1965," *The Musical Quarterly* 78, no. 4 (1994), 774–781.

16. Jack Hamilton, *Just Around Midnight* (Cambridge, MA: Harvard University Press, 2016), 3; 8–11.

17. Andrew Flory, *I Hear a Symphony: Motown and Crossover R&B* (Ann Arbor, MI: University of Michigan Press, 2017), 69–71.

18. Editorial Staff, "R&B Now Soul," *Billboard*, August 28, 1969.

19. Rick T., in discussion with the author, November 20, 2011; Bill W., in discussion with the author, June 1–2, 2020; Bruce C. in discussion with the author, June 8, 2020; Stan W., in discussion with the author, December 20, 2011; Michael P., in discussion with the author, October 4, 2019; Scott F., in discussion with the author.

20. Bibb E., in discussion with the author, November 13, 2011.

21. Pat K., in discussion with the author, November 15, 2019.

22. Matthew Lassiter, *The Silent Majority: Suburban Politics in the Sunbelt South* (Princeton, NJ: Princeton University Press, 2007), 1–2.

23. Merle Black and Earl Black, *The Rise of the Southern Republican* (Cambridge and London: The Belknap Press of Harvard University Press, 2002), 5; 75; 115; 326; Gabriel Winant, "Glenn Beck, Park 51 and the Politics of Hallowed Ground," Salon.com, August 30, 2010, last accessed at http://www.salon.com/2010/08/30/beck_park51_hallowed_ground/, on May 19, 2014.

24. Martin Luther King Jr. "Letter from Birmingham Jail," 1963, last accessed at https://letterfromjail.com/ on November 11, 2021.

25. "US House Passes Anti-Lynching Law Over 100 Years After First Attempt," BBC News, February 27, 2020, last accessed at https://www.bbc.com/news/world-us-canada-51663053, on July 4, 2021.

26. Nia-Malika Henderson, "Race and Racism in the 2016 Campaign,: CNN Politics, September 1, 2016, last accessed at https://www.cnn.com/2016/08/31/politics/2016-election-donald-trump-hillary-clinton-race/index.html, on July 4, 2021; Vanessa Williamson and Isabella Gelfand, "Trump and Racism: What do the Data Say?" Brookings Institute, August 14, 2019, last accessed at https://www.brookings.edu/blog/fixgov/2019/08/14/trump-and-racism-what-do-the-data-say/, on July 4, 2021; Lisa Desjardins, "What Exactly Trump Has Said About Race," PBS News Hour, August 22, 2017, last accessed at https://www.pbs.org/newshour/politics/every-moment-donald-trumps-long-complicated-history-race, on July 4, 2021. "Thug" statement made on April 28, 2015. False statement statistic made in November 2015. Statements on Judge Gonzalo Curiel made between May and June 2016. Statement about Mexican immigrants made on February 25, 2015. Statement in Dimondale, Michigan on August 19, 2016.

27. Williamson and Gelfand, "Trump and Racism."

28. Glenn Thrush and Maggie Haberman, "Trump Gives White Supremacists an Unequivocal Boost," *The New York Times*, August 15, 2017; Eduardo Bonilla-Silva, "'Racists,' 'Class Anxieties,' Hegemonic Racism, and Democracy in Trump's America," *Social Currents* 6, no. 1 (2019), 14–31.

29. *Shelby County v. Holder*, 570 U.S. 529, 2013, last accessed at https://www.supremecourt.gov/opinions/12pdf/12-96_6k47.pdf, on November 12, 2021; Charles W. Mills, "Racial Liberalism," *PMLA* 123, no. 5 (2008), 1391; 1385.

30. John H., in discussion with the author, September 20, 2019; Victor F., in discussion with the author, September 30, 2019; Andrew L., in discussion with the author, April 8, 2020.

31. Marcia P., in discussion with the author, December 6, 2019; Jimmy F., in discussion with the author, September 25, 2019; Victor F., in discussion with the author; Walter S., in discussion with the author, October 4, 2019; Mills, "Racial Liberalism," 1394.

32. Ellis B., in discussion with the author, September 26, 2019; Jimmy F., in discussion with the author.

33. Ron R., in discussion with the author, June 9, 2020; Henry I., in discussion with the author, October 30, 2019; Marcia P., in discussion with the author; Michael P., in discussion with the author.

34. Victor F., in discussion with the author; Ellis B., in discussion with the author; Andrew L., in discussion with the author; Ron R., in discussion with the author.

35. Miche B., in discussion with the author.

36. Miche B., in discussion with the author, Joseph J., in discussion with the author, January 30, 2020; Cheryl J., in discussion with the author, January 9, 2020; Rhonda E., in discussion with the author, February 26, 2020.

37. Ann W., in discussion with the author, November 9, 2011; Patricia J., in discussion with the author, March 9, 2020; Michael P., in discussion with the author; Bill W., in discussion with the author.

38. Ann W., in discussion with the author; Victor F., in discussion with the author; Bob S., in discussion with the author, September 25, 2019; Bob R., in discussion with the author, December 31, 2011.

39. Eric Burdon, "An 'Animal' Views America." *Ebony*, December 1966; Bibb E., in discussion with the author; Bret Eynon, interview with Madison Foster, July 1978, 32, Contemporary History Project: The New Left in Ann Arbor, Bentley Historical Library, The University of Michigan, Ann Arbor, MI; Bob C., in discussion with the author, December 13, 2011; Bruce C., in discussion with the author; Bret Eynon, interview with Todd Gitlin, September 16, 1978, 19, Contemporary History Project: The New Left in Ann Arbor, Bentley Historical Library, The University of Michigan, Ann Arbor, MI; Larry R., in discussion with the author, October 4, 2019.

40. Joseph J., in discussion with the author; Bill W., in discussion with the author; Scott F., in discussion with the author.

41. Rhonda E., in discussion with the author.

42. Victoria Valentine, Interview with James Forman, *Emerge* 7, no. 6 (April 1996), 26, James Forman Papers, Box 92, Folder 1, The Library of Congress, Washington, DC.

43. Ta-Nehisi Coates, "The Case for Reparations," *The Atlantic*, May 21, 2014.

44. Scott F., in discussion with the author; Ed B., in discussion with the author, June 23, 2020; Edgar S., in discussion with the author, June 25, 2020.

45. Ron R., in discussion with the author; Henry I., in discussion with the author; Larry R., in discussion with the author.

46. Rose W., in discussion with the author, April 26, 2020; David S., in discussion with the author, September 16, 2019; Victor F., in discussion with the author.

47. Mary R., in discussion with the author, May 11, 2020.

48. Ed B., in discussion with the author; David P., in discussion with the author; Carol B., in discussion with the author, October 2, 2019; Emily W., in discussion with the author, June 30, 2020; Ellis B., in discussion with the author; Henry I., in discussion with the author; Rose W., in discussion with the author.

49. Jimmy F., in discussion with the author; Walter S., in discussion with the author; Victor F., in discussion with the author.

50. Larry R., in discussion with the author.

51. Mary R., in discussion with the author; Ellis B., in discussion with the author; Victor F., in discussion with the author; Walter S., in discussion with the author.

52. Marcia P., in discussion with the author; Patricia J., in discussion with the author; Clara A., in discussion with the author, May 29, 2020; Bob S., in discussion with the author.

53. Carol A., in discussion with the author; Edgar S., in discussion with the author; Cheryl J., in discussion with the author; Scott F., in discussion with the author; Rhonda E., in discussion with the author.

54. Joseph J., in discussion with the author; Ed B., in discussion with the author.

55. Miche B., in discussion with the author.

56. Edgar S., in discussion with the author; Ed B., in discussion with the author.

57. Michael P., in discussion with the author; Patricia J., in discussion with the author; Emily W., in discussion with the author.

58. Bill W., in discussion with the author; Marcia P., in discussion with the author; Bruce C., in discussion with the author.

59. Bruce C., in discussion with the author; Bill W., in discussion with the author.

60. Larry R., in discussion with the author; Clara A., in discussion with the author; Edgar S., in discussion with the author; Cheryl J., in discussion with the author.

61. Chart editors responded that the removal occurred because of the single's heavy bass track and the fact that Columbia Records had not been promoting it on country music radio. Lil Nas X responded that, while he respected the decision, many contemporaneous country hits also featured heavier bass tracks, and that he believed the single "leans more toward country. Of course it's easier to get seen [as a rap song]." *Billboard* editors' attempts to claim that the move was strictly racially neutral and dependent on musicological specifics and promotion tactics are very much in keeping with broader attempts at color blindness. But the realities of selling a younger Black artist within a genre that is coded as white are anything but neutral, which Lil

Nas X clearly indicates in his otherwise conciliatory response. Michaelangelo Matos, "How SoundScan Changed Music, Driving Metal, Rap, and Alt-Rock Up the Charts," *Billboard*, June 10, 2021, last accessed at https://assets.billboard.com/articles/business/9585482/how-soundscan-changed-music-charts-success, on July 13, 2021; Rob Havilla, "How SoundScan Changed Everything We Knew About Popular Music," *The Ringer*, May 25, 2021, last accessed at https://www.theringer.com/music/2021/5/25/22452539/soundscan-billboard-charts-streaming-numbers, on July 13, 2021; Gary Trust, "Ask *Billboard*: How Does the Hot 100 Work?" *Billboard*, September 29, 2013, last accessed at https://www.billboard.com/articles/columns/ask-billboard/5740625/ask-billboard-how-does-the-hot-100-work, on July 13, 2021; Joe Levy, "Chart Beat: Inside the 'Old Town Road' Charts Decision," *Billboard*, September 19, 2019, last accessed at https://www.billboard.com/articles/business/chart-beat/8530110/inside-the-old-town-road-charts-decision, on July 13, 2021.

62. Scott Carlson, "Mapping a New Economy," *The Chronicle Review*, May 12, 2014, last accessed at http://chronicle.com/article/Mapping-a-New-Economy/146433, on May 22, 2014.

63. Coates, "The Case for Reparations."

Bibliography

I. ARCHIVAL COLLECTIONS

Alan Freed Collection. ARC-0006. The Rock and Roll Hall of Fame Library and Archives, Cleveland, Ohio.

Amzie Moore Papers. Wisconsin Historical Society Library, Archives, and Museum Collections, Madison, Wisconsin.

Apollo Theater Oral History Project. Columbia University Rare Book and Manuscript Library, New York, New York.

Atlantic Recording Corporation Records. ARC-0031. The Rock and Roll Hall of Fame Library and Archives, Cleveland, Ohio.

Bluefield Auditorium Posters. ARC-0084. The Rock and Roll Hall of Fame Library and Archives, Cleveland, Ohio.

Bret Eynon Papers, 1966–1977. 85166. Bentley Historical Library, University of Michigan, Ann Arbor, Michigan.

Contemporary History Project: The New Left in Ann Arbor. 85141. Bentley Historical Library, University of Michigan, Ann Arbor, Michigan.

James Forman Papers. The Library of Congress, Washington, DC.

Jerry Wexler Papers. ARC-0007. The Rock and Roll Hall of Fame Library and Archives, Cleveland, Ohio.

Leadership Conference on Civil Rights Collection. The Library of Congress, Washington, DC.

Mary King Papers. Wisconsin Historical Society Library, Archives, and Museum Collections, Madison, Wisconsin.

Milt Gabler Papers. ARC-0003. The Rock and Roll Hall of Fame Library and Archives, Cleveland, Ohio.

National Visionary Leadership Project. American Folklife Center, The Library of Congress, Washington, DC.

Ralph Bass Papers. ARC-0055. The Rock and Roll Hall of Fame Library and Archives, Cleveland, Ohio.

Russell B. Nye Popular Culture Collection. Special Collections, Michigan State University Libraries, Michigan State University, Lansing, Michigan.
Specialty Records Collection. ARC-0048. The Rock and Roll Hall of Fame Library and Archives, Cleveland, Ohio.
Voices of Civil Rights Project Collection. American Folklife Center, The Library of Congress, Washington, DC.

II. ORAL HISTORY INTERVIEWS

A. Carol. Interview With Beth Fowler. Telephone Interview, February 24, 2020.
A. Clara. Interview With Beth Fowler. Telephone Interview, May 29, 2020.
A. Ken. Interview With Beth Fowler. Telephone Interview, November 22, 2011.
B. Carol. Interview With Beth Fowler. Telephone Interview, October 2, 2019.
B. Ed. Interview With Beth Fowler. Video Interview, June 23, 2020.
B. Ellis. Interview With Beth Fowler. Telephone Interview, September 26, 2019.
B. Lori. Interview With Beth Fowler. Telephone Interview, January 7, 2020.
B. Miche. Interview With Beth Fowler. Video Interview, April 5, 2020.
C. Bob. Interview With Beth Fowler. Written Response to Interview Questions, December 13, 2011.
C. Bruce. Interview With Beth Fowler. Video Interview, June 8, 2020.
E. Bibb. Interview With Beth Fowler. Written Response to Interview Questions, November 13, 2011.
E. Rhonda. Interview With Beth Fowler. Telephone Interview, February 26, 2020.
F. Jimmy. Interview With Beth Fowler. Telephone Interview, September 25, 2019.
F. Matt. Interview With Beth Fowler. Video Interview, June 23, 2020.
F. Scott. Interview With Beth Fowler. Video Interview, April 20, 2020.
F. Victor. Interview With Beth Fowler. Telephone Interview, September 30, 2019.
H. John. Interview With Beth Fowler. Telephone Interview, September 20, 2019.
I. Henry. Interview With Beth Fowler. Telephone Interview, October 30, 2019.
J. Cheryl. Interview With Beth Fowler. Telephone Interview, January 9, 2020.
J. Joseph. Interview With Beth Fowler. Telephone Interview, January 30, 2020.
J. Patricia. Interview With Beth Fowler. Telephone Interview, March 9, 2020.
K. Pat. Interview With Beth Fowler. Telephone Interview, November 15, 2019.
L. Andrew. Interview With Beth Fowler. Video Interview, April 8, 2020.
M. Najee E. Interview With Beth Fowler. Written Response to Interview Questions, November 20, 2011.
P. Marcia. Interview With Beth Fowler. Telephone Interview, December 6, 2019.
P. Michael. Interview With Beth Fowler. Telephone Interview, October 4, 2019.
R. Bob. Interview With Beth Fowler. Written Response to Interview Questions, December 31, 2011.
R. Larry. Interview With Beth Fowler. Telephone Interview, October 4, 2019.
R. Mary. Interview With Beth Fowler. Video Interview, May 11, 2020.
R. Ron. Interview With Beth Fowler. Telephone Interview, June 9, 2020.
S. Bob. Interview With Beth Fowler. Telephone Interview, September 25, 2019.

S. Bruce. Interview With Beth Fowler. Telephone Interview, September 24, 2019.
S. David. Interview With Beth Fowler. Telephone Interview, September 16, 2019.
S. Edgar. Interview With Beth Fowler. Video Interview, June 25, 2020.
S. Fran. Interview With Beth Fowler. Detroit, MI, November 15, 2011.
S. Walter. Interview With Beth Fowler. Telephone Interview, October 4, 2019.
T. Jeff. Interview With Beth Fowler. Written Response to Interview Questions, November 5, 2011.
T. Rick. Interview With Beth Fowler. Telephone Interview, November 20, 2011.
T. Tony. Interview With Beth Fowler. Telephone Interview, November 9, 2011
W. Ann. Interview With Beth Fowler. Written Response to Interview Questions, November 9, 2011.
W. Bill. Interview With Beth Fowler. Video Interview, June 1–2, 2020.
W. Emily. Interview With Beth Fowler. Video Interview, June 30, 2020.
W. Rose. Interview With Beth Fowler. Video Interview, April 26, 2020.
W. Stan. Interview With Beth Fowler. Written Response to Interview Questions, December 20, 2011.
W. Tyrone. Interview With Beth Fowler. Written Response to Interview Questions, November 4, 2011.

III. COURT RULINGS AND POLICIES

"Brown et al. v. Board of Education of Topeka et al." *The Eyes on the Prize Civil Rights Reader: Documents, Speeches, and Firsthand Accounts From the Black Freedom Struggle*, edited by Clayborne Carson, David J. Garrow, Gerald Gill, Vincent Harding, and Darlene Clark Hine. New York: Penguin Books, 1991.
"Code of Ethics Adopted by the National Association of Real Estate Boards, June 6, 1924." http://archive.realtor.org/sites/default/files/1924Ethics.pdf. Last Accessed on February 6, 2020.
"Equal Employment Opportunity: Title VII of the Civil Rights Act of 1964." https://www.usda.gov/oascr/civil-right-laws-authorities. Last accessed on June 16, 2021.
Equal Justice Initiative. "Red Summer of 1919." https://eji.org/reports/online/lynching-in-america-targeting-black-veterans/red-summer. Last Accessed on September 7, 2019.
Johnson, Lyndon B. "Special Message to Congress, March 15, 1965. National Archives and Records Administration, The Lyndon B. Johnson Library and Museum." http://www.lbjlib.utexas.edu/johnson/archives.hom/speeches.hom/650315.htm. Last accessed on May 16, 2019.
"New Voting Restrictions in America." *Brennan Center for Justice at New York University of Law.* http://www.brennancenter.org/new-voting-restrictions-america. Last accessed on June 2, 2019.
"Shelby County v. Holder." 570 U.S. 529, 2013. https://www.supremecourt.gov/opinions/12pdf/12-96_6k47.pdf. Last accessed on November 12, 2021.

The Civil Rights Act of 1875. "History Art and Archives, United States House of Representatives." https://history.house.gov/Historical-Highlights/1851-1900/The-Civil-Rights-Act-of-1875/. Last accessed on June 16, 2021.

The Civil Rights Act of 1964. "Office of the Assistant Secretary for Administration and Management, U.S. Department of Labor." https://www.dol.gov/agencies/oasam/civil-rights-center/statutes/civil-rights-act-of-1964. Last accessed on May 25, 2021.

"Voting Rights Act of 1965. August 6, 1965. The Martin Luther King Jr. Research and Education Institute, Stanford University." https://kinginstitute.stanford.edu/encyclopedia/voting-rights-act-1965. Last accessed on June 2, 2021.

IV. FILMS AND FILM CLIPS

Bernard, Sheila Curran, and Sam Pollard. *"Eyes on the Prize" Two Societies: 1965–1968*. Blackside, 1990.

Bradley, Ed. "Interview With Little Richard." *60 Minutes*, 1985. https://www.youtube.com/watch?v=JmdpmM6mhBg. Last accessed on March 15, 2021.

Csaky, Mick. *American Masters: Sister Rosetta Tharpe: The Godmother of Rock and Roll*. PBS, 2013.

Frankie Lymon and the Teenagers. "I'm Not a Juvenile Delinquent." *The Big Beat*, 1956. https://www.youtube.com/watch?v=ZsBSsdAhnxE. Last accessed on September 14, 2020.

Griffin, Merv. "Interview With Little Richard." *The Merv Griffin Show*, October 18, 1971. https://www.youtube.com/watch?v=qyPHSsw7tiQ. Last accessed on March 15, 2021.

Hackford, Taylor. *Ray*. Universal Pictures, 2004.

Howard, Ron. *The Beatles: Eight Days a Week, the Touring Years*. Imagine Entertainment, 2016.

Mangold, James. *Walk the Line*. 20th Century Fox, 2005.

Neville, Morgan. *The Hitmakers: The Teens Who Stole Pop Music*. Peter Jones Productions, 2001.

Shankman, Adam. *Hairspray*. New Line Cinema, 2007.

"The Beatles Encounter a Segregated America in 1964." http://www.cbsnews.com/videos/the-beatles-encounter-a-segregated-america-in-1964/. Last accessed on May 21, 2014.

The Dick Clark Saturday Night Beechnut Show. March 7, 1959. https://www.youtube.com/watch?v=Qpkn6SOy0l8. Last accessed on November 4, 2018.

The Secret of Selling the Negro. Sarra Productions, 1954.

Vecchione, Judith. *Eyes on the Prize: Fighting Back: 1957–1962*. PBS Home Video, 1986.

Waters, John. *Hairspray*. New Line Cinema, 1988.

V. RECORDINGS

Adler, Lou, Herb Alpert, and Sam Cooke. "Wonderful World." Keen, 1959.
Ballard, Hank. "Work With Me, Annie." Federal Records, 1954.
Bartholomew, Dave, and Pearl King. "I Hear You Knocking." Imperial Records, 1955.
Berry, Chuck. "Maybellene." Chess, 1955.
Berry, Chuck. "Oh Baby Doll." Chess, 1957.
Berry, Chuck. "School Days." Chess, 1957.
Bradford, Janie, and Berry Gordy. "Money (That's What I Want)." Tamla, 1959.
Burnette, Johnny, and Dorsey Burnette. "Waitin' in School." Imperial, 1957.
Cooke, Sam. "You Send Me." Keen, 1957.
Davis, Maxwell, Aaron Collins Jr., and Sam Ling. "Eddie My Love." RPM, 1956.
Domino, Fats, and Dave Bartholomew. "The Fat Man." J&M Studio, 1949.
Gilliam, David. "A Teenager's Romance." Verve, 1957.
Goldner, George. "I'm Not a Juvenile Delinquent." Gee, 1956.
Jordan, Louis, and Ellis Lawrence Walsh. "Saturday Night Fish Fry." Decca, 1949.
Kohlman, Churchill. "Cry." Okeh Records, 1951.
Leiber, Jerry, and Mike Stoller. "Charlie Brown." Atco Records, 1959.
Leiber, Jerry, and Mike Stoller. "Get a Job." Ember Records, 1957.
Leiber, Jerry, and Mike Stoller. "Jailhouse Rock." RCA Victor, 1957.
Leiber, Jerry, and Mike Stoller. "Yakety Yak." Atco, 1958.
Lymon, Frankie, Herman Santiago, and Jimmy Merchant. Frankie Lymon and the Teenagers. "Why Do Fools Fall in Love?" Gee Records, 1956.
Mann, Kal, and Dave Appell. "Teach Me How to Twist." Cameo-Parkway Records, 1962.
McGhee, Stick. "Drinkin' Wine Spo-Dee-O-Dee." Atlantic Records, 1949.
Merrill, Bob. "(How Much Is) That Doggie in the Window?" Mercury, 1953.
Morton, George, Jeff Barry, and Ellie Greenwich. "Leader of the Pack." Red Bird, 1964.
Penniman, Richard, and Dorothy LaBostrie. "Tutti Frutti." Specialty Records, 1955.
Perkins, Carl. "Blue Suede Shoes." Sun Records, 1956.
Pitney, Gene. "He's a Rebel." Phillies, 1962.
Pomus, Doc, and Mort Shuman. "A Teenager in Love." Laurie Records, 1959.
Ram, Buck. "The Great Pretender." Mercury Records, 1955.
Robinson, Smokey, and Berry Gordy. "Bad Girl." Chess/Motown Records, 1959.
Robinson, Smokey, Pete Moore, and Marv Tarplin. "The Tracks of My Tears." Tamla, 1965.
Rose, Fred. "Honest and Truly." Decca Records, 1952.
Rose, Vincent, Larry Stock, and Al Lewis. "Blueberry Hill." Imperial, 1956.
Stone, Jesse. "Shake, Rattle and Roll." Bill Haley and His Comets. Decca, 1954.
Stone, Jesse. "Shake, Rattle and Roll." Joe Turner. Atlantic, 1954.
Ward, Billy, and Rose Marks. "Sixty Minute Man." Federal Records, 1951.
Weiss, Stephen, and Bernie Baum. "Music! Music! Music!" London Records, 1949.
Williams, Hank. "Cold, Cold Heart." MGM Records, 1951.

VI. DIGITAL PROJECTS AND OTHER ONLINE SOURCES

Alan Freed Archives. http://www.alanfreed.com/wp/archives/archives-moondog-1942-1951/.

Carmichael, Stokely. "Black Power." Berkeley, California, October 29, 1966. https://www.blackpast.org/african-american-history/speeches-african-american-history/1966-stokely-carmichael-black-power/. Last accessed on June 17, 2021.

"Elvis and Race in 1950s America." *TeachRock.org*. http://www.teachrock.org/lesson/elvis-and-race-in-1950s-america/. Last accessed on June 22, 2016.

Garvey, Michael. "Oral History With Mr. Amzie Moore, Black Civil Rights Worker." The University of Southern Mississippi Center for Oral History and Cultural Heritage Digital Collections, 31. http://digilib.usm.edu/cdm/ref/collection/coh/id/5707. Last accessed on July 17, 2013.

"Greensboro Sit-Ins: The Sit-Ins Spread." *The Greensboro Sit-Ins*. https://greensborositinsalegacy.wordpress.com/2017/04/06/the-sit-in-spreads/. Last accessed on December 9, 2020.

"Intermarriage Across the U.S. by Metro Area." *Pew Research Center*, May 18, 2017. https://www.pewresearch.org/social-trends/interactives/intermarriage-across-the-u-s-by-metro-area/. Last accessed on June 16, 2021.

King, Martin Luther, Jr. "Advice for Living." April 1958. The Martin Luther King, Jr. Research and Education Institute, Stanford University. https://swap.stanford.edu/20141218225520; http://mlk-kpp01.stanford.edu/primarydocuments/Vol4/Apr-1958_AdviceForLiving.pdf. Last accessed on July 2, 2021.

King, Martin Luther, Jr. "Letter From Birmingham Jail." 1963. https://letterfromjail.com/. Last accessed on November 11, 2021.

"Motown Museum: Home of Hitsville U.S.A." https://www.motownmuseum.org/story/motown/. Last accessed May 21, 2019.

National Association for the Advancement of Colored People. "A Letter to President Woodrow Wilson on Federal Race Discrimination." August 15, 1913, NAACP Records, The Library of Congress. https://www.loc.gov/exhibits/civil-rights-act/segregation-era.html. Last accessed on September 12, 2019.

"November 1964: SNCC's Waveland Conference." SNCC Digital Gateway. https://snccdigital.org/events/snccs-waveland-conference/. Last accessed on May 25, 2021.

Oliver, Kitty. "The Beatles, Race and Segregation." *The Beatles Story*, February 1, 2018. www.beatlesstory.com. Last accessed on April 7, 2021.

Snyder, Thomas D. "120 Years of American Education: A Statistical Portrait." *Center for Education Statistics*, 1993.

"Student Nonviolent Coordinating Committee (SNCC) Actions, 1960–1970." Mapping American Social Movements Project, University of Washington. http://depts.washington.edu/moves/SNCC_map-events.shtml. Last accessed on December 8, 2020.

"Whites Believe They Are Victims of Racism More Often Than Blacks." *Tufts University News Release*, May 23, 2011. https://now.tufts.edu/news-releases

/whites-believe-they-are-victims-racism-more-o%20on%20June%2027. Last accessed on June 27, 2021.

Williamson, Vanessa, and Isabella Gelfand. "Trump and Racism: What do the Data Say?" *Brookings Institute*, August 14, 2019. https://www.brookings.edu/blog/fixgov/2019/08/14/trump-and-racism-what-do-the-data-say/. Last accessed on July 4, 2021.

VII. PUBLIC HISTORY SOURCES

MLK Exhibit Guide. The Rock and Roll Hall of Fame Museum, Cleveland, Ohio.
Motown Museum: Hitsville, USA, Detroit, Michigan.
Stax Museum of American Soul Music, Memphis, Tennessee.
Sun Studio, Memphis, Tennessee.

VIII. NEWSPAPER AND MAGAZINE ARTICLES

"A Bold Boycott Goes On." *Life*, March 5, 1956.
"A New $10 Billion Power: The U.S. Teen-Age Consumer." *Life*, August 31, 1959.
"Are Teen-Agers Growing Up Too Fast?" *Jet*, May 19, 1955.
"Battle Against Tradition: Martin Luther King, Jr." *The New York Times*, March 21, 1956.
Billboard charts, 1953–1964.
"Charting the Charts." *On the Media*. WNYC, October 23, 2009. http://www.wnyc.org/story/132541-charting-the-charts/#transcript. Last accessed on April 12, 2018.
"Child Star Grows Up." *Ebony*, December 1959.
"Education Held Integration Key." *The New York Times*, May 20, 1956.
"Montgomery Boycotters Usher in New Era of Democracy For South." *Chicago Defender*, December 26, 1956.
"Montgomery's Patience Praised by Boycott Chief." The *Washington Post and Times Herald*, December 7, 1956.
"Prepare for Boycott Trials." *Chicago Defender*, March 30, 1956.
"R&B Now Soul." Editorial Staff. *Billboard*, August 28, 1969.
"R&R Still Beams Plenty of Life." *Billboard*, January 18, 1960.
"Race Urged to Keep Faith In Its Fight: Rosa Parks Makes Plea In Capital." *Chicago Defender*, June 9, 1956.
"Rock-and-Roll Called 'Communicable Disease.'" *The New York Times*, March 28, 1956.
"Rock 'n' Roll: The Sound of the Sixties." *Time*, May 25, 1965.
"Should Teen-Agers Have Steady Dates? Survey Reveals 'Going Steady' Is Increasing Among Teens." *Jet*, October 1, 1959, 24–26.
"Teen-Age Stars Who Prefer School to Dollars." *Jet*, November 1, 1962, 58–60.
"The Costly Hazard of Young Marriage." *Life*, April 13, 1959, 119–130.

"The Forgotten 15,000,000." *Sponsor*, October 10, 1949.
"The Forgotten 15,000,000, Part Two: How to Build Negro Sales." *Sponsor*, October 24, 1949.
"The Reverend Martin Luther King." *Chicago Defender*, March 25, 1956.
"The South: A Universal Effort." *Time*, May 2, 1960.
"US House Passes Anti-Lynching Law Over 100 Years After First Attempt." *BBC News*, February 27, 2020. https://www.bbc.com/news/world-us-canada-51663053. Last accessed on July 4, 2021.
"White Girls Take Lead in Mixed Dating, Says Coed." *Jet*, November 27, 1958.
"Yeh-Heh-Heh-Hes, Baby." *Time*, June 18, 1956.
Anderson, Trezzvant W. "How Has Dramatic Bus Boycott Affected Montgomery Negroes?" *The Pittsburgh Courier*, November 23, 1957.
Anderson, Trezzvant W. "How Has Dramatic Bus Boycott Affected Montgomery Negroes?" *The Pittsburgh Courier*, December 4, 1957.
Anderson, Trezzvant W. "How Has Dramatic Bus Boycott Affected Montgomery Negroes?" *The Pittsburgh Courier*, December 21, 1957.
Ashbury, Edith Evans. "Rock 'n' Roll Teen-Agers Tie Up the Times Square Area." *The New York Times*, February 23, 1957.
Barrett, George. "Bus Integration in Alabama Calm." *The New York Times*, December 22, 1956.
Barrett, George. "Montgomery: Testing Ground." *The New York Times*, December 16, 1956.
Booker, James. "Who is Martin Luther King?" *New York Amsterdam News*, March 31, 1956.
Brown, Lloyd L. "Brown v. Salina, Kansas." *The New York Times*, February 26, 1973.
Bundy, June. "Desegregation of Chart Categories Earmarks '56'." *Billboard*, January 26, 1957.
Burdon, Eric. "An 'Animal' Views America." *Ebony*, December 1966.
Burley, Dan. "People Are Talking About." *Jet*, June 14, 1956.
Carlson, Scott. "Mapping a New Economy." *The Chronicle Review*, May 12, 2014. http://chronicle.com/article/Mapping-a-New-Economy/146433. Last accessed on May 22, 2014.
Carthew, Anthony. "Shaggy Englishman Story: British Long-Hairs Are Proud of Setting a New Tonsorial Style—But the Barbers Are Crying." *The New York Times*, September 6, 1964.
Coates, Ta-Nehisi. "The Case for Reparations." *The Atlantic*, May 21, 2014.
Cobb, James C. "Even Though He Is Revered Today, MLK Was Widely Disliked by the American Public When He Was Killed." *Smithsonian Magazine*, April 4, 2018. https://www.smithsonianmag.com/history/why-martin-luther-king-had-75-percent-disapproval-rating-year-he-died-180968664/. Last accessed on June 16, 2021.
Cobb, James C. "The Voting Rights Act at 50: How It Changed the World." *Time*, August 6, 2015.
Cunningham, Evelyn. "Martin Luther King, Jr.: 'A Young Minister Marked for Leadership.'" *The Pittsburgh Courier*, April 7, 1956.

Desjardins, Lisa. "What Exactly Trump Has Said About Race." *PBS News Hour*, August 22, 2017. https://www.pbs.org/newshour/politics/every-moment-donald-trumps-long-complicated-history-race. Last accessed on July 4, 2021.

Emerson, Gloria. "British 'His and Her' Hairdos Blur 'Him-Her' Line." *The New York Times*, July 23, 1964.

Freed, Alan. "The Big Beat Has Arrived: Izzy Rowe's Notebook." *The Pittsburgh Courier*, 1955.

Gavin, Bill. "No Musical Color Line." *Billboard*, April 25, 1964.

Havilla, Rob. "How SoundScan Changed Everything We Knew About Popular Music." *The Ringer*, May 25, 2021. https://www.theringer.com/music/2021/5/25/22452539/soundscan-billboard-charts-streaming-numbers. Last accessed on July 13, 2021.

Henderson, Nia-Malika. "Race and Racism in the 2016 Campaign." *CNN Politics*, September 1, 2016. https://www.cnn.com/2016/08/31/politics/2016-election-donald-trump-hillary-clinton-race/index.html. Last accessed on July 4, 2021.

Hsu, Hua. "Pale Fire." *The New Yorker*, July 18, 2016.

Hutchinson, Louise. "Barber Gives Scare to Five Fuzzy Singers: Rolling Stones Roll Out of His Way." *Chicago Tribune*, June 12, 1964.

Kaleem, Jaweed. "How Did the Weakened Voting Rights Act Impact Election Results?" *The Los Angeles Times,* November 8, 2016.

King, Jason. "I'll Take You There: R&B From NPR Music." *The Mix: NPR Music*, February 10, 2014.

Levy, Joe. "Chart Beat: Inside the 'Old Town Road' Charts Decision." *Billboard*, September 19, 2019. https://www.billboard.com/articles/business/chart-beat/8530110/inside-the-old-town-road-charts-decision. Last accessed on July 13, 2021.

Mahler, Jack. "No Mercy From Mersey? Beatles Have Launched a New Redcoat Invasion." *Billboard*, April 25, 1964.

Martin, Joe. "Hit Tunes and Good Talent are Keeping the Boxes Busy: The Pops." *Billboard,* March 15, 1952.

Matos, Michaelangelo. "How SoundScan Changed Music, Driving Metal, Rap, and Alt-Rock Up the Charts." *Billboard*, June 10, 2021. https://assets.billboard.com/articles/business/9585482/how-soundscan-changed-music-charts-success. Last accessed on July 13, 2021.

Miller, Zeke J. "Why Martin Luther King Jr.'s Lessons About Peaceful Protests Are Still Relevant." *Time*, January 12, 2018.

Phillips, McCandlish. "Campuses in North Back Southern Negro Students." *The New York Times*, March 20, 1960.

Phillips, Wayne. "Integration: A Pattern Emerges." *The New York Times Magazine*, September 29, 1957.

Phillips, Wayne. "Montgomery is Stage for a Tense Drama." *The New York Times*, March 4, 1956.

Pophan, John N. "Violence Shuts Clinton School." *The New York Times*, December 5, 1956.

Poston, Ted. "This is Montgomery." *The Baltimore Afro-American*, July 21, 1956.

Poston, Ted. "This is Montgomery: No Hat in Hand." *The Baltimore Afro-American*, August 25, 1956.

Richardson, Cliff. "Mixed Dancing Baffles Cops in Houston Texas" and "Integrated Houston Dance Draws 4,000." *The Pittsburgh Courier*, August 18, 1956.

Rolontz, Bob. "Hit Tunes and Good Talent Are Keeping the Boxes Busy: Rhythm & Blues." *Billboard*, March 15, 1952.

Rowland, Stanley. "Southern Youths Back Integration." *The New York Times*, January 1, 1956.

Samuels, Gertrude. "School Desegregation: A Case History." *The New York Times*, May 8, 1955.

Samuels, Gertrude. "Why They Rock 'n' Roll—And Should They?" *The New York Times*, January 12, 1958.

Sippel, Johnny. "Hit Tunes and Good Talent are Keeping the Boxes Busy: Country & Western." *Billboard*, March 15, 1952.

Sitton, Claude. "Group Maps Plans on Freedom Rides." *The New York Times*, June 1, 1961.

Sitton, Claude. "Not Token Freedom, Full Freedom." *The New York Times*, June 9, 1963.

Sitton, Claude. "Troubled Actors in the Little Rock Drama." *The New York Times*, October 5, 1958.

Smith, Mychal Denzel. "Donald Sterling's Impolite Racism." *The Nation*, April 28, 2014.

Stern, Mark Joseph. "North Carolina's 'Monster' Voter-Suppression Law is Dead." *Slate*, May 15, 2017.

Thrush, Glenn, and Maggie Haberman. "Trump Gives White Supremacists an Unequivocal Boost." *The New York Times*, August 15, 2017.

Trust, Gary. "Ask *Billboard*: How Does the Hot 100 Work?" *Billboard*, September 29, 2013. https://www.billboard.com/articles/columns/ask-billboard/5740625/ask-billboard-how-does-the-hot-100-work. Last accessed on July 13, 2021.

Trust, Gary. "Chart Beat." *Billboard*, July 9, 2018. https://www.billboard.com/articles/columns/chart-beat/8464454/drake-hot-100-record-nice-for-what-scorpion. Last accessed on June 8, 2021.

Winant, Gabriel. "Glenn Beck, Park 51 and the Politics of Hallowed Ground." *Salon.com*, August 30, 2010.

Winston, Michael R. "Opinion: Sit-Ins in the District in the 1940s." *The Washington Post*, November 14, 2011.

Yarborough, Chuck. "Rock Hall Offers Free Admission, Programs on Martin Luther King Jr. Day." *The Plain Dealer*, January 7, 2016.

IX. BOOKS, JOURNAL ARTICLES, AND DISSERTATIONS

Alexander, Michelle. *The New Jim Crow: Mass Incarceration in the Age of Colorblindness*. New York: The New Press, 2012.

Altschuler, Glenn C. *All Shook Up: How Rock 'n' Roll Changed America.* New York: Oxford University Press, 2003.

Bailey, Beth. "Rebels Without a Cause? Teenagers in the 1950s." *History Today* 40, 2001, 25–31.

Baraka, Amiri. *Blues People: The Negro Experience in White America and the Music That Developed From It.* New York: Morrow Quill Paperbacks, 1963.

Barnosky, Jason. "The Violent Years: Responses to Juvenile Crime in the 1950s." *Polity* 38, no. 3, 2006, 314–344.

Beals, Melba Patillo. *Warriors Don't Cry: A Searing Memoir of the Battle to Integrate Little Rock's Central High.* New York: Washington Square Press, 1994.

Berman, Ari. *Give Us the Ballot: The Modern Struggle for Voting Rights in America.* London: Picador, 2016.

Berry, Chuck. *Chuck Berry: The Autobiography.* New York: Harmony Books, 1987.

Bertrand, Michael T. *Race, Rock and Elvis.* Champaign, IL: University of Illinois Press, 2000.

Biondi, Martha. *To Stand and Fight: The Struggle for Civil Rights in Postwar New York City.* Cambridge, MA: Harvard University Press, 2003.

Black, Merle, and Earl Black. *The Rise of the Southern Republican.* Cambridge and London: The Belknap Press of Harvard University Press, 2002.

Bonilla-Silva, Eduardo. "Color-Blind Racism in Pandemic Times." *Sociology of Race and Ethnicity* 1, no. 12, 2020.

Bonilla-Silva, Eduardo. *Racism Without Racists: Color-Blind Racism and the Persistence of Racial Inequality in America.* Lanham, MD: Rowman & Littlefield, 2009.

Bonilla-Silva, Eduardo. "'Racists,' 'Class Anxieties,' Hegemonic Racism, and Democracy in Trump's America." *Social Currents* 6, no. 1, 2019, 14–31.

Brackett, David. "The Politics and Practice of 'Crossover' in American Popular Music, 1963 to 1965." *The Musical Quarterly* 78, no. 4, 1994, 774–797.

Branch, Taylor. *Parting the Waters: America in the King Years, 1954–1963.* New York: Simon & Schuster, 1988.

Breines, Wini. *Young, White, and Miserable: Growing Up Female in the Fifties.* Boston: Beacon Press, 1992.

Browne-Marshall, Gloria J. *The Voting Rights War: The NAACP and the Ongoing Struggle for Justice.* Lanham, MD: Rowman & Littlefield, 2016.

Cahn, Susan. *Sexual Reckonings: Southern Girls in a Troubling Age.* Cambridge, MA: Harvard University Press, 2007.

Cantor, Louis. *Dewey and Elvis: The Life and Times of a Rock 'n' Roll Deejay.* Champaign, IL: University of Illinois Press, 2010.

Cantor, Louis. *Wheelin' on Beale: How WDIA-Memphis Became the Nation's First All-Black Station and Created the Sound that Changed America.* New York: Pharos Books, 1992.

Caro, Robert. *The Passage of Power: The Years of Lyndon Johnson.* New York: Knopf/Doubleday Publishing Group, 2012.

Caro, Robert A. "Autherine Lucy at the University of Alabama: How the Mob Won." *The Journal of Blacks in Higher Education* 37, 2002.

Catsam, Derek. *Freedom's Main Line: The Journey of Reconciliation and the Freedom Rides*. Lexington, KY: The University Press of Kentucky, 2008.

Chalmers, David. *And the Crooked Places Made Straight: The Struggle for Social Change in the 1960s*. Baltimore: The Johns Hopkins University Press, 1996.

Chapple, Steve Chapple, and Reebee Garofalo. *Rock 'n' Roll is Here to Pay: The History and Politics of the Music Industry*. Lanham, MD: Rowman & Littlefield Publishers, 1978.

Charles, Ray, and David Ritz. *Brother Ray: Ray Charles' Own Story*. Cambridge, MA: Da Capo Press, 2004.

Cleaver, Eldridge. *Soul on Ice*. New York: Delta Trade Paperbacks, 1999.

Cohen, Lizabeth. *A Consumer's Republic: The Politics of Mass Consumption in Postwar America*. New York: Vintage, 2003.

Colley, Zoe A. *Ain't Scared of Your Jail: Arrest, Imprisonment, and the Civil Rights Movement*. Gainesville, FL: University Press of Florida, 2012.

Countryman, Matthew J. *Up South: Civil Rights and Black Power in Philadelphia*. Philadelphia: University of Pennsylvania Press, 2007.

Davis, Angela Y. *Blues Legacies and Black Feminism: Gertrude 'Ma' Rainey, Bessie Smith, and Billie Holiday*. New York: Vintage Books, 1998.

Delmont, Matthew. "Dancing Around the 'Glaring Light of Television': Black Teen Dance Shows in the South." *Southern Spaces*, September 29, 2015. https://southernspaces.org/2015/dancing-around-glaring-light-television-black-teen-dance-shows-south/. Last accessed on September 13, 2019.

Delmont, Matthew F. *The Nicest Kids in Town: American Bandstand, Rock 'n' Roll, and the Struggle for Civil Rights in 1950s Philadelphia*. Berkeley & Los Angeles: University of California Press, 2012.

Delmont, Matthew F. *Why Busing Failed*. Berkeley and Los Angeles: University of California Press, 2016.

Delmont, Matthew F., and Jeanne Theoharis. "Rethinking the Boston 'Busing Crisis.'" *Journal of Urban History* 43, no. 2, March 2017, 191–203.

D'Emilio, John. *Lost Prophet: The Life and Times of Bayard Rustin*. New York: Simon & Schuster, 2003.

Donohue, John J., III, James J. Heckman, and Petra E. Todd. "The Schooling of Southern Blacks: The Roles of Legal Activism and Private Philanthropy, 1910–1960." *The Quarterly Journal of Economics* 117, no. 1, February 2002, 225–268.

Driskell, Jay Winston, Jr. *Schooling Jim Crow: The Fight for Atlanta's Booker T. Washington High School and the Roots of Black Protest Politics*. Charlottesville, VA: University of Virginia Press, 2014.

Dudziak, Mary. *Cold War Civil Rights: Race and the Image of American Democracy*. Princeton, NJ: Princeton University Press, 2002.

Ennis, Philip H. *The Seventh Stream: The Emergence of Rocknroll in American Popular Music*. Middletown, CT: Wesleyan University Press, 1992.

Evans, Sara. *Personal Politics: The Roots of Women's Liberation in the Civil Rights Movement and the New Left*. New York: Vintage Books, 1980.

Fairclough, Adam. *To Redeem the Soul of America: The Southern Christian Leadership Conference & Martin Luther King, Jr.* Athens, GA: The University of Georgia Press, 1987.
Farmer, James. *Lay Bare the Heart: An Autobiography of the Civil Rights Movement.* Fort Worth, TX: TCU Press, 1998.
Feldstein, Ruth. *Motherhood in Black and White: Race and Sex in American Liberalism, 1930–1965.* Ithaca, NY: Cornell University Press, 2000.
Flory, Andrew. *I Hear a Symphony: Motown and Crossover R&B.* Ann Arbor, MI: University of Michigan Press, 2017.
Foner, Philip. "The Battle to End Discrimination Against Negroes on Philadelphia Streetcars: (Part I) Background and Beginning of the Battle." *Pennsylvania History* 40, no. 3, 1973, 261–291.
Fong-Torres, Ben. "Ray Charles." *The Rolling Stone Interviews, 1967–1980*, edited by The Editors of *Rolling Stone*. New York: Rolling Stone Press, 1981.
Ford-Smith, Honor. "Unruly Virtues of the Spectacular: Performing Engendered Nationalisms in the UNIA in Jamaica." *Interventions* 6, no. 1, 2004, 18–44.
Frazier, E. Franklin. *Black Bourgeoisie.* New York: Simon & Schuster, 1997.
Freund, David. *Colored Property: State Policy and White Racial Politics in America.* Chicago: University of Chicago Press, 2007.
Garofalo, Reebee. "Crossing Over: From Black Rhythm & Blues to White Rock 'n' Roll." In *R&B, Rhythm and Business: The Political Economy of Black Music*, edited by Norman Kelley. New York: Akashic Books, 2005.
Garofalo, Reebee. "Popular Music and the Civil Rights Movement." *Rockin' the Boat: Mass Music and Mass Movements*, edited by Reebee Garofalo. Cambridge, MA: South End Press, 1999.
George, Nelson. *The Death of Rhythm and Blues.* New York: Penguin Books, 1988.
Gerard, Charley. *Jazz in Black and White: Race, Culture, and Identity in the Jazz Community.* Westport, CT: Praeger, 1998.
Gerber, David A. "Education, Expediency, and Ideology: Race and Politics in the Desegregation of Ohio Public Schools in the Late 19th Century." *The Journal of Ethnic Studies* 1, no. 3, 1973, 15–16.
Gillett, Charlie. *The Sound of the City: The Rise of Rock And Roll.* Cambridge, MA: Da Capo Press, 1996.
Gilmore, Glenda Elizabeth. *Defying Dixie: The Radical Roots of Civil Rights.* New York: W.W. Norton & Co., 2008.
Gordy, Berry. *To Be Loved: The Music, the Magic, the Memories of Motown.* New York: Warner Books, 1994.
Green, Hilary. *Educational Reconstruction: African American Schools in the Urban South, 1865–1890.* New York: Oxford University Press, 2016.
Greene, Christina. *Our Separate Ways: Women and the Black Freedom Movement in Durham, North Carolina.* Chapel Hill: University of North Carolina Press, 2005.
Gregory, James. *The Southern Diaspora: How the Great Migrations of Black and White Southerners Transformed America.* Chapel Hill, NC: University of North Carolina Press, 2005.

Grossman, Lawrence. "George T. Downing and Desegregation of Rhode Island Public Schools, 1855–1866." *Rhode Island History* 36, no. 4, 1977, 104.

Guglielmo, Thomas A. *White on Arrival: Italians, Race, Color, and Power in Chicago, 1890–1945*. New York: Oxford University Press, 2003.

Guralnick, Peter. *Last Train to Memphis: The Rise of Elvis Presley*. New York: Little, Brown and Company, 1994.

Guralnick, Peter. *Sam Phillips: The Man Who Invented Rock n' Roll*. New York: Back Bay Books, 2016.

Hague, Euan. "'The Right to Enter Every Other State'–the Supreme Court and African American Mobility in the United States." *Mobilities* 5, no. 3, 2010, 331–347.

Hale, Grace Elizabeth. *A Nation of Outsiders: How the White Middle Class Fell in Love with Rebellion in Postwar America*. New York: Oxford University Press, 2011.

Hale, Grace Elizabeth. *Making Whiteness: The Culture of Segregation in the South, 1890–1940*. New York: Vintage Books, 1998.

Hall, Jacquelyn Dowd. "The Long Civil Rights Movement and the Political Uses of the Past." *The Journal of American History* 91, no. 4, March 2005, 1233–1263.

Hamilton, Jack. *Just Around Midnight: Rock and Roll and the Racial Imagination*. Cambridge, MA: Harvard University Press, 2016.

Harris, Fredrick C. "The Rise of Respectability Politics." *Dissent* 61, no. 1, 2014, 33–37.

Haynes, Bruce D. *Red Lines, Black Spaces: The Politics of Race and Space in a Middle-Class Suburb*. New Haven, CT: Yale University Press, 2001.

Higginbotham, Evelyn Brooks. "African-American Women's History and the Metalanguage of Race." *Signs: Journal of Women in Culture and Society* 17, no. 2, 1992, 251–274.

Higginbotham, Evelyn Brooks. "Re-Thinking Vernacular Culture: Black Religion and Race Records in the 1920s and 1930s." In *African American Religious Thought: An Anthology*, edited by Cornel West and Eddie S. Gladue Jr. Louisville, KY: Westminster John Knox Press, 2003.

Higginbotham, Evelyn Brooks. *Righteous Discontent: The Women's Movement in the Black Baptist Church, 1880–1920*. Cambridge, MA: Harvard University Press, 1993.

Himes, Joseph S. "Negro Teen-Age Culture." *The Annals of the American Academy of Political and Social Science* 338, no. 1, 1961, 91–101.

Hinton, Elizabeth. *From the War on Poverty to the War on Crime: The Making of Mass Incarceration in America*. Cambridge, MA: Harvard University Press, 2016.

Hunter, Tera W. "'Sexual Pantomimes,' the Blues Aesthetic, and Black Women in the New South." *Music and the Racial Imagination*, edited by Ronald M. Radano, Philip V. Bohlman, and Houston A. Baker. Chicago: University of Chicago Press, 2000.

Ian, Janis. *Society's Child*. New York: Tarcher, 2008.

Jackson, John A. *Big Beat Heat: Alan Freed and the Early Years of Rock & Roll*. London: Schirmer Trade Books, 1991.

Jackson, Kenneth. *Crabgrass Frontier: The Suburbanization of the United States*. New York: Oxford University Press, 1985.

Jacobson, Matthew Frye. *Whiteness of a Different Color: European Immigrants and the Alchemy of Race.* Cambridge, MA: Harvard University Press, 1999.

Joel Foreman, Ed. *The Other Fifties: Interrogating Midcentury American Icons.* Champaign, IL: University of Illinois Press, 1997.

Jones, Martha S. *All Bound Up Together: The Woman Question in African American Public Culture, 1830–1900.* Chapel Hill: University of North Carolina Press, 2009.

Jordan, William. "'The Damnable Dilemma': African-American Accommodation and Protest During World War I." *The Journal of American History* 81, no. 4, 1995, 1562–1583.

Joseph, Peniel E. *Waiting 'Til the Midnight Hour: A Narrative History of Black Power in America.* London: Macmillan, 2007.

Joyce, Thomas. "The 'Double V' Was For Victory: Black Soldiers, the Black Protest, and World War II." Dissertation, The Ohio State University, 1993.

Katznelson, Ira. *When Affirmative Action was White: An Untold History of Racial Inequality in Twentieth-Century America.* New York: W.W. Norton & Company, 2005.

Kelley, Blair L. M. *Right to Ride: Streetcar Boycotts and African American Citizenship in the Era of Plessy v. Ferguson.* Chapel Hill, NC: University of North Carolina Press, 2010.

Kelley, Robin D. G. *Hammer and Hoe: Alabama Communists During the Great Depression.* Chapel Hill, NC: University of North Carolina Press, 2015.

Kelley, Robin D. G. *Race Rebels: Culture, Politics, and the Black Working Class.* New York: Simon & Schuster, 1996.

Kingsbury, Paul. *BMI 50th Anniversary: The Explosion of American Music 1940–1990.* Nashville, TN: The Country Music Foundation, 1990.

Krause, Kevin M., and Thomas J. Sugrue, eds. *The New Suburban History.* Chicago: The University of Chicago Press, 2006.

Kunzel, Regina. "Pulp Fictions and Problem Girls: Reading and Rewriting Single Pregnancy in the Postwar United States." *The American Historical Review*, 1995, 1465–1487.

Lashua, Brett. "In the Moondog's House: Alan Freed, Leo Mintz, and the 'Invention' of Rock 'n' Roll." *Popular Music, Popular Myth and Cultural Heritage in Cleveland: The Moondog, The Buzzard, and the Battle for the Rock and Roll Hall of Fame.* Somerville, MA: Emerald Publishing, 2019.

Lassiter, Matthew. *The Silent Majority: Suburban Politics in the Sunbelt South.* Princeton, NJ: Princeton University Press, 2007.

Lebovic, Sam. "'Here, There and Everywhere': The Beatles, America, and Cultural Globalization, 1964–1968." *Journal of American Studies* 51, no. 1, 2017, 43–65.

Lee, Taeku. *Mobilizing Public Opinion: Black Insurgency and Racial Attitudes in the Civil Rights Era.* Chicago: University of Chicago Press, 2002.

Leppert, Richard, and George Lipsitz. "Age, the Body and Experience in the Music of Hank Williams." In *All That Glitters: Country Music in America*, edited by George H. Lewis. Bowling Green, OH: Bowling Green State University Popular Press, 1993.

Levine, Lawrence. *Black Culture and Black Consciousness: Afro-American Folk Thought From Slavery to Freedom.* New York: Oxford University Press, 2007.

Levitin, Daniel. *This Is Your Brain on Music: The Science of a Human Obsession.* New York: Plume Printing, 2006.

Lewis, George H. "Ghosts, Ragged But Beautiful: Influences of Mexican Music on American Country-Western and Rock 'n' Roll." *Popular Music and Society* 15, no. 4, 1991, 85–103.

Lipsitz, George. "Land of a Thousand Dances: Youth, Minorities, and the Rise of Rock and Roll." *Recasting America: Culture and Politics in the Age of Cold War*, edited by Lary May. Chicago: University of Chicago Press, 1988.

Lipsitz, George. *Time Passages: Collective Memory and American Popular Culture.* Minneapolis: University of Minnesota Press, 2001.

Lopez, Ian Haney. *Dog Whistle Politics: How Coded Racial Appeals Have Reinvented Racism and Wrecked the Middle Class.* New York: Oxford University Press, 2014.

Lucander, David. *Winning the War for Democracy: The March on Washington Movement, 1941–1946.* Champaign, IL: University of Illinois Press, 2014.

Lydon, Michael. *Rock Folk: Portraits from the Rock 'n' Roll Pantheon.* New York: Citadel Press, 1971.

MacDonald, J. Fred. *Don't Touch That Dial! Radio Programming in American Life from 1920 to 1960.* Stanford, CT: Wadsworth Publishing, 1979.

MacLean, Nancy. *Freedom Is Not Enough: The Opening of the American Work Place.* Cambridge, MA: Harvard University Press, 2006.

McDermott, Stacy Pratt. "'An Outrageous Proceeding': A Northern Lynching and the Enforcement of Anti-Lynching Legislation in Illinois, 1905–1910." *The Journal of Negro History* 84, no. 1, 1999, 61–78.

McGirr, Lisa. *Suburban Warriors: The Origins of the New American Right.* Princeton, NJ: Princeton University Press, 2002.

McGuire, Danielle. *At the Dark End of the Street: Black Women, Rape, and Resistance—A New History of the Civil Rights Movement from Rosa Parks to the Rise of Black Power.* New York: Knopf, 2010.

Messenger, Cory. "Record Collectors: Hollywood Record Labels in the 1950s and 1960s." *Media International Australia* 148, no. 1, 2013, 118–126.

Miletsky, Zebulon Vance. "Before Busing: Boston's Long Movement for Civil Rights and the Legacy of Jim Crow in the 'Cradle of Liberty.'" *Journal of Urban History* 43, no. 2, 2017, 204–217.

Miller, Karl Hagstrom. *Segregating Sound: Inventing Folk and Pop Music in the Age of Jim Crow.* Durham, NC: Duke University Press, 2010.

Mills, Charles W. "Racial Liberalism." *PMLA* 123, no. 5, October 2008.

Mitchell, Michele. *Righteous Propagation: African Americans and the Politics of Racial Destiny After Reconstruction.* Chapel Hill, NC: The University of North Carolina Press, 2004.

Muhammad, Khalil. *The Condemnation of Blackness: Race, Crime, and the Making of Modern Urban America.* Cambridge, MA: Harvard University Press, 2010.

Muller, Mary Lee. "New Orleans Public School Desegregation." *Louisiana History: The Journal of the Louisiana Historical Association* 17, no. 1, Winter, 1976.

Myers, Andrew. "The Blinding of Isaac Woodard." *The Proceedings*, 2004.

Nagin-Brown, Tomiko. *Courage to Dissent: Atlanta and the Long History of the Civil Rights Movement.* New York: Oxford University Press, 2012.

Norton, Michael I., and Samuel R. Sommers. "Whites See Racism as a Zero-Sum Game That They Are Now Losing." *Perspectives on Psychological Science* 6, no. 3, 2011, 215–218.

Ongiri, Amy Abugo, *Spectacular Blackness: The Cultural Politics of the Black Power Movement and the Search for a Black Aesthetic.* Charlottesville, VA: University of Virginia Press, 2009.

Otis, Johnny. *Upside Your Head! Rhythm and Blues on Central Avenue.* Middletown, CT: Wesleyan University Press: 1993.

Owram, Doug. *Born At the Right Time: A History of the Baby Boom Generation.* Toronto: University of Toronto Press, 1996.

Painter, Nell Irvin. *Sojourner Truth: A Life, A Symbol.* New York: W.W. Norton & Co., 1996.

Palladino, Grace. *Teenagers: An American History.* New York: Basic Books, 1996.

Payne, Charles M. *I've Got the Light of Freedom: The Organizing Tradition and the Mississippi Freedom Struggle.* Berkeley and Los Angeles: University of California Press, 2007.

Payne, Charles M. "View From the Trenches." In *Debating the Civil Rights Movement, 1945–1968,* edited by Steven F. Lawson and Charles M. Payne. Lanham, MD: Rowman & Littlefield Publishers, 2006.

Pecknold, Diane. *The Selling Sound: The Rise of the Country Music Industry.* Durham, NC: Duke University Press, 2007.

Reid, John B. "'A Career to Build, a People to Serve, a Purpose to Accomplish': Race, Class, Gender, and Detroit's First Black Women Teachers, 1865–1916." *The Michigan Historical Review*, 1992, 1–27.

Remmers, H. H., and D. H. Radler. *The American Teenager.* Newport, RI: Charter Books, 1957.

Robertson, Diarra Osei. "Cash Rules Everything Around Me: Appropriation, Commodification, and the Politics of Contemporary Protest Music and Hip Hop." *Soul Thieves: The Appropriation and Misrepresentation of African American Popular Culture,* edited by Tamara Brown and Baruti Kopano. New York: Palgrave Macmillan, 2014.

Robins, Wayne. *A Brief History of Rock, Off the Record.* London: Routledge, 2016.

Robinson, Sean. "Revitalizing Northwood: Morgan State University's Role in Economic and Community Development." *Re-envisioning Higher Education's Public Mission*, edited by A. Papadimitriou and M. Boboc. New York: Palgrave Macmillan, 2021.

Ross, Barbara Joyce. "JE Spingarn and the Rise of the NAACP, 1911–1939." *Atheneum* 32, 1972.

Rothstein, Richard. *The Color of Law: A Forgotten History of How Our Government Segregated America.* New York: Liveright Publishing, 2017.

Roussell, Aaron K., Henne K. S. Glover, and D. Willits. "Impossibility of a 'Reverse Racism' Effect." *Criminology & Public Policy* 18, no. 1, 2017, 477-504.

Roy, William G. "'Race Records' and 'Hillbilly Music': Institutional Origins of Racial Categories in the American Commercial Recording Industry." *Poetics* 32, nos. 3–4, June–August 2004, 265–279.

Runowicz, John Michael. *Forever Doo Wop: Race, Nostalgia, and Vocal Harmony*. Amherst, MA: University of Massachusetts Press, 2006.

Self, Robert O. *American Babylon: Race and the Struggle for Postwar Oakland*. Princeton, NJ: Princeton University Press, 2005.

Shaw, Arnold. *Honkers and Shouters: The Golden Years of Rhythm and Blues*. New York: Macmillan, 1978.

Shaw, Arnold. *The Rockin' 50s: The Decade That Transformed the Pop Music Scene*. New York: Hawthorn Books, Inc., 1976.

Singh, Nikhil Pal. *Black Is a Country: Race and the Unfinished Struggle for Democracy*. Cambridge, MA: Harvard University Press, 2005.

Smith, Suzanne E. *Dancing in the Street: Motown and the Cultural Politics of Detroit*. Cambridge, MA: Harvard University Press, 2009.

Sokol, Jason. *There Goes My Everything: White Southerners in the Age of Civil Rights, 1945–1975*. New York: Vintage Books, 2007.

Solinger, Rickie. *Wake Up Little Susie: Single Pregnancy and Race Before Roe v. Wade*. London: Routledge, 2013.

Spitz, Bob. *The Beatles: The Biography*. New York: Little, Brown and Co., 2012.

Springhall, John. *Youth, Popular Culture, and Moral Panics: Penny Gaffs to Gangsta-Rap, 1830–1996*. London: Palgrave-McMillan, 1999.

Star, Larry, and Christopher Alan Waterman. *American Popular Music: From Minstrelsy to MP3*, 3rd ed. New York: Oxford University Press, 2009.

Stewart, James S., James Brewer Stewart, and Eric Foner. *Holy Warriors: The Abolitionists and American Slavery*. London: Macmillan, 1996.

Stewart, Shelley, and Nathan Hale Turner. *The Road South: A Memoir*. New York: Grand Central Publishing, 2002.

Sugrue, Thomas. *Not Even Past: Barack Obama and the Burden of Race*. Princeton, NJ: Princeton University Press, 2010.

Sugrue, Thomas J. "Breaking Through: The Troubled Origins of Affirmative Action in the Workplace." *Color Lines: Affirmative Action, Immigration, and Civil Rights Options for America*, edited by John David Skrentny. Chicago: University of Chicago Press, 2001.

Sugrue, Thomas J. *Origins of the Urban Crisis: Race and Inequality in Postwar Detroit*. Princeton, NJ: Princeton University Press, 2005.

Sugrue, Thomas J. *Sweet Land of Liberty: The Forgotten Struggle for Civil Rights in the North*. New York: Random House, 2008.

Swenson, John. *Bill Haley: The Daddy of Rock and Roll*. New York: Stein and Day, 1982.

Theoharis, Jeanne. *The Rebellious Life of Mrs. Rosa Parks*. Boston: Beacon Press, 2015.

The Oral History Association. "General Principles for Oral History." oralhistory.org.

Tosches, Nick. *Hellfire: The Jerry Lee Lewis Story*. New York: Grove Press, 1998.

Trounstine, Jessica. *Segregation by Design: Local Politics and Inequality in American Cities*. Cambridge, UK: Cambridge University Press, 2018.

Turner, Ike, and Nigel Cawthorne. *Takin' Back My Name: The Confessions of Ike Turner.* London: Virgin Books, 1999.
Turner, Steve. *A Hard Day's Write: The Stories Behind Every Beatles Song.* London: Carlton Books, 1994.
Tushnet, Mark V. *The NAACP's Legal Strategy Against Segregated Education, 1925–1950.* Chapel Hill: University of North Carolina Press, 1987.
Valocchi, Steve. "The Emergence of the Integrationist Ideology in the Civil Rights Movement." *Social Problems* 43, no. 1, February 1996, 116–130.
Wallach, Jennifer Jensen. *Getting What We Need Ourselves: How Food Has Shaped African American Life.* Lanham, MD: Rowman & Littlefield, 2019.
Ward, Brian. "By Elvis and All the Saints." *Britain and the American South: From Colonialism to Rock and Roll,* edited by Joseph P. Ward. Jackson, MS: University Press of Mississippi, 2003.
Ward, Brian. *Just My Soul Responding: Rhythm and Blues, Black Consciousness, and Race Relations.* Berkeley and Los Angeles: University of California Press, 1998.
Washburn, Pat. "The 'Pittsburgh Courier's' Double V Campaign in 1942." Presented at the Annual Meeting of the Association for Education in Journalism, 1981.
Weems, Robert E., and Robert E. Weems Jr. *Desegregating the Dollar: African American Consumerism in the Twentieth Century.* New York: New York University Press, 1998.
Werner, Craig. *A Change is Gonna Come: Music, Race and the Soul of America.* New York: Penguin Putnam, 1998.
Wexler, Jerry, and David Ritz. *Rhythm and the Blues: A Life in American Music.* New York: St. Martin's Press, 1994.
Whitburn, Joel. *Top R&B/Hip-Hop Singles: 1942–2004.* Menomonee, WI: Record Research, 2004.
White, Charles. *The Life and Times of Little Richard: The Quasar of Rock.* New York: Da Capo Press, 1994.
White, Frances E. *Dark Continent of Our Bodies: Black Feminism and Politics of Respectability.* Philadelphia: Temple University Press, 2010.
Willett, Edward. *Janis Joplin: Take Another Little Piece of My Heart.* Berkeley Heights, NJ: Enslow Publishers, 2008.
Williams, Juan, ed. *My Soul Looks Back in Wonder: Voices of the Civil Rights Experience.* New York: Sterling: 2004.
Wise, Tim. *Colorblind: The Rise of Post-Racial Politics and the Retreat from Racial Equity.* San Francisco: City Lights Books, 2010.
Wolcott, Victoria W. *Remaking Respectability: African American Women in Interwar Detroit.* Chapel Hill: University of North Carolina Press Books, 2013.
Woo, B. "Racial Discrimination and Mental Health in the USA: Testing the Reverse Racism Hypothesis." *Racial and Ethnic Health Disparities* 5, 2018, 766–773.
Zak, Albin. *I Don't Sound Like Nobody: Remaking Music in 1950s America.* Ann Arbor, MI: University of Michigan Press, 2010.
Zinn, Howard. *A People's History of the United States, 1492–Present.* New York: Harper Perennial Modern Classics, 2005.

Index

1968 Presidential Election, 296
2016 Presidential election, 7, 14, 298–99, 305–6
2020 Presidential election, x, 304–6

Abramson, Herbert and Miriam, 51
Acuff-Rose Music, 56
Advertising. *See* marketing
affirmative action, 68n53, 321
"Affluent Society," The, 41–45, 138
Allen, Rex, 62
Alt-Right violence, 299–300
American Bandstand, 191–96
American Broadcasting Company (ABC), 142–43, 191–92, 251
American Society of Composers, Authors, and Publishers (ASCAP), 50, 55
Andrews Sisters, 48
Animals, the, 229–30, 312
Anka, Paul, 179, 197
Apollo Theater, 269–71, 295
appropriation, white, of Black music, 11, 12, 75–78, 108–9, 111–12, 115, 117–19, 121–22, 124–26, 130n88, 134n154, 141–45, 152, 179, 194–95, 197, 198n8, 231–33
Arbery, Ahmaud, 316
Armstrong, Louis, 47

"aspiring class," 42–43, 46, 79–81, 84–85, 116, 138, 235, 243–44
Atlanta Compromise Speech, 80
Atlantic Records, 9–10, 51, 70, 96, 99, 106, 115, 133, 144, 150
Avalon, Frankie, 143, 177, 179–80, 197
Ayler, Albert, 231

Baker, Ella, 237
Baker, LaVern, 101, 104, 113, 114, 264
Baraka, Amiri (LeRoi Jones), 37
Bartholomew, Dave, 61
Bass, Ralph, 54, 99, 267
Beatles, The, 216–19, 226–33, 271–72, 278
Bennett, Boyd, 98
Bennett, Tony, 60, 62
Berry, Chuck, 3, 76, 78, 97, 101, 124, 141–42, 149–52, 180–82, 221, 226–27, 229–32, 267, 269
Bevel, James, 237–38, 248
Biden, Joseph, 304
Big Beat, The, 142–43, 190, 191, 199n14
Billboard charts, 16–17, 19, 25, 54, 57–63, 63n1, 73–76, 96, 110, 119, 122, 134–35, 139–41, 144, 148, 152, 178–79, 182, 184–88, 196–98, 207–8, 214–17, 227, 250, 278, 293–94,

326–27, 331–32; content analysis method of, 16
Birmingham campaign, 241, 243–44, 247–49, 256–57, 259–60, 262
Birmingham church bombing, 1963, 244
Blackboard Jungle, 99, 187
Black Bourgeoisie, 42
"Black Cabinet," 35
Black Codes, 32
Black Lives Matter (BLM), x, 7, 298, 306–7, 313, 323–24
Black Nationalism, 4, 29–31, 81–82, 290
Black Panthers, 292–93, 328–29n13
Black Power, 1, 8, 29, 64, 208, 224–25, 261, 290–94, 316, 320
Black press, 32, 36, 45–47, 89–91, 93, 146, 161, 172, 185–87, 312
Blayton, J.B., 54
blockbusting, 210–11
blues music, 82–83, 106, 116, 118–19, 127–28n34, 217, 284n149, 294, 326
Boone, Pat, 112–14, 119–21, 134–35, 149, 179, 193, 229
Boston busing crisis, 10, 22n16
boycotts, public streetcars, 32–33
Braden, Anne, 250, 255–56
British Invasion, 214–16, 219, 226–33, 312
Broadcast Music, Inc. (BMI), 50, 55, 57, 61, 145, 151
Browder v. Gayle (1956), 90
Brown, Esther, 157
Brown, James, 294–95, 312–13
Brown, Michael, 298
Brown, Nappy, 113
Brown, Oliver, 157–58
Brown, Ruth, 97, 104, 112, 116, 144
Brown v. Board of Education of Topeka (1954), 2, 12–13, 74, 133n140, 157–58, 170
Bryan, Hazel, 160, 195
Bush, George, 300
Bush, George W., 300

busing campaigns, school desegregation, 20n6, 22, 38, 140, 171, 174–75, 325
Butler, Jerry, 115

"call and response," 52–53, 83
Cameo-Parkway Records, 207
Capitol Records, 48, 69n74
Carmichael, Stokely, 288, 290–92
Carroll, Diahann, 85
Carter Family, The, 47
Cash, Johnny, 2
Cash Box, 16, 99
Central High School, Little Rock, AK, 139, 159–62, 164, 169, 172, 176, 195
Chaney, James, 258
Charles, Ray, 2, 84, 106, 115, 123, 144, 197, 215–16, 272
Charms, the, 96–97, 112–13, 134n157
Checker, Chubby, 143, 192–93, 207–8
Chess, Philip and Leonard, 51, 149
Chess Records, 51, 149, 267
Chords, The, 96–97, 112
churches, Black. *See* respectability politics; and gospel tradition, 52–53, 83–84, 224, 295; support for civil rights organizing, 32, 94, 234, 244, 256
Civil Rights Act of 1875, 32
Civil Rights Act of 1964, 4, 10, 18, 249, 251, 253, 288, 296, 313, 315–16
Civil Rights Act of 1968, 44, 68n57, 315
CKLW-Windsor, 218, 233
Clark, Dick, 182–83, 191, 193, 196, 219
Clark, Jim, 290, 296
Cleaver, Eldridge, 208
Clovers, The, 61, 99
Clyburn, James, 304
Coasters, The, 150, 181–83, 188–89, 249, 266
Coates, Ta-Nehisi, 5–7, 314, 327
coded language, 6, 20n6, 289, 296, 298, 300
Cold War, 39, 89, 173–74, 239–40, 246; anxiety over, 25, 85, 187, 208;

political leverage, 30–32, 67n37, 156, 158, 174, 239, 255–56
Cole, Nathanial Adams (Nat King), 49, 58
color-blind racism, 3–9, 41, 93, 100–102, 166–68, 174–75, 218–23, 296–98, 302–11, 317–18, 331
Columbia Broadcasting System (CBS), 48, 229
Columbia Records, 47–48, 69n74, 70n94, 112, 146, 331n61
Colvin, Claudette, 87, 89
Committee on Civil Rights, 38
Communist Party USA (CPUSA), 29, 65n10
Como, Perry, 60, 99, 113
concerts: integrated, 152, 208, 264–65, 270–74; segregated, 124, 229, 263–76; segregated, challenges to, 267–70
Congress of Industrial Organizations (CIO), 42
Congress of Racial Equality (CORE), 4, 26, 29–31, 39–41, 235, 240, 247, 254; and desegregation tactics, 31; and respectability politics, 17
Connor, Eugene "Bull", 244, 247–49, 256–57, 259, 296
consumer boycotts, 28–29, 64n8
consumer collectives, 28
consumer culture: Black middle class, 17, 41–42, 45–47, 116, 140, 146–47, 220, 234–36; and citizenship, 28, 45–47, 55, 234–36, 254, 266; teenagers, 120, 138, 145–48; white middle class, 17, 102, 120–21
Contours, the, 220
Cooke, Sam, 1, 76, 143, 151–52, 181–84, 186, 192, 215–16
Cooper v. Aaron (1958), 160
Council of Federated Organizations (COFO), 254, 257
Counter Intelligence Program (COINTELPRO), 292
Country and Western, *Billboard* chart, 8, 16, 58–60, 62, 63n1, 110, 117, 122–23, 125, 139, 144, 150, 181, 199n16, 214, 217, 327, 331n61; content analysis of, 16
country and western music:Black appeal, 17, 117–18, 122–24; cover records, 110; creation of rock and roll, 63–64n7, 118, 145, 149; crossover records, 59–62, 73, 98; genre, 55–56, 71n110, 127–28n34; record labels, 47, 53, 56–57, 70n94
cover songs, 17, 60–62, 72n120, 74, 76–78, 96–98, 108, 110–17, 120–25, 130n88, 134n157, 135n159–160, 141, 143–44, 148, 150, 177, 179, 196, 207, 226–30, 327
Crew Cuts, the, 112–13
Crosby, Bing (Harry Lillis), 48
crossover records, 8–9, 16, 53–54, 59–63, 72n120, 74–75, 77, 96–108, 112, 115, 121–23, 133n140, 137–39, 141, 143–44, 148, 194, 199n16, 214–17, 220; and creation of rock and roll, 17, 78, 108, 117–18, 124, 139, 142, 144–45, 196, 214
Crudup, Arthur, 2, 124

dancing, interracial, 142–43
Danny and the Juniors, 144, 199n17
Darin, Bobby, 178, 194
dating, 137–38, 143, 147, 181–87; interracial, 34, 143, 152, 168, 268, 288, 303, 318–19
Decca Records, 26, 47–48, 69n74, 73–74, 98, 106, 111, 118, 145; "Hill Billy" series, 70n94; "Sepia" series, 25, 47, 70n94
deejays, 2, 9, 60, 63n1, 77, 99, 105, 108–10, 178–79, 191, 196–98n8, 227, 246, 274; Black, 43, 54, 101, 217, 233, 249
Del-Vikings, The, 152
desegregation: Black student experiences, 18, 140–41, 155–56, 161–66, 168–69, 172, 176–77, 180–82, 184, 195, 212; desegregation,

white student experiences, 18, 166–67, 170–72, 176
desegregation campaigns: interstate transportation, 26–27, 38, 240; public transportation, 17, 74, 86–87, 89–91, 93–94; schools, 5, 17–18, 34, 139–40, 153–60, 163, 173, 176; streetcars, 31–33
Dexter Avenue Baptist Church, 74, 88
DiMucci, Dion, 186
Dinkins, David, 37
Dinning, Mark, 152
Dion and the Belmonts, 101, 152, 186, 193
"Dixiecrats," 38
Domino, Fats (Antoine Dominique, Jr.), 1, 3, 61, 99, 106, 112–13, 121, 122, 124, 125, 134n154, 134–35n157, 135n159, 144, 145, 197, 268–69
Dominoes, The, 61–62, 104
"Don't Buy Where You Can't Work" campaigns, 28, 64n8
doo wop, 97–98
Dot Records, 56, 112, 113, 120–21
Double "V" campaign, 36–38
Douglass, Frederick, 29, 32, 316
Downing, George T., 153–54
Drifters, the, 144, 150, 217
Du Bois, William Edward Burghardt (W.E.B.), 34, 86, 155
Duke, David, 299–300

Eckford, Elizabeth, 160, 195
Ed Sullivan Show, the, 122, 227, 230
Eisenhower, Dwight D., 160, 181
Electric and Musical Industries (EMI) Records, 48
Ellington, Edward Kennedy (Duke), 47, 51
equalization lawsuits, 155–58
Ertegun, Ahmet, 51, 99, 106
Evans, Leonard, 54
Everly Brothers, 144, 199n16
Executive Order 8802, 35
Executive Order 9981, 38

Fabian, 143
Farmer, James, 29, 39–41
Faubus, Orval, 159–60, 176
Federal Housing Administration (FHA), 43–44, 211
Fellowship of Reconciliation (FOR), 26, 39–40
Flamingos, the, 117, 120, 135n160
Floyd, George, 15, 301, 307–8
Foley, Clyde "Red," 112, 123
Fontane Sisters, 113
Forman, James, 40, 238–39, 243, 245, 247–48, 251–53, 258, 259, 261–62, 297, 313–14
Four Preps, 144, 199n17
Fourteenth Amendment, 10, 30, 36, 40, 158, 174
Four Tops, 221, 312
Four Tunes, 96–97
Francis, Connie, 144, 152, 177, 192, 199n17
Freed, Alan, 10, 60, 77, 108–9, 117, 118, 120–21, 141, 144–45, 148, 150, 152, 190, 191, 196, 264–65
Freedom Rides, 26–27, 240, 250, 260; media coverage of, 27, 241
Freedom Summer. *See* Mississippi Freedom Summer
friendships, interracial, 163, 165–69, 172–73, 176, 207, 209–10, 212–14, 225, 303–4, 317, 324, 326

Gabler, Milt (Milton), 26, 47–48, 98, 106, 111–12, 118, 120–21, 145
Gandhi, Mohandas (Mahatma), 5, 30, 39, 41, 90, 262
Gant, Cecil, 53
Garvey, Marcus, 34, 81
Gaye, Marvin, 233, 294, 313
Gee Records, 137
Gene and Eunice, 113
gentrification, 323–24
Gibbs, Georgia, 113, 114, 120
G.I. Bill. *See* Serviceman's Readjustment Act of 1944

Gilbert, Eugene, 198n4
Ginsburg, Ruth Bader, 303
girl groups, 192–94, 205n146, 215, 217, 220–22, 227–28, 269, 311
Gitlin, Todd, 102, 312
Glen, Artie, 62
Glen, Darrell, 62
Goldner, George, 190
Goodman, Andrew, 258
Gordy, Berry, 1, 58–59, 124, 148–49, 192, 215–16, 218–26
Gore, Lesley, 215
gospel music, 1, 2, 50, 52–53, 62, 83–85, 105, 109, 118, 122–24, 151, 216–22, 224, 289, 294, 327
Grand Ole Opry, 56, 123
Great Society, 21n7
Greensboro Four, 236–38, 242, 245
Groove Records, 70n94
Gunter, Cornell, 182–83

Hairspray, 2
Haley, Bill, 97–99, 105, 111–12, 117–19, 122, 134n154, 197
Hank Ballard and the Midnighters, 107, 114, 207
Harrison, George, 226, 229
Head, Wilson, 38
Helms, Bobby, 199n16
Heyer, Heather, 300
Hightower, Little Donna, 73
hillbilly music. *See* country and western music
Hilltoppers, the, 113
Holly, Buddy, 192, 226
Horn, Bob, 191
Hot 100 chart, *Billboard*, 141, 152, 178, 179, 182, 184, 186, 198n6, 207, 214–20, 223, 227, 250, 278n44; content analysis of, 16; and desegregation of charts, 17–18, 139, 144, 196–97; and re-segregation of charts, 19, 217–18, 293, 326–27
Houser, George, 26

housing segregation, 43–45, 58–59, 64n8, 175, 208–13, 296, 315
Houston, Cissy, 85
Hunter, Ivory Joe, 114, 144, 264

Imperial Records, 61
Impressions, the, 115, 215–17
Ink Spots, The, 73–74
Isley Brothers, the, 227

Jagger, Mick, 105, 232
"jail without bail," 239, 241, 280n72
James, Etta, 113
Jan and Dean, 215
Jarvis, Al, 191
Jeffrey, Sharon, 245
Jet magazine, 161, 168, 185, 187, 268
Johnson, Lyndon Baines, 19, 21n7, 249, 251, 259, 288
Johnson, Marv, 220
Johnson, Roland, 73
Jones, Quincy, 44
Jordan, Louis, 25–27, 47, 53, 118, 231
Journey of Reconciliation, 26–27, 31, 32, 38, 240
jukeboxes, 16, 50, 58–59, 63n1, 77, 100–101, 181
Justis, Bill, 199n16
juvenile delinquency, 182, 187–90

Kaye, Sidney M., 50
Kennedy, John Francis, 240, 248–49, 253, 262
Kennedy, Robert, 240, 255, 287
Keynote Records, 70n94
King, B. B. (Riley), 38, 83–84, 123–24, 230
King, Ben E., 215
King, Jr., Martin Luther, 3, 74, 93–95, 105, 121, 125, 173, 237, 241, 246, 249, 259, 288, 290, 297, 314, 315; and the Montgomery Bus Boycott, 88–91; and respectability politics, 17, 88–89

Kinks, the, 229, 233
Knight, Gladys, 85, 267, 269
Knight, Merald "Bubba," 267, 269
Ku Klux Klan (KKK), 90, 258, 272, 297, 299

labor organizing, 17, 42, 85, 202n71, 251–52
"Law and Order," Republican strategy, 20n6, 296
Leadership Conference on Civil Rights, 4, 158
Leiber, Jerry and Mike Stoller, 150–51, 180–81, 188–89
Lennon, John, 105, 226–27, 229
Lewis, Jerry Lee, 3, 11, 78, 117, 123, 141, 144, 199n16
Lewis, John, 259, 261–62, 291, 297
Lewis, Smiley, 98, 113
liberalism, racial, 6, 8, 10–11, 14–15, 31, 275, 289, 291–93, 296–99, 301–10, 314–15, 319–20, 322–26
Life magazine, 89, 145–46, 184–85
Lil Nas X, 327, 331n61
Little Anthony and the Imperials, 117, 193–94
Little Richard (Richard Penniman), 76, 78, 85, 101, 105, 119–21, 124, 135n160, 141, 142, 221, 226, 229, 231–32, 269
Little Rock, AK, desegregation of Central High School, 94, 139, 159–62, 169, 172–73, 176, 181, 195, 262, 270
Lombardo, Guy, 73–74
Loving v. Virginia (1967), 288
Lowe, Jim, 199n16
Lucy, Autherine, 160
Lymon, Frankie, 117, 137–38, 142–43, 148, 182, 190, 192, 193

March, Little Peggy, 215
March on Selma, 4, 19, 259
March on Washington, 1963, 245, 248–51

March on Washington movement, 1941, 35–36
marketing, 10, 13, 56, 73, 141–43, 145–46, 151, 220–21; to Black consumers, 25, 45–47, 51, 54–55, 60, 77, 99, 116, 138, 217–18, 235, 288; cross-racial, 28, 50–51, 60, 75, 108, 148–53, 179, 181–82, 187–88, 266; segmented, 45–46, 53, 63n7, 73–74, 110, 127–28n34, 217–18, 288; to teenagers, 137–38, 141, 144–46, 148–52, 177, 180, 184, 198n4; to white middle class, 49, 58, 111, 113–14, 118, 137, 143, 148–50, 191–92, 196, 222–23
marriage: interracial, 7, 34, 168, 288, 317–18; teen, 184–85, 205n137
Marshall, Thurgood, 29, 40, 155–58, 160
Martha and the Vandellas, 220, 233
Martin, Trayvon, 298, 323–24
Martin Luther King, Jr. Day, 1–3, 297
Marvelettes, the, 220–21
massive resistance, 4, 20n6, 139–41, 153, 158, 164, 170–71, 177, 237, 239–40, 242–43, 254, 257, 259–60, 272, 298
Mathis, Johnny, 49
Mayfield, Percy, 60
McCain, Franklin, 236–37
McCartney, Paul, 226–27, 229–31
McGhee, Stick, 52
McGuire Sisters, 120
McPhatter, Clyde, 144, 180
McVea, Jack, 54
Mercury Records, 48, 69n74, 70n94, 112–13
Meredith, James, 240–41
Miller, Mitch, 146
Milton, Roy, 53
Mintz, Leo, 108
Miracles, the, 220, 223–25
Mississippi Blues Commission, 326
Mississippi Freedom Democratic Party (MFDP), 251–52, 282n106

Mississippi Freedom Summer, 253–59, 290; media coverage of, 257; murders, 258
Mitchell, Guy, 123
Montgomery Bus Boycott, 4, 74, 86–91, 93–94, 106, 259, 262, 301
Montgomery Improvement Association (MIA), 88–89, 94
Moondog Ball, 110
Moondog Show, The, 108–9
Moore, Amzie, 37, 253, 262
Morgan, Irene, 38
Morgan v. Virginia (1947), 26, 38
Moses, Bob (Robert), 251
Motown Museum, 2
Motown Records, 1, 58, 124, 149, 214, 216, 218–26, 228, 230–33, 242, 271, 273, 310, 311
Muste, Abraham (A.J.), 39

National Association of Advancement for Colored People (NAACP), 4, 17, 27, 37, 40, 242, 247, 248, 253, 254; and housing integration, 44; and integration mission, 29, 31, 34–35, 38; and lunch counter sit-ins, 235–37; and the Montgomery Bus Boycott, 86–88; and respectability politics, 17; and school desegregation cases, 154–58, 160, 161
National Association of Real Estate Boards, 43–44
National Broadcasting Company (NBC), 48, 111
National Negro Network, 54
National Negro Rights League, 34
Nelson, Ricky (Eric), 135n154, 143, 144, 152, 177, 178, 181, 182, 186–87, 199n17
Nelson, Sandy, 152
New Deal, 34–35, 161
New Orleans Citizens Committee, 32
Newton, Huey, 292
Nixon, E.D. (Edgar Daniel), 87–88
Nixon, Richard, 20n6, 296, 298, 306

nonviolence, ideology, 26–28, 38–41, 74, 90, 96, 235–39, 250, 254, 257–58, 260–62, 288, 301
nonviolent direct protest, 4, 5, 15, 30, 38–41, 63, 95–96, 173, 209, 233–36, 239–41, 249, 259–61, 263, 288, 295; media coverage of, 18, 40, 74, 236–37, 239–43, 246, 252, 259, 261, 270, 301; opposition to, 40–41, 235–36, 290; as organizational tactic, 18, 38–41, 74–75, 139, 234–36, 239, 259; white appeal, 27, 30–31, 39, 41, 74–75, 235, 239–40, 252, 261–63

Obama, Barack, 7, 21n7, 297, 298, 304–6, 308, 315
Odetta, 44
Okeh Records, 58, 70n94, 112
Open Schools movement, 202n72
oral histories, methods, 13–16, 18–19, 22n23, 305
Orioles, The, 62
Otis, Johnny, 84, 124–25

Packard, Vance, 104–5
Paige, Patti, 96
Parks, Rosa, 17, 74, 87–88, 121, 125, 314
payola radio scandal, 196–97
Penguins, the, 113
Perkins, Carl, 117, 122–23, 268
Peter, Paul and Mary, 215
Phillips, Dewey, 2, 9, 77, 109–10, 198n8
Phillips, Sam, 2, 57, 124, 198n8
Pitney, Gene, 101, 205n146
Pittsburgh Courier, 36, 89, 93, 109, 268–69
Platters, The, 97–98, 104, 113, 122, 150, 224
Plessy, Homer, 32
Plessy v. Ferguson (1896), 32–33
policing, racist, 15, 33–34, 189–90, 214, 242–43, 250–52, 297–98, 301–2, 306–9, 323–24

pop records, Black appeal, 17, 59–60, 98–99, 116–18, 122, 152, 181, 196, 199nn16–17, 215, 230–31
Presley, Elvis, 2–3, 11, 76, 78, 105, 117, 122–26, 141, 144, 188, 199n16, 215, 226; and appropriation of Black music, 122, 124–26
Preston, Frances Williams, 57
Price, Lloyd, 197

Quakers, 39–40, 67n38

"race records," 50, 55, 58, 70n94, 83–84, 100–101, 111, 141
radio stations, Black-oriented, 54–55, 99–101, 217
Randolph, Asa Philip, 35, 248
Ray, 2
Ray, Johnnie, 56, 58–60
RCA Victor, 47–48, 69n74, 70n94, 113
Reagan, Ronald, 20n6, 300
record labels: consolidation, 28, 47–49; independent, 50–51, 54, 56–58, 62–63, 99, 103, 111, 113, 143, 148–49, 196, 216–17, 219–20; major, 9, 18, 47–50, 55–56, 58, 70n94, 77, 103, 108, 110–11, 113–15, 120, 141–43, 177–79, 196–97, 216, 287, 326
records, production, 47–49
redlining, 43–44, 64n8, 175, 208–10, 303–4, 315
Reeves, Martha, 220
reformers, Black middle class, 74, 79–86, 104–7, 115, 125, 128n34, 154
respectability politics, 5, 8, 78–86, 97, 106, 125, 167–68, 174, 295, 302; and Black churches, 79, 81–85; and Black pride, 74, 79–80; and the Montgomery Bus Boycott, 17, 74, 86–91, 94, 125–26; and music, 17, 75–76, 78, 82–84, 108, 110, 115–16, 124–26, 142, 149, 220, 222–23, 232, 287; and nonviolent action, 139–40, 259–60; opposition to, 95–96; and white appeal, 17, 74–76, 79–81, 87–92, 139
restaurants, protests, 41, 234–37, 239, 241–42, 245, 249, 251
restrictive covenants, 44
rhythm and blues (R&B) *Billboard* chart, 8, 16, 18, 25, 58–62, 63n1, 96–97, 112–14, 117, 119–20, 122, 135n160, 138–39, 141, 143–44, 148, 150–52, 180–81, 184, 186, 188, 196, 199nn16–17, 207–8, 214–17, 220, 293–94, 327; content analysis of, 16
rhythm and blues (R&B) music: crossovers, 59–62, 64n7, 73–74, 96–99, 112–14, 117, 119–20, 122, 125, 135n160, 138–39, 141, 143–44, 148, 150–52, 180–81, 184, 186, 188, 194, 196, 199n16, 207–8, 214–17, 220; genre, 1, 9, 48, 51–53, 76, 97–98, 102–3, 105–8, 116, 185–86, 217–18, 220–21, 229, 273–74, 294; radio stations, 54–55, 98–100; white consumer appeal, 17, 54–55, 59, 61–63, 76–78, 97–110, 113–14, 122, 141, 145, 180, 185–86, 191, 198n8, 214, 219–22, 230–31, 273
Richards, Fannie, 153–54
Robbins, Marty, 123, 150
Roberts, John, 302–4
Robinson, Jo Ann, 87
Robinson, Smokey, 220, 223–25, 227
Rock and Roll: An American Story, 2
Rock and Roll Hall of Fame, 1, 16, 61
Rodgers, Jimmie, 47, 199n16
Rolling Stones, 105, 229–30, 232–33, 293
Rooftop Singers, the, 215
Roosevelt, Franklin, 34–35
Rose, Fred, 56, 73
Ross, Diana, 220, 222, 224
Royal Teens, 152
Rupe, Art, 51, 151, 177
Rustin, Bayard, 26–27, 39–40, 248
Rydell, Bobby, 177, 178, 180, 194, 197, 207–8, 214, 218

Sam and Dave, 272
satyagraha, 39
"schlock" rockers, 17, 141, 143, 144, 177–78, 180, 197, 207–8, 218
schools, private, 153–54, 159
Schwerner, Michael, 258
Seale, Bobby, 292
separatism, 31–32, 35, 54–55, 154–56, 292, 295
Serviceman's Readjustment Act of 1944, 43, 68n53
Seville, David, 144, 199n17
sexual violence, 29, 64n8, 78–79, 87
Shelby v. Holder (2013), 7
Sherrod, Charles, 252, 261
Shirelles, the, 192, 269
Shirley Gunter and the Queens, 112
Simone, Nina, 293
Sinatra, Frank, 60, 124
Sinclair, John, 92, 107–8, 147–48
Sister Rosetta Tharpe: Godmother of Rock and Roll, 2
sit-ins, 41, 208, 234–42, 245, 253–54, 262, 270, 272
Six Teens, 148
Smalls, Robert, 32
Smith, Mary Louise, 87
Smith-Robinson, Ruby Doris, 238–39, 243, 259
SNCC Legacy, 13, 325–26
Sony Music Entertainment, 69n74
Soul, *Billboard* chart, 19, 294
soul music, 215, 217, 294–95
SoundScan, 326–27
Southern Christian Leadership Conference (SCLC), 4, 237, 241, 247–48, 254, 259
Southern Manifesto, 158
Southern strategy, 296
Soviet Union, the, 67n37, 156
Specialty Records, 51, 60, 143, 151–52, 177
Spector, Phil, 115, 215, 216, 228
Spelman College, 81

Spencer, Richard, 300
Starr, Kay, 59–61
Starr, Ringo (Richard Starkey), 226, 229–30
Stax Museum of American Soul Music, 2
Stewart, Shelley, 249
Storm, Gale, 113
Strong, Barrett, 220
Student Nonviolent Coordinating Committee (SNCC), 4, 7, 18, 208, 233–34, 237–63, 265–66, 270, 275, 280n72; shift to Black Power, 261, 288, 290–91, 293; and student involvement, 243–45, 247; tactical divisions, 251–54, 257–58, 260–61, 291–92; Waveland retreat, 251–53, 261
Students for a Democratic Society (SDS), 102, 245, 260–62, 312
suburbs, segregated, 43–45, 68nn57–58, 102, 131n103, 189, 209–13, 242–43, 288, 296
Sun Records, 57, 124
Sun Studio, 2
Supremes, The, 217, 220–22, 311–12

"Talented Tenth," 79–80
Taylor, Breonna, 15, 301
Taylor, Zola, 97
teenage identity, 137–38, 140, 143, 145–52, 166, 177, 179, 181, 191, 197
Teen Queens, 148, 186
Temptations, the, 220–21, 224, 233, 269–70
Tin Pan Alley, 56
Truman, Harry, 38, 41, 156
Trump, Donald, 14–15, 297–301, 305–6, 308–9
Truth, Sojourner, 32
Turner, "Big Joe," 98, 111–12, 117, 144, 197
Turner, Ike, 134n154, 267–68
Twist, the, 178, 207–8, 290

Uggums, Leslie, 146, 161
United Negro Improvement Association (UNIA), 34, 81–82
Universal Music Group, 69n74
Universal Pictures, 48
University of Alabama, 139, 159–60
"uplift," racial, 5, 79–82, 84, 115, 125, 294
Urban League, 27, 29, 31, 247
urban rebellions/uprisings, 295–96, 298

Valli, June, 62
Vee, Bobby, 192
Vincent, Gene, 122, 226
Vocalion Records, 70n94
voting rights, 4–5, 7, 12, 18, 34, 208–9, 248–51, 253–55, 259, 261, 275, 288–89, 302–3, 315–16
Voting Rights Act, 4, 7, 18, 19, 255, 257–59, 288, 302–3, 315–16

Walk the Line, 2
Wallace, George, 171
Warren, Earl, 157
Washington, Booker T., 80
Washington, Dinah, 60
Waters, John, 2
WCHB-Inkster, 54
WDIA-Memphis, 43, 54, 109, 124
Wells, Ida Barnett, 32
Wells, Mary, 220

WERD-Atlanta, 54
Wexler, Jerry, 9–10, 51, 53, 97, 99, 106, 124, 150, 178, 223
WHBQ-Memphis, 109
White Citizens Councils, 19, 159, 297
Williams, Andy, 215
Williams, Dootsie, 44
Williams, Hank, 56, 60
Williams, Nat, 43, 54
Williams, Tony, 97–98
Willis, Chuck, 112, 194–95
Wilson, Jackie, 180, 192
Wilson, Woodrow, 34
WJW-Cleveland, 108
WLAC-Nashville, 54
Women's Political Council, 86–88
Wonder, Stevie, 220
Wood, Randy, 56, 112, 274
Woodard, Isaac, 38
World War II, 28, 30, 47–48, 55–56, 66n28, 235, 254, 256; Black employment during, 42; and Black patriotism, 35–36, 39; and Black soldiers, 35, 43; and Black veteran organizing, 37–39; and juvenile delinquency, 187; and origins of the civil rights movement, 36–37, 156; prisoners of war, 37–38

Zinn, Howard, 254, 261

About the Author

Beth Fowler is an associate professor of teaching in the Irvin D. Reid Honors College at Wayne State University in Detroit, Michigan. Her research interests include popular culture and consumerism, the U.S. civil rights movement, youth culture, urban history, gender and sexuality, and twentieth-century U.S. and African-American History.

www.ingramcontent.com/pod-product-compliance
Lightning Source LLC
Chambersburg PA
CBHW021339300426
44114CB00012B/1007